Jerry:
Been a long
Hartford has been
good for us. loved
your wife & you
as a couple. ☆☆☆
all the best
Jack

The Odyssey

of a

Polish Patriot

IN THIS BOOK

For Nellie

Her Children

Their Children

And All Who Follow

Wanda, Nellie, Kazimierz, Ludwik

ACKNOWLEDGMENTS

I am extremely thankful to the many folks who helped me write this book. In particular, I would like to thank the widow of Ludwik Skoczylas, the former Nellie Smith of Carlisle, England, for her wonderful tales and recollections of events, large and small, that occurred during the tumultuous era of World War II. Her amazing memory and cheerful intellect made the writing of her husband's story an interesting and enjoyable task.

I am also indebted to her daughter, Wanda and son, Kazimierz, for granting me permission to visit their mother on a weekly basis for chats about their father and his experiences both on and off the field of battle. The pictures, documents and letters the family made available to me were extremely helpful in writing the story of this extraordinary man. Extra thanks go to Kazimierz for his effort in helping with the early editing of the book. In addition to all the help both son and daughter provided, I will be forever grateful to them for allowing me to become a part of their family for a while.

Thanks go out to Piotr Hodyra of Poland and Peter Sikala of England for providing me with important information and documents concerning Ludwik's military career.

Special thanks go out to my wife, Pat for understanding the amount of time it took to write this book, my daughter, Michelle and her husband, Steve McCoy, grandchildren Colleen Nelson, Ben, Ethan and Katie La Plante along with volunteer Linda Feldman for guiding me through the technicalities involved and to my good friend, Noel Kelliher, for supporting and encouraging my effort to write.

Thank you
Dziekuje Ci
Jack

FORWARD

I must have walked past him on the street, sat in a church pew near him, even bagged his groceries at the super-market. Many times, I am certain, I encountered him, but I did not know him.

I was a youth in the 1950's and Ludwik Skoczylas was in his early middle life, an ordinary man who lived near the center of town with his wife and young family. Virtually no one knew his story.

When Jack La Plante began gathering material for his book, "Stories from the Fifties, East Hartford Style," I had the opportunity to read many of the submissions before they went to press. One, written by Ludwik's son, Kazimierz, impressed us both in that it contained a paragraph that began, "As a young man, my father escaped from Poland during the Nazi invasion. He did it by riding on the top of railroad cars at night and hiding during the daytime."

Kazimierz told, in the briefest, but starkest of details, of his father's dangerous journey in the early days of war-torn Europe as he made his way first to France and then to England where he became a pilot in the Royal Air Force. There he met and married his beloved Nellie, overcame a horrible automobile accident, flew Special Operation flights into occupied Europe, survived a tragic crash into the sea and some years after the war ended, emigrated with his young family to the United States. Kazimierz went on to finish his story of growing up in East Hartford in the fifties. But from those few lines about his father, Jack sensed a much larger story; the story of a man's love for his country and how he helped destroy the tyranny that threatened the freedom of the western world. It is the story of a seemingly ordinary man, compelled by circumstances, who accomplished extraordinary things in his life.

In telling this story, we all get to know Ludwik Skoczylas.

It has been said that history is only an approximation of the past; there is much we will never know. Jack's challenge was to try and discover what no one knew by using logical suppositions and the educated guess work of a dedicated researcher to narrow the probabilities of what took place, an intuitive process of elimination to reach beyond the scant facts available to write scenarios that were within the definite realm of actuality.

In great matters, Erasmus wrote, "It is enough to have tried." In Ludwik's Skoczylas' case, it went far beyond that. His was a supreme effort. In his quest to help regain Poland's status as a free society, his dedication to that cause was relentless. Only when the reality of the grinding forces of history made that cause impossible did he suspend his actions. The victorious western nations that he had fought so valiantly alongside were not able to save Poland from the Soviets.

Ludwik was left with a bitter reality. For him and his young family to survive, he would have to abandon a beloved but now hopeless past, for an uncertain, but promising future. He would take them to America.

For post-war immigrants arriving in the USA, there was the storied "American Dream" to experience living in a better world, full of freedom and opportunity.

Ludwik had another dream; that one day, his beloved Poland would also be free and full of opportunity. From the end of WWII, through the Cold War, the Gdansk shipyard revolt, the fall of the Soviet Union and Poland's new independence, some forty-five years would pass. Ludwik would not live to see his dream become a reality. His wife and three children would. And that would have been enough for him.

Noel Kelliher

The Odyssey

of a

Polish Patriot

Part One

SPECIAL DUTIES
FLIGHT 1586

Base Campo Casale

Italy

Ludwik
Skoczylas

The Liberator crossed the coast of Italy just after dawn and headed south over the Adriatic Sea. Its destination was Campo Casale, a makeshift airfield on the eastern coast of southern Italy and near the city of Brindisi. It was the home base of the Polish "Special Duties Flight 1586," a special operations air unit that was part of the Mediterranean Allied Air Forces covering the Mediterranean region during World War II. The plane was piloted by Ludwik Skoczylas and had a crew of six other Polish patriots. They were returning from a successful nighttime mission into the interior of northern Italy. They had dropped supplies by parachute to a band of friendly partisans who were fighting and winning the battle against the Germans still in their country. It was January 19, 1945.

Warrant Officer Pilot Skoczylas and his crew had made several sorties into enemy territory in the year or so they had been stationed on the "heel" of Allied controlled southern Italy. Flying mostly at night to avoid detection by deadly German night fighters and countless anti-aircraft gun emplacements, the crew had delivered money, medical supplies, food, clothing, arms, ammunition and several agents to partisan groups throughout the Mediterranean region. Drops had been made in Yugoslavia, Greece, Crete, Austria, Romania, northern Italy, and most importantly to the crew, their beloved homeland of Poland.

Ludwik had Zygmunt Weyne, his co-pilot, take over the controls. He removed his helmet and earphones, stretched out his legs and relaxed. It had been another long mission and he was tired.

This one had been uneventful, and he was grateful for that. He closed his eyes and let the rhythmic hum of the plane's four powerful engines lull him into a peaceful semi-nap. He wondered how many more missions they would have to fly and if their luck would hold out. Their American-made Liberator had been hit and damaged by flak and bullets on more than a few of their missions. The crew had survived engine problems, storms, freezing temperatures and partial failures of the plane's electrical and hydraulic systems. Ludwik had always believed that his superb crew, good fortune, and answered prayers were the reasons they had made it safely back to base every time. Some of their missions had been extremely difficult—especially the one to Warsaw some months ago. That had been a ride into hell; an unforgettable dance with the devil. It had shaken his heart and soul, but he had survived.

There was still an hour or so left on the return flight. Zygmunt could take it the rest of the way. For now, a little rest was in order for him. Keeping his eyes closed, he thought about his wife, Nellie, and their son, Kazimierz, back home in England. That only lasted for a few minutes. Beginning to doze, he found himself going over the tragedy that was Warsaw and the part he had played in it.

The uprising had started in the late summer of 1944. The underground Polish Home Army, along with thousands of forest partisans and eager, able bodied citizens of Warsaw had risen up against their Nazi oppressors and their brutal occupation of Warsaw and the country. They had begun a valiant and desperate attempt to regain control of their capitol. The fighting had been fierce and the Poles had held their own for some time. Though outmanned, there had been hope for a victory. A victory that was highly dependent upon the Allied Forces providing badly needed support. Especially air support. The crews of Special Duty Flight 1586, along with other Allied squadrons in the area, were ordered to drop needed supplies into the Polish occupied parts of the city.

The drops would be made under the cover of darkness. Nightly sorties to the city dropped weapons, ammunition and medical supplies to the outnumbered Polish forces. All available planes at the base had made the nearly 1600 miles round trip at least once. It was what every Polish airman in Campo Casale had been waiting for; a chance to be a direct part of the fight for their beloved Warsaw. Unfortunately for Ludwik and his crew, their plane had not been among those available. They were waiting for their ground crew to finish overhauling two of the plane's four engines. All other ground crews were too busy servicing their own planes to help them. It had been crushing to the crew not to be involved in the operation.

Patriotic fervor had swept through the entire Polish squadron. Many of the airmen's families were still living in or near Warsaw. Some flight crews had even discussed the idea of crash-landing their plane after making their drop and joining the fight on the ground. Some even considered parachuting into parts of the city still under Polish control. The feeling among most was if they were going to die in this war, then let it be in the battle for Warsaw. To die there, with their Polish brethren, would be an honor. When the command in Campo Casale heard of this talk, they had moved quickly to remind the men how important their mission was and that they would be needed to continue it. All of this meant little to Ludwik's crew. They were not going. They would have to wait for their plane to be readied. Their ground crew, feeling the urgency to fight also, began to work long shifts. They even ate and slept in the plane's hangar.

In the first few weeks of the Warsaw uprising, sixteen Allied crews were lost to heavy anti-aircraft fire and enemy night fighters. Many of them were Polish crews. That disturbing fact did not deter Ludwik and his men. They still hoped to be part of the battle. When word came down from the Polish High Command in London that consideration was being given to cancel the almost suicidal flights, an outcry went up from the men in Flight 1586.

They felt it was almost their sacred duty to continue the fight. They begged their commanding officers to convince London to continue them. Many in London understood the men's need to fight for something of their own. They knew the importance of that. They also knew that Warsaw had become a lost cause in the minds of many. The Germans were systematically destroying the city and had surrounded the hard fighting, but overmatched Polish forces that were now backed up to the Vistula River. And there was no help coming from the Russians who were sitting on the opposite side of the river, a few miles from the action. The Red Army was content to watch the Poles being eliminated. They also knew the Germans were suffering heavy losses at the same time. They wanted a softened up German force to be the one waiting for them when they decided to launch their attack.

The general staff of the Polish Air Force realized that flying supplies to Warsaw would not be enough. Bombing raids were needed against the Germans. They didn't have the number of bombers left in Italy to get that accomplished. American and English bombers based in England could reach Warsaw and bomb the Germans, but wouldn't have enough fuel left to return. The distance was too great. The English government tried to convince the Russians to let Allied bombers land and refuel at their airbases after bombing the Germans. The Russians refused. They would wait until the battle had been won, at a heavy cost to the Germans, before agreeing with the English request. Their leadership wanted the Polish forces destroyed. Besides their desire to face a weakened German force, they knew the day was coming when their armies would control Poland and didn't want any organized Polish force left to challenge them. When the outcome of the battle clearly favored the Germans, the Russians finally relented. Permission was given to land Allied bombers at their bases to refuel. Encouraged by this change in Russian policy, the Polish High Command sent orders to Campo Casale to continue their supply runs

4

to Warsaw. Once again, Special Duties Flight 1586 made ready their planes for more missions to their beleaguered capitol. This time, Ludwik's reconditioned plane would be among them. He remembered the joy that he and the crew had felt when they were ordered to take part in the battle. To have done nothing to help in the great uprising would have created a lifetime of misery and regret for every one of them. That disappeared as soon as their loaded plane lifted off the ground and headed north into the Adriatic night. They were no longer bystanders in the battle. Now, they had become participants.

Ludwik opened his eyes. They were tearing with pride thinking of that day and the crew's joy and enthusiasm when they had learned they were going to Warsaw. His sleep had not turned into the one he needed, but he was glad to be awake. He felt very proud to be a member of this crew. And he wanted to tell them. He put on his earphones, cleared his voice, and said, "Gentlemen, it is an honor to serve with you." There was a long moment of silence in the plane and then a proud, "Long live, Poland!" reply came from an unidentified crew member. Ludwik smiled and looked at Zygmunt, who nodded his head in approval. It had been a good moment, one filled with profound respect. Ludwik took off his earphones. He really was exhausted. Sleep was again just a few heartbeats away. He knew he would probably dream of Warsaw some more. He usually did. That mission was the one that seemed to be the centerpiece of all his dreams. It wasn't that he lost much sleep over the dreams, it was just that when he dreamt, Warsaw always seemed to make an appearance. This time the dream began with the briefing at Campo Casale reminding everyone that it was a long flight to Warsaw. The quickest route would take them over the city of Krakow. And that was dangerous. The Germans had a night fighter base there.

The air would be filled with those fighters seeking out the much slower planes of Flight 1586 as they came through one by one.

Each converted bomber would be flying alone to Warsaw and would remain alone for the entire mission. ......The dream then moved on to the flight itself.

Nearing the airspace of Krakow, Ludwik went into a climb that would put them above the patrolling night fighters in the area. Witold Zurawski, his navigator, began searching for the signal from Warsaw that would guide them to the city. The Liberator made it through the Krakow gauntlet without any contact with the enemy. The sleek bomber sped its way north over Polish soil toward its target. It was a moonless sky. The black, anti-spotlight painted fuselage of the B24 blended perfectly into the night sky. Less than half an hour later, Witold picked up the radio signal from Warsaw. He homed in on it and gave Ludwik his new heading. It wasn't long before a dim, orange glow appeared far off in the night. Ludwik knew it was a fire. He hoped it wasn't Warsaw. As they closed, the orange glow began to spread in size. It seemed the entire horizon was on fire. Only a large city could burn like that. It had to be Warsaw.

Ludwik brought the Liberator down and begin the run to the drop zone located in a small park by the Vistula River on the river's west bank. It would be marked by men and women lying on the ground in the form of a cross; each holding a large torch. Ludwik wondered if anyone was still alive down there in all that fire. Approaching the outskirts of the city, he maintained his altitude of 300 feet and followed the river into the burning capitol. Hopping over bridges hiding in a smoky haze was tricky and tested Ludwik's skill. He left the river where it fronted the suburb of Praga and crossed into the city proper. Using the light from the inferno, he dodged a church steeple and a few burnt out buildings still high enough to kill them all. He ordered the bomb bay doors opened. Two crew members, secured with ropes to the inside of the fuselage, made ready to push out the long, metal canisters filled with arms, munitions and medical supplies. As the doors opened, the heat from the flames below roared into the belly of the plane. With it came the smells of a dying city. It became hard to breathe. Sweat poured out of every pore in Ludwik's body. He could see German soldiers on the ground pointing at the plane as he flew toward the park and the "cross" that lay waiting for them. Ludwik knew the park well. He had frequented it many times before the war.

Slowing his plane to a vulnerable 130 miles per hour to enable the successful deployment of the parachutes, he spotted the "cross" straight ahead. On his order, Zygmunt hit the "go" button that lit the green light in the bomb bay area. The two harnessed men pushed out the containers one after another. All parachutes opened perfectly forming a mushroom- like parade down to the drop zone. The "cross" was now on its feet and scrambling to open the precious containers as they landed around them. The last few began to drift past the park and toward the buildings beyond. That's when the Germans spotted them. They began firing with everything they had. Ludwik goosed the throttle and raced away across the city.

Sgt. Gagala, the tail gunner, radioed his report on the drop saying all but three containers were in friendly hands. They had done well. They had completed a nerve-wracking run over the city in good shape. No casualties and very little damage to the plane as far as they knew. That being said, there was very little joy in their survival. They knew their success wasn't going to matter much. Warsaw was lost. An air of despair mingled with the smoky residue of fire and death hung inside the plane as it flew silently through the Polish night.

Accelerating out of the city, Ludwik banked the Liberator west, climbed to a safe altitude and began a long, slow turn south; far away from the hell that was Warsaw. No one said anything.

They had just seen what none of them had thought possible. Their capitol, their adored center of Polish culture, filled with family and friends, was being destroyed.

The Warsaw missions to aid the uprising ended with the surrender of all Polish forces in the early autumn of 1944. Ludwik never made another flight to the city. There were, however, many other missions into different areas of Poland and other occupied countries in southern Europe. One of them was the mission into northern Italy that Ludwik and his crew was returning from.

Ludwik woke with a start as the plane shook and wobbled through a patch of turbulent air. The Warsaw nightmare was forgotten. There was flying to finish. Ludwik put his earphones back on and asked Zygmunt for an update. Zygmunt advised him they were less than one hundred miles away from base and their fuel was running low. Assuming control of the aircraft, Ludwik instructed Zygmunt to lower flaps 20 degrees, the first step in a normal approach for a landing. The turbulent air was making it difficult to hold the control wheel steady. It was also drawing curses and growls from the crew who were being tossed around in the plane behind the cockpit. Ludwik shouted for everyone to secure themselves and tie down anything that could cause damage. A moment later, a crackling radio produced an advisory message from the base warning them that a large, severe thunderstorm was rolling over the airfield and heading directly out to sea toward them. They were advised to climb to fifteen thousand feet, get over the top of the storm and then follow it back to the base as it churned out to sea. They further advised a homing signal would be sent out to guide them in case remnants of the storm obscured the field. Ludwik acknowledged the message and pulled back on the control wheel to gain altitude. There was no response. He eased the wheel slightly forward and then back again hoping it would engage. No luck! He could maneuver the wheel forward and side to side, but that was it. He tried several more times to no avail.

There would be no climbing over the storm! And no hope of flying around it. It was just too large, and their fuel was dangerously low. He would have to continue his descent through the storm and hope to find enough daylight near the ground to land.

The monstrous, inky clouds of the storm swallowed the Liberator with an ear-splitting roar of thunder. Gigantic flashes of lightning tore through the air around them. Sheets of pounding rain made visibility and hearing almost impossible. The Liberator was buffeted by swirling winds and tossed around like a leaf on a windy, fall day. Ludwik couldn't remember flying in a storm like this. He tightened his grip on the wheel. He knew the airfield was close. He had to maintain control of the plane. Minutes passed and his struggle continued. It took all his strength to hold the plane steady in its descent. Only the homing signal from base gave him some idea of where the base was. He could only pray they would be able to see the landing strip in time before they ran out of fuel. That's when Zygmunt advised him the gas gauges read empty. Ludwik would be flying a large glider any second now. He had been trained to fly gliders, but not any the size of the Liberator and never in conditions like this. The homing signal suddenly grew quite loud and Ludwik realized he was passing over the base. The altimeter read fifteen hundred feet. He would have to make his turn back to the airstrip quickly before the engines sputtered out of gas. He accomplished the difficult maneuver and headed back with a strong tail-wind from the storm. He ordered full flaps for landing, hoping the runway would come into sight quickly as he went down. The landing would now be in the direction of the sea. The end of the runway was only yards from a small cliff that plunged down onto a narrow beach. Ludwik prayed he would have enough runway to stop. There would be no "touch and go" option because of the plane's inability to climb and the lack of fuel.

They would wind up in the sea or on the small, rocky beach if they ran out of runway. He preferred the water. It would be dangerous, but if the plane bellied down on the water's surface, they might have enough time to get out. He silently asked Mary, the Blessed Mother, to help him.

The plane's altitude kept dropping. At 800 feet the turbulence ended and the rain lessened considerably. The hazy outlines of hangars came into view. As he cleared them, he spotted the runway just off to his right. He quickly maneuvered the plane in line with it and dropped down to land. There was less than half of the runway left. Three of his engines sputtered to a stop. They were out of fuel. He calmly announced for the crew to "prepare for crash landing."

The Crash

Most of the runway was made of corrugated steel plates that had been hammered deep into the Italian soil. They were very narrow and could prove tricky when wet. And today, they were very wet! The speed of the landing and the wet runway caused the plane to skid when he applied the brakes. Realizing he didn't have enough time to stop, he released the brake and let the plane hurtle off the runway. It splashed hard into the sea on its belly, skipped high in the air and smashed back down on the water. The plane leveled out on the surface and began taking water. It was a hundred yards from shore.

Ludwik was pinned to his seat by the steering wheel. It had been driven back into his chest when the plane impacted the water. He was dazed, but still conscious. His head had slammed down hard on the steering wheel. Bits of glass and plastic from the shattered control panel had rocketed into his face. Blood streamed from his forehead and covered his face, neck and chest. He could taste it as it ran over his mouth. Looking to his right, he saw his friend, Zygmunt, slumped over in his seat and still strapped in it.

He was either dead or unconscious. His first thought was to free himself from the steering wheel and get him out. The wheel was crushing his chest. Using his free arms and hands, he tried to push the wheel forward and work his body free and get out of his harness. The Liberator began listing heavily to his side. He could see that the cockpit window next to his friend had been shattered and was open to the sea. In that instant, a large swell of water crashed over the plane's nose. Water splashed into the cockpit dousing both him and Zygmunt from head to toe. Then the plane began to sink. The fuselage behind Ludwik seemed to groan as it filled with water. He desperately tried to free himself. He felt dizzy as the cold water of the Adriatic began to slosh over his boots and move upward toward his knees. Then another large swell lifted the plane's nose and cockpit out of the water and momentarily halted the plane's downward slide. That's when Ludwik saw the bright light approaching. It was moving rapidly toward him. There was someone standing on it or just behind it. A woman! She was dressed in a glowing, white garment. She wasn't standing on the light or just behind it, she WAS the light! He had seen statues of her dressed exactly like that. It was Mary, the Blessed Mother, and she was headed directly for the sinking Liberator. She extended her arms toward the plane, the palms of her hands facing upward as the plane slowly sank under the waves. She began motioning her hands in a slow, upward movement. It was like watching a skillful conductor gently imploring an orchestra to slowly raise the volume of a lovely melody. Ludwik's skin began to prickle uncontrollably. He never took his eyes off her as he went under. As he did, the cold Adriatic suddenly turned warm, and he felt like he was floating away from the world. His last thought before losing consciousness, was that Mary would save him.

The two American Army Air Force men in the motor launch were making their way through the choppy sea headed for their base when the Liberator crashed into the water just ahead of them.

The startled Americans didn't hesitate. They sped toward the plane hoping they might find survivors that had made their way out into the water. As they neared the plane, they turned on the launch's powerful spotlight to help them locate any of the crew. One of the Americans, a sergeant from the all-black supply and maintenance battalion stationed next to Campo Casale, trained the spotlight on the plane's cockpit. The sergeant saw movement in the far side of the cockpit. It was Ludwik, frantically trying to free himself. The other soldier saw him also. He opened the throttle on the launch and moved quickly to the plane. As they came closer, the plane suddenly lurched sideways towards them and a piece of the cockpit window fell into the sea. They could see two men in the cockpit. The one closest to the launch looked to be dead. He was strapped into his seat. The other seemed to be wedged between his seat and the control wheel. He was no longer moving. The American handling the searchlight jumped into the water with his already inflated life jacket and paddled the short distance to the open cockpit. It was quickly filling with water. The wings of the plane were almost under the surface and the rest of the aircraft would be in seconds. The American reached in and grabbed the slumped-over aviator with one hand and unbuckled his strap with the other. He pulled the man out of the plane and quickly moved him through the dancing water to his friend in the launch. In short order, the first airman was in the boat. The American swimmer turned back to the plane for a second effort only to see the cockpit disappear under the waves. It was too late for the other aviator. The American held on to the bobbing launch and rested, looking at the space a few yards away where the plane had been. He closed his eyes and cursed the stupid war. He opened them to climb back into the launch and ......there he was! Gasping for air, and thrashing in the water, the other man in the cockpit had somehow escaped and was blindly looking for something to hold onto. The amazed American paddled to him, circled behind, reached over his head and grabbed the front of his leather helmet to keep his

12

face out of the water. The man went limp in his grasp. The soldier in the boat threw his friend one of the launch's lines and in a few anxious minutes, both waterlogged men were aboard. Ludwik Skoczylas had survived!

The bed was warm and comfortable. Only the sound of someone's retreating footsteps echoing off the corridor walls in the hospital interrupted the blissful silence around him. He didn't have to open his eyes to see where he was. He knew by the smell. He had been to the hospital many times before to visit some of his fellow aviators that had been wounded or become seriously ill. Some of them were still here. He was grateful to be alive, but he wasn't sure if he would stay that way. He wasn't afraid to die. He just didn't want to die here, in Italy. The fact that men died was not the only thing that worried Ludwik. When you died, you died! So be it. But, while a death of a Polish airman was a sad and tragic event, it was made worse by the fact that he would not be buried in Poland, the beloved homeland. The best that could be done for him in Italy was to have some friends sprinkle a little Polish soil on his grave. Sacks of the soil had been gathered over time by Polish airmen that had made covert night landings on fields in Poland to retrieve prisoners, agents, wounded partisans, German weapons and maps locating German positions. While most of the crew were busy loading what and who they had come for, a few others jumped out of the idling plane with shovels and sacks to gather and bring back the prized soil. In minutes, the cargo and soil were on the plane. Moments after that, the plane was lifting off in the darkness and returning to Italy. Ludwik appreciated the symbolism of it all but prayed that he would not die here. If he had to die, he wanted it to be at home with his family or shot out of the sky over Poland. He could still taste the sea in his mouth, a briny souvenir from his life and death struggle in the water. Every inch of his lean, muscular frame ached, especially his chest and lower abdomen. His face was covered with bandages.

He had sustained several cuts from flying pieces of shattered cockpit glass. He remembered the impact, the pain, his struggle to free himself, the flooding water, his friend, Zygmunt, and of course, the Blessed Mother in her "LIGHT." He could not remember escaping the sinking plane but believed the "Lady" was responsible for it. He thought about the rest of his crew. All good men; loyal, professional and dedicated to the cause. Their faces drifted by him in his thoughts. He whispered their names to God and hoped it wasn't too late for Him to help them. ....Witold Zurawska, navigator, Edward Gagala, tail gunner, Stanislaw Slowik, radio operator, Andrzej Wandzel, flight mechanic, Jan Czarnata, flight engineer and Zygmunt Weyne, co-pilot and bunk mate.

Had they survived? Was he the only one that had? Would he survive? No answers now, but he knew they would come soon. More prayers were in order instead. Ludwik had always been deeply religious and understood the power of prayer. His Catholic upbringing had ingrained in him a love for Christ with a special adoration of Mary, His Holy Mother. He prayed for the safety and well-being of his crew. Halfway through his next prayer asking God to forgive the men their sins if they had perished, he fell off into a deep sleep. He could do no more.

Crew of B24 Liberator

KH 151 GR-S

Lost January 19, 1945

Ludwik Skoczylas

2nd row   far right

Rest and Reflection

Sergeant Mechanic Wandzel stood at the foot of the bed. He was holding onto the bed frame and staring at Ludwik's chart trying to decipher the notes scribbled on it in the timeless, messy manner that most hurried physicians seemed to use.

"Good to see you, Andrzej," Ludwik said quietly.

"Ahhh, Ludwik, glad you made it my friend. How do you feel?"

"Good enough, my friend. And you and the others?"

The lack of military formality between the two men was typical of the Polish Air Force. Rank had no real meaning with most of the men. They were friends first and foremost. Officers and enlisted men both shared the same dream; to win back the brief but wonderful independence that Poland had gained after World War I.

The sergeant lowered his head for a moment then said, "Edward is dead. His body washed up on the shore. Stanislaw and Witold are missing. Zygmunt and Jan are here in the hospital. They are not allowed any visitors. I got out of the plane through a break in the fuselage about ten feet from Edward's position in the tail. I never saw him. I have some cuts, bruises and a broken ankle. God was with me," the sergeant replied. He raised the crutch that had been resting on the bed frame and gave his friend a sad smile.

"How long have I been here?" asked Ludwik.

"Three days," the flight mechanic answered.

Three days. And two men still missing! Probably dead by now. Ludwik was shaken by that. He hoped their bodies would eventually wash ashore like Edward's had. Then they could all be buried together at the base with the honor they deserved.

He had lost three good friends. Three more men that would never see their homeland again. A surge of guilt ran through him. He had been the pilot that put the plane in the sea. If only he had seen the runway sooner. If only he could have managed to loosen the controls and climb over the storm. He knew he had done the best he could considering everything that had happened. He also knew he would have to live with the fact that men had died while he was at the controls. It was a sad moment for him.

Days passed. A week went by. Then two weeks. The pain from the deep bruises on his chest had lessened considerably. His facial cuts were healing nicely. The hospital care, along with the almost daily letters from Nellie, had done him well. Andrzej visited every day and brought updates on the other two survivors. They were improving. Concussions, cuts and a few broken bones aside, the hearty Polish lads would be up and about soon. Their flying days, like Ludwik's, were over for now.

News arrived daily on the steady advance of the Allied forces squeezing the life out of the Nazis. Hitler's armies were being crushed by the Russians closing in from the east and the American, British and other allies, including Polish forces, from the west. They were all positioned inside Germany now and it was only a matter of time before the war ended. The slaughter would soon be over and Hitler's "thousand-year Reich" gone in a relatively few ugly years. That was the welcome news. The worrisome news was that a large Russian bear was now prowling the Polish countryside and he was very, very dangerous.

On January 22nd, Flight 1586 was given orders from the Polish High Command in London to cease flights into occupied Europe. The "Special Duties" squadron was further ordered to "stand down" for the immediate future. All operational and support equipment was to be inspected, repaired and refurbished.

Ground crews were to conduct a thorough inspection of their respective aircraft. Each plane would then be cleaned, lubricated, repainted and fueled. The order did not receive a "high priority" label; just said to get everything done in an orderly manner. Command at Campo Casale knew that the "stand down" order also meant some sorely needed rest for the flight crews. They were to be given some leave on a rotating basis. Those not on leave were to be considered off-duty.

Everyone at Campo Casale hoped that Special Duties, Flight 1586 had flown its last mission. More than five years of war seemed like a lifetime for many of the veterans who had managed to survive. Their prayers of returning home would soon be answered. The important question now was, would they be allowed to return to Poland? Stalin, the Russian dictator, was already making demands about the post-war borders in Eastern Europe and seemed very unlikely to favor any plan for Poland's return to independence. The memory of the Russians refusing to help the Poles during the Warsaw Uprising last October had shown he cared little for the Polish people.

On February 15th, the question of where "home" would be after the war was answered. Probably not in Poland. At the Yalta Conference in Crimea, the United States and England agreed that post-war Poland would be controlled by the Soviet Union with a Russian promise of free elections shortly after the war ended. Ludwik knew that promise was a lie.

He also knew what awaited him and his family if he chose to return to Poland with them. Imprisonment for him was almost certain, exile with the family to the Russian gulags probable and his execution would be no surprise. There had been many reports of those things happening in Poland. He also didn't believe the fact that Nellie and the children were English citizens would make any difference in their treatment by the communist government.

The men and women of the Polish Armed Forces throughout Europe were stunned, disappointed and angered by the decision of their allies to give Poland to the Russians. It was a betrayal, plain and simple by the very people they had fought side by side with for years. Their anguish was shared by many in the Allied military. While understanding the political reasoning that prompted the give-away, keeping Stalin in the fight, it was hard for them to watch a valued and respected ally lose its country after fighting so hard to regain it.

Immediately after the Yalta concessions were made public, all Polish airmen at Campo Casale were ordered to turn in their weapons for "reconditioning." The Polish Command had decided not to leave any weapons in the hands of their emotional countrymen. They worried that some might take their own lives in frustration and anger after hearing their country had been given away; that their sacrifice and blood had been for nothing. They knew the number of Polish casualties, military and civilian, was already in the millions. No need to add to it.

Everyone at Campo Casale was outraged by the agreements made at Yalta. Heavy drinking and anger became the unofficial order of the day. Some of it even spilled over into the quiet confines of the hospital.

Ludwik's personal plans for post-war life had been dramatically changed by Yalta. The future for him and millions of other Poles had been decided in an arena of appeasement. He would be with Nellie and Kazimierz, but not in Poland. In was no different in his mind to what had happened when the British were fooled into agreeing that Czechoslovakia's Sudetenland should be ceded to Germany to appease Hitler. Six months after that decision, Germany controlled all of Czechoslovakia. And that had been just the first step in establishing their dominance over the rest of Europe.

Now history was repeating itself. Poland had been given away in the hope of pacifying Stalin and his Russian Soviet Union.

Ludwik's disappointment in the Yalta decision was tempered somewhat by knowing that a home in England was waiting for him. He knew that Nellie's family would help him find his way. There would be opportunity for him after the war. That would not be the case for most of his fellow Poles. Their choice of returning to Poland and all its uncertainties or starting a new life in a foreign land without their loved ones, would be filled with frustration and bitterness. He vowed that he would do what he could to help as many of his comrades as possible. His door in England would always be open to any Pole that walked down his street looking for a friend.

The world was about to regain some sense of sanity and millions of people were going to celebrate the beginning of a new life with their loved ones. Many would rejoice with unabashed, patriotic pride in their victory and get on with life in their own country. His people, left like a sacrificial lamb, would have to deal with the loss of their freedom once again. Ludwik wondered when, if ever, it would be Poland's turn to celebrate its return as a free country. With that in mind, he knew he would have to simplify his plan for the immediate future. Poland would have to wait for now. First, he needed to regain his strength quickly. He would have to work hard on what had made him who he was; a determined individual with a firm belief in discipline, hard work and prayer. All concepts he had learned being raised on a family farm. It was important that he remain calm, measured and patient. He had been through something similar to this sort of thing before in England after being struck down by a drunk driver and nearly losing his life.

He knew from that experience physical pain would eventually disappear over time. What he didn't know was if he could handle the pain he felt in his heart about the loss of his beloved homeland.

Before long, he was on his feet and walking around the hospital. The daily walks were great therapy for him. It was good to be on the move. The pain in his chest had subsided considerably, but there was still discomfort in his abdomen and ribs. Luckily, none of the ribs had been broken. The cuts on his face had healed nicely. Only an occasional itch from a shrinking scar or two gave him any bother.

The walks always included a stop at the hospital library. It was a small but very comfortable room. It was his favorite place in the building. It had a large window that faced the airfield and sea beyond. There was a couch for reading and a desk for writing. Both were arranged so one would have a view out the window. Hundreds of books, written in Italian, Polish and English, were available. They were neatly arranged in cedar bookcases tailored for the patients. The bottom three shelves in each were three feet plus off the floor making it much easier for a wheelchair patient to reach a book. That considerate detail was appreciated by Ludwik. He respected the thought that had gone into it. He admired the craftsmanship of the men that had created the bookcases. They were true artists. He would run his hands along the smooth, pegged joints connecting the shelves to the frame and then over the well-cut figurines of children and animals along the top. All perfectly cut and smooth to the touch. Everything about the bookcases was exceptional. In England, the maker of bookcases like these were called people with a "good turn of hand." He had been described as one of those people by his English in-laws and their friends. It was well known that he could build or repair anything. He was also known as a master of taking things apart and putting them back perfectly. No matter how intricate the item was. He also enjoyed the smell of the bookcases. The cedar was strong and very sweet. It brought a sense of home to him. Made him relax. He'd sit on the couch, close his eyes and let the aroma take him back in time. Back to Poland and the farm he had grown up on. He could see the kitchen with its hand-made cedar table and chairs.

He could see the bedroom he shared with Karol, his younger brother. It had a cedar storage chest at the foot of the bed. The heavy mattress and duvet on the bedframe were supported by cedar planks spread across underneath. He remembered falling asleep every night with the pleasant smell of those planks making its way up to and through the thick mattress. The cedar and its aroma also brought to life images of his family going about their daily life on the farm. There were nine people in the family. Three boys, four girls and their parents. He was the oldest boy. He hadn't seen the family in nine years. He left the farm at the age of seventeen to attend Poland's prestigious naval academy but had returned home after one year and a summer because of financial hardship. He finished his university education in Warsaw at a technical university while helping to run the farm on his off months. In 1936, he left home for good and joined the navy's Fleet Air Arm as a reconnaissance pilot. Shortly after the Germans invaded in 1939, he was ordered out of the country with thousands of other airmen to live and fight another day.

While the library and its bookcases gave Ludwik many happy moments, it didn't compare with the enjoyment he experienced reading the letters from his young wife, Nellie. They arrived almost daily. Her words were little treasures to him. They were delicate, beautiful and filled with love. He read them with care again and again. He could picture her dark, curly hair, beautiful eyes and full lips. She was his "cyganka," the gypsy-looking love of his life. She liked to use a combination of Polish and English words to weave her stories of the family's daily life in Carlisle, his future home. The city, located a few miles from the Scottish border, had never suffered a German air raid. Life had been fairly normal there for some time.

Her letters always began with the same poignant Polish greeting of "Moj najdrozszy." The words, meaning, "My Dearest," were enough by themselves to lift his spirits.

He always felt the love that poured out from Nellie's heart when she put her pen to paper and wrote those two words. They were very special to him.

Ludwik was released from the hospital near the end of February and placed back on active duty. Most of his days were spent with the three other surviving crew members who had also been released. They would breakfast together and then report to the airfield to become familiar with their new plane, another B24 Liberator. They met and worked with their ground crew on a variety of matters. None of which was urgent. The squadron was still in "stand down" status. Ludwik, always interested in the mechanical end of things, spent most of his time reviewing what he already knew about a Liberator and its systems.

After lunch, the crew would meet in the barrack's day room to play cards, throw darts and exchange any news they had concerning the war and the situation at home. Much of the news was discouraging. Russian rule was going to be difficult. More difficult than they thought. The new occupiers were going to change the country's way of life with a new political and social system that did not allow much individual freedom. People were already being forced to accept the communist system and swear allegiance to a communist government. Poland's short-lived period of democracy, now dead, was going to be buried by the "collective good" of communism. Ludwik wondered if the new political system would be a threat to the existence of the Catholic Church in Poland. He remembered the threat Mussolini was to the church in Italy before being killed by his own people.

The news from England was also unsettling. Under pressure from labor unions, the English government had begun to talk openly about the Polish presence on the island becoming a problem economically. The English people, who had once admired the Poles as heroic allies in the struggle against Germany, were now beginning to worry about the large number of them that might remain in England and take their jobs. It was very apparent to the men at Campo Casale that when the war ended, they would be fighting other "battles" should they decide to remain in England. Ludwik told his crew to concentrate on their duties. He reminded them the war was still on and Flight 1586 had to maintain its readiness.

The average daily temperature at Campo Casale had improved to a steady seventy plus degrees. Duties at the base were lightened and additional free time given to the men. Going to the beach became a regular routine; a good place to escape the hum-drum days on base. The men set up picnic tables for their lunch, beer drinking and card playing. The main topics of conversation were usually about home, women and what they were going to do after the war.

Ludwik enjoyed the friendly group activities. Flight and ground crews mixed comfortably with each other. The feeling of brotherhood had always been strong among the men and Ludwik felt good to be a part of it again. He loved listening to the stories of home, family, holidays, sweethearts and traditions. He was always amused by the younger airmen and their inflated tales of female conquests, daring deeds and drunken escapades. He had been their age once and knew how the art of embellishment worked. He also knew it could earn you lots of good-natured verbal abuse that always increased proportionally to the number of beers consumed by the abusers. When it became too loud, and it always did, he would leave the noise and find a comfortable, quiet spot to relax. Enjoying the quiet, he would read a few of Nellie's letters and think about his families in England and Poland. From time to time, he would gaze up the coastline to where the base runway led to the sea. His plane was still under water there. Just a hundred yards from the rocky beach at the end of the runway. The tail section had broken off and lay some yards away from the rest of the fuselage. Divers had confirmed that.

The bodies of Witold and Stanislaw had not been found. The sea had refused to give them up. Every time he thought of those two, he would pray for their souls. Edward Gagala, their tail gunner, had already been buried at the base cemetery. Most of the squadron had assembled there earlier in February on a cool, misty morning to witness the customary "sprinkling of Polish soil" on his gravesite. Andrzej, walking on crutches, had gone to the ceremony to represent the crew who were still confined to the hospital and unable to attend.

Saying Goodbye

He had given Ludwik a detailed account of the ceremony. He said the squadron commander had addressed the squadron from the platform on the parade grounds next to the cemetery. He read the names of the three men and praised their heroism, sacrifice and love for Poland. He said the lost men would always be considered heroes of the homeland and defenders of Warsaw. Everyone assembled there was asked to remember the three and all the others that had given their lives in the war. He went on to praise the four survivors of the crash and all the rest of the squadron for their performance in the last two years. He said the squadron had performed brilliantly in their mission to supply partisan groups throughout occupied Europe with the arms, munitions, agents and essential supplies that in no small part, had aided in the defeat of the Germans. He finished by expressing the hope shared by every Pole alive that the decisions made at Yalta would in time be reversed and they would all live to see a free Poland again. As he stepped back on the platform and faced the flag, a small band of musicians stood up and began playing the national anthem. Everyone snapped to attention, faced the flag and saluted. Andrzej said it was a proud moment. Everyone held their salute until the last note was played. He said there were more than a few who had wept, and he had been one of them.

After the anthem ended, all the men were marched to the gravesite. A song was sung to honor Edward, Witold and Stanislaw by one of the band members.

"And the sprinkling on Edward's grave?" Ludwik asked.

"I had the honor," Andrzej answered.

"I'm glad it was you," Ludwik said.

Andrzej said, "As soon as the dirt hit the grave, someone shouted, "NIECH ZYJE POLSKA!" and then as one, everyone shouted the same words as loud as they could. It was as if they wanted Edward to hear them."

Ludwik had heard the last part of the ceremony. A nurse had opened the window facing in the direction of the gathering. His eyes had moistened as the sound of the "Mazurek Dabrowskiego" came floating through the mist and onto the airfield. The national anthem carried with it the spirit of Polish fight, defiance and pride. The words in the anthem had moved him and helped to lessen the profound sadness he felt over the loss of those three good men.

He had bowed his head to give thanks to Mary, the Blessed Lady for his survival. He would always believe she had freed him from the submerged plane and made his rescue possible.

He was told that two Americans had pulled him and Zygmunt from the water, but no one knew or had asked how he managed to escape the sinking plane. He knew that didn't matter. They wouldn't believe it anyways. In his heart, he believed that three people had saved him; the two Americans, whoever they were, and most importantly, the Lady that had answered his prayers.

Dreams

It had been a month since the crash. Ludwik had been released from the hospital and placed on restricted duty. He had tried in vain to get the names of the two Americans that had pulled him out of the water. He asked the medics that had come for him in the ambulance if they knew who they were, but they said there had been no time for that. They could only say they were two black Americans.

Ludwik was back in his quarters at the barracks. At first, everything was as it always had been. After a few days however, things changed. He began having trouble getting a good night's sleep. And that made his days a little difficult. He was tired most of the time. The quiet hospital routine of rest and relaxation had worked well for him. He had enjoyed the leisurely pace of recovery, good care, time in the library and friendly exchanges with his crew and other patients. It had all become a comfort to him. He had dreams in the hospital, but they were always silent and never lasted long. Sleep had always won out. The dreams came and left quickly. They were like short, silent-movies. That pattern continued the first two nights in the barracks. On the third night, the short, silent-picture shows morphed into full length movies featuring the sights and sounds of war on night missions into German-occupied territory; tracer bullets, exploding ack-ack shells, pinging flak, roaring engines, screaming men, and a plane bouncing like a soccer ball. Enough noise and fright for a lifetime.

Sometimes the images gave way and there was nothing but sounds that came from places unseen. Dark places. People praying in a group that grew louder and louder as if they were closing in on him, a wolf howling off in the distance, a train whistle screeching its way toward him, a child sobbing uncontrollably. The sounds didn't need pictures. They were upsetting by themselves. Maybe even more so.

Ludwik was an intelligent man. He surmised it was no coincidence that the quiet dreams in the hospital had suddenly turned ugly in the barracks. Barracks were built to house warriors not patients. Comfort and relaxation had not been considered a necessity in their construction. Basic need and functionality had. Stark reminders of war were everywhere in his quarters. His leather flight helmet and fur-lined, leather flight jacket hung in his tiny, no door closet. His flight gloves lay on the room's one chair, his boots tucked neatly underneath. On top of the desk was his flight log, an empty pistol holster wrapped neatly beside it. The pistol had been turned in to the squadron armorers under the pretense of "inspecting" and "cleaning" it. An obvious excuse to prevent pilots from committing suicide after the depressing news of the Yalta giveaway of Poland to the Russians. Everything in the room reeked of war; a daily reminder of who he had been before the crash and who he was once again. Maybe that was one of the reasons for the dreams. Maybe it was the almost six years at war finally catching up to him.

The dreams, now full-fledged nightmares, became more complex. They might start about incidents while flying then suddenly switch to episodes on the ground and then switch quickly back to the air. The terrifying flight into the inferno that was Warsaw would suddenly switch to a run and hide chase in a forest and then move on to the crash in the Adriatic. On other nights, the dreams remained fixed on a single episode. There was one that hounded his soul. It happened on a mission to drop an agent into Poland; a mission that went horribly wrong. Seconds after the agent had jumped, his parachute became entangled in the plane's tail and rudder assembly. The poor man was dragged through the freezing night air like a fish hooked by an angler in a trolling boat. Ludwik tried to shake him loose by waggling the plane's wings but was unable to free him. To make matters worse, the parachute lines entangled in the tail rudder assembly made the aircraft very difficult to fly.

Ludwik had to use all his skill to get back to the base. He never knew if the agent died from exposure or his body's impact on the ground when the plane landed. The most agonizing part of it all for Ludwik was that he had been powerless to save the man. It was one of the few times in his life that he had experienced such helplessness. He had been raised by his parents with the idea that there always was an answer to a problem. All one needed was logic, determination and time. Unfortunately, time and circumstance in this instance had denied him that process. A man had died a horrible death and he, Ludwik Skoczylas, had failed, in his mind, to save him.

Bednarz

Dr. Jozef Bednarz was a medical doctor that had received additional training in the field of psychiatry. He was the only doctor that had any background in that field at Campo Casale. That made him the doctor that airmen experiencing emotional issues came to for help. It didn't matter the rank of the man or what his duty was. Bednarz had learned quickly that the mind of a man, any man, could be wounded as badly as his body might. While his background in psychiatric treatment was limited, he did the best he could to help the man get through a problem and remain fit for duty. His method was simple and direct. Probe gently, listen carefully, take notes, analyze the situation and then guide the man through discussions that would give him some understanding of why things were the way they were. Along the way, he would look for any repressed memories of a troubled past that the war had brought out. He would recommend ways to deal with the identified problems and chart the man's progress through subsequent consultations. With his limited experience treating patients with emotional issues, his prescription for improvement was somewhere between good discussions, a pat on the back and a little medication. He never allowed himself to become too close to an individual. He needed to remain objective.

It was his charge and responsibility to get the man back on duty quickly and to that end, he had been successful. There were some men he would have preferred to spend more time with but there was a war going on, and orders were orders. It was that part of the job that bothered him. Only the men that had become a danger to themselves and others were kept away from duty. They were the ones that might compromise the safety of an entire crew.

One of Bednarz's duties was to periodically conduct mental fitness checks on the pilots of Flight1586 to insure they were fit to fly. Ludwik's checkup was scheduled in a few weeks, but he had requested an earlier date to make sure the sudden bouts with nightmares weren't a sign of a more serious issue; either mental or physical. The squadron's "stand down" status seemed to be a good time to address those possibilities. There was plenty of time open for a good chat with the doctor. Ludwik had only seen him once in all the time he had been stationed at Campo Casale and that had been more of a physical exam than an interview to check his mental status.

Bednarz's office was just before the library in the hospital. Ludwik felt a familiar sense of comfort as he walked down the corridor toward the office. He was early so he decided to stop in the library, relax on the couch and have a cigarette. He was pleased to see no one was there. He felt relaxed. He walked past the couch to the window. He stood there gazing out at the airstrip and the sea. There was nothing moving. No planes, no trucks, no people. Not a bird in the sky. The sea shone like glass and seemed fixed to the shore. It was beautiful. He thanked God for the day. He thanked Jesus for his sacrifice then asked Mary for the courage to do good so he would be worthy of her son's promise of eternal life. Just as he finished his request, he sensed he wasn't alone in the room. A familiar tingle began to spread over his body. The hair on his arms seemed to be moving. Something was happening. Someone else was there.

He turned toward the open door of the library and caught a quick glimpse of a young woman passing by in the corridor. He didn't get that good a look at her, but something told him he had seen her before. He walked slowly to the doorway to see if she was still in the corridor, but she was gone. There was no other room in the direction she was headed, just the exit door at the end of the corridor. He had not heard the door being opened or closed. He went to the door, opened it and stepped outside. She was nowhere in sight. It was hard to believe she had disappeared so quickly. Puzzled, he went back into the library and sat on the couch. The skin on his body continued to prickle. He felt it was somehow connected to the appearance of the woman. He tried to remember what she looked like from the brief glimpse he had of her. He thought she was young, slight in figure, dark haired and olive skinned. She was wearing something brown. That's what he remembered. At least that's what he thought he remembered. He got up and went to the window. He stared long and hard at the sea and began to question himself. Had he really seen someone? Maybe he hadn't. Was this all connected somehow to his nightmares and lack of sleep? Was his mind conjuring up visions now? She had seemed real. And the skin on his arms was still prickling. What had caused that? That's when he remembered the shepherdess in brown being strafed by the Messerschmitt in Poland and the shepherdess who waved to him outside a train station in Romania. The ones that his friend, Josef and he had come to consider might be the Blessed Lady or someone sent by her to help them make their way to France. He remembered well the prickling of his skin on both those occasions. The same sensation he had experienced under the water after his crash and now again here in the library. Ludwik told himself to be rational. While he truly believed that the Blessed Lady had saved him from drowning and had answered his prayers across Europe years ago, he found it hard to believe she had any connection to today. Still, there was the prickly skin and now bumps on his arms.

31

He wondered what Bednarz would say about this. He might think delusion had set in. Maybe it had. That would be a problem concerning his fitness to fly. Then again, if he was becoming delusional and seeing things, it might be good to get it out in the open now before he went home. He decided to wait a while and see how things went.

"So. What brings you to me so early, Ludwik?" Bednarz asked.

"I'm not sleeping well. Lots of nightmares."

Bednarz smiled at the pilot and said, "Let me welcome you into the "Sick and Tired of War," fraternity. From what I hear, the war is about to end. My guess is the next time you fly a plane, you'll be returning it to a base in England."

Ludwik smiled back and said, "I'll believe that when I'm doing it. The war isn't over, and I need to be sure I'm alright to fly. I need your help to make that happen."

Bednarz measured carefully the honest request. It surprised him. He wasn't used to a pilot asking for help. He found that refreshing. Usually, the pilots lied through their teeth to keep flying. It was that important to them. They were a proud bunch.

Opening his notebook, he scribbled the following in his notepad: good eye contact, good body language, requesting help—nightmares!

He told Ludwik that notetaking would be part of the process no matter the issue; physical, emotional or both. Ludwik nodded his understanding. Bednarz continued, "Lots of pilots here are considering a stay in the Air Force after the war. They seem to think flying is their best chance of making a living. From what I've read of your record, your performance as a pilot has been quite excellent.

Better than most, I would say. How do you feel about remaining in the service? Making a career of it."

While that sounded like a re-enlistment pitch to Ludwik, he knew it probably wasn't. He asked the doctor for a minute to think about it. Bednarz agreed. Ludwik felt the doctor might be fishing for an emotional answer, that he probably was very keen on the manner and tone of his reply and not necessarily the answer itself. It was a question that certainly could have provoked an emotional response from an overtired, burnt-out pilot. Especially one that was recovering from a crash. The question also called into play the degree of confidence a pilot had in himself to perform his duty. It was a clever way to open an evaluation. He respected that. He thought this exchange might be good for him and hoping it wouldn't take that long. Especially in getting rid of the nightmares. He relaxed and answered the question.

"Thanks for the time. Let me say, I love to fly. I wanted to fly the first time I saw a plane. I wasn't even a teenager then. I was working in the fields on our farm when it flew over us. Everyone stopped working to watch it. None of us had ever seen a plane before. I was fascinated. The pilot put on a show. I knew then I would fly someday. And here I am. As far as remaining in the Air Force, I just want to finish my duty to Poland as a pilot. After that, I'm not sure. There are other things that interest me. I'm sure God will help me decide."

Bednarz added another entry in his book: Intelligent, confident, articulate, religious. He asked Ludwik to take the other pad and pencil on the desk and write down the following three categories: people, places, and events. And under each category list at least five examples. Then circle three that he considered to be most important. He said he would return in ten minutes.

After Bednarz left, Ludwik moved to the doctor's vacated chair and began writing. He wasn't sure what the purpose of it meant, but he began. The words came quickly. Under "People" he listed Nellie, Kazimierz, Mary, Jesus, Josef, Basha, Bodil, mother, father and Zygmunt. Under "Places" he listed Poland, Mazanki, Warsaw, Carlisle, Budapest, Gdynia, Puck, Blackpool, Praga, Deblin and the Naval Academy. Finally, under "Events" he wrote invasion, solos, graduations, weddings, births, anniversaries, contests, parades, holidays. He looked carefully over his selections for a few minutes and then circled "Nellie," "Mary" and "Poland."

Bednarz smoked his pipe slowly. He enjoyed the view of the sea from the library. Days like today always seemed to have a calming effect on him. Nature had a way of doing that. It always reminded him of what life had to offer if men, including himself, could just get in step with its rhythm. Or more precisely, get back in step with its rhythm after this calamity of war ended. He wondered how long it was going to take for himself to accomplish that. A glance at his watch told him it was time to return. He tamped the tobacco down into the pipe's bowl, took a long look out at the sea and headed back to the office. Skoczylas interested him. His file indicated he had attended the Polish Naval Academy. Obviously a very bright individual. His record was excellent. A definite asset to the Polish Air Force. If Poland was to ever regain its independence, then men like him would be needed to carry its torch. He was that impressive.

Ludwik had returned to his seat and was mulling over what had occurred in the library earlier. Or what he thought had occurred. Another person with him to verify the woman's presence would have helped. Someone like Josef who had been witness with him to the two unusual appearances of a lady shepherdess in a brown robe on their odyssey across southern Europe in 1939.

"I should spend a little more time in our library. It has a beautiful view," the doctor stated as he walked into the room. "It's the kind of place a man needs to be in from time to time."

He was not only speaking to Ludwik, he was speaking to himself. He was a true member of the "Sick and Tired of War" fraternity. He had joined it a few years ago while treating bomber crew personnel in England. His work there massaging the bruised minds of young Polish airmen had taken a toll on him. It was the reason he had requested the transfer to Italy. He thought the change of scenery would refresh his energy. It had helped for a while, but the work was still the work. There was always a steady stream of tired, tense and troubled men seeking help. Their faces may have been new, but their problems were the same. He looked at the tired face across from him and hoped this one's mind hadn't been damaged much. There was way too much potential here. His instincts told him that this man could do lots of good in a world that was in dire need of it. It struck him that the probability was high that he would be treating veterans like him long after the war was done. And that he would do the very best he could for all of them. After recording Ludwik's picks, Bednarz decided to briefly discuss the two women Ludwik had circled.

"Who are Nellie and Mary?" he asked.

"Nellie is my wife and Mary is the mother of Christ," Ludwik responded.

"Do you and Nellie have any children?"

Ludwik smiled broadly and said, "We have a young son. His name is Kazimierz. He will be two soon. The last time I saw him he was only two days old. Just before I left to join Flight 1586 in Derna."

Bednarz knew that Mary was an important figure to the Polish people. The highest saint in the minds of most. He always felt that religion had a place in therapy, but he usually preferred to keep it in reserve and only use it if an individual might have already benefitted from it. He had never been that personally involved in religious observance and knew his faith wasn't that strong. He was, however, interested as to why Mary had been one of the pilot's choices.

"Anything in particular about Mary?"

"She is my spiritual friend. I pray to her more than anyone else. If it wasn't for her, I wouldn't be here."

The answer piqued Bednarz's interest. He almost asked why that was but something held him back. For a second, he thought it was fear. Dismissing that, he decided not to pursue it today. Maybe the next time. He was concerned if he asked about it today, it would take more time than he wanted to give in a first meeting. He always preferred recording a first impression of a man then taking time to thoroughly review the man's file before their next session. With Skoczylas, he would engage him in a lengthy discussion designed to learn what might be at the root of this onset of nightmares. It interested him that in the five plus years of war the man had experienced, there was no mention of nightmares being a distraction in his file. It was only now they had surfaced. He decided that sleeping pills were in order to help Skoczylas catch up on his sleep for a couple of nights; see if the nightmares continued then. Pills were only a short-term answer. Couldn't take them every night the rest of his life. He needed to discuss the nightmares with him. What they were about? And were there any other reasons besides the war that might be contributing to them? He decided one more question for today was in order. He asked Ludwik why he had chosen "Nellie," "Mary," and "Poland."

Ludwik spoke slowly in a quiet voice, "They are my heart, my soul, my country. They are what I love the most. They are what I believe in."

Bednarz recorded the answers, closed the book and told Ludwik to report back to him at 1300 hours, two days from now. He handed the pilot two sleeping pills, one for tonight and one for tomorrow night. He added that he would be available for any "emergency consultation" the rest of today and tomorrow.

After Skoczylas left, Bednarz outlined his plan to counsel him. He decided to wait to bring up "Mary" and why he had said she was the reason he was here. Instead, he would ask the pilot to talk about his upbringing in Poland. Let him pick a starting point and go from there. Normally, he would never take much time for this, but with the "stand down" status, time was available. He decided he was not only going to be more thorough in this case; he was going to use it to get back on track to being the physician he was supposed to be. He knew he had missed helping others the way he should have, but his orders had always been to "get them back in the air ASAP!" No need for that now.

Ludwik dawdled through his second cup of coffee in the officer's mess. The lady by the library and his prickling skin was on his mind. He had talked to a priest in Italy five years ago about the two other instances that had produced the same body reaction. At that time, he had felt strongly that it had something to do with the Blessed Lady answering his prayers. After his rescue from drowning by the Lady, the onset of nightmares, and now the library incident, he was beginning to wonder about it all. He had gained a little insight spiritually from the priest on his first two "encounters" years ago. Maybe it was time for a little clinical insight. He would think on it.

37

Ludwik spent the next two days trying to figure out what had gone wrong with the controls of the Liberator that had crashed. He and his ground crew took apart the steering system of a decommissioned Liberator to see if they could find a clue as to why the controls had locked up the way they had on that awful day. While it had been a thorough and rigorous inspection, they had found no clues.

Ludwik realized the answer to the crash lay at the bottom of the sea a hundred yards or so from the end of the runway. There would be no raising the plane for an inspection. It had found its final resting place. The answer to the mystery of the jammed controls would never be known. Just like the mystery of the two missing crewmen. Divers had searched a week for them, but the sea had not relented.

The sleeping pills had helped. Ludwik had taken the recommended one a night just before "lights out." Sleep had come quickly both nights and had blissfully lasted close to eight hours each time. The nightmares had patted his pillow both nights, but the pills had kept them at bay.

All the news was good. The need for Flight 1586 to fly into danger again was very slim. There didn't seem to be any doubt that the war's end was imminent. And if that was the case, Ludwik would be going home soon and that fact reinforced the need for help in combatting the nightmares. He didn't want to carry them into his bedroom. He knew that sleeping pills were only a stop-gap measure. He needed advice, some tips on how to deal with the nightmares after he no longer wore a uniform.

Bednarz was pleased that Ludwik had had two decent nights of sleep. He looked much better. That meant sleeping pills did not have an adverse effect on him. They were good for occasional use. He asked Ludwik if he didn't mind talking a bit about growing up in Poland. Ludwik was surprised by the suggestion.

He wasn't sure what, if anything, it had to do with his ability to pilot a plane, but if it was going to help him cope with ugly nightmares in the future, he was willing to go along. At least for now.

Farming or Flying

The thirty-year old pilot said his early days were spent growing up on farms. The first one was near a village called Kurylowka. It was located on the banks of the San River in southeastern Poland. It was owned by an uncle on his mother's side. When he was seven, the family moved to a farm of their own outside of Mazanki, another small village, hundreds of miles to the north. Not too far from East Prussia. The farm had more than thirty acres of land. It was part of the vast plain that ran through most of north central Poland. Sugar beets were the major money crop of the region. They were also the main source of income for the family. In addition to sugar beets, the family had an extensive vegetable garden and raised a variety of livestock that included chickens, goats, pigs, a few cows, and two horses.

Bednarz was born and raised in the city of Krakow. He was a city boy. He knew very little about farms and the operation of one. Especially one that was in the business of growing and harvesting sugar beets. He had questions; how large was the family? What role did family play in the operation of the farm? And at what age were the children expected to take part?

Ludwik found himself enjoying the conversation. He hadn't really talked about farming with anyone for years. Not even when he was with Nellie's family in England. Talk there was always about the war, politics, family, and the local economy. It was nice having a conversation about a time and place that had been free of the madness that was today's world. The only real worry then was how nature was going to behave.

Farming had been the main focal point in his life until he graduated from university and joined the navy. Then it became a thing of the past as he moved into the next chapter of his life.

"There were seven children in the family. I was the eldest son. Karol Jr. and Sebastian were my brothers. There were four girls, Josefina, Kasha, Albinka and Maria. Josefina was the oldest child."

"You being the eldest son had some added responsibility, I presume?" asked Bednarz.

"It did. My father expected me to take over the farm one day. I understood that."

"But you never did. Any problem with that?"

"No. Not with that. I do have guilt that I wasn't there for them when the Germans invaded."

"Guilt can weigh heavily on one. I have lived with it ever since we were ordered out of the country and I had to leave my family," Bednarz said.

"We have all felt that guilt," Ludwik mused.

"You have managed it well all these years," Bednarz offered.

"Did we have a choice?" Ludwik asked.

"No, we did not," Bednarz answered. "We were ordered to leave. All I am saying is there have been many good men that guilt has devoured over the years. A war and a long absence from family can cause severe damage. Many took to the "drink" as a result.

"Is that a warning?" Ludwik asked.

"Not for you. You have made it through the war in good health and a family waits for you. Those are two very encouraging positives."

"I have been very fortunate," Ludwik responded.

"Do you think you can live with the fact that you were not there for your family?" Bednarz asked.

"I don't think it will drive me to drink," Ludwik answered.

"I don't either," Bednarz agreed. "I want to concentrate on the present issue. The nightmares. I'm interested in you keeping a positive attitude. I believe that getting the source of the nightmares out into the open will help. As will some medication."

Ludwik thought for a moment and said, "Prayer will help me also."

"Good to keep that in mind if nightmares and guilt join forces against you," Bednarz offered. He was impressed that Skoczylas had already figured out a way that might help him deal with leaving the family and his country. Faith in prayer could certainly help a person. It was critical for one to feel there was someone or something he or she could turn to in troubled times. Not to feel alone and without "weapons." He felt Skoczylas' faith might be his "ace in the hole" so to speak.

Bednarz changed the subject and asked, in general terms, to describe life growing up on a farm. He thought it might give him a little more background to delve into and see if there were things in Ludwik's life other than war that might be contributing to the sudden emergence of powerful nightmares. It was something he rarely took the time to explore with pilots or crew members. They were needed in the air. Time and circumstance had always demanded that. But with the war ending and Flight 1586 in "stand down," time was now available.

41

He wanted this evaluation to be more comprehensive, more personal and to a large degree, much more honest.

The first thing that Ludwik mentioned was how farm work had made him strong. And strength, especially in his hands, wrists and arms was essential in handling the controls of the planes he flew. He said anyone who flew a B24 for more than a few hours would attest to that. He felt that hard work on a farm wasn't that bad once you realized it was a means to an end. That it put food on the table and money in your pocket. He believed farming was an education unto itself. If you worked hard for something, your chances of getting it were good; that farm work taught you the importance of organization and routine. That doing the little things made the bigger things much easier to do.

He said with seven children and a hired man or two, chores were divided up according to age. The harder chores obviously went to the older children and the hired help. By the time children reached the age of ten, they were milking the cow, feeding livestock, mucking stalls, gathering eggs, picking and canning fruits and vegetables and doing all the odds and ends around the house, barns and coops. And by the time they became teenagers, they knew how to seed, irrigate, tend, hoe, harvest and transport the crops to market. They also understood that success only came with a willingness to work hard every day.

As for himself, he believed by the time he became a teenager, there wasn't anything he couldn't do. That there was always a way to get something done. No matter what it was. All one needed was time, concentration, patience, and most importantly an even temperament. He had learned early when people became emotional there was very little they could accomplish.

Ludwik stopped. He realized he was lecturing Bednarz on farming. He started to apologize, but the doctor just waved him off and said to continue the "lecture" for a while longer.

Ludwik continued. He said he had learned a great deal from his parents. They were not school educated, but they knew how the world of farming worked. They were practical, logical and very patient; especially when a problem arose. They taught him that failure was always a possibility, but never an option; even when it looked like it might be the inevitable outcome. There was always an answer. If not today, then tomorrow.

Bednarz was impressed by the choice of those words. He'd make a note of them later and star them for possible use in sessions with other men who were looking to work their way out of a problem but had given up trying.

"When did you begin to consider not being a farmer?" Bednarz asked.

"I believe that started after a few years in school. School opened my eyes to other things in the world. There seemed to be so much more to life than farming. Not that farming wasn't an honorable thing to do. I just wasn't sure I wanted to do it my entire life."

"What happened to the farm after the war began?"

Ludwik grimaced for a moment before answering, "The farm is near East Prussia. Lots of Germans still living there. Many farms hired German help. When Germany invaded, many of them turned on the Polish farm owners. They either killed them or drove them off the land. When the German army arrived, they finished the job of removing the Polish farmers."

"And your family?" Bednarz asked.

"They were fortunate no one was killed. They were allowed to take one horse and a wagon, pack what they could on the wagon and leave immediately. They set out for my uncle's farm in Kurylowka. The journey took six weeks. Two weeks into it, the Russians invaded. That made everything worse. They were caught between the Germans behind them and the Russians ahead of them. And then, somewhere along the way, they ran out of food and had to beg to eat before they reached my uncle's farm. They're still there today. Hopefully, they can get the farm in Mazanki back after the war."

"I hope so too. Let's break for ten minutes," Bednarz said.

Ludwik left for the library and Bednarz retreated into his inner office to jot some notes down on Skoczylas' account on farming and the unfortunate exodus his family had been forced to make. Finished with that, he lit his pipe and relaxed. He had to appreciate the fact that this man, like so many others, not only had to face the uncertainty of war, but had to find the inner strength and courage to fight the helplessness he must have felt about leaving his family. He thought about his own family. He had left his father and two sisters when the order came to evacuate. His mother had passed the year before. It had been a lot to deal with. It still was. He knew first-hand how hard it could be on a man to leave his family behind. He had experienced many sleepless nights himself because of the guilt he felt. He was impressed that Skoczylas had managed to perform his duty so well under the tragic circumstances forced on him by the war. He had seen men broken by far less. The fact that he had not broken down spoke volumes about his character. Bednarz felt the pilot's immediate future would be fine. When the war ended, a home would be waiting for him. Those two facts alone would light a few candles of hope in his future. His major concern was the long-term effects of the war; that the recent onset of nightmares might be a harbinger of troubled times ahead.

44

"Two more questions for today. I'm assuming most of your nightmares are war related. Would that be a correct assumption?"

Ludwik agreed it most definitely was. He said a few of them only carried sounds. Bednarz asked him for examples. Ludwik thought a bit then said, "whistles, steam trains hissing and chugging, dogs barking and snarling, someone crying, footsteps approaching, people praying in a language he didn't understand."

"All of these occurring recently and not before?" Bednarz asked.

"Just recently."

"Your records indicate a long period of time from the start of the war until you reached France. Might some of the sounds and nightmares come from that period. The sounds you just described have very little to do with flying. More with trains and places you might have been."

"Could be," Ludwik answered.

"We should talk about that time. But not today. Last question. When did you decide to be a pilot?"

"I think when I was around twelve. I was hoeing weeds in a sugar beet field. Sometime late in the morning I heard a distant buzzing sound. It sounded like crickets. I didn't pay much attention to it. No one else in the field did either. That all changed when the buzzing got louder. I stopped my hoeing and looked toward the road by our house. I expected to see a machine moving around there. There wasn't one. Then someone yelled, "It's in the sky!" It was coming our way. It looked like a giant bug with two sets of wings, one on top of the other. I could see a man seated in it. I had heard of airplanes in school, but this was the first one I had ever seen. It was just cruising along.

Suddenly it turned, dropped its nose and dove straight at us. The buzzing became a roar as the plane approached. Everyone dove into the dirt. The plane zoomed over us no higher than a tall tree. Its single engine screamed pure power. I rolled over onto my back and watched the pilot take the plane majestically straight up at the heavens and then turn to level out. He was putting on a show for us. I was hoping for a repeat performance. Everyone jumped to their feet in anticipation of another zooming flyby. I decided to stand my ground this time to get a better look. The pilot had other plans. He came straight at us much higher than his first pass. He rolled the plane over upside down and then rolled it back upright. I was rooted to the ground in absolute awe at the maneuver. It was like watching magic. The pilot waggled the plane's wings, waved at us and sped away like an arrow shot from a bow. I watched the plane until it was out of sight, then realized my father was yelling at me to get back to work. I only had one thought in my mind the rest of the day. I wanted to fly."

"Did you ever get to fly a plane like that?" Bednarz asked.

"Quite a bit. They were used to train pilots in Poland and in England. They're called "Tiger Moths.""

"Did you have to qualify in England?"

"We all did. We had to prove to the English that we knew how to fly."

"You mentioned that your early education in Poland taught you about airplanes."

"We learned a little about them. Mostly that they were one example of how the world was quickly changing and that machines of all sorts were at the forefront of that change. And that Poland needed to be a part of it. That day in the field was in 1926.

Look at where we are today. How fast was that? That plane was the perfect example of how machines were changing the world. I wanted to be a part of that change."

"And here you are," Bednarz said. "I think that's enough for today. Let's take tomorrow off and I'll see you on Friday. 1300 hrs."

Ludwik had supper that night with Zygmunt. The co-pilot said rumor had it that passes were coming for this weekend and that replacements for their crew were here. Ludwik wondered if they were veterans. Zygmunt said they likely were not. They had just finished training in England. He asked how the evaluation was going with Bednarz and that he had heard that the evaluations had morphed into multiple sessions with an emphasis on post war concerns. He thought that was a good idea. Ludwik said he wasn't sure about it.

Bednarz spent most of the morning Friday updating the files of the men he was seeing. He was thinking of presenting each man a copy of their file before they left Campo Casale. His hope was they might find his notes, comments and recommendations useful someday. It was the least he could do to say, "Thank you for your service." He would of course, keep the original files for official purposes.

Ludwik spent his morning Friday before meeting with Bednarz by relaxing on the beach and writing a letter to Nellie. He usually sent her two a week. They were never long. He still had problems with his English but had shown improvement in the past few months. He remembered the first note he had written her. A friend who knew English had to help him. The note was short and written on a torn-off cover from a pack of cigarettes that was wrapped around some chocolate. The note read, "Hello, my pet. Dinner tonight. Your house. Cheerio. Ludi." He had used trickery to deliver the note. He had Nelly believing they would meet in the field next to the airbase Saturday at noon. He had a surprise for her.

While she stood in the field waiting for him. he flew over the field and dropped the note and chocolate at her feet. She always said she loved the delivery almost as much as the chocolate.

Besides writing the letter to Nellie, he spent quite a bit of time thinking about his "encounter" with the young woman by the library in the hospital. That was giving him more thought than the nightmares. He had weighed the pros and cons of opening-up to Bednarz concerning his "history" with the Blessed Lady. He was not sure if the timing was right for that exchange. He knew if the war was still on in its fury, an exchange like that could be problematic. Chances would be good his flying status would be questioned. On the other hand, with the war coming to an end and the doctor seemingly more interested in his well-being after the war, it might be the right time to discuss it with him. Get this thing out in the open. He thought about the spiritual opinion on his "experiences" he had received from the priest in Italy some years ago. It had come without any judgment. It was just an opinion by the priest for him to consider. It had crossed his mind recently that it might be good to get a clinical opinion on the matter. Hopefully, an opinion that didn't carry a judgment. Like the priest had done. He would have to weigh the possibility that it might affect his evaluation. He didn't think it would, but one never knew for sure. He left the question of broaching the subject with Bednarz up to the doctor. If Bednarz brought Mary into the conversation, he would put everything about her on the table. And he wouldn't lie to the man. If he lied today, he probably would have to lie tomorrow to cover it up. He had learned that early in life from his father. He could hear his father now; "Lies make good people bad people."

1300 hours found Ludwik watching Bednarz pour him a strong-smelling cup of coffee. He took his coffee black now. The tasteless powdered milk the Air Force used had made the change easy.

He thought about the conversation he had with Zygmunt concerning the extended evaluations Bednarz was conducting these days. He decided to ask him about it.

"Has the Air Force ordered you to extend these sessions now that the war is nearing its end?"

Bednarz said no. That it was his idea. Ludwik asked why.

Bednarz didn't hesitate, "Most of you will be out of uniform soon. Maybe I can help you with the transition to civilian life."

Ludwik politely asked, "Why would anyone need help going home after this?"

Bednarz rolled a pencil back and forth on the table then answered, "Because the day will come for many, maybe even you, when the horrors of war will come back to haunt them."

Ludwik appreciated Bednarz's point. He had heard about the men from WWI who never regained the normal life they once had after experiencing the traumatic and insane world of the trenches. The answer to his question had been a good one.

Bednarz's first order of business was to have Ludwik list a few of the worst nightmares/conscious thoughts he was experiencing. Ludwik began with a very troublesome one; the real-life dropping of a Polish agent from his plane over occupied territory only to have the man's parachute become entangled in the plane's tail and no matter how hard he tried, he couldn't shake him loose and save his life. And then there was the crash into the Adriatic. That was followed by dreams of fog and creatures that lived in them. Some coming out of the fog and grabbing him. Sometimes flinging him high into the sky. Others, with ax handles in their hands would chase him into woods where he was forced to hide.

Bednarz asked him if they were any common ones. Ones that occurred more than the others. Ludwik said the most common ones involved the missions. Especially the one over a burning Warsaw during the Uprising. That was the one that woke him up in a sweat and a very dry throat. He was guessing the dry throat meant he had been yelling in his sleep. Another one had him at a crossroads in a foreign place without money and no idea of how to get to where he had to go.

Bednarz listened intently and jotted down his usual notes. He said he would document both categories, dreams and thoughts, and fit what was mentioned under each then add any others that came up later. Done with that, he suggested they talk about the missions. He felt Ludwik had a story to tell about the war and his part in it. That it might be helpful to tell it to someone like him. Someone who might have a bit of useful advice. He said his first piece of advice would involve a willingness on Ludwik's part to get his story out. Every chapter, good or bad. Not to bury it, but to own it.

The Blessed Lady

They spent the next half hour discussing the missions. Bednarz made his notes then changed the subject to Ludwik's strong religious faith. It had become evident to him in their discussions that Ludwik's faith had been a driving force in his ability to handle what the war had wrought on him. He felt it would be central to Ludwik's ability to handle what awaited him in the future. For now, while he believed Ludwik's nightmares would diminish with sleep-aided medication, it probably would be the man's faith that would see him through in the long run. He was Catholic also but had lost what faith he had after working with so many emotionally crippled men and asking God "Why?" a thousand times it had to be this way. He decided to expand this business of faith with Ludwik.

50

"You mentioned the other day that Mary was the reason you were here. Would you care to expand on that?" Bednarz asked.

There it was! Bednarz had brought Mary into play. It was all or nothing now. Truth or lie. He would be speaking to a man of science. He wasn't sure what the man was going to think. The thought that the story of his "experiences" with the Blessed Lady might influence a negative evaluation raced through his mind, but after a few moments of hesitation, he decided to open the door to Bednarz. Let him in. The doctor had just said it would be good thing to tell his story.

"When our plane went into the sea, the controls collapsed back onto my chest and pinned me to the seat. I could not get out. As the plane sank, I asked Mary for help. Almost immediately a bright light came toward me. There was a woman standing in the light. She was waving her hands upward. The cold Adriatic suddenly turned warm, and I felt like I was floating away from the world. My body was prickling all over. Before blacking out, I remembered thinking the Lady had come to save me."

"You were pulled out of the water by an American," Bednarz said.

"True, but he did not free me from the cockpit," Ludwik answered.

"Isn't it possible that you freed yourself as you were blacking out? That the light you saw was the instrument panel shorting out. That maybe subconsciously you asked Mary for help at the same time you freed yourself. I know she has appeared to children in both Portugal and France with a message for the world. The church has documented these events and classified them as real-life miracles. This rescue in the Adriatic by our Lady seems a bit of a stretch. Wouldn't you agree?"

"I understand why you or anyone would feel that way," Ludwik answered. "It doesn't alter my belief that it was her. In all honesty, there were three other times that I thought that maybe she, or someone she sent, was with me. Those I am not sure of."

Bednarz took a long, hard look at Ludwik before asking in a very measured voice, "What other times?"

"The most recent was just the other day. Before my first session with you. I was in the library looking out the window. It was quiet and it looked like the world was standing still. Nothing was moving. Then I felt a presence near me and my skin began to prickle. I thought I saw a young woman pass by in the corridor. She looked familiar. I went into the corridor, but she was gone. I went through the exit door that leads to the airfield. She wasn't there. That's when I began to think it all had been my imagination. The thing that I found interesting was the prickling sensation. That had happened only three times before in my life; after the crash, and twice five years ago after a young shepherdess, who resembled the woman in the corridor, came into my life. Olive skinned, dark haired, young and wearing a similar long, brown robe with a hood folded on the back of her neck."

Bednarz stared at Ludwik. His eyes were not dancing or averting like eyes usually did when a liar spoke. Just a normal blink or two. Four possible encounters with the mother of Jesus Christ! What was this all about? He had dealt with other men who claimed some extraordinary episodes with God, Jesus, Satan and a few angelic women. Those men had lost their sense of reality. They were unfortunate, emotionally spent, casualties of war. He didn't feel Ludwik was in that category. He was sure about that. But this…. this was indeed quite an amazing story. He had to hear more. He asked Ludwik if he thought the woman he saw or thought he saw, by the library, was the same woman he had seen twice before five years ago.

He then asked Ludwik if he thought that woman might be the Blessed Lady. He said it was difficult for him to believe that it was. Ludwik knew what Bednarz was thinking. The look on his face told him that. He would try and answer the questions as best he could.

"If I may, I'll take your comment first. You said it is very difficult to believe. I suppose it all depends on what you believe and how much you believe. My faith has always been strong. I believe Mary saved me from drowning. That will never change. Do I think the woman by the library and the two women I saw five years ago are the same? Perhaps the Lady herself? I don't know if they are the same woman. I do know all three looked very much alike and my body's reaction to them was the same. The only times in my life I have had that reaction. Was she the Lady? I don't know that, but I hope she was."

Bednarz asked Ludwik for a few minutes to record some notes concerning the discussion so far. Ludwik smoked while he recorded. There was little doubt in Bednarz's mind that Ludwik was sincere and fully in control of his emotions. The matter of his rescue from the sea by the Blessed Lady was obviously hard for him to believe. Ludwik was holding fast to his rescue by the Lady, but to his credit, had admitted he wasn't sure about the other women, all very similar in appearance and most curiously of all, having caused him to have a physical reaction that was the same each time. The only times in his life he had experienced that. He had to admit there was lots here to discern. He knew the mind always had a way of making life interesting. And if imagination and coincidence turned out to be the underlying factors for all of this, which he thought it probably was, he wasn't that worried about the man's future or the man's ability to fly. One thing was for certain; the man had an extraordinary faith. Especially in the Blessed Lady. Why wouldn't that be an asset to any man? It had obviously helped him through the war. He had a feeling there was something here for him to learn.

Something he was missing. He needed to do some serious thinking. He decided to table discussion on the matter for a while. He waited until Ludwik finished his Pall Mall then said, "I want you to know that your evaluation will be recorded as positive, and you are cleared to fly. As far as our discussion today, it will be between the two of us and nothing on the record about being saved by the Blessed Lady or anything else. I do think you have a story that needs to be told. I believe it's important you tell it now. Please consider doing that. See you Monday, 1300 hours."

Ludwik left feeling good about sharing the Blessed Lady experience and the recent real or imaginary encounter with the young woman outside the library. He was comfortable with Bednarz. They were more than doctor-patient now. The doctor had made no judgement on the accounts given to him. It would be interesting to see what he had to say about it all on Monday. He made sure the package with the three sleeping pills were safely tucked into his jacket pocket and headed for the hangar where his new plane waited. Another B24.

The only thing left to do on the plane was painting it the dull black non- reflective paint that all Flight 1586 planes needed for their night flights into occupied Europe. The belly gun turret had been removed, a separate hatch had been installed for the parachutists, flame-dampers had been welded on to hide the flame from the engine exhaust and black-out curtains were in place all along the sides of the fuselage from cockpit to tail gunner.

When he got to the hangar, he was greeted by the three young replacements that had just arrived from the special-ops training base in England. All were very eager to wreak havoc on the Germans. He remembered that thirst for revenge. Jan, one of the regular crew members, informed Ludwik the entire crew was getting overnight passes into Brindisi. Good until Sunday evening. For Ludwik, a good night's sleep on a cushy, civilian bed would be most welcome.

Between the pills and a fresh set of sheets, he had high hopes for a great night's rest. He looked forward to mingling with civilians and enjoying the charm of Brindisi once again. He would wear his uniform on Saturday but change into his civilian clothes for church and whatever else a sunny, warm Sunday might bring to a man who needed practice being a civilian. He entertained the possibility of spending time with the replacements and getting to know them but understood that young men needed room to be young men. He would stay with Zygmunt.

Brindisi

Brindisi offered an assortment of attractions. The former capitol of Italy had parks, restaurants, museums, theatres, beaches and of course, women. Ludwik's plans were simple. Dinner and drinks with his co-pilot on Saturday night, a good night's rest, attend mass Sunday morning and get in a little sightseeing Sunday afternoon. The two married men had enjoyed each other's company in Brindisi before. They both knew the younger men would be after some more exciting endeavors. Probably spend most of their time and money supporting the local prostitutes. The sex business had become an important part of the economy in war-torn southern Italy and healthy young lads with money were dependable repeat customers. It was going to be interesting listening to their stories on the way back to base. That is if they were able to remember anything.

Most of the older, married men in the squadron had families that were still in Poland. While many stayed loyal to their wives, others had fallen victim to their basic needs and the separation that war brought on. Most of the men had been away from home and their wives the better part of five years. Time and the pull of nature had pushed them into the shadows of unfaithfulness. They had learned to live for the day and not worry about tomorrow.

Others, stronger in their resolve, understood how important it was to remain faithful. Ludwik stood front and center with them.

The truck sat idling inside the main gate Saturday morning. Ludwik and Zygmunt were fifteen minutes early and waiting for the rest of the crew to arrive. The driver of the truck, a sergeant Antocak, stepped out of the cab and joined them. He was a tall, good looking, blond lad that was in his early twenties. He opened a pack of the popular, hard-to-get, American cigarettes called Lucky Strikes. Ludwik knew the cigarettes were rarely seen in the hands of a Pole. He wondered how this young sergeant had been able to get them. Both he and Zygmunt declined the sergeant's offer to join him in a smoke. They looked on with interest as the young man lit his cigarette with an American made Zippo lighter. That piqued Zygmunt's curiosity. He asked the sergeant how he came to have both the American lighter and American cigarettes. The young man proudly said they were both given to him last week by some Americans soldiers he had picked up outside of Brindisi. They were drunk and staggering alongside the road. He took them down the coast to their base and let them off at the main gate. One of them gave him six packs of the American cigarettes and another gave him the Zippo as thanks for the lift. The one that give him the cigarettes told him they were worth their weight in gold; that a carton of them got a man the company of a woman for a weekend and a pack got him "serviced." He said the Italian women were good at what they did, and they knew how to convert the cigarettes into cash and food. The sergeant said he spoke some English but didn't understand what it all meant until he brought the cigarettes with him into Brindisi the next day. That's when he found out what "serviced" meant. All he had to do was show the cigarettes and the smiles from women got very big and very inviting. He said he didn't have enough cigarettes for a weekend with a lady, but he did get "serviced" twice, once in an alley and once on the beach under the stars.

He saw one of the women the next day trade in her haul of cigarettes in broad daylight for a pile of lira from a fat man sitting on a bench in a park. He said he found out that a pack of cigarettes usually brought enough lira for a loaf of bread or two with enough pasta and soup to feed a family of four for two days. The sergeant thought it was a win-win situation for everyone involved.

Ludwik knew Antocak was thinking with another part of his body much lower than his brain, but he was young and didn't know better. He wouldn't judge the young man. It was what young men did. Antocak's story of sex for cigarettes was a sad one. So many women forced into a life like that in order to survive. Casualties of war themselves.

The rest of the crew led by Andrzej and Jan arrived just in time before the truck was scheduled to leave. The gate guards ambled over to check their passes. Ludwik greeted each new man by his first name and watched them spring into the back of the canvas covered deuce and a half. Jan and Andrzej followed them. They were going to act as guides for the newcomers. Ludwik and Zygmunt got into the cab with Antocak.

The trip into Brindisi was quick. The excited chatter of the new men grew in intensity with every passing mile. Ludwik was glad he had dropped the idea of spending time with them. They were planning other things and letting the world know about it. Zygmunt elbowed Ludwik gently as the happy noise from the back made its way into the cab. He had a big smile on his face. The last time Ludwik had seen a smile like that from Zygmunt was after their successful drop in northern Italy last January. Just a few hours before hitting the storm that put them into the Adriatic. There would be no storm and crash today. The weather was perfect. Sunny and mild. The only crash he would experience was tonight when he hit that cushy, civilian bed. He began to get little excited. He hadn't been on pass for some time.

This short weekend in Brindisi would be his third since arriving at Campo Casale last year. He checked his cap to make sure it was at the right angle and began to hum a little "Too ra loo ra loo ra, too ra loo ra lie." It was his favorite part of the first song he had learned to sing in English while participating in the weekly Saturday night sing-along at Nellie's home in Carlisle.

The truck stopped at an entrance to the walled city called the Porta Mesagre. Ludwik assembled the men outside the entrance and wished them all a good stay. He reminded them that the truck would leave from this very spot tomorrow at 1700 hours. He said he hoped to see them at mass tomorrow at the Chiesa di San Paolo. It was located in the "Old Town" section of the city where he and Zygmunt would be staying. Jan said he would do his best to get the replacements there.

The crew walked through the cobblestoned entrance and entered Brindisi. Ludwik and Zygmunt turned left on via Della Liberta and headed for the inner harbor. The other five turned right and passed through a stone arch leading to a staircase that went down into the city. There was a woman standing on almost every step. Business started early in Brindisi. Ludwik wondered how many of the men would reach the bottom of the stairs by themselves.

The huge, ancient Castello Sevo dominated the row of buildings that overlooked the inner harbor. It always reminded Ludwik of the old castle back home in Mazanki, where he had played as a youth almost every Sunday after mass. There weren't many people in the street. A few of the locals were sweeping the area in front of their small shops getting ready for the day. There wasn't a uniform in sight. The men who wore them would be sleeping off the results of a lively Friday night out on the town. Reaching the old castle, the two turned right onto via St. Aloy. The street ran parallel to the waterfront for a short distance before turning toward central Brindisi.

It was a quiet, well-kept street filled with the charm that only antiquity and history could bring. They headed for the inn/restaurant called "Fabbri's." It was run by a family of the same name. They had stayed there before. It was an affordable and comfortable place in this part of "Old Town." It offered rooms that had balconies high enough to view both the inner and outer harbors of the port city. The restaurant was well known for its seafood menu, homemade breads and pastries. It had been in the hands of the Fabbri family for some time. The building had survived WWI aerial bombings, Mussolini fascists, WWII bombardments, German, British and American occupation and a wide variety of Allied airmen and soldiers stationed at nearby bases like Campo Casale.

The three-story enterprise was also home to three generations of the Fabbri family. The restaurant's bakery and ovens were in the basement. The first floor held the inn's lobby and reception desk, an open kitchen and a small dining area that held eight tables. There was an entranceway at the rear of the dining area that led to a courtyard holding a dozen more dining tables. Each table was adorned with an olive-drab umbrella that looked suspiciously American. Most likely a payoff for some favor provided by the Fabbris. The family was well known to have lots of connections to the black market and was very capable of some high-stakes wheeling and dealing.

There were a few select rooms for overnight guests on the second floor. The street side ones overlooked Brindisi's beautiful harbor. They were the most expensive and usually available because of that. The third floor housed three generations of the Fabbri family. They had a separate entrance in the back of the building. Lodgers and diners used the main entrance on the street side. The restaurant had always stayed open late into the night; even when "blackouts" had been mandated. The Fabbris had "come upon" a stash of heavy, black curtains somehow and were able to keep the local authorities happy by using them during "blackouts."

The happiness of the authorities was then guaranteed by the family's generous donations that landed in the pockets of the right official. It was business as usual for the family.

Alcohol was tough to find in Brindisi except for a few places like Fabbri's. Imports were almost impossible to get because of the war. Most places in Brindisi only offered local wines and beer. And forget the pasteurization. Yet, at Fabbri's, one only had to ask if anything "stronger" was available. It usually was. They always managed to have a little something on hand. For the right price, of course. Scotch whiskey, American bourbon and English gin topped the foreign imports. Additional luxuries such as cigarettes, pipe tobacco, women and other pleasure-producing items were always available.

The threat of a German air raid had long since passed. As a matter of fact, lights from homes and businesses along both sides of the inner and outer harbors of Brindisi had illuminated the water for a few weeks now. The local merchants had been hustling to help change the economic mode of the city from survival to recovery. Helping that recovery were the hundreds of Allied servicemen stationed in the area. With the war nearing its end, soldiers and airmen from Poland, England, New Zealand, Australia, France, Canada, South Africa and the United States were coming into the city with their pockets full of the money they had no time to spend while the fighting was in full force. While some locals disliked the idea of so many "occupiers" in their city, most of them were very happy to take their money.

All guests were welcomed with open arms, smiles, friendly faces and good manners. The Fabbris had turned every welcome into an art.

"Ludwik, Zygmunt, jak sie macie, moi przyjacielu?" Ricardo Fabbri shouted as he spotted the two familiar Polish pilots. He followed that with and an Italian, "That's all the Polish I know, my friends."

He laughed at himself and said, "I know how to say, "How are you my friends in five different languages. Good for business, don't you think?"

"Very good for business," answered Zygmunt in Italian. He and Ludwik had decided to let him take care of the essentials for a stay here. He had been in Italy for two years and his Italian was very good. Zygmunt clicked his heels, bowed and said to the Italian, "Let's do business my faithful and honest friend."

Ricardo's smile stretched almost ear to ear and with a twinkle of mischief in his eyes, he asked, "What kind of business are you interested in?"

The look told the two pilots everything they had known about Ricardo was the same. He was still dealing in the seamier side of life. And that undoubtedly meant the black market or the parlors of pleasure were in play here.

Ludwik had understood Fabbri's question. He passed his answer on to Zygmunt who repeated it in Italian, "A couple of quiet rooms overlooking the harbor, a decent breakfast tomorrow and one night in a comfortable, clean bed WITHOUT company."

"Still the same two respectable Polish gentlemen," the rotund Italian chuckled. "I suppose you both want to know if the masses at San Paolo's are at the same time. They are. And yes, I have two adjoining rooms, our family suite, on the street side. They share a bath and a balcony. Whatever bottle you buy here in the restaurant, bring it upstairs. Enjoy it on the balcony while you admire our harbor. It will help you relax, improve your chances for a good night's rest or for whatever "ELSE" might suddenly appeal to you."

Fabbri was always trying to sell you something. Both pilots understood that. Buying a bottle of something was part of the deal staying here.

"Do you want the money up front?" Zygmunt asked.

"Always, my friend. You two are honorable men, but unfortunately, this God-awful war has turned men like you into liars and thieves."

Ludwik and Zygmunt liked and respected Ricardo despite his ties to the black market. He had led his family through two wars and a calamitous period of political and social upheaval. He had taken his family out from the uncertainty of life and into a future filled with promise. His family would do well after the war. It wasn't going to be that way for most families in Italy and the rest of Europe. It certainly wouldn't be that way in Poland. The future there would be filled with uncertainty and worry. Not to mention fear. The irony of it all was not lost on the two airmen. These Italians, once the enemy, a vanquished enemy at that, were going to be all right. At the same time, their people back in Poland, on the side of the soon-to-be victorious allies, would not be able to share the same kind of future. They would not be all right.

Ludwik brought his suitcase and jacket carrier into the room. Zygmunt's room was on the other side of the bath and shower they both shared. The room was sparse. It had no windows, but it did have a large, glass sliding door that opened onto a balcony. The door was covered by a thick, black curtain. Sliding the curtain and door open, Ludwik stepped onto the balcony. The air was warm and smelled of the sea. The street below had begun to stir with activity. A dusty looking mule, looking bored and half asleep, slowly clopped its way in his direction. It was pulling an old man sitting on an old wagon covered by an old tarp. The old man, also looking bored and half asleep, sat motionless behind the mule.

Mule, old man and wagon gradually came to a stop just in front of
the balcony. The old man just sat there and waited. He only moved
when he turned to greet two men who appeared from under the
balcony and approached him. Ludwik recognized them immediately.
They were Ricardo's sons. Both in their thirties. They looked healthy
and had obviously managed to escape the wrath of war. Ludwik
heard the word "lira" mentioned. Negotiations were taking place
between a buyer and seller. The old man nodded his head a few times
then accepted a small bag from one of the brothers. The other
brother flipped the tarp off the wagon exposing bales of hay and
sacks of flour. From his view overhead, Ludwik could see three
crates tucked neatly between the hay bales and flour sacks. Ludwik
assumed the crates were filled with bottles of homemade wine. He
was wrong. The crates were filled with bottles that had labels on
them. Most certainly imports. And all were protected by the hay bales
and sacks of flour. A good idea. A broken bottle of imported spirit
was a significant loss of income. The brothers, along with a few
scrappy looking boys that had appeared magically, quickly had the
crates and sacks of flour off the wagon and into the building. It took
only five minutes. Unloaded, the old man snapped the reins and the
mule dutifully plodded away. It had been a quick and efficient piece
of business. Ludwik admired that.

His attention moved to the inner harbor just beyond the row of
buildings across the street. The water shone a beautiful greenish-blue
that sparkled in the morning sun. A few sailboats, their mainsails fully
extended, moved gracefully over the water headed out to sea. He was
struck by how similar the boats were to the gliders he had flown back
home in Poland. Sleek, silent instruments made by man and powered
totally by the winds; a gift from God. It made one feel alive and for a
moment, at peace with the world. He stepped back into his room and
carefully removed the items of clothing he had packed into his
suitcase. He neatly folded each item into thirds before placing them

in a drawer of the room's Waterfall dresser. He removed the tan slacks and brown jacket with the matching shirt and tie from the jacket carrier and hung them in the small closet next to the dresser. Those were his clothes for Sunday. It had been a while since he had worn civilian clothes. He had been wearing some kind of uniform almost daily for a decade. His first uniform was that of a cadet at the Naval Academy, his second as a member of the navy's Fleet Air Arm and now, a member of the Polish Air Force. He was always proud to represent the mother country, no matter what military branch he was part of. The responsibility that came with the uniform meant a great deal to him. Wearing it every day never seemed to be a burden. It had always been an honor for him to put it on. Tomorrow, he would practice being a civilian and dress the part. Today, he would remain Warrant Officer Ludwik Skoczylas, 792341, pilot, Special Duties, Flight 1586, Squadron 301.

In the bathroom, after washing and drying his face, Ludwik took a good look at himself in the mirror over the sink. He was surprised by what he saw. His scar had company now. Lots of company. He had aged; not dramatically, but noticeably. He was beginning to resemble the farmers from his father's generation. Faces weathered into creases and wrinkles from decades of fighting the cold winters and hot summers of Poland. A branding by nature. Looking old way before their time. He was only in his thirties. But today, he was looking like fifty.

The scar was a souvenir he had picked up at Bramcote Air Base in England after colliding with an automobile while pedaling one of the base bicycles he rode to and from the airstrip. The furrows and lines accompanying the scar had to be the result of flying those tension filled, night missions into enemy occupied Europe. He didn't feel sorry for himself. It was what it was. The more he thought about it, the more he realized it was a small price to pay for the opportunity to avenge the loss of his country.

Just a few wrinkles and crinkles in the skin to look at. No big deal. He had survived. So many others had either been killed or so physically disfigured, that death probably would have been a better outcome. No, he would never complain. He did not have the right to do so.

Back in his room, he knelt beside the bed and began to pray. He thanked God for today and for all of his days, asked Him to forgive him his sins and give him the strength and courage to do what was right so he would be worthy of God's promise of eternal life. He thanked Jesus for his sacrifice and said he was sorry for his pain, suffering and humiliation. Finally, he asked Mary to watch over his family and asked her to pray for Poland's return to independence.

Zygmunt entered the bathroom from his room on the other side and saw Ludwik kneel to pray. He watched him make the sign of the cross, close his eyes and begin. He said nothing; just watched in admiration and respect for his friend. The man never seemed to waver in his faith. Anyone experiencing the last five years might have questioned the existence of God. His friend was not one of them. He would never be one of them.

As Ludwik finished, Zygmunt turned on the water to announce his presence and began to wash his hands.

"Are you going to wear the uniform today?" he asked Ludwik.

"I am. Just for today," his friend answered.

"I will also," Zygmunt replied.

The Vista Porto was a quick walk down the narrow cobblestoned street. The aptly named restaurant had a beautiful view of the harbor. The view included a dozen or so brightly colored sailboats anchored a short boat ride away from the dock area.

The picturesque view and the warm sun lent an air of relaxation and comfort to the two Polish pilots. It was a world away from the boring greyness of the airbase.

They chose a wood-fired, crusty, white fish with a generous side of calamari, oysters and clams. It was a nice change from the meat, potatoes and kapusta they ate almost daily at the base. Ludwik ordered a small bottle of unlabeled white wine to compliment the seafood. He knew his drinking had to be moderate for a while. He didn't want to mix too much wine with the sleeping pill he would take tonight.

The two men lifted their glasses toward each other and toasted Poland. As they took their first sip, the bells of San Paolo cathedral and every church throughout Brindisi announced the arrival of noon. And from somewhere across the harbor, a single bell rang out, synchronizing its beautiful, mellow tone with the ringing chorus of the city. The symphony of the bells lasted only a few minutes, but the peace it brought to the two men lingered. They sat quietly, deep within their own thoughts. Then, as one, they raised their glasses again. Ludwik toasted "peace." Zygmunt toasted "home."

Their lunch was enjoyable. The bread was a meal unto itself. The crusty ends bordered a delectable, soft middle that just melted in their mouths. The Italian bakers had a knack with the ovens. They were the best when it came to baking breads. The bread, the olive oil it was dipped in, the flakey, white fish and all the sides were a meal fit for royalty. To eat like this and be served by a courteous waiter, a civilian, was a rare treat; a long way from a mess hall in the military.

Ludwik suggested that Zygmunt finish the small bottle of wine while they enjoyed the pleasant view of the harbor and the comfortable weather a little while longer. He would order a coffee.

Zygmunt was happy to comply. He took the extended stay at the table and relaxed atmosphere to ask his friend about the scar on his face and how he had acquired it.

Ludwik was surprised by the question. It had been three years since the accident. No one had asked him about the scar in the past two years. It wasn't that noticeable anymore. At least he didn't think so. Zygmunt had proven him wrong. At one time, the question would have bothered him, but not anymore. Initially, the scar was hideous to look at. It was a dark, jagged line that ran down the left side of his face from his ear to the corner of his mouth. It was very noticeable and had made him extremely self-conscious for some time. As time went by, he began to realize the scar meant very little to most observers and nothing to the people who loved him. He had heard others, outside of his new family and friends, talking about the scar as if it had been earned in combat. It hadn't. It had been "earned" as a consequence of being in the wrong place at the wrong time. Being caught in the path of a wayward, out of control Austin Seven Ruby. It had almost ended his life.

Memoirs of a Guinea Pig

"The scar has a story. You interested?" Ludwik asked his friend.

"I like stories," Zygmunt replied.

"It happened in April 1942. I had just completed a practice nighttime exercise over the North Sea and was returning to the barracks at Bramcote with the crew. We were all riding our bicycles. It was dark and that was the problem. The base was in "blackout." The driver of the car that hit us was a doctor that was very drunk and driving with only his parking lights on.

He came racing around a corner and never saw us. He plowed through most of the crew. One man was killed and I had a severe facial injury. The accident put me in the hospital for a long time. I was transferred from Bramcote to Sussex for treatment. There I underwent a new medical procedure that made me a member of a very "special group." One that opened the door to my marriage."

Ludwik was enjoying the interest on his friend's face. It wasn't that much different from the interest shown by Bednarz on his story of the Blessed Lady. He sipped his coffee while Zygmunt finished his wine. He waited for the questions he knew were coming.

"What was that "special group" you were part of?" Zygmunt asked.

Ludwik said it was called the "Guinea Pig Club." He said because his injury was so serious, he had to have his entire jaw repaired by a relatively new procedure called "plastic surgery." The bone in his lower jaw had been crushed almost beyond repair and that had made him a prime candidate for the new medical technique. He and some other airmen whose faces had been horribly burned in bombing raids were placed into a group where stitching, wiring, skin grafting and insertion of plastic material was being used to rebuild destroyed bone, tissue and skin. It was the RAF's first attempt to treat catastrophic facial injuries with this new, experimental procedure. That was the reason the patients were called "guinea pigs." He said the patients served as pioneers of a sort and what was learned from their treatment served as the foundation for improved plastic surgery technique. In his case, he had dozens of stitches, skin grafts from his leg to his face, teeth removed, plastic inserted into his jaw and an extensive bit of wiring used to hold everything in place. The entire process was done by a Canadian specialist by the name of Dr. Archibald McIndoe. He said he was given a certificate of honor from the Queen Victoria Hospital in Sussex for being a graduate of the club. After his release, he underwent months of checkups and adjustments from the surgery in McIndoe's London office and that period of time opened the door to his marriage.

"How so?" Zygmunt asked.

"I had been seeing Nellie, at the time of the accident and when she got word of it, she came with a friend to visit me in the hospital at Sussex. She became very upset when she saw me. She put her head on my chest and sobbed like a baby. I didn't know until then how much she cared for me. It was very moving. It made me realize how much I really cared for her. I proposed to her a few months later after I had been released from the hospital and put on off-duty status pending the results of my rehab. I had some leave coming and was hopeful I could get enough time for a wedding and maybe even a short honeymoon. She said she wanted to marry me but had to discuss it with her parents. A week later, I took a train to Carlisle to ask her parent's permission to marry her. Her mother was not in favor of it. She said Nellie was too young and not ready for marriage. She said her daughter knew nothing about the world of a married woman. I told her I was twenty-seven and would teach her. I would teach her how to cook, sew, can food, wash and iron clothes, plant a garden and anything else it took to help her become a wife and my partner. I told her I might die in the war and that both of us dearly wanted the time, whatever time God would give us, to be with each other. Nellie's father was a WWI Air Force veteran and understood those sentiments. He convinced his wife that Nellie and I were a good match."

"Did you marry her right away?" asked Zygmunt.

"No, you know how the military works. It took a lot of paperwork and a little help from a few people to get the go-ahead."

"How long did it take, and did you get time for a little honeymoon?"

69

"It took three months. We were married in September 1942. And we had a weeklong honeymoon in the Lake District."

Ludwik's marriage interested Zygmunt. He remembered those early days in England when the only way a Pole could marry an English woman was to get her pregnant. He asked Ludwik how he had managed to get permission to marry his Nellie. Ludwik read his intent and laughed. He said Nellie wasn't pregnant, but they still got permission to marry from a high source.

"Your commander gave you permission?" asked Zygmunt.

Ludwik laughed and said, "Would you believe I got permission to marry from General Sikorski himself?"

"How on this earth did you arrange that?" a startled Zygmunt asked.

"I didn't. My little "cyganka" did. While I was being treated as an outpatient, she wrote a letter to Sikorski. She told him she wasn't pregnant, but wanted to marry me before the war took one or both of us. She wrote of my service, my accident and her parents' approval. Nellie has a way with words. She is an honest and truthful soul. Sikorski must have been impressed by her request. He sent her a telegram giving us permission to marry. How about that? She sent the general a piece of our wedding cake as a way of thanking him. I was surprised she didn't get the man to attend the wedding. My superiors at Bramcote were amazed by Sikorski's orders commanding them to let me marry and get the time off for a honeymoon."

"How did that go?" a thoroughly entertained Zygmunt asked.

"Everyone thought I was related to the general. They took care of me. Piotr Gaj, my commanding officer, was my best man. When Sikorski died in the plane crash off Gibraltar, his body was brought to Newark for burial. Piotr oversaw organizing a "fly over" as a salute to honor him. Our squadron was assigned the duty. Nellie was there. She had been invited by Piotr. I'd like to think my participation in the "fly over" and Nellie attending the funeral procession had something to do with her letter. Most of the people attending the services were dignitaries from the English government and Allied forces, including of course, members of our provisional government and military command. It was quite an honor for us."

"That was a sad day for Poland. He was a good man," Zygmunt added. Ludwik agreed. A sad day indeed. The man had been a driving force in getting the English to agree that the Poles should have their own military units commanded by their own officers.

They split the bill and left for a stroll around Brindisi's Old Town. Zygmunt wanted to stretch his legs out in a fast walk, but Ludwik found himself preoccupied with thoughts generated by their conversation of the scar and Nelly's letter. He decided to walk casually along the harbor by himself, find a comfortable place to relax and let his mind do most of the walking. He found a small park that overlooked the harbor. The park's walkway near the water was busy with people and too noisy for him. The other end of the park was at the top of a grassy incline some distance from the water. He spotted an empty bench there facing the harbor. Rather than use the path that circled up to it, he went directly up the grassy incline to claim the bench before someone else got there.

The view was spectacular. Sailboats and motorized craft made their way up and down the harbor and past a dozen or so multi-colored sailboats anchored just off the shore. White and brown stucco dwellings shone in the afternoon sun on the opposite side of the harbor. This was a good place to relax and think.

Two small groups of uniformed men from God only knew where huddled at each end of the walkway. Probably trying to figure out what to do next. Like him, they were all attempting to find a way to forget, for a while, the world that had brought them here.

The sound of giggling and laughter interrupted his thoughts. A young couple was approaching the bench on the flower lined, dirt path that circled the park. A young American Army officer in his handsome, belted brown uniform strolled hand in hand with a slim, black haired, beautiful Italian girl. Her dark eyes sparkled with excitement. An Italian "cyganka" in a white dress! Like Nellie, his beautiful "gypsy." The two were thoroughly enjoying the challenge of trying to communicate with each other; the American in his American English and the girl in her romantic Italian. He made no effort in trying to communicate with them other than to offer both a smile and an understanding nod. He watched them move on down the path teasing each other with funny sounds that sounded like words. Their mutual amusement with each other's antics was a beautiful thing to watch. Made him think of his first time with Nellie. Their long stroll along the river Eden in Carlisle. He lit a cigarette, sat back on the bench and let his thoughts return to those days.

1940

It was the fall of 1940. He had escaped from France with thousands of other Polish airmen and made it to England in late June of that year. It was the year his life would change dramatically.

It had been a race with the Germans to the French port of St. Jean de Luz. He and a few others were among the last to arrive at the small port. The Germans arrived the day after their ship sailed. It had been that close.

The voyage to England had been frightful. Thousands of men crammed on top of each other, horrible food, and the constant threat of being bombed or torpedoed. For most, the smell of vomit coupled with the constant pitching of the ship and bad food made the voyage a test of one's manhood. After arriving in Liverpool, he was sent to Blackpool with hundreds of other men. They had nothing but the clothes on their backs. There had been no room on the ship for luggage. He was put to work, with pay and new RAF fatigues, building P.O.W. camps for a month. Then he was sent to a transition school at Blackpool where he was introduced to English culture and the RAF. Learning English and the RAF way of flying were the priorities. All foreigners, regardless of rank, spent the next few months there. After that, he was sent to the Kingstown Aerodrome just outside the northern city of Carlisle for refresher flight training. The fact that he had attended the Polish Naval Academy and later earned his wings in the Polish Navy's Fleet Air Arm, meant little to the British. He had to prove he really knew how to fly an airplane and fly an airplane the Royal Air Force way.

In Poland, he had been an officer. In England, he was still a pilot, but only given the rank of sergeant. He completed his refresher flight training soloing in a biplane known as the "tiger moth." It was similar to one of the many planes he had flown to earn his wings in Poland. He was quick to learn the English necessary to fly English planes. Many hours on his own were devoted to the study of English schematics explaining the functions of all systems in the aircraft he was going to be flying. Unfortunately, that enthusiasm for learning was not shared by some of his countrymen. Lives were lost on training flights because a Polish pilot forgot the simple difference between "left" and "right" and "up" and "down." Confusion at critical moments misreading English gauges that were in feet rather than meters and forgetting that the English throttle required a push as opposed to a pull in Polish planes, resulted in scores of accidents and tragic crashes. At one point, there was serious discussion about transferring any Polish trainee that couldn't master the English necessary to pilot a plane out to a ground service unit.

In Poland, pilots learned to communicate in the air by using hand signals. In England, they had to learn how to use a radio. If they were communicating with a Polish instructor, everything was fine. If the instructor was English, it was a different matter. And that was when understanding English became a matter of life and death. Especially when flying at night in formation where hand signals were useless. There was no room for error. One pilot's mistake could prove to be fatal for his crew and other crews in planes close by.

He liked Carlisle. It was a nice city. It had castles, parks, bridges, the usual assortment of pubs and restaurants, friendly people and lots of pretty, young girls. It was much smaller than Warsaw and Liverpool and that added to its appeal. One wasn't overpowered by size, noise and congestion. There was little of military significance within its limits and that was a blessing. While the air raid sirens went off from time to time, not one bomb was ever dropped on the city. The German planes flying overhead were usually on their way to bomb the Newcastle shipyards some sixty miles away to the east.

Many a knowing English and Polish airman used the anxiety and fear generated by the air raid sirens to get a little bit closer to their dates in order to "protect" them. He always thought how strange it was to see young men and women smiling as they headed off to some dark corner of the city when the sirens went off. He always made his way to a shelter. He had experienced how it was when the bombs actually fell. He remembered the stampede of screaming men, women and children in Warsaw during the first days of the invasion. The look of terror in the eyes of those huddled closely together in the basement of the Hotel Bristol as dozens of enemy bombers approached the city. He remembered the desperate, hopeful prayers of people praying not to die while their children, feeding off that fear, whimpered in innocence besides them. He remembered his own terror of being trapped in a Praga cellar with friends as bombs exploded in Warsaw then in the neighborhood where he and Josef

74

had taken shelter. He would never forget the helplessness, frustration and anger he felt because he could do nothing about it. He and Josef had survived that day. The others had not.

Nellie

The best thing about Carlisle was Nellie. He remembered the day they met. He was in Carlisle on pass with another pilot, Karol Lucas. They had just been issued brand new dress uniforms and were wearing them for the first time in public. They were both hoping to catch the eye of one of the many pretty girls that lived and worked in the city.

In those early days of the war, Polish airmen and soldiers that had made it to England were treated as heroes by most of the English people; men who had already felt the brunt of war, survived, and escaped to fight with the Brits against the Nazis. That perception, coupled with the new uniforms, made them very attractive to many of the women in the city.

While happy with the attention from the women, Ludwik always remembered to respect the feelings of the local men. Especially the ones in uniform. He could imagine what it would be like if the situation was reversed, and English soldiers and airmen had arrived in Poland to help his country fight to keep its freedom.

That being said, he was always open to meeting any unattached woman and enjoying her company. And there were plenty of attractive and unattached ladies in Carlisle. They always seemed to have a smile for any Polish serviceman that passed them on the street.

That brought his thoughts back to Nellie and her story about their "accidental" meeting in the park next to the river walk. She and her good friend, Jean Graham, had set up what amounted to be an ambush of the first Polish twosome that came their way. Luckily, he had been in that twosome. Both the girls were young, not quite eighteen. Nellie was working for the Air Ministry just outside of Carlisle and coincidentally, right next to the Kingstown Aerodrome where he was stationed. Jean held a clerk's position in the city's Civic Centre. They had worked together in a local biscuit factory for a year and had become good friends. Neither of the two had ever heard of Poland until refugees from there began arriving in England after the German invasion in 1939. Sympathy was high in England for the Polish people who had lost so much. Nellie and Jean felt the same way. That sympathy turned into excitement when Polish soldiers and airmen began arriving in England to join the war effort. The two girls became mesmerized by the appearance of so many dashing, young foreigners in Carlisle. The fact that England was at war did not alter their fantasies concerning romance. It only intensified them.

Nellie, Jean and a few other girls had devised a scheme to say hello to the new arrivals. To be close to them. They would take shortcuts through alleys in order to pass them face to face on the street. "Hello, Polish man!" was their usual greeting to them.

Most of the men just smiled and waved as they passed by each other. And that reaction was all the girls needed. It was enough to set them off on a giddy flight of excited chatter sounding quite like a flock of starlings gathering to roost for the night. If any man stopped to talk with them, they ran away like the inexperienced girls they were. Just not ready for that kind of social interaction.

The girls also liked to walk around the Civic Centre area with all its shops, pubs and restaurants and make believe they were interested in what was displayed in the windows. All the while keeping an eye out for the Polish lads. A short walk from the Centre brought them to the English Street train station where they would flirt with the Polish soldiers hanging out of the open windows on their Scotland bound train.

As they grew bolder over time, they discovered that the two best places for meeting the newcomers were in the parks or on the walkways that ran along the river Eden. Massive crowds in the city proper were fun, but the noise and bustle on the streets made it hard to stop and chat. The pace in the parks and along the river was much slower and quieter. A long walk along the river gave couples a good chance to have a meaningful conversation. Even with the differences in language, it really was the best chance to meet and get to know one other.

The day quickly came when Nellie and Jean decided that being almost eighteen was old enough to start being a woman. They didn't want to run away giggling like schoolgirls anymore. They wanted to meet some young men. Especially some Polish young men. They chose the parks, and the river walks to do that. Their approach was simple. Dress nice, look attractive and say "hello." Jean suggested they sit together on a bench and wait for a Polish twosome to come by. And it had to be a twosome. Any more than that would seriously impair their reputation.

On one warm and sunny Saturday afternoon, their plan worked. That was the day Ludwik got to meet the girl he would marry. Nellie told him later that she and Jean met downtown and walked over the bridge that led to Rickerby Park to set up their "ambush." They would wait on a bench for two Polish men to come walking by and attempt to start a conversation. He remembered having a good laugh when she mentioned they wanted to meet men who looked like movie stars and were war heroes. She said that most people in Carlisle shared those feelings. Especially the women. And it was not unusual for parents of a daughter or son to encourage them to bring home any well behaved, Polish soldier or airman for tea. Show them their appreciation and support for their part in the war effort. Make the Poles feel welcome in their "adopted" country. That idea was also shared by her father. To Nellie that meant she would be doing her civic duty in bringing home an "ally" for tea. Very patriotic.

Their strategy was good. They chose a bench that had a good view of the bridge crossing the river from the Civic Centre to their side. They could spot anyone coming across the bridge and have plenty of time to decide if they were worth executing their plan.

The city was filled with movement that day. Much of it was military. Convoys of trucks carrying men north to their bases in Scotland rumbled periodically over the bridge. There were lots of Polish airmen out and about on the streets. Most were from the Kingstown base next to the Air Ministry where Nellie worked. They were the ones that Nellie and Jean had high hopes of meeting. Maybe entice them into a long walk and then home for tea.

It wasn't long before they spotted Karol and Ludwik coming across the bridge. They were hoping the two were headed for the river walk. If they were, they would have to pass by their bench and with some encouragement from them, might stop and have a chat. Their hopes were realized when the men turned right and headed toward them. Nellie waited until they were within an arm's reach and said, "Hello, Polish man." Jean followed with a well-practiced, "Jak si masz." The Polish, "How are you?" stopped them on the spot.

Ludwik remembered just staring at Nellie. She had beautiful, black, curly hair. Just like the cygankas, the attractive gypsy women back home in Poland. He had always been intrigued by them; spent many a night dreaming about them in his teenage years. He liked the way Nellie's eyes sparkled when she smiled. He knew she was young; but not that young. She had nice legs, was well dressed and had a bosom that showed promise. He was interested. That interest was not shared by Nellie. She said her first impression of him was that he appeared to be a little arrogant, a little "stiff" with his white gloves and all. She told him later that he acted like he had some place to go and was already late. She said she knew he was staring at her but avoided eye contact when she looked at him. She said she was more interested in Karol at first, but he had his eyes on Jean.

Karol was the one that got things rolling between the four when he pointed to the cemented stone wall across from the ladies and said in his best English, "Sit please?" That brought an outburst of laughter from the girls followed by a nod and a very loud, "YES, PLEASE!" After a few awkward moments of finger pointing and primitive English with Nellie offering, "me Nellie, her Jean." And Jean offering, "me Jean, her Nellie," the ladies were introduced. The men responded by standing at attention smartly to introduce themselves. Ludwik went first. He clicked the heels of his shiny shoes together, bowed from his waist and said, "I am Ludwik Skoczylas. Honor to meet you." Nellie was speechless. He seemed to be from another world with all that clicking and bowing. She had never seen a man do that. The other airman introduced himself in the same manner. His name was Karol. He had a great smile and was just as polite as the first man.

By this time, both girls had noticed that each man had wings stitched on the front of their blue gray jackets. That meant they were pilots. They were not only attractive, they were grown men.

While Nellie had been more interested in Karol initially, the tall, well-built Ludwik no longer seemed aloof and bored. Nellie took a closer look at him. He had thick, wavy, brown hair, smooth skin, piercing light blue eyes and a friendly smile. She had been mistaken. He was perfect!

Karol pointed to the stairs leading to the river walk and bowed once again, sweeping an arm in an invitation for the girls to accompany them down to the river. Their plan had worked! All four went down the steps. Karol motioned for Jean to join him while Nellie, curiosity and interest now aroused, waited for Ludwik to join her. It was the beginning of a relationship that would quickly evolve into romance.

After their walk using broken English and Polish words that brought lots of laughter, Nellie knew she was going to invite Ludwik home for tea. It took a while to get the invitation across to him. She got it done by pulling out a little notebook from her purse and writing her address with next Saturday's date and a time under it. She then drew a knife and fork under that. He got the message and said yes. In his broken English, he asked her if she liked chocolates. She said yes. He then asked, in that same charming, broken English, if she could meet him on that same day at noon. She wasn't sure what he was saying so she gave him the notebook and pen. He wrote a misspelled Saturday and the numbers 1200 under it. Knowing now she worked at the Air Ministry, he drew a map showing that building and the runway next to it. He marked an X between them and pointed at her. She understood. The X was on the field between the Ministry and airfield. He wanted her to be there next Saturday at noon. She smiled and nodded her head yes.

She went home excited with the prospect of Ludwik meeting her father who was a RAF veteran. She knew he had some pictures of his service. Communication between Ludwik and him would be a problem, but the pictures would help with that. She also had a feeling the Polish pilot knew more English than he let on.

The week went by slowly. Every day she got off the bus and walked by the field on her way to work. She pictured in her mind how they would meet on Saturday. She would wait for him in the lush, green field wearing her bright, yellow dress. He would come to her jogging across the field in his dashing blue-gray uniform. She would run to meet him and leap into his arms. He would swing her around once or twice before putting her gently down. They would embrace. He would kiss her. A long, sweet kiss. Just like in the movies. Very romantic!

Nellie was early on Saturday. It was cool. A typical October day in the far north region of England. Normally, she would be with Jean on Saturday, but not today. Today she would be with her Polish pilot. Jean had wanted to tag along for the midday adventure, but Nellie had decided this "special" meeting would be between her and Ludwik. It was quiet standing in the field. She could see the main gate to the airfield some distance off to her right. There was a small guardhouse there. Two guards were sitting on chairs outside the door. A long line of brown barracks was just a short distance away inside the gate. Nellie assumed Ludwik would be exiting there. She focused her attention on the gate and waited for him to appear. Her concentration was interrupted by a distant drone of engines high overhead. Covering her eyes with one hand to block out the sun, she looked up and saw a formation of three biplanes approaching the base. She watched in admiration as they broke off into some sort of maneuver left, get back into formation, peel off into another maneuver right and then head off into the distance.

She watched them disappear into a bank of clouds and then returned her attention back to the gate. It was close to noon. Uniformed men were gathering there. She hoped Ludwik was one of them.

She never heard the plane approaching until it passed over her a few hundred feet above the field. Startled, she watched it climb straight up, turn on its side and slowly come around to make another pass over the field. It was lower this time and coming straight at her. The pilot waggled the plane's wings as he approached and then did the strangest thing. He leaned out of the cockpit and waved to her. It was Ludwik! He went past her, banked the plane sharply left and came back toward her a third time. One of his arms was hanging out of the cockpit. He was holding something in his hand. He dropped it just as he zoomed by. She waved to him and watched the plane climb quickly to join the other two planes that had returned. She watched them fly out of sight again then turned and ran to the package. It was covered in cigarette wrappers that had elastics wrapped around it. There was a note written on one of the wrappers. It read, in English, "Cheerio my pet. See you tonight." She was impressed with the note and his surprise fly-by. Inside the package was a small bundle of chocolate. Another surprise! And for that, she was also impressed. She loved her sweets.

"Buona sera!" The friendly greeting from the young Italian couple walking by him snapped Ludwik out of his daydream. He returned their greeting with a "Buona sera" of his own and then watched the two lovers continue on down the path, their arms locked around each other's waist. They only had eyes for each other. A beautiful thing.

He remembered listening, with much amusement, to Nellie's boastful, humorous rendition of that Saturday meeting in the park; from the planning of the "ambush" featuring the "Hello, Polish man," her initial dislike of him and their fun-filled walk by the river Eden trying to communicate with each other. He could still picture her dark eyes dancing with excitement and joy whenever she spun her version of the day's events; every sentence accompanied by a mischievous, very contagious stream of laughter.

Ludwik missed her terribly but knew they would be together soon. Patience was the key. He had plenty of that. Their time was coming. It would be good again. That he knew for sure. He got up from the bench, straightened his tie, adjusted his cap as he always did, and walked briskly out of the park. There was energy in his step. Zygmunt would be waiting for him later at Fabbri's but more importantly, his wife and son were waiting for him in Carlisle. He only stopped once in his walk that afternoon. That was to enjoy a cigarette and watch the sun creep closer to the horizon out at sea and turn the sky into a glowing, reddish orange. It had always been one of his favorite views. A perfect intro to the night; dinner with a friend, a little wine, intelligent conversation and then welcoming a good night's sleep in a real bed.

The meal, wine and conversation had been excellent. The good night's sleep in a real bed was another matter. He had fallen asleep quickly, but in little more than an hour, everything changed. Dreams, bits and pieces at first; faces, clouds, country roads, workers in a field, walking in a fog, his heart pounding, huge hands appearing from nowhere and dragging him deeper into the fog, fighting to free himself from their iron grip, unable to do so, a bolt of lightning splitting the fog apart as the hands hurled him high into the sky. Falling head over heels into the sea. Sinking under the waves then blinded by lights. Floating back toward the surface. Hearing screams from the darkness below. Then nothing. Now flying over the English Channel. The plane shaking, sputtering, bouncing; losing altitude at an alarming rate. The water below suddenly churning, building and rising upward toward the plane.

He was sitting next to Marian Krol, a good friend. Marian was the pilot. He was the co-pilot. Marian was fighting with the controls of the Halifax. He was trying to bring the crippled bomber back to their base at Bramcote. The plane had been hit badly by flak over Calais on the French coast. It had been a struggle keeping the plane in the air since then. It shuddered repeatedly as it slowly made its way across the Channel. Ludwik's eyes were fixed on the white cliffs of Dover. In a few minutes, they would be over them and able to crash land on one of the fields just beyond. Marian's hands were locked on the wheel, straining to keep it back and not let the plane nose over and drop into the water. Ludwik kept yelling for him to hold on. Marian's swollen fingers began to bleed from under his fingernails. He began screaming that he could not hold on much longer. The skin behind his fingernails suddenly split open and fountains of blood spurted into the air. The blood splattered all over the instrument panel, then poured down onto the floor of the cockpit. It formed a dark-red puddle that quickly spread across the floor toward his boots. Marian began losing his grip. He screamed at Ludwik for help, but Ludwik was frozen in his seat. The plane suddenly nosed over and began to spin its way down toward the rising water. Ludwik was helpless. He closed his eyes and waited to die. The last thing he remembered was Marian screaming, "Help me, Ludi! Help me!" The scream jarred him awake. His entire body was swimming in sweat. He threw the covers off and swung his legs over the side of the bed. He sat in the dark trying to figure out what had happened. Then he knew. He had forgotten to take his pill. Cursing himself, he got up, walked across the room, opened the balcony door, and stepped out into the Brindisi night. Feeling a little lightheaded, he took a deep breath of the salty air and extended the exhale. It was something he often did to compose himself. He sat on one of the two thatched chairs provided by the Fabbris for their guests to sit and enjoy the harbor view. He reached for the cigarettes and lighter he had left on the wrought iron table after dinner.

Saturday's Dream-Sunday's Remembrance

He wanted to think about the dreams while they were still fresh in his mind. Maybe find something to help Bednarz's analysis.

His first thought was how Marian Krol had made it into his dreams. While they were friends, they had never flown with each other. As far as he knew, Marian was still alive. Nellie had mentioned him in one of her last letters. He had been awarded the Air Medal for Bravery for action performed in the line of duty some months ago. He had landed a smoking, heavily damaged bomber at his base in England. The plane had skidded off the runway, gone through a fence and come to a stop in a cow pasture. When the base firemen and medics entered the cockpit, they found Marian unconscious at the wheel, both hands locked tight on it. It had taken two men to pry his hands loose. He became an instant hero for landing the crippled Halifax and saving the lives of the entire crew. That had to be Marian's connection to the nightmare. He thought about the fog. He remembered something about a woman crying in a fog that he couldn't find and help. Him being in the water probably had something to do with his crash into the Adriatic last January; his struggle to free himself, the bright light that was Mary and floating away in water that had turned from cold to warm. He wondered what Bednarz might have to say about these things. For now, it was up to him to try and get some sleep. Two cigarettes and one pill later, he was back in bed and sound asleep. He dreamt again, but this time it was about Nellie, her warm body and eager lovemaking.

After Sunday mass at the Cathedral, Ludwik and Zygmunt took a ferry boat ride around the inner and outer harbors of the city. The boat was full of men in uniform. Americans, Australians, New Zealanders, South Africans, Poles, Brits and others were all crammed together against the railings on the two-deck ferry.

A few men had ladies with them. They were given the choice spots along the railings. Ludwik was pleased to see that men still knew how to be courteous.

The sight of the uniforms crowded on the decks of the ferry brought back vivid memories to Ludwik of his narrow escape by ship from France in late June of 1940. General Sikorski had issued orders from London for all Poles in France to get to ports along the Atlantic coast and make ready for evacuation by sea. He was one of the last ones to make it. His small group of four had lost their transportation and had to walk through the night with German tanks and infantry prowling in the area. Fortunately, they were picked up by Polish scouts in the morning and brought to a convoy headed for the coast. It had been an anxious two day wait there for a ship to arrive before the Germans did. The nearly four days aboard that ship had been taxing. The ship was packed shoulder to shoulder on deck by many of the five thousand men that had made it aboard. Men were sick every day and night as the ship plowed its way through heavy seas on the way to England. It didn't help matters when the only thing you had to eat and drink was foul tasting mutton and milk-curdled tea. He remembered the constant smell of vomit and how it slushed along the deck and sometimes flowed over your boots. God forbid, you slipped and fell into that river of shit. You risked being thrown overboard if you did.

The trip on the Arandora Star, a luxury liner, pressed into service by the British for the evacuation, was one he never forgot. He had been pained to learn the ship was sunk a few weeks later off the coast of Ireland by U-boats. Sixteen hundred people lost their lives. Ironically, many were German prisoners of war headed to Canada for internment in POW camps. Another example of madness run rampant in the world.

The ferry slowly made its way toward shore and by far, the tallest structure in Brindisi. It looked to be a tower of some kind. It was the only stop the ferry was to make on the two-hour excursion. As they neared the dock, a guide explained in Italian, then in English, that the tower was a monument dedicated to the memory of all the Italian sailors that had lost their lives in WWI. He said their number exceeded six thousand.

"Warsaw lost more people in two weeks," Zygmunt murmured.

"Sadly so, my friend. Sadly so," Ludwik responded.

The long, winding staircase to the top took a while to manage. The view of the sea and city was worth the effort. It also served as another reminder of a time past for Ludwik. He and Basha, his Hungarian lady, used to climb the long, winding, stone staircase in the bell tower of St. Stephen's cathedral in Budapest to enjoy a spectacular view of the city. They used to play a game of trying to describe the person making the echoing footsteps coming up the staircase to their spot. And their total surprise one day when Willie, a German embassy worker and former suitor of Basha's, appeared in the doorway with a warning that events were unfolding in Budapest that put both of them in danger.

Ludwik lit a cigarette and took in the view of the Adriatic. His thoughts still lingered on his time in Budapest with Basha. He had heard that she and her family had left the city and had gone to one of the Greek islands. The family had been good to him during his time in Budapest and if it wasn't for the war, he might have stayed on and made a life with them. But that was five years ago. A lifetime in war. Duty, fate and circumstance had driven him to France and then England where he had found Nellie and her family. He was part of that family now. He hadn't prayed for his friends in Budapest for some time. He would also pray for Willie, the German embassy worker, who had risked his life to warn him that trouble was coming his way.

Wearing civilian clothes today had proven to be an uplifting experience for both men. They agreed that it was good to feel like a civilian again. They had blended in easily with the Italians at mass and enjoyed assuming the role of locals in the sea of uniforms on board the ferry boat. Zygmunt said for the first time in over ten years of service, he felt the urge to leave the military and return to civilian life. His only concern was where that was going to be. Ludwik understood that completely. Every Pole would be faced with that question when the war ended. Would it be back to Poland or find another place?

They said goodbye to old man Fabbri and strode off to meet the others at the Porto Mesagre. They had seen the crew at mass, but all five of had begged off the ferry ride offer. Ludwik and Zygmunt had laughingly wondered if the new men would return to the same women they had just left or if they would be on the streets looking for new recruits to play with.

All five were waiting for them outside the entrance. Jan and Andrzej looked rested and ready to go. They knew how to pace themselves. The three new men looked like they hadn't slept or eaten all weekend. They would sleep well tonight. Ludwik hoped he would do the same.

Ludwik and Bednarz discussed the dreams for over an hour. Bednarz was impressed that Ludwik had been able to remember them. Even tie them to events that had happened. He thought it might be a good sign. Not too different from getting things off one's chest in real life. He told Ludwik that having dreams about his experiences in war would always be part of his life. The question was how much of an effect they would have on him.

If he could manage dreams like he did this weekend and have a sleeping pill or two handy for help, he was going to be fine. If things ever got out of hand, he would have his file to bring to a more qualified physician than he was. It might help that doctor in his evaluation and diagnosis. He knew there wasn't a whole lot more he was qualified to offer. He did feel it would help Ludwik if he got his story out; his "odyssey" from the invasion to now. He would make his notes, offer a few suggestions and add it to the file. The business of Ludwik's "encounters" with the Blessed Lady he would stay away from. He did not want his reluctance to believe that those events had happened interfere with their discussions. He would never question a man's faith. Especially a faith like Ludwik's. A faith that he had lost. He would listen to Ludwik's story, ask questions and make copious notes for the file. It really was all he could do. Time was not on their side. Ludwik would be going home soon.

Painting a Picture

"I'd like to hear a little about the Naval Academy and then anything else that comes to mind after that. A chapter or two from your "story" so to speak. Peacetime or war time."

Ludwik nodded. "I loved the school. It was another world to me; a world that helped change my life. Most farm boys were expected to be farmers for the rest of their lives and there I was at one of the best universities in Poland learning to be something else. I was surprised my parents, especially my father, had even considered the idea of me not being a farmer. I didn't know that any money had been saved by them, but when the new government made school possible for anyone, they made sure we all went."

"I do remember thinking that while education was opened for all, only the well-to-do would be able to send their children to university," Bednarz commented.

"That is exactly what happened," Ludwik said. "Still, when it became too expensive to continue at the Academy, my mother encouraged me to attend the less expensive Technical University in Warsaw. I helped on the farm as much as I could during those years. My brothers chose to stay on the farm and not attend university. My sisters stayed in school until they were sixteen. Not being able to see my family after the invasion was hard; even harder when we were ordered to retreat to the Romanian bridgehead hundreds of miles away from them. Our orders were to hold fast there until planes from France and England arrived in Romania. Then some of us would cross the border and fly the planes back into Poland. At that point, I knew it was going to be almost impossible to get to my family. When the Russians invaded, everything got worse. We were ordered to get out of the country as fast as we could and make our way to France. It took a long time for a friend and I to cross most of southern Europe to get there. During that time, we had no way of finding out what was happening to our families."

"You haven't seen them for six years then," Bednarz deduced.

"Correct, but I know where they are. I had written a letter to my uncle in Kurylowka when I was in England asking if he had heard anything about them. One of my sisters wrote back and said the family was there. And believe it or not, I did have sort of a visit with them a few months ago."

"A few months ago? 1944? How was that possible?"

"We were assigned a mission to southern Poland. We had to drop an agent and supplies to a partisan group along the San River. The drop zone was not far from my uncle's farm. I had lived on that farm before my father moved us to Mazanki. I knew exactly how to get there. All I needed was a little moonlight. I had plotted the farm's position on the river as soon as I found out about the mission.

I had my crew load two extra cannisters full of food and medicine for the family."

"That's amazing. How did the drop go?"

"It went well. The farm was on the biggest bend of the river. We just followed the river east to the bend. There was some moonlight that helped us find the farm. We had to make another pass after we located it. We made the drop from five hundred feet. It was a good drop. I know they must have heard us. I hope they found the cannisters before anyone else did. They will not be writing about it in any letters. Too dangerous to do that. God willing, they'll tell me if they got the cannisters when I see them."

"Was the drop authorized by your squadron?" Bednarz asked.

"The mission was," a smiling Ludwik answered.

Bednarz loved the story. He almost wished he could have been a part of something like that. What a wonderful way to remind people they had not been forgotten. The whole crew must have enjoyed helping the family of one of their own. He would not note any part of the drop. No need to cause undue trouble with the war nearing its end. He might have done the same thing if it was his family, and he was the pilot. He hoped the cannisters had been found by the family.

"How about your stay at the Academy?"

The Academy was a year-round operation," Ludwik said. "Before my first year started, we were required to attend summer training."

"What kind of training?"

"It was mostly a physical endurance exercise; lots of long marches, sleepless nights and obstacle courses. Tons of push-ups, sit-ups, squats, that sort of thing.

It was a pre-curser to the basic training we got at the Academy. We did receive some rifle and small arms instruction. It was expected that if you had to, you would be able to join army units and help in a fight. We also received lots of survival training. That was especially important for any of us wanting to be a pilot. If your plane went down in enemy territory, they taught you how to survive and get back to your lines. A few of the instructors were aviators who had experienced just that in WWI. One of them had broken an arm and leg in a crash behind enemy lines and still managed to get back to his base. They were excellent instructors. That training was very helpful later when the war got going and my friend and I had to make our way over land to France. The rest of the instructors just yelled at us."

"The way of the Army," Bednarz chuckled.

Ludwik went on to describe some of the abrasive treatment all naval cadets had to endure from their Army instructors. Every order had someone screaming in your face. Not very pleasant, but not unlike what you encountered in the first weeks at the Academy from their instructors.

"How did you feel about that?"

Ludwik smiled and said, "It only reinforced my conviction that being in the Navy and hopefully flying a plane for them was the only way to go. No one up there in the sky to yell at you like that. I also knew the clean air in the sky had to be much better than the slime and rot in the trenches."

"Why did you leave the Academy?"

"Like I said before, it became too expensive for my parents."

"And how did you feel about that?"

"It was......... disappointing, but I understood. I received a good education in Warsaw and had the time to help the family on the farm during those years. It was a fair trade. My mother was happy I was in school and my father respected the fact that I put a lot of time in on the farm."

"Any friendships made at the Academy?"

"Many. My best friends were a family from Sopot not far from the academy. I met them in Copenhagen the summer after my first year. I was close to one of them. Her name was Bodil. She was a student also. Her father and brother were pilots. They taught me how to fly gliders and planes way before the Navy did. Bodil and I were in Warsaw together just before the war started. I never saw her or her family after that."

Bednarz entered the following notes on Ludwik: (lost friends at start of war, handled it well, showed maturity and ability to move on)

Ludwik said he had a question. Bednarz said that questions were always welcome. Ludwik asked when the discussions would end concerning his pre-war life. He said he was not sure how they would help with the nightmares and loss of sleep. He wanted to take the doctor's advice and get his war experience out in the open and see where that led. To see how it felt. To test it out on someone that might have some tips on how to handle any problems that surfaced in their give and take sessions. He asked Bednarz what he thought about this.

Bednarz picked up his pencil and twirled it around in his fingers for a few seconds, put it down and clasped both hands together on the desk. He thought for a few moments then answered, "This time, you, not me, asked for the evaluation. You had some concerns about your ability to fly and command because of nightmares and lack of sleep. Your honesty in asking for help is impressive.

As you probably know, many of your fellow airmen would never be that honest if they knew their flight status was on the line. With the war at its end and the Flight probably done with missions, I felt I had the time to help you and a few others get ready to return to the world. The real world. I believe a more thorough discussion of who

93

you were in the past might be beneficial. I want to help you handle the flashbacks that will almost certainly be part of your life for some time. If you feel this is unnecessary and all you need from me is a "clean bill of health" to get you back in the air, I can do that. In my opinion, you are fit to fly. I do have some concerns about the long-range effects of your service. Learning about who you were before the war is important for me to understand who you are now. Painting a picture so to speak."

Ludwik appreciated that. He liked this man. He was sincere. And he had a point. Life after the war was something he had not thought much about. It might be a good idea to follow his lead. He had time to do that now. There was not much else going on at the base anyhow. He knew there was no one back home in the family who could help him the way this man might. Maybe he would find a few ghosts he never knew he had. It would be interesting to see. He decided to let the doctor lead. He would follow.

"Thank you for your confidence in me. I meant no disrespect with my question," Ludwik said.

"Right. Let us get back to the Academy and your family then. Did the Academy give you any time off? Weekends, holidays? And was there a problem with anyone in your family that kept you away from home?"

"No problems with my family. Most of my holidays were spent writing papers, doing research and reading. My family understood. I did spend some time with the family I met in Denmark.

Their daughter, Bodil, and I became very fond of each other. I guess one might have called us "sweethearts." Frankly, I was more interested in seeing her than my family at the time. I was eighteen then. I did write home some but did not get many letters in return.

When I did receive one, it was usually written by one of my sisters and always said the farm was doing well and not to worry. She said mother wanted me to better myself with an education. That the farm would always be there. My father could not read or write that much also, so I never heard from him. But I knew his heart was with me. He always wanted me to be a man and be in charge of my own life. He never asked me to return and help when I was at the Academy. When I left the Academy and came home, he was pleased to see me. I was happy about that. I was a bit concerned that I might lose my place in the family and the respect I had from my brothers and sisters for being the oldest son."

Bednarz noted: (possible father/son relationship problems?) He went on, "Let's talk more about the Academy. How did you manage to get accepted there and what made you pick aviation?"

"I scored number one on the "Matura." When the navy notified me that I had been accepted at the Academy, I jumped at the chance immediately. I knew I could learn to fly there and be like one of my heroes who were all aviators. Stanislaw Skarzynski and Marian Plonczynski were two of them. They were always in the news for their flying. Skarzynski was a WWI army hero that had learned to fly after the war. He became one of the best pilots in Poland. He won many awards competing in air shows all over Europe. Plonczynski was the most famous sport club flyer in all of Poland. I wanted to be like them. The Academy opened the door for me to try. Even though I didn't finish there, the experience eventually helped me become a pilot. Flying has been my life the past eight years. I never became a pilot like them, but who has?

Now, I think I would like to finish my duty as a pilot and go home to my family in England. Then I can think about the future. I'm not sure if flying or joining the RAF is what I want to do after the war. It's a possibility, but I will have to discuss it with my wife.

95

There are some other things that interest me. I enjoy working on automobiles. I did a lot of that in France before we had to get out. Maybe operating an automobile repair shop would be a good business for me."

Bednarz respected the fact that Ludwik realized he had options and had been thinking of them. That was good. He was impressed by his words, "I would like to finish my duties as a pilot." Like everyone else, he was sick of the war. And yet, here he was, still anxious to continue his duties with Flight 1586.

Bednarz was aware of the importance of a high score on the "Matura" by an individual. It was the measuring stick used by universities in Poland to help determine the potential of an applicant. It reflected the comprehensive, educational achievement of the individual up to that point in time. He had to marvel at how this "farm boy" had managed not only to get accepted into the prestigious Naval Academy, but how he had become a pilot and war hero…. A real war hero. No doubt about that. All those missions supplying partisans in occupied Europe was proof enough. He had survived much. The questions he had at the moment were twofold: would all those missions cost the pilot psychologically in the future and would the guilt about leaving his family and country raise its ugly head somewhere down the road. He knew the missions had taken a toll. He was not sure about the guilt. He asked him again about leaving his family behind after the invasion and then having to leave the country entirely.

"I could have stayed in Warsaw to fight with the army. Maybe even tried to get home and be with my family, but our orders sent us to the Romanian border to wait for the French and English planes. Then we could get into the fight; bomb the German supply lines, maybe provide support for our ground troops. Unfortunately, our allies let us down. When the Russians invaded, we were ordered into

96

Romania to live and fight another day. That order was hard to obey. It meant leaving everyone behind. There were many tears. Much guilt. When we found out that we would be sent to an internment camp in Romania, three of us decided to cross the border on our own. We did not want to take the chance that we might be stuck there for a long time. The guilt and shame for leaving would have been too much then. We had to find a way to fight. Once we crossed the border however, one of the other two men had a change of heart and decided to find his outfit and join them in internment. My friend, Josef and I then took off on our own. When Sikorski later ordered all Poles to leave Romania and get to France before the Germans or Russians intimidated the Romanians into keeping us in the camps, Josef and I were already on our way to France."

Bednarz felt that while that journey undoubtedly had some interesting episodes, he wanted to finish up compiling information on Ludwik's Academy experience and his life up to the war first.

"What did you study at the Academy?" Bednarz asked.

"Engineering."

"Your instructors?"

"They were excellent. Most of them were navy. Some were civilians. My classes included physics, mathematics, basic seamanship, navigation principles, shipboard systems, hydrography and international law."

"How were your grades?"

"My grades were very good."

"Any classes involving aviation?"

"Just a basic introductory course."

"Any regrets about those days?"

"None at all. I learned a lot, found out what life in my new world was like and made some great friends in and outside of the Academy. I wished I could have graduated from the Academy and gone on to flight school, but it all worked out in the end."

Bednarz put his pencil down and decided to change the subject and see where it led.

"It's amazing to me how quickly everything fell apart in '39. Did anyone in your circle have any idea about what might happen?"

"There was lots of talk about a possible invasion. I was stationed at Deblin then. Some of the pilots there had witnessed the buildup of German forces on our borders for some time. There was lots of speculation about what it all meant. It was the main topic of conversation between everyone on the base. Reconnaissance missions along the coasts and borders of Germany and East Prussia kept bringing back more and more information on the buildup. I believe most of our command thought it was German intimidation trying to get back the corridor into Prussia. Command didn't seem to be that concerned. I think they thought if trouble started, our forces and equipment were up to the task. I wasn't sure about that. I had seen their planes over the Baltic. It wasn't hard to notice their capabilities. They were much faster than our planes. They could fly higher than anything we had. And there were so many of them. When they invaded, they came in numbers we couldn't handle. And as you know, it didn't take them long to disprove our command's assessment of our capabilities. We just didn't have enough."

"My feeling is that we were just not ready," Bednarz added.

"True. Our battle plan to fight an invasion was poor. Very poor. Our supply of petrol and ammunition was pretty much wiped out in the first few weeks. We couldn't refuel or rearm our planes and vehicles. The whole supply operation was a sham. We had no choice but to retreat. When the Russians invaded, it was over. They only thing left to do then was follow orders and get out of the country."

Bednarz shifted the conversation back to Ludwik's time at the naval academy. He wanted to get as much information about those days and other pre-war experiences before he got into Ludwik's war time experiences. He had decided to give Ludwik and the other airmen he was treating the best he had while he could. He had always wanted to do more for the men he had "treated." He wanted to give men like Ludwik a little ammunition to help fight off the stress he knew they were going to experience sometime down the road in the future. And for that, he needed more information.

He liked Ludwik. He felt the present situation with the nightmares was controllable. He was doing it now with sleeping pills. It was the man's future he was concerned with. The important question was would the nightmares dwindle to an acceptable, intermittent few or would they become an overpowering, disruptive influence in the man's life? He felt that creating a conversation designed to motivate bringing out in the open his experiences would be helpful. He was a firm believer that repression always resulted in varying degrees of depression. His job of putting men back into the cockpit with emotional issues was at an end. His assessment of their mental state had always been influenced by the need for their services. The standing order had always been to get them back in their planes. There was no need for that now. It was time to think more of their future.

Seaman Cadet

Ludwik continued the session discussing his limited experience at the Academy. His first academic year completed, his class was assigned to sail on the "Iskra," the Academy's training vessel that summer. The purpose of the sail was to teach the basic skills of seamanship to the cadets. Its officers and crew numbered around twenty and carried seventy to eighty cadets. All crew members, officers and sailors alike, were career navy men with years of experience sailing the beautiful "tall ship." The cadets performed their duties under the watchful and demanding eyes of their instructors. There was plenty to learn about handling a real sailing ship. If you were not on duty on the bridge, deck, or galley, you were in your quarters reading and studying the ins and outs of sailing. Each cadet was asked to put into practice what he had learned in the classroom. Instead of walking the grounds from one class to another on shore, the cadets hustled from one deck to another learning their trade at sea. While the ship was their classroom, the Baltic Sea was their playground. Using the stars for navigation, steering the ship, reading depth and current charts, tying knots, painting the vessel, and climbing the heights of the three masts were just a few of the dozens of skills and duties each cadet had to master on the cruise. It was well known that if you were not a sailor before putting out to sea on the ship, you would be one after it returned to port.

In early June of 1933, the "Iskra" raised anchor in Gdynia, caught a stiff westerly breeze and moved gracefully through the Baltic Sea along the coastline. It passed the Hel peninsula and its heavily fortified base and entered waters off the coast of Germany. With cadets scrambling like ants up and down the climbing nets, the ship tacked north and headed to Copenhagen, Denmark.

Shore leave was rotated. Ludwik was in the first group. Emphasis was placed on appearance and behavior when going ashore. They were expected to look and behave like gentlemen and future officers of the Polish Navy. The cadets were also reminded that a "brig" was part of the ship. Anyone who wound up in it had to face the possibility of dismissal from the Academy.

Ludwik said he had been taught to be responsible by his parents at an early age and understood and respected what it meant. In this case, it meant staying sober and obeying the local laws.

The time in Copenhagen was not only a reward for worthy sea duty, it was a lesson in how to represent your country in a foreign land. The cadets had been warned they would be tested in every port they visited. The test in Copenhagen would be the competition between them and the local men for the company of the women who frequented the pubs dockside. Strangers, especially young ones like them, usually had the honor of buying the drinks for the ladies while the locals had the honor of taking them home. The Danish men knew the cadet's shore leave was just for a few hours each day the ship was in port. They would let the cadets pay for the drinks that would loosen any distaff resistance later. It was smart strategy. It would have been a different story if the cadets were on "overnight" pass. Then it would have been a "no holds" barred competition between the two groups. High testosterone levels would rule the day's behavior and that could be disastrous for a cadet.

Ludwik said he waited to see which way most cadets went. Then he went in the opposite direction. He went right by several pubs located dockside where trouble in a tight dress smiled at him from every doorway. His plan was to get off the dockside street and get up into a neighborhood where a friendly smile might be an honest one.

He wanted to find a place that didn't have cadets; maybe meet some natives, perhaps even a woman; one that wasn't interested in playing young lads along, but one that was just....... interesting.

On a quiet, narrow, cobblestoned street, he found the perfect place. It held no cadets and had the look of respectability. It had a large, rusty anchor nailed over a sign that read, "Café Sommerer." He took a small table in the rear of the dining area and began examining the menu.

The two men and young woman sitting in the opposite corner of the café had taken immediate notice of Ludwik as soon as he walked through the door. They were all well acquainted with the dress-white uniform of a cadet from the Polish Naval Academy. The oldest man signaled the bar maid over and ordered a mug of beer sent over to Ludwik. In a short minute, she had the frothy mug in front of the sailor. She smiled at his puzzled expression and pointed to the trio across the way. He thanked her and looked at his new friends. They were staring at him. Only the young woman was smiling. He acknowledged their goodwill with a nod of his head and raised the mug towards them. They returned the thank you gesture with their own nods, raising their mugs in kind. One man, the one with the gray hair, moved a chair out from an unoccupied corner of the table and motioned for Ludwik to join them. Ludwik was intrigued with the prospect of meeting some locals and learning a little about Danish culture. He would also have someone to lean on when ordering his food. Mug in hand, he weaved his way around some empty tables and joined them. He thanked them with some polite Polish words. They stared blankly at him. It was an awkward moment. That changed quickly when the young woman raised her mug and clinked it against Ludwik's. Smiling brightly, she said in perfect Polish, "Welcome to Copenhagen and the beautiful country of Denmark." They were Polish! He could see that now. It was in their eyes, cheekbones and skin. He was "home" with these people. He introduced himself. The older man shook his hand. His name was Piotr Pastula. He was the father of the other two. Jozef and Bodil. Both were smiling broadly and enjoying the moment.

Piotr explained the family had been in Copenhagen for three days. They were leaving for home in the morning. Their home was in Sopot, the middle city in the "Trojmiastro" (three city area) on the

102

Baltic coast. It was bordered on the north by Gdynia and by Gdansk on the south. The family was very familiar with the coming and goings of the men from the Polish Naval Academy. They were sailors also. The three had sailed their boat from Sopot to Copenhagen along the same route the cadet "tall ship" had taken.

Ludwik was delighted with this good fortune. He was encouraged to order the bratwurst, potatoes and cabbage. The family ordered the same. Jozef called for another round of beer and advised Ludwik he was their guest and no money should leave his pocket. He said he would be offended if a guest offered to pay; especially a young man committed to service for his country.

Jozef, about ten years Ludwik's senior, admired the young man and his polite manners. Bodil, a few years older than Ludwik herself, thought he was the most attractive young man she had ever seen. She was struck by his appearance and immediately thought ahead to the time when they had all returned to Poland. She knew she would ask this young man to come and visit her in Sopot. Jozef could see the interest in his sister's eyes. She had taken a liking to this handsome, young man. As for himself, he would be interested in learning what this lad was being taught at the Academy. He wondered if the cadet understood just how important he and all the other young men in Poland were to the country's future. He wondered if he knew about the dangerous developments that were occurring in Germany, East Prussia and the Soviet Union. His family certainly did. The three of them had been to Germany and East Prussia. National Socialism, with its uniforms, swastikas, storm boots and ugly politics, promised trouble for Poland's newly gained independence. The Soviet Union was no less a concern. What the Bolsheviks had done to the Tsar, his family and the ruling class, had demonstrated the ruthlessness they possessed. The Russian cry for communist revolution was heard loud and clear by anyone who could read and think. One thing was certain. Wolves were circling the flock that was Poland.

Jozef was an experienced pilot. He flew gliders and planes at the numerous, very popular air shows throughout Europe including Germany and East Prussia. His father, an ex-pilot, served as mechanic, advisor, and money manager. Bodil joined them from time to time and served as interpreter. She spoke six languages. She tutored young ladies from wealthy families that had made their money in the growing shipping industry along the Baltic coast. The family cruise had been a welcome diversion for all of them. And now, with Ludwik at the table, Jozef knew another "diversion" for his sister was in the works. He would see to it that the two youngsters spent some time alone with each other today.

After the meal and second beer had been finished, Piotr and Josef decided to leave Bodil and her new-found interest for a while. Ludwik was only mildly disappointed that he wouldn't be able to talk more with the two men. He would, however, have the happy consolation of being with a very pretty, very intelligent, young woman. Jozef told him that Bodil would be good company for him and that he would be the same for her.

As the men rose to leave, Piotr reminded Ludwik the bill was not his to pay. He left money on the table to take care of it. It was agreed that they would meet in three hours at dockside where Ludwik's ship was anchored. Ludwik was impressed with the two men. They were already what he wanted to be. Successful men who were pilots. They had treated him with trust and respect by leaving him alone with Bodil. He felt duty bound to treat their young lady with the same respect they had given him.

Bodil

Bodil was a slim, blond, freckled faced beauty. Her light blue eyes twinkled with mischief and adventure. The smile she wore was not only generous, but it was also genuine. There was an attractive, athletic quality about her. She was tall. Somewhere around five feet seven inches. In addition to her physical attributes, she was intelligent, confident and very friendly. Like Ludwik, she was a leader. Knew how to handle herself. She was very comfortable in the company of men. The two were a good match. He knew it and so did she.

Bodil saw quickly that her father and brother had taken a liking to Ludwik. Especially when they left her in his company. She knew they would never have left her alone with anyone that was suspect. Their instinct about Ludwik was shared by her. This was a nice young man. She would find out more about this sailor from Poland. She put Ludwik at ease by telling him she was her own boss and not to worry about her brother and father. And besides that, she said they both liked him. She asked Ludwik to order another beer for them. He knew it would be his last one today. It would not be good if he reported back to the ship "unfit" for duty.

When Bodil learned that Ludwik was interested in aviation, she was quick to tell him of her experiences at the air shows with her brother and father. Ludwik became genuinely excited as he listened to her description of the shows, her brother's flying skills and her father's service as a pilot in WWI.

He sipped his beer slowly and listened with great interest as this lovely girl spun the story of her family. She was amazing! He wanted to know more about her. He told her that. She said all he had to do was ask. When he did, she laughed and told him to enjoy the rest of her story. She said after finishing her elementary education in Poland, she attended schools in France and England.

She said that only as a matter of fact and with a genuine appreciation for her good fortune. There was nothing arrogant about her. While her foreign education had been exciting and wonderful, her heart and soul had always remained in Poland. She believed that her generation, their generation, would be the one that would make this new and free Poland a great country. She said she had developed a keen interest in languages early on and that had become the focal point of her education. At present, she was preparing for a teaching position by tutoring young Polish girls in French and English. She said her mother had passed away a few years ago after a long illness and the three family survivors had taken a vow to live their lives to the fullest in memory of her. The sailing trip to Denmark was just one example.

The slow walk through the narrow streets brought them to a bridge that crossed a canal. At the other end of the bridge was a bicycle rental shop. Bodil headed straight for it. She rented the bikes before Ludwik had any idea what she was doing. Ludwik said he would follow her lead and she replied, "You might be sorry for that!" They pedaled leisurely around the city and wound up on a street called the "Stroget." They stopped for a tea break at a sunny, outdoor café packed with young people. Within minutes they both learned that neither had a romantic partner. Ludwik found the tea good, but that bit of information even better. The prospect of returning to the ship and never seeing her again suddenly became an issue. Bodil quickly put his mind at ease by mentioning that she would like to show him her home in Sopot sometime in the future. Ludwik said he would like that as long as it was approved by her father. She said he would.

The two toasted each other with their teacups to seal the agreement. That brought a rollicking roll of laughter from both. They were enjoying the day and their newly acquired friendship. Bodil asked him if he had ever heard the term, "Little America" while at the Academy. He said he hadn't. She told him that was what the three-city area of Danzig, Sopot and Gdynia was known as.

It was like the United States of America in that it had a growing "melting pot" form of population. She said many foreigners were coming to work and live in those cities. She felt the entire area represented the "new" Poland; the beginning of a Poland that she envisioned becoming a leader in Europe and eventually in the world. Her enthusiasm was infectious. She seemed so mature for her age. Ludwik had been mostly concerned with his "survival" as a student to be looking that far ahead. In a few short hours, she had expanded his outlook on life.

Ludwik thought of his recent years of schooling including his time at the Academy. Many of his instructors had spoken about the same ideas that he was hearing from Bodil. Their words were being reinforced by this beautiful, young woman from Sopot. He was very impressed. Both agreed it was exciting times for Poland. They decided to make an informal pact between themselves. Each would contribute to the new, independent Poland. She would teach the next generation of children to be literate and well informed and he would fly to defend those opportunities. They would become "partners" in the business of transforming an agrarian society into an educated, industrial one; one that promised opportunity for all.

They toasted each other with another "clink" of their cups, finished their tea and left. They cycled slowly back to the ship. Neither was in a hurry to get there. When they did, they found Bodil's father and brother strolling down the long walkway that ran parallel to the line of vessels tied up alongside it.

The four stopped a few yards from the bow of the "Iskra." The Pastula family stepped back on the walkway to admire the ship. Its masts towered far above all the others anchored in that picturesque assembly. It was majestic in appearance. Its gangplank had already been lowered to the walkway and several cadets were in the process of boarding. It was time to say goodbye.

Bodil blurted out to her brother that Ludwik was going to be a naval aviator hoping the comment would earn a few more minutes with Ludwik. Both Piotr and Jozef congratulated Ludwik on his choice of pursuing aviation. Jozef suggested it might be nice if the three men could find some time in the future to talk about aviation. Ludwik said he would love that. Jozef suggested Bodil give the cadet their phone number while he and their father returned the bikes. Bodil laughed as she pulled out a slip of paper from her jacket. It had their address and phone number on it. She had written them down while having tea with Ludwik earlier. Jozef laughed and said, "So. You had already made plans to invite Ludwik. I should have known. Why did you wait so long?"

"Respect for my father and much older brother," she shot back. She handed the slip to Ludwik and walked over to her men. She kissed each one on the cheek and whispered to Jozef to take his time.

There wasn't much to say. Ludwik agreed to write her with the dates he could visit. She promised to write back. They held each other's hands, kissed one another on both cheeks and said goodbye for now.

Ludwik Skoczylas, Seaman Cadet

The orders came as a surprise to Special Duties Flight 1586. Their stand down" status had become permanent and 1586 had been redesignated to become part of Squadron 301. There was no longer a need for any more missions into occupied Europe. The officers and men would now serve as part of the transportation wing of Bomber Squadron 301.

The Allies were closing in on the Nazis. It would not be long before the war ended. News had come into Campo Casale that certain Nazi officials were trying to negotiate a surrender with the Allies and Hitler had not been seen. An air of excitement and anticipation swept over the entire base. The thought that their mission was at an end brought tears of joy to many. It also brought out the bottles of vodka that had been stashed away for just this occasion. The drinking was fast, furious and widespread. It did slow somewhat when a rumor crept through the ranks that the squadron might be reassigned to a base in the Far East to help fight the Japanese. It was a semi-sobering reminder that while the fighting in Europe was ending, it continued hot and heavy in the Pacific. The slowdown in drinking only lasted a few hours. Then the thought of reassignment was dismissed. Glasses were hoisted again; to Poland, to family and to all their comrades who had lost their lives.

Ludwik reported to Dr. Bednarz for what he hoped to be a session that would add something significant to his file. He had celebrated quietly with Zygmunt in the barracks. He only drank one tumbler of vodka while his friend poured and sipped his way through half the bottle. It might have been different if he wasn't on doctor's orders to avoid excessive amounts of alcohol while on medication. That made it even more surprising to see the unopened bottle of wine and pair of sparkling wine glasses sitting on the doctor's desk when he entered the office.

Bednarz sat smiling in his chair behind the desk. The tools of his trade, the pad and pencil, were noticeably absent. Ludwik smiled as he greeted the doctor and took his seat.

"Just a small toast, my friend," Bednarz offered as he twisted the cork out from the unlabeled bottle of local red wine. Ludwik watched as the doctor poured a little bit of the grape into each glass.

"To Poland, our families and our brothers," the doctor toasted as he raised his glass toward Ludwik.

"To the future and a return one day to the freedom we fought so hard for," Ludwik answered.

The pinging of the glasses echoed off the walls. It was a warm and friendly sound. The glasses were emptied quickly.

"Good news!" the doctor said as he recorked the bottle.

"Indeed. Been thinking about the future all day," Ludwik responded.

"Peace, family and home?" Bednarz asked.

"Of course," Ludwik replied.

"And your night, my friend?"

"Not bad. Enough sleep."

"Things will get better now. I'm sure of it. Still willing to continue?"

"Yes. Better than getting drunk like the whole base is going to be."

"That is well said, my friend. There's going to be a lot of emotion here in the next few days. Unfortunately, some of it will include anger and sadness. Lots of men not going home.

110

I'm going to suggest the sessions become more frequent and last a little longer. I want to hear your story and fatten your file." The wine and glasses were put away. Out came the notebook and pencil. Bednarz headed the top sheet with the date; March 1st, 1945.

The Pastulas

He began, "What about your relationship with the family you met in Denmark and the years you spent after leaving the Academy. It doesn't have to be detailed, but just say what comes to your mind."

"The Pastulas became my second family in Poland. Bodil and I became very close during those years, but our relationship never really developed into anything more than a dear friendship. She saw other men during that time and eventually became romantically involved with an older man who was an officer in the Navy. They were planning to be married in the summer of 1940. When an invasion looked likely, his ship was ordered to make its way to England. That ended their wedding plans. She was with me and a few friends in Warsaw the days just before the Germans invaded. I remember her crying as she left to go home and join her father and brother in Sopot. He had called the hotel in Warsaw where we were staying and told her a German invasion was imminent and she needed to get back to Sopot with all haste. They were going to fly to Sweden and stay with friends as soon as she got back. I believe they planned to stay in Sweden until the hostilities ended. Her brother had moved their personal plane under some trees a good distance from the runway at the airfield that housed all the planes of their sport flying club. The plane was fueled and packed with as many clothes and personal items they could squeeze into it."

"Was it a good plane?"

"It was a rebuilt American Curtis Robin. A beautiful plane. They had refitted it from nose to tail. I flew it many times."

"Have you heard from them at all?" Bednarz asked.

"Not a word. I'm sure they made it to Sweden. They may have even flown to England from there to be close to her fiancé."

With some prompting from Bednarz, Ludwik went on discussing his relationship with the Pastula family. He described in detail how he had managed to spend time with them, work on the family farm, attend Technical University in Warsaw, and learn how to fly at the sport club that Piotr and Jozef belonged to. He said it was a busy time in his life and one of the reasons his relationship with Bodil never became a romantic one. He never really had the time to make that happen. It had been difficult for both at first, but as time passed, the romance they thought they had slowly changed into a strong and loyal friendship. There was a profound feeling of respect and understanding for what each wanted to accomplish with their lives. The cornerstone of their relationship had been laid with the informal pact they had made with each other in Copenhagen; that they would support one another in becoming important players in the development of the new Poland. She would teach and he would fly. She was proud of him when he earned his wings and he was proud of her when she taught her first youngsters how to speak not only their native language, but also French and English. And when she met the man of her life, he was happy for her. He even agreed to be in the wedding party. Unfortunately, the war ended those plans.

"No misgivings about seeing her in love with another man? No hint of anger or maybe a little jealousy?" Bednarz prodded.

"None whatsoever," Ludwik responded. "There was too much love of another kind. A deep-seated feeling of respect and friendship."

Into the Air

Ludwik said both Piotr and Jozef had taken a genuine liking to him even after they knew that Bodil and he would never be more than close friends. They enjoyed and encouraged his enthusiasm for flying. Jozef told him how much he was reminded of himself as he watched him become a flyer. By the time the Pastulas were done with their schooling, he had become an accomplished aviator. They taught him to fly gliders first before airplanes. Their methods were not much different than the ones used by the Polish military in training new pilots.

Ludwik said Piotr had a great deal of influence in the flying community; both civilian and military. His record as a pilot in WWI was well known and he had become one of the more prominent members of the air club outside of Sopot. His professional and social credits went a long way in convincing influential people to grant a favor or two for him from time to time. Ludwik said the World War I veteran made good use of that to further his career as a pilot. And when he graduated from technical university, Piotr advised him to join the Navy and apply for Fleet Air Arm training. Ludwik said the veteran had friends in the Fleet Air Arm and would see to it that he got his chance to fly for the Navy. Ludwik said he enlisted immediately.

Because of his prior basic training at the Academy, it was arranged by Piotr for him to bypass that phase and move right into the flight training program conducted at Puck. Piotr recommended Ludwik as one of the most promising young pilots he had seen. That recommendation had gone a long way with the naval officials. Ludwik was given time to be with his family in Mazanki before reporting to Puck and the naval aviation flight school. It didn't matter that he had already obtained a civilian pilot's license.

He had to pass the rigorous training regimen at Puck to earn his wings as a pilot in Poland's Fleet Air Arm.

Flight school was an absolute joy for Ludwik. His classes in aerodynamics, mechanics, flight principles and others provided a measure of challenge as the weeks passed, but he was always up to the task. His experience at the Naval Academy, coupled with the expert training he had received from the Pastulas, facilitated an understanding of the process used by the Navy to train pilots. There were only two phases of training at Puck he hadn't received from the Pastulas. They were ballooning and parachuting. Balloons, tethered and untethered, were used to practice the fundamentals of flight and navigation learned in the classroom. Some balloons were the one basket, hot air ones. Others came in the form of large, shark fin dirigibles powered by motors. Each had its own purpose. Both were at the mercy of the wind and required strong manual handling.

Parachuting techniques were begun with land drills that included how to exit a craft safely, deploy the parachute, control its descent and land safely. The land drills progressed to tower jumps hanging onto a cable and sliding down to the ground and using proper landing techniques. Following that, he was put into the harness of a fully enveloped parachute, hoisted high in the air and then dropped to the ground to practice a controlled descent. The cadets were then put into planes they had to jump from and deploy their parachutes. The training on balloons and parachuting was followed by learning how to fly gliders. Two-man trainers were used at first. Controlled by foot pedals and a joystick, the glider was pulled by cable across a grass field and into the air by a sport plane. After the necessary altitude was reached, the cable was released, and the glide began. It only took a few trips for the instructors to realize that Ludwik was already an accomplished glider pilot.

Ludwik had always been fascinated when flying gliders. It was an amazing, almost hypnotic experience becoming a part of the heavens that way. He loved being up there; to be free and far away from the noise and clutter that was earth. He always wondered if birds enjoyed flight as much as he did. He didn't think so. They were just birds and took to flight because nature dictated it. Because God had planned it that way. He, on the other hand, considered it to be a privilege to be able to glide through the sky like one of those creatures. He loved the soothing sound of air slipping by the canopy and over the wings as he turned, dove and circled his way across God's doorstep. He was always disappointed when the time came to land. Then the flight became all business as he swooped silently down towards a grassy runway far below.

He said radios were not part of the initial training. The early training planes didn't even have them. At that time, it was felt by Fleet Air Arm that pilots without radio communication would learn to be more alert, be able to improvise and take initiative on their own. The Navy wanted pilots who were not only intelligent and physically fit, they wanted pilots who could react quickly to any situation. His prior experience in flying gliders and planes with and without radios with the Pastulas in Sopot, put him heads and shoulders above the other trainees. The sport club experience coupled with his mature demeanor and education made him a natural leader; one the younger, less experienced trainees could follow. He became a model for them. If there was a need to have a trainee demonstrate a specific skill, or answer a difficult technical question, he was usually the one the instructors called on.

"How did you communicate in the air with other pilots?" Bednarz asked.

"There was a series of hand signals taught to the trainees so instructors in the front cockpit of the trainers could relay their

115

commands to students sitting behind them in the rear cockpit. Learning how to communicate by radio came later in the training cycle."

"Were the textbooks at Puck difficult?"

"Not really. I was a quick learner and kind of enjoyed reading them and the manuals. I used to practice repeating out loud out important info to myself. Winning my wings and becoming a pilot in the Navy became the single, most important thing in my life."

He went on to say that one of the more critical concepts taught to the trainees was the idea that if you saw and identified the enemy first, you would have a distinct advantage over him. The instructors taught him to search the sky in a measured sequence to locate planes far away and determine the speed they were moving at. One of them told him he had exceptional eyesight; that he could see things that most people could not. The instructor said he stood at the top of his group when it came to scanning the sky and finding planes way off in the distance and that his night vision was listed as "superior." In ground practice, he could find and identify objects at night before anyone else.

"So, you had good genes. That must have been one of the reasons you wound up with Special Duties," Bednarz said.

"It was. One of my instructors in England a few years later said I would be a good fit with them. He said that's where my eyes belonged. And here I am."

He said the primary mission of the Fleet Air Arm was to gather intelligence for ships of the Polish Navy. Their pilots flew two-man float planes on reconnaissance missions to gather that information. The skill of taking off and landing on the sea was only taught to trainees that signed up for it. He was not one of them.

He was one of the many pilots in the Fleet Air Arm trained to fly land-based planes used for reconnaissance missions over the sea and along the coastline. He said there were some problems in learning to fly those types of planes. Many of the trainers they had were overused and well worn. Some were close to ten years old. They were very similar to the first plane Ludwik had seen when he was a young boy. A few were dangerous to fly. Even the more experienced instructors had difficulty at times. There were a few crashes. Some fatal. He experienced a serious problem himself on a qualifying solo flight. His plane's engine stalled out and he was forced to make a powerless landing. His experience flying at Sopot enabled him to drop the plane like a glider onto the runway without incident. The feat was noted on his record with generous praise for landing the plane under very stressful circumstances.

"What type of plane was used as trainers?" Bednarz asked.

Ludwik said they were bi-planes that had two open cockpits, one behind the other. Each had a separate windshield and individual controls. The instructor sat in the front. The trainee sat in the rear. The aircraft had a fixed wheel assembly and propellers made of wood. Its frame was made of light steel and thin wood covered by plywood and canvas. Power came in the form of a 4 cylinder, air-cooled, 120 horse powered engine. While the plane's air speed was relatively slow, it more than made up for its lack of speed with its maneuverability. He said he had flown a similar model at the sport flying club at Sopot. Outside of the near fatal stall, he had a rather easy time earning his wings on the biplane.

Bednarz asked Ludwik if he had ever dreamt about that near fatal incident. Ludwik said he thought about it occasionally over the years, but never had any nightmares or dreams concerning it.

Bednarz noted: (near death training flight in peacetime did not cause nightmares)

"How was your life after you became a pilot?" asked Bednarz.

"It was great. Those years were good ones. I stayed close with the Pastula family. We spent a lot of time together. I visited them often on weekends when I was off duty. We usually went to the sport club together or Bodil and I went into Sopot to have fun with friends. I was flying gliders a lot then. Bodil flew with me from time to time. She loved the glider flights."

"Where were you stationed with the Fleet Air Arm and what did the Navy have you doing?"

"I was stationed at Puck. My main duty was to fly reconnaissance missions along the Baltic coastline from Germany to Lithuania. Occasionally they had us flying overland along the borders of the Soviet Union and Germany looking for any suspicious military movement that might constitute a threat."

"Did you see your parents and siblings?"

"Not often. I wish I had seen them more. I was too busy flying and spending time with Bodil and her family. When the war started, all chance for me to go home ended."

Ludwik Skoczylas

Polish Navy

Fleet Air Arm

Part Two

Josef Przyba

"Did you have other friends in the years before the war?"

"I did. Good friends in my unit and some old friends from university in Warsaw. The city was so beautiful then. I loved it there. We all did. It embodied everything that was us. We called it "Paris East." You could feel the excitement when you walked through the neighborhoods. The streets were alive with people. Shops, markets, flowers, music, and entertainment seemed to be around every corner. Trolleys, automobiles, trains, horse and carriage; Warsaw had it all. It was the perfect combination of tradition and change. The old ways and the new ways. All you had to do was watch a motorcycle roar past a horse and carriage on Ujazdowskie Avenue to see that."

"Any friends in particular?"

"Josef Przyba," Ludwik answered.

"Who was he?"

"He was stationed with me at Deblin. He was an Air Force pilot training to qualify as a navigator. I was there learning to fly light bombers. The Navy was considering using them because of their long-range capability. Josef and I met each other in Warsaw on pass one weekend and hit it off very well. We always went together to Warsaw after that. Sometimes we met Bodil and some of her friends there. She and a few others were with us in Warsaw just before the war started. We managed to get her and two of her friends out of the city early when word came that war could break out anytime. Josef and I were still in the city when the Germans attacked on the 1st. We didn't get out of Warsaw until later that day. We were just across the river in Praga looking for a way to get back to Deblin when the second air raid hit. We were together every day after that until we got to France."

"How long was that?" Bednarz asked.

"More than half a year," Ludwik answered.

"Did you serve with him in England?"

"No. I stayed in England to train as an RAF bomber pilot. He was sent to Morocco from France to train as a bomber plot.

"Did you get a chance to see your family after the invasion?"

"No. I was supposed to see them the week after the war began."

"You must have been worried about them."

"Yes, of course. Our farm was close to the East Prussian border. I knew the Germans might get there quickly. There wasn't much I could have done for them. I called a friend in Mazanki to get word to them, but never got a call back. Josef and I listened to the radio and tried to find out what was happening. There was a lot of confusion. We knew the early morning air raid had been turned back by our planes. That gave us some hope, so we decided to wait out the afternoon and see what happened. That's when we got caught in the second raid.

Bednarz remembered the confusion himself that Friday. There were unsubstantiated radio reports and rumors flying all over the country. He was in southeastern Poland visiting friends that day. After the attack, he left them to be with his father in Krakow and two sisters It had been an anxious time for him.

"So, your escape from Poland began when?" Bednarz asked.

"It began that afternoon when the bombs fell and people started dying," Ludwik answered.

Before the Storm

Ludwik left Bednarz after an hour and walked over to the officer's mess. He left with a full belly and three bottles of beer. It was another sunny Italian day. He decided to walk to the beach with his beer and spend the afternoon alone. He found a shady spot under a young palm not far from where his Liberator sat under water. It wasn't long before his thoughts turned back to his conversation with Bednarz earlier about the first days of the war.

While events in East Prussia and Germany had increased the tension between Poles and Germans, there was still a feeling throughout much of Poland that an all-out war was remote. There was also a certain air of confidence shared by both the Polish military and public that if a war did break out, it would be short lived and end in a resounding victory for Poland. That was the atmosphere Josef and he found themselves in just before the war began.

They were at the train station waiting for Bodil and her friends. It was Wednesday, August 30th. Ludwik's plan was to stay in Warsaw with them for a few days and then visit his family in Mazanki.

It had been unusually hot that summer of 1939. Farmers had to start harvesting crops late in July for fear of losing them to the excessive heat. It was that kind of heat that greeted Bodil and her three friends as they detrained and met Ludwik and Josef. The four were joining Ludwik and Josef for a long weekend in the city. All six were staying at the Hotel Bristol on Krakowskie Przedmiescie, one of the main thoroughfares in Warsaw. Their stay at the expensive hotel had been arranged and paid for by Bodil's family. It wasn't the first time they had made a stay possible for Bodil and Ludwik along with a group of their friends.

The family had a substantial investment in the bank that owned the hotel. They had used their influence to have suites reserved for Bodil, Ludwik and their friends through the weekend. It promised to be a relaxing, fun filled, few days.

Warsaw seemed particularly colorful and alive that day. Flowers were everywhere. They overflowed the balcony boxes that jutted out from apartments and businesses along the streets. They spilled over from pots adorning the lamp posts that dotted the walkways in the city and along the river Vistula. The public parks showcased meticulously manicured gardens that were alive with petals and blossoms of white, red, yellow, purple and assorted other colors, all carefully arranged to compliment the abundant green of the freshly cut grass. The shops, markets, cafes, theatres, banks and government buildings bustled with the movement of commerce, entertainment and politics. It was Warsaw at its finest; the center and very essence of Poland's proud past and promising future. It was good to be young, Polish, and part of this great city.

After checking in at the hotel, the group decided on a walk to the Vistula. During the walk, Ludwik noticed numerous posters plastered on buildings and advertising columns with the message, "STOP HITLER!!!" Other posters displayed a large, clenched fist with the same caption underneath. Near each poster was an appeal to the general public for contributions to the national defense. Nationalism was stirring strong in the hearts of his countrymen. It made him proud. He knew if there was a fight, his fellow Poles would respond with courage and confidence. He just wondered if they knew, like he did, about the substantial size and formidable capability of the opposition. He had witnessed the buildup of the German forces during his reconnaissance missions along the border the past few months. It had been worrisome. Especially in the number of armored units along Poland's western border.

He hoped it was just "posturing" by the Germans in their attempt to intimidate Poland into returning land they had been forced to cede to Poland in the aftermath of WWI.

He was also very concerned about the technological advances the Germans had made in developing new aircraft. He had met a few of those planes in the skies over the Baltic and on the German border. They were fast; much faster than the planes Poland had. Even their bombers flew faster than some of the fighters Poland had. They flew at altitudes unreachable by anything the Poles could put in the sky. Their fighters had canopied cockpits, retractable wheels and carried tremendous firepower from an assembly of cannons and machine guns. It was a new and very dangerous German Air Force. And while he was confident that his fellow Polish pilots could match up with the German pilots or any other pilots in the world, he worried that the Germans were now flying warplanes that were probably the best in the world.

The group of young professionals sat on the grass in the shade of a row of trees that ran parallel to the walkway along the Vistula. Ludwik and Josef represented the Polish military. Bodil, Marta and Stephanie were teachers. Franz was an artist. Bodil had brought a bottle of vodka and some small glasses from Sopot for a gathering such as this. They sipped their vodka, smoked and entertained each other with a lively discussion of the many recent political events in Germany and East Prussia that were casting something of a shadow on Poland's future. Hitler seemed to be hell bent on getting back German land lost in the treaty after WWI. He was making promises through his underlings in East Prussia that German rule would be returning soon. Polish students had been attacked by Nazi party members in Danzig. German "tourists" had been arrested and accused of spying on Polish military bases and the most disturbing development of it all was the movement of large forces in East Prussia, Czechoslovakia and Germany toward their border.

Ludwik, Bodil and Josef were of the view that war was probable. All the signs pointed to it. The other three disagreed. They felt that Poland was too strong militarily and with France and England as allies, it would be more than enough to deter Hitler from attacking their homeland. Josef smiled and quietly suggested that all civilians, including them, might consider making emergency plans to get out of harm's way if an attack should happen. Marta, a teacher of language, answered that with, "And where should we go to do that?" No one answered. The small group of friends stared blankly down at the Vistula and waited for someone to break the silence. It was the young artist, Franz, who did. He said, quite dramatically, there was NOTHING to fear because the country was protected by the likes of Ludwik and Josef. Then he bowed in their direction. Everyone laughed, happy the somber moment had been destroyed. Bodil raised her glass and proposed a toast to Ludwik and Josef. Her three friends joined her in the tribute. Bodil walked over to Ludwik, kissed him and said, "My hero, will you save me?" Ludwik kissed her back and said, "Of course, my dear."

The river walk was crowded with young women leisurely pushing baby carriages along its way. Many of them were wearing white or light-colored summer dresses and pushing black carriages. Others, dressed in black and dark colored dresses were pushing white carriages. It was like watching a movie; everything in black and white. The women stopped from time to time to chat, peer into the other's carriage, and congratulate each other for producing such a beautiful child. Franz, the artist, was struck by the scene unfolding before him. He marveled at the symmetry produced by all the black and white. He remarked that he'd like to paint that scene; maybe call it something like "A Warsaw Checkerboard." Ludwik and Bodil decided to leave the others and join the parade of black and white. It was a peaceful stroll. The air was filled with that special kind of happiness and love only a baby could bring to the world.

They could feel the energy. It was pure, honest and strong. It was beautiful. Perfect. Mother and child. Love personified.

Bodil said she hoped to be a mother someday but was worried about the future. She felt "bad times" were coming and that would push those plans aside. Ludwik agreed. He felt those "times" might be just around the corner. He took both of Bodil's hands into his own and urged her to make plans like Josef had suggested. He said he knew that she and her family had the means to get out of harm's way in a hurry. She smiled and nodded her agreement. She squeezed his hands and said, "Enough talk about that. Let's go dancing tonight."

The square in Old Town Warsaw was filled with people that night. It was another warm, summer evening. Ludwik and Josef were immaculate in their dress uniforms. Bodil, Marta and Stephanie looked like movie star triplets in their white, brightly flowered, summer dresses. Only Franz remained in the casual, relaxed attire he had worn all day. His untrimmed beard and uncombed hair set him apart from the masses in the square. The slim, anemic looking artist wasn't there to dance. He just wanted to relax, sip his wine and conjure up future paintings by watching the night unfold.

The string ensemble gaily played the favorite foxtrots and waltzes of the day. The music echoed gently off the high, stone-walled buildings that surrounded the square and fluttered back down onto a milling crowd. Dancing couples moved romantically under lighted lamp posts that stood just outside the circle of tables filled with the well-dressed gentry of Warsaw's growing well to-do society.

Fun, more than romance, moved Ludwik and Bodil onto the dance area. Franz had changed his mind and decided to dance also. He was a little more interested in romance than fun. He danced with Marta, Stephanie and anyone else who caught his fancy.

The young man had plenty of luck finding dance partners but was not doing that well in starting a romantic adventure.

The six friends shared two tables that had been brought together by the wait staff. Each table had lighted candles on them. It was a nice touch that helped lend a little more atmosphere and enjoyment to the evening. Drinks included beer and wine. There was plenty of money being spent at the tables in the square. Recent times had been good for many residents of Warsaw. Businesses were flourishing and people were making money. Jobs, while not in abundance, were available for both those with an education and those with a strong back. The old guard businessmen were mixing well with the next generation of young entrepreneurs busy transforming their ideas into businesses of their own. Life was good for many in Warsaw.

The night clerk at the desk in the hotel had a message waiting for Ludwik when he returned from the evening out with his friends. It was from Bodil's father, Piotr. It read: "URGENT, call me IMMEDIATELY. No matter the time." Ludwik was alarmed by the word "URGENT." He thought it would be best if he made the call with no one there except Josef. He called Bodil over, gave her a hug and whispered in her ear to return to the lobby as soon as the ladies were comfortable. She started to ask why, but he put a finger on her lips and said to give him at least fifteen minutes. Ludwik caught Josef's eye and nodded his head toward the desk. Josef nodded back in return and lingered in the lobby while the three women and Franz headed upstairs to the suites. The two men sat in the lobby and exchanged thoughts about what Piotr might have to say. Josef thought that Bodil's brother might have met with some misfortune. Maybe something had happened to their home in Sopot. Maybe there had been a fire or an accident with the plane. Ludwik thought otherwise. If those things had happened, he felt that Piotr would have asked for Bodil, not him. No, he was guessing Piotr had gotten information through his military contacts that was important.

Probably about the German their build up on the borders. Ludwik had always feared that Hitler wasn't bluffing with all his oratory and veiled threats against the homeland. He knew things were simmering with the Nazis when they signed the non-aggression pact with the Soviet Union last week. It was a warning sign that they were up to no good. And then just a few days ago, Bodil's fiancé and his ship had left Gdansk with two other ships for parts unknown. No, something had happened or was about to happen.

A curious, somewhat anxious, Bodil, appeared in the lobby. She became very alarmed when told her father had left a message for Ludwik and not her. Her immediate reaction was that something had happened in the family, but then wondered why her father wanted Ludwik to call him and not her. Ludwik said it was time to find out. He made the call. Piotr answered immediately. He obviously had been waiting by the phone. He had bad news. Main roads to Poland were filled with German tanks. Huge artillery pieces called "super guns" had been loaded on trains pointed in the direction of Poland. They were accompanied by heavy mortar and ammunition trains. Other trains had been seen moving out from Berlin loaded with troops, anti-aircraft guns, field artillery and full field kitchens. Reports from friendly foreign press members indicated that most of the German troops in Berlin had left. In addition, Polish agents in Czechoslovakia had reported a large movement of German motorized infantry crossing the country and headed toward the Czech-Polish border. All this news, coupled with the knowledge of the massive build-up of Germans along the East Prussian border meant invasion was imminent. He said there was absolutely no other way to look at the situation. War was about to happen. He asked Ludwik to make sure Bodil left immediately for Sopot. Ludwik was to find transportation for her and her friends and get them out of Warsaw. He said that Jozef, at the very moment, was moving their plane away from the hangar area to the other side of the runway.

It was to be parked in a space between trees keeping it out of sight from any attacking planes. Piotr's hope was to pack the plane with what they could, take all the money they had and get out of Poland before the attack began. He said he would speak to Bodil for a minute and tell her they were going to Sweden and that she needed to get home now! He said he knew she would argue with him about staying, but there wasn't any time for that discussion. Ludwik wished Piotr good luck and gave the phone to Bodil who was waiting anxiously, her faced filled with worry and fear. The conversation didn't last long.

"What does it all mean?" she asked Ludwik.

"It means the time has come for you to leave Poland. The Germans are coming. You need to be with your family and friends in Sweden. Get packed and be ready to leave immediately. Inform your friends. Wait for me here. I will be trying to find you some transportation."

Finding transportation was easier than Ludwik thought it would be. The lobby clerk, a young man named Viktor, owned an old French lorry parked outside and was willing to drive Bodil and her friends to Sopot. He said he was very tired however and thought it would be best if he slept awhile. The stack of money in Ludwik's hand changed his mind quickly. Staring at the money, he said it would be his honor to drive the small group to Sopot immediately, no questions asked. He said there was room for one passenger in the cab and the others could ride in the open back. It had sideboards and would be safe.

He felt the night was warm enough for them to lay out in the back and be comfortable enough. Ludwik said they had to leave immediately. Viktor answered he was about to go off duty and would start the drive when everyone was ready.

Josef wasn't surprised by the news. He cursed Hitler, the Nazis and Germany in general, as he sprinted up the stairs to retrieve Franz.

To his surprise, the young artist was not in the suite. There was no sign of him. His travel bag lay unopened on the sofa. Josef could only hope the young man would get back before the ride left. He was sure Ludwik would not wait for him. He left the bag in place and returned to the lobby.

When Ludwik saw the condition of the lorry in the back alley, he knew there was a chance the old pile of rust and ruin wouldn't make it to Sopot. He didn't want to waste time in trying to locate another ride, so he told the young clerk to drive until daylight, get them away from Warsaw then bring them to the nearest railroad station. They could finish the trip on a train. He said Bodil would pay him when his driving had ended and not before. Viktor said he understood. Then he asked Ludwik what the emergency was. Ludwik told him it was a family matter and all he had to do was drop them off and get back to the hotel and see him.

It took some stern prodding by Ludwik, Josef and Bodil to convince Marta and Stephanie that leaving immediately was important. The two women insisted that the idea of invasion was only a threat. Bodil told them that her father, who had important friends in the military, had information that proved otherwise and if they didn't get on the truck now, she would leave without them. She also said they would be leaving without Franz. There would be no waiting for him. That convinced the two to load their baggage and climb aboard.

Ludwik smiled to himself. Bodil was now in charge. She would take care of things. That was her character. She was a leader. With the two friends on board and Viktor warming the lorry's engine, Bodil came to him and Josef. She hugged them both; Josef first and then Ludwik. She clung to her dear friend for a few extra moments and told him she would call the hotel as soon as she got home. They kissed each other's cheeks. And then with a light kiss on his lips, she stepped away.

Before climbing into the cab, she turned and said, "Be strong. Fly for us and our Poland and may God be with you." Ludwik nodded and waved for Viktor to get going. The lorry rattled its way down the back alley, shifted gears and lumbered out onto the street. Ludwik and Josef remained in the alley until the sound of the tired and groaning old lorry could no longer be heard. Then they walked to the hotel entrance and sat on the front steps. The doorman had retired long ago. The street was empty. Warsaw was asleep. They sat quietly in the silence of the night smoking and talking softly. They discussed the probable tactics of the Germans. They agreed when the planes came it would be in daylight. Probably a little after dawn. Easier to bomb targets you could see. They wondered what effects an air raid would have on the people of Warsaw. The thought of that sent a chill through each of them.

"What now, my friend?" Josef asked.

"Time to call the base," Ludwik answered.

The line stayed busy for fifteen minutes. It was after three in the morning. Something was happening. When Ludwik finally got through to his training command center, he was told that a full alert had been ordered for the base. All fighter pilots not on base had to return immediately. Word had gone out for them.

They were to fly their planes to the designated secondary base in the countryside and prepare for action. All support personnel were in the process of loading onto trucks and headed for that same base. The bombers, including the reconnaissance planes, had already been flown south to their secondary base and that he should get to that field no later than 1500 hours Friday. All student pilots, training personnel and instructors on pass or leave were ordered to report back to Deblin no later than 1100 hours Friday morning.

They were to remain on base and await further orders. The instructors were to take charge of all trainees if and when an attack occurred. Ludwik asked the officer if Command felt this was going to be the real thing. The officer said he wasn't sure, but if it wasn't, the base would be getting a realistic drill for the real thing if it ever came. He then hung up on Ludwik.

"IF IT EVER CAME!!!!!" Ludwik yelled into the silent phone. "He doesn't think it's going to happen," he said to Josef.

"What are the orders?" Josef asked.

"For you, back to base by 1100, Friday. For me, back by 1500 Friday at the secondary base. I'll go back to Deblin with you first, pick up my gear and hopefully my pay."

"Let's get some sleep," Josef said. He was exhausted. Too much dancing and now, too much anxiety.

"Let's hope the morning brings a good breakfast with some strong coffee without sirens announcing another war," Ludwik wearily added.

Ludwik slept and dreamt of the day when he saw his first airplane. It was all very clear to him. He was working in the family sugar beet field with his father and the hired help. It was a hot and muggy day. The Polish bi-plane glided down gracefully, picked up speed and roared straight at him. He dove to the ground as it whizzed overhead and then watched it climb straight up into the sky. The maneuver both startled and amazed him. He hoped the plane would return for another pass. He watched it make a lazy left turn, lose altitude and head back in his direction. The pilot was going to put on a show for him. Ludwik was excited. He watched the plane approach. It looked different to him this time. He thought it was moving faster than before. Then he realized it was not the same plane coming his way.

It was a sleek German Messerschmitt 109. His heart began pumping wildly and an icy fear gripped his body. He stood transfixed in the field as the 109 bore down on him and opened fire with its machine guns. The bullets churned a path of destruction directly toward him. The air became filled with exploding dirt and shattered vegetation. He tried to turn and run but couldn't move. The plane closed in. It was after him. No one else. He closed his eyes and yelled for his mother. She didn't answer. He dropped to his knees and asked Mary to save him. That's when he woke up.

His watch read 0800. He had slept about four hours. He looked over at Josef. He was still asleep and snoring like it was the end of the earth. He always snored. But when he drank, he snored like a train. Ludwik wondered how he had managed all this time to escape with his life when he snored like that in a barracks filled with men who liked to sleep. He quickly forgot the snoring and assessed the situation. They were still alive, and no sirens had gone off. On his way to the bathroom and shower, he shook his friend to wake him. Josef mumbled something that sounded very unpleasant. After the shower, he dressed and packed his backpack. He wanted to be ready to leave in a hurry. Josef appeared to be on his way to consciousness with his usual groans of resentment for being awakened. Ludwik made it worse by slamming the door on the way out.

The immediate order of business was to take a brisk walk to get the body going and then get a cup of strong coffee and enjoy the first-class trappings of the dining room. It took him twenty minutes and two cups of coffee before deciding to leave and talk with the Blessed Lady in her house next door to the hotel. He needed to pray.

The Church of St. Joseph of the Visitationists was just a few steps away from the hotel. It was his favorite church in Warsaw. It had been named after an order of Catholic nuns called the Visitationists who had a special adoration for the Blessed Mother Mary.

Like the nuns, he had a special place in his heart for her also. He always felt there was a spiritual connection with her. It had all started when he was a child. He would talk to the small statue of Mary in their orchard. He loved her smile. It comforted him. He even made it his job to clean the statue whenever nature soiled it. It had always made him feel good. It was like helping a friend and knowing the friend would always be there for him.

Ludwik knelt before a statue of the Lady in one of the side altars near the rear of the church. Her open arms and gentle smile welcomed him. The loft that once held the organ played by Fryderyk Chopin was just a few feet above her. The great musician had played that organ during the special "children's masses" held there long ago.

Keeping his voice at a respectful level, he began his prayers, "Please, Mary, give us the strength and courage to do what is right so we may be worthy of your son's promise of eternal life."

"Amen," a familiar voice added. It was Josef. Ludwik smiled at the sound of his friend's voice behind him. He continued by asking Mary to help Bodil and her friends get home safely, to protect his own family in Mazanki and to give the people of Poland the courage to stay together when the Germans invaded. Then he stood, bowed his head, and thanked Mary, Jesus and God for the day. He closed his eyes and stayed standing for a full minute. Falling back down on his knees, he slowly began reciting his trilogy of prayer. First, it would be the "Our Father," to be followed by the "Hail Mary" and finishing with the "Hail, Holy Queen." He was joined by Josef. Their low, manly voices created a pleasant hum at the side altar. A few moments later, a small group of elderly women entered the church behind them. They all held rosary beads. They prayed silently for a moment there. Then they began to slowly shuffle single file toward the main altar. Their wooden rosary beads danced deftly in their withered hands as they made their way down the long, central aisle.

The rhythmic clicking of their beads and quiet voices began to merge with the voices of the two men. The soft, mellow sounds of prayer began to fill the air inside the church.

Finished with their prayers, the men made the sign of the cross, stepped back from the altar and bowed before Mary. The sound of the rosary beads clicking in unison at the main altar followed them out the main entrance and into the day. Ludwik knew it was going to take more than faith, hope and love when the fighting began, but he fervently understood and believed that prayer was a powerful ally.

Josef packed his bag while Ludwik brought his downstairs to be checked. Josef followed suit a few minutes later and joined Ludwik in the dining room. They both ordered a full breakfast and shared a pot of coffee. Their conversation centered on the fate of the three women who had left in the middle of the night and the idea that a call to Bodil's family and their own family might be in order after breakfast. Ludwik was particularly keen on hearing from Bodil. If she didn't call him soon, he would try her home in Sopot before leaving for his base. He suggested to Josef they check the lobby after breakfast to see if there were any messages. They could also call their families then.

Because there was no phone at home, Ludwik would have to call the store in Mazanki and leave a message for his family saying he would call them at the store around six o'clock tonight. That would give the store owner, who knew him and his family well, time to send someone out to the farm and relay his message.

Josef knew it was too late to call his father because he would be at work. He would call him later today or at noon tomorrow from Deblin. He knew his father would be home then. He always came home for lunch on Fridays to cook a special meal of fish to honor his faith's requirement that no meat be eaten on that day.

He had been doing that for as long as Josef remembered. He felt it was necessary to make sure his father knew where the nearest air raid shelter was and to urge him to be ready, with provisions, to get there when the sirens sounded. He also wanted to discuss an escape plan over the mountains with him.

It was midmorning. There was a drum and bugle band playing patriotic music somewhere down the street from the hotel. Finished with their food, the two men strode out onto the street and walked casually toward the music. It was a beautiful day. They found a bench in a small park to sit, smoke and enjoy the music. They talked about Bodil and her friends, the disappearance of Franz and the various scenarios that might play out when the attack came. Josef hadn't finished his training as a navigator so it stood to reason he would be sent back to his unit; wherever they may have been deployed. That could mean being used as the pilot he was or becoming a spare crew member; even being assigned to a ground crew. He would know tomorrow. Anything was possible now. Depending on the need, he could even be assigned to an Army unit to fight as an infantryman. That possibility was a little bit scary to him. In any event, he would have to wait for those orders when he returned to Deblin. Ludwik hoped he would be flying recon missions with his training unit.

The red trolley car discharged its passengers by the news stand across the street from the park. Many of the passengers stopped to buy the papers that were headlining the full-scale mobilization of the military and the threat of war. There didn't seem to be any sign of panic among them as they glanced at the front page. Most simply folded the paper under their arms like they did every day and went to their jobs. It was business as usual in the city. Ludwik had mixed feelings about the newspaper scene across the street. On the one hand, it was comforting to see people going about their business. Just like any other day. On the other hand, they all appeared to be too innocent and trusting. Almost like children.

137

Even with the news of impending war tucked under their arms, they went about their lives like nothing would happen to them. That was uncomfortable to Ludwik. He stared at the ground and listened. Everything sounded as it always had. He let it all come to him. The trolley clanging as it glided away, shoes scuffing and marching their way to work, voices talking, a friendly laugh, the warning beep of an automobile; it was all there. A normal day. Even the drum and bugle band playing at this early hour didn't seem that unusual. The government had bands like that playing every day in Warsaw hoping to drum up the patriotic spirit of the people. He wondered how many of these good people would die when the attack came. Would there still be cars, buses and trolleys carrying Poles to work in Warsaw? Would the life of this great city, with all its history and culture, continue? Would his family and friends survive? Would he survive?

"Ludwik, are you praying again?" Josef chuckled out between deep drags on his cigarette. The first thing Ludwik looked at when he raised his head was the sky. It was overcast. A good thing. "Just thinking, my friend," he answered.

Josef smiled and said, "Well, you think, I'll watch the women."

"Forming a picture to paint like our friend, Franz?" Ludwik asked.

"I wonder what happened to him?" Josef wondered.

"Maybe he got lucky last night," Ludwik joked.

All the streets that led to the large market square in Warsaw's Old Town were filled with people browsing, eating and shopping. The square itself was busy with people doing the same. Ludwik could not stop picturing in his mind the damage an air raid would do to the congestion of souls in the large square and on the narrow, crowded streets feeding into it. There would be no place to hide.

Old Town, near the river Vistula, was the "heart and soul" of the city. It was where people went to congregate, socialize, eat, be entertained and shop. Its streets were filled with art, music, history and small businesses. Many of the craftsmen, vendors and shop owners were Jewish. Ludwik had gotten to know a few of them while attending the Technology University in the city. He wondered how they felt about these dangerous times.

He was surprised by the indifference many people in Old Town seemed to have concerning the German threat and the general mobilization of the country's military. People didn't seem to be worried. Merchants were only interested in coaxing potential customers, like them, into buying something. One elderly, grey bearded gentleman offered the opinion that "whatever God had in store for the world, he had in store. There was nothing that man could do about it." Josef and Ludwik nodded, smiled politely, and moved on.

"I hope that England and France will want to do something about it," Josef remarked to Ludwik.

"They walked away from Czechoslovakia last year," Ludwik answered.

"True, but that country is half German. We're not," Josef replied.

"What do you think East Prussia and Danzig are?" Ludwik asked.

Warsaw, the Final Hours

They headed for Kramer Rubenstein's tailor shop on Nalewki Street. Kramer had tailored uniforms and suits for them in the past. He did excellent work. An interesting and educated man, Kramer had taken a liking to Ludwik and had become a friend. He wasn't really part of the orthodox, old-line, Jewish citizenry in Warsaw.

Neither were his parents. They respected their religion but were far from viewing it as the dominant part of their lives. Kramer was always open to a friendly discussion of issues other than Jewish ones. He had been a university student before entering his father's tailoring business and understood and appreciated politics and economics. He was well versed in the potential of a free and democratic Poland and eager to be part of it. Ludwik considered him to be more Polish than Jewish.

Kramer was very much aware of the danger to Jews if the Germans ever controlled Poland. It was painfully obvious to him what the Nazi party and its Jew-haters were up to. He had been born in Germany and raised in Ulm on the Danube. His father had fought in the German Army during the Great War with distinction before becoming the excellent tailor he was. His mother ran a small bakery. Their customers were mostly non-Jewish. The Rubenstein family had been highly respected by their community in Ulm. When the Depression engulfed the country in the early 1930's, Kramer's father decided to help their customers through the hard times. Jews and non-Jews alike. Credit was offered to their regular customers. In many cases, bread was given free of charge to those with small children. Clothes were made or repaired for little or no cost. The extension of good will by the Rubenstein family saved more than a few German families from destitution. The family continued their unselfish acts of kindness throughout the early years of the Great Depression. It all stopped when the Nazis gained control of the government. Discrimination against Jews quickly became a priority of the Nazis. Most people in Ulm, even close friends of the Rubensteins, became wary, then fearful of interacting with them at any level. The prolific and unrelenting anti-Semitic propaganda being put out by the Nazi-controlled media made it difficult for the ordinary German to ignore. They got the message. It was unhealthy to consort with Jews, German or not.

It was wise to distance themselves from them. Some non-Jews secretly admitted to Kramer's parents that they feared for themselves and their families if they continued to support the Rubenstein businesses. Kramer's father was quick to see what the future was going be for a Jew in Nazi Germany. He sold both businesses and moved the family to Warsaw and safety. That "safety" was now in jeopardy. Kramer knew it and had tried to convince his parents to leave Poland. Both had refused. His mother argued there were too many Jews in Warsaw for the Germans to handle. She wasn't worried. His father said he wasn't moving anymore. For anyone.

Ludwik tried to explain to Kramer the urgency of the times and that it was very likely the Germans would invade soon. Kramer totally understood the gravity of the situation. He expressed hope that the Polish military could hold off the Germans until help came from France and England. If that failed, he would join the Polish forces in defending Warsaw. Josef suggested to Kramer that when the Germans invaded, he might then be able to convince his parents to head south to Hungary or Romania. He knew Kramer had a car. Ludwik agreed and said to Kramer that at the very least, he should fill the car with petrol and be ready to leave quickly. The lanky, dark bearded, bespectacled Kramer said it would be smart to do that, but he didn't think his parents would change their minds. He shook hands with Ludwik and Josef and told them to come back soon after the "trouble" with the Germans was over. The two men walked back across the square and headed to the hotel.

The main avenue in Warsaw was crowded with people; more so than usual this late in the morning. They seemed to be just milling about in groups rather than moving from one place to another. Excited volleys of voices peppered the air all along the street. People were exiting the buildings and pushing others off the sidewalks and into the street with their bulk. Everyone seemed to be engaged in some sort of conversation. Some were subdued. Others were not.

A few were beginning to escalate to a point of animated hostility. Josef wanted to get engaged with a group to find out what was happening, but Ludwik grabbed his arm and said they would find out when they got to the hotel. As they drew near the building, they saw a large crowd in front. Some people were carrying signs. Just then, a drum and bugle ensemble marched its way around a corner two buildings past the hotel and stopped in formation on the street. They just stood there. There were no cars, trolleys or horse drawn carriages in sight. Something was happening. Ludwik and Josef quicken their pace to the hotel. Before they got to the door, the crowd in front moved toward the musicians in the street. They began to shout, "We are not Czechs. We will fight! We will make Germany pay." On cue, the band broke out into a rousing version of the "Mazurek Dabrowskiego" and everyone stopped in their tracks. When the anthem was finished, the band and a large crowd of people began to move toward Castle Square and Old Town. They were joined by smaller groups of people that had left their work and come out into the street. The drummers beat a steady cadence as the growing crowd marched and shouted out their promise to fight the Germans. Ludwik wondered if all this commotion meant that war had started and if so, why had there been no air raid.

The lobby of the hotel was filled with people all engaged in very quiet, serious conversations. As Ludwik and Josef made their way to the front desk, they overheard comments of "they'll pay", "it won't last long" and "may God help us."

"Are we at war?" Ludwik asked the clerk.

"No, we are not at war, sir," was his response.

"Then, what's this commotion about?" Josef asked as he jerked his thumb back at the people in the lobby. The clerk said that in the last hour or so, radio broadcasts had reported that skirmishes between

Polish and German forces had occurred on the Czech border. In addition to that, violence in Danzig between Germans and Poles had been allowed to escalate without interference by the authorities. The broadcast had gone on to say that the Polish government would have everything under control in short order. He said the people in the streets were marching to Old Town to show their support.

Ludwik turned to Josef and said, "It won't be long now. You call home first. I want to see if this gentleman has any messages from Bodil or Viktor for me."

Josef looked at his watch. It was noon. His father didn't usually come home Thursdays, but it was worth the try. Friday might be too late.

Josef's father was pleasantly surprised by his son's call. He told Josef there was lots of stirring about on the streets of Krakow. The people there had also heard the news on the radio concerning alleged border skirmishes and civil unrest in Danzig. He said his school had closed for the day, but he was to report back after lunch for a meeting of the school staff and then finish his cleaning as he normally did.

Josef told him to have a backpack full of provisions close by at all times. He read off a list of items he felt would be helpful if it became dangerous. It included the following: knife, fork, spoon, several books of matches, flashlight, small blanket, canteen, money, non-perishable canned food, tea bags, socks, underwear, suspenders, candle, some rope, warm cap, gloves, fishing line and hooks.

Mr. Przyba was chuckling by the time his son had finished the list. Josef asked him what was so funny. His father wanted to know what the suspenders were for because he never wore his. Josef said he could use them as straps in fashioning a smaller pack to be carried on one's backpack or for making a tripwire to alert him at night that someone was in the area. That was met with silence on the Krakow end of the line.

143

Then a serious voice said, "Do you expect me to be in the forests and mountains any time soon, my son?"

"Father, you are fit enough to be there if you must. Remember our hiking trips to the mountains?"

"Of course, I do. We lived off the land and streams, didn't we?"

"You may have to do it again. Hungary is just over the mountains."

"I understand, my son. Will I see you again?"

"God willing, father. I will call if I can. Stay well. I love you."

There was no message from Bodil. Ludwik listened to Josef speaking with his father. He was impressed to learn that both men had extensive experience living in the wild. It might come in handy for Mr. Przyba if he decided to make a run for the mountains. He hoped the man didn't have to, but if he did, there was a chance he could make it.

It took close to a half hour and several calls before Mr. Piorowski answered the phone in Mazanki. There was an excited response by the store owner when Ludwik identified himself. It had been a few years since the two had spoken. Ludwik had always been a favorite of the man. Ludwik asked how the summer had been in the village and the farms around it. Piorowski said most of the crops had been harvested early because of the unusual heat wave this year. It had been a poor season for the sugar beet farmers. He was hoping next year's crop would be better. He knew if farmers made money, he made money. Ludwik didn't ask him if he was aware of the very real threat of invasion. He could tell by the man's voice that he wasn't. He asked if word could be sent to the Skoczylas farm to send someone to the store at six o'clock so he could talk to them. The store owner agreed to do that. Ludwik thanked him and hung up.

144

He wondered how Mr. Piorowski would be treated by the Germans if they ever got to Mazanki. The man was one of many Poles with German blood in his family. He also wondered how Piorowski and others with German ties in the region would behave toward the all-Polish natives if the Germans were successful. He was well aware of what was happening in Danzig. There had been bad blood between Germans and Poles in that city for some time. More worrisome than that was the fate of the 300,000 or so Jews in Warsaw if the Germans somehow prevailed. The Jews had a long history of being made the scapegoats for all problems a society had.

Finished with their calls, both men went upstairs to their suite on the second floor. Josef needed to pack his backpack. If trouble came to Warsaw, they would need to move fast. Everything had to be ready. Backpacks and suitcases would be secured in the lobby when they were out. It would be easier to retrieve them there rather than risk running up the stairs during an air raid to get them. That little delay could be deadly. Bags and packs would stay with them at night.

The suite had been impeccably cleaned, beds made and the curtains drawn open. The kitchen and dining area in the suite were immaculate. Ludwik enjoyed this luxurious hotel. Tomorrow, it would be back to the bare-bone barracks life of a pilot. He sat comfortably on the large sofa chair in the dining room, lit a cigarette and waited for Josef to finish his business in the bathroom. He thought they might walk down to the train station after lunch, buy their tickets for tomorrow and pick up the afternoon edition of the Warsaw Gazette. Then maybe a short stroll down to the Vistula. Read the paper and see what the rest of the day might bring.

Josef came out of the bathroom wearing a very large smile. Putting a finger to his lips, he motioned Ludwik over. He pointed to the bathroom wall and cupped one hand to his right ear. Ludwik went to the wall and listened. There were people in the suite next door.

145

The suite that Bodil and her two friends had shared for a short time last night. It didn't take Ludwik long to recognize the urgent and rhythmic thumping of an intense lovemaking session. He had to stifle a laugh when he heard an excited female voice shout, "Franz, Franz, don't stop!" He also left the bathroom with a smile.

"Well, now we know Franz is alright," Ludwik said.

"Couldn't be better," Josef added.

The tickets to Deblin leaving Friday morning were given to Ludwik and Josef free of charge. The ticket seller said it was an honor to meet the two men and that he hoped they would fight well when the invasion came. Ludwik saw the benefit of the uniforms and suggested they always stay in them. Josef agreed.

Coffee and some "paczki" in Old Town were what the two men decided on before heading down to the Vistula to relax, read the paper and watch the ladies go by. The band and demonstrators had gone from the square, and everything looked and sounded rather normal. The doughnuts were especially tasty. Each man had one with his coffee. Josef said they reminded him of his younger days in Krakow eating his mother's version of the paczki. He and his father used to help prepare the dough for her. Then he would watch her work her magic creating the delicious dessert.

"How far is it to the mountains from Krakow?" asked Ludwik.

"Somewhere between eighty and a hundred miles."

"Do you think your father could make that trip on foot?"

"Absolutely. The only problem might be the weather. If he went in late fall, he might run into some cold conditions. If he left within a few weeks or so, it would be much easier."

"Interesting. Let's pick up the newspaper after the coffee and head down to the river," Ludwik said.

"Yes sir!" Josef answered.

"Remember, we don't do rank between us my friend. Let's keep it that way."

"Yes sir," the young plot shot back.

The Warsaw Gazette's headline read, "The Homeland is Threatened!" Accounts of civil unrest and attacks on both Poles and Jews in Danzig was the underlying story on one side of the front page. On the other side was an article about a young Pole who had been shot at by German troops as he drove his motorcycle along a remote country road near the border. The young man had accidentally come upon German troops camouflaging tanks in woods across a small field in what he thought was Polish territory. Several Germans had opened fire at him, but he had escaped unharmed.

Ludwik's reaction to the ominous headlines and front-page articles was that they just underlined the obvious. The unrest in East Prussia and Danzig was old news. The escalation of that unrest was the "new" news. Piotr had made that clear with his phone call. It was plain to see what the Germans were up to. They wanted that corridor of land back that had been given to Poland after WWI. That had made Poland next on Hitler's list. France and England were threatening retaliation if Hitler attacked. So far, they had only watched as the Nazis swallowed Austria, the Sudetenland and most of Czechoslovakia. Their indifference had to have been a clear message to Hitler that there was no real interest by the two countries in trying to stop him. And if Hitler believed that, then the homeland was in trouble. Ludwik knew how important a second front on Germany's western border would be for Poland.

All he could hope for was when Germany attacked his country, the French and English would live up to their promises. Josef broke up Ludwik's thoughtful analysis of the day's events by saying, "Let's go down to the river and find some pretty girls."

Ludwik nodded and replied, "That's good thinking, my friend. Company for dinner would be nice tonight."

They spent the first few hours walking back and forth along the Vistula enjoying the weather. The young mothers with their baby carriages were back in force and black and white were once again the dominant colors. Josef remarked that Franz's idea of a black and white painting featuring the young women of Warsaw pushing their prize possessions was a good one. He wondered if the Sopot artist would do what he said.

"Why don't we ask him," Ludwik said.

"He's probably still exercising in Bodil's suite," Josef answered.

Ludwik pointed ahead and said, "Take a look."

Franz was sitting on the hill, a large sketching pad on his lap. He was sketching a beautiful, long-legged girl posing on the river walk in front of him. She was dressed in a white summer skirt and a white blouse covered with black polka dots. She wore shiny, black, patent leather shoes and a thick black belt that circled a very thin waist. She had black hair that tumbled halfway down her back. She looked to be in her late teens. Both of her hands were on the handle of a black baby carriage. Ludwik was impressed. Franz was a man of his word. He had said he wanted to paint a black and white collage and here was the beginning of it. Josef was much more impressed by the young woman's beauty and curvaceous body. He knew she had to be the one that had frolicked with Franz earlier in the hotel. He was already a tad jealous.

"Good to see you again, Franz," Josef shouted.

Franz dropped his pencil on the pad, smiled broadly, got up, walked down to the path and shook hands with the two airmen. He looked back at his model and said, "Georgina, come meet my friends."

Ludwik stepped forward, clicked his heels together, bowed and kissed her hand.

"My name is Ludwik Skoczylas. An honor to meet you."

Josef introduced himself in the same manner.

Georgina smiled and said, "Are you staying at the Hotel Bristol also?"

"We have the suite next to Franz's," Josef answered. He smiled first at her and then at Franz. He was letting Franz know nothing would be said about the suite belonging to Bodil and her friends.

"We met at the square last night," Franz nervously interrupted. "She was wearing this dress and I thought it was perfect for my painting. I'm going to sketch her wearing different outfits. I'll paint them all black and white. We went to her apartment across the river in Praga last night. She shares it with her sister. Her sister had this baby carriage and let us borrow it for the sketching. I brought Georgina to the hotel this morning to meet the ladies, but they had left. Their door was unlocked. They must have forgotten to lock it. I used my room key to get my bag."

Ludwik took Franz aside and walked a few yards away from Josef and the girl. He explained the events of last night. He said all three ladies were probably in Sopot as they spoke. Franz just shook his head in disbelief. He said he still couldn't bring himself to believe an attack was coming. Ludwik sighed and put his arm around him. He told him that when the attack came, he should stay away from anything that had military value like bridges, railroads and roadways.

149

If he got caught in a building, he should stay away from windows. If he was out in the open, he could use the sewers or recently dug ditches in the parks for cover. And when the sirens sounded, he should get to cover immediately.

Franz had an incredulous look on his face as he listened. He thanked Ludwik for his concern and advice. Then he asked if it would be alright if he and Georgina used Bodil's suite tonight. Ludwik smiled and said, "Of course. It's already paid for. Just keep the noise down this time." Franz's face betrayed his guilt, but he recovered quickly, chuckled and promised to do just that. They shook hands once more.

Josef was talking to Georgina and complimenting her on how good she looked. She was liking that very much. Ludwik came over to say goodbye to her. Josef reluctantly did the same.

"What were you talking about?" Josef asked.

"If they could hold the noise down tonight when you were in the shower."

"That's not funny. A repeat performance I do not need. It's not fair. Did you see the legs on that woman?"

"They're not hard to notice," Ludwik responded.

"I'm thinking Café George for supper," Josef suggested.

"Good by me. Maybe you should take that shower now before "Picasso" and "Legs" return. I'm going to check for messages and wait a while in the lobby for my family to call me."

"Shower sounds good to me," Josef said as he glanced back toward Franz and Georgina.

Ludwik caught his glance and said, "Try the cold water first. It's better for your health and your present state of mind."

Josef laughed and mumbled something about how a woman could make a man forget a war was about to happen.

There were no messages and no calls. Ludwik was not surprised by the no call from Mazanki. A day working the farm was long and hard and sometimes went longer than six o'clock. He thought there was a chance someone might call later in the evening so he decided to have dinner in the hotel and let the lobby know where to find him If he didn't hear from them before he left Warsaw, he would write them as soon as it was possible.

He was relatively sure his family would be all right. They had always managed to take care of themselves. They were strong and very resourceful. His father would know what to do. Bodil was another matter. She had the means to call but hadn't. That was a little concerning. Viktor, the hotel clerk that had driven her out of Warsaw, had not reported to work yet. Ludwik decided to try and reach Bodil at her home in Sopot. The phone rang for a long five minutes. Probably on their way out of the country. He wondered what time of day the Pastulas left to avoid contact with German planes. He thought flying out at night would have been a good move. If in fact they had decided to do that, then tonight would be the night. Then again, if Piotr was that certain the Germans were coming, they would already be in Sweden.

Josef was tired. He hadn't taken his shower yet. He was glad they were staying in the hotel for dinner. A nice meal, a few drinks and a good night's rest would be better than carousing until the early morning hours. Ludwik was surprised that Josef was more interested in rest than in partying. He let his friend have the honor of reserving a table in the dining area while he went upstairs to get ready for the evening.

Ludwik finished his shower, brushed down his dress uniform carefully and ironed one of his dress shirts. Then he cleaned and polished his shoes. He wanted to look good tonight. He had a feeling it would be some time before he would be dining at the Bristol again. Josef was in no hurry to do the same. He lay on his back smoking a cigarette and daydreamed about Georgina's long legs.

The food was superb. The service top notch. It certainly did not hurt to be associated with one of the hotel's prime investors. Ludwik hoped he would be able to thank the Pastula family one more time for arranging all his stays here. They had been good to him in so many ways.

Before pouring a second cup of coffee for Ludwik, the waiter announced he had a note for him. It was from Viktor. He was at work and looking for Ludwik. Josef said they should skip the coffee and have another drink. Ludwik agreed and headed out to the lobby.

The news was good. The lorry had made it all the way to Bodil's home in Sopot and back. Viktor had been paid handsomely and there had been no problems. He handed Ludwik an envelope. Before opening it, he asked the young man if he had seen any other family member in Sopot. Viktor said Bodil's father was there. Ludwik asked him what Piotr looked like and was given a perfect answer. Satisfied that what he was being told was the truth, Ludwik shook the clerk's hand and thanked him. Before returning to the dining area, he opened the envelope and found a note. It was from Bodil. It was very short. It read, "I am safe. I will be gone shortly. We will miss you terribly. Love, Bodil."

Both Ludwik and Josef drank a little more than usual that night. They offered toasts to Bodil, her family, to each other, each other's family and of course, to Poland. They left the dining room close to midnight very drunk and very tired. Both stumbled into the suite.

152

Josef collapsed on his bed fully clothed and began snoring immediately. He was loud. Ludwik undressed, turned off the lights and knelt beside his bed to pray. He bowed his head and asked Mary, the Blessed Mother to keep his family safe. His prayer kept being interrupted by Josef and his snore. It was becoming more like a roar with every breath he took. He was roaring to the heavens now. Ludwik finished his prayers, crawled into bed and slept.

The roar woke him. It was deafening. He opened his eyes and looked at the clock. 0550 hrs. He couldn't believe Josef was still snoring that loud. He peeked over at him in the dim, morning light. He was lying where he had fallen on the bed. Stiff as a statue. His mouth was closed; the roar not his! It was outside and overhead. Ludwik jumped out of bed. It was planes; fighters, by the sound of it. They were low and moving fast. Lots of them. They were headed north; north toward Mazanki and his family. Then the sirens went off! The initial blast went through him like an electric shock. The mournful, undulating electronic waves of sound seemed to sweep through the suite from all directions. Ludwik thought about turning on the lights, then realized he might be helping a German bombardier. He stood transfixed on the spot and listened to the wail of the sirens; a long, high pitch, a slow, fading pitch, a high pitch, a fading pitch; each cycle repeating the same message; get up, find cover, get up, find COVER, danger coming, DANGER coming, RUN and HIDE!

The wailing rhythm pulsated throughout the city. This was no drill. Not at this time of day. The beast was on its way! The hour had arrived. Ludwik made the sign of the cross and asked God for the strength and courage to fight well. He walked to his comrade's bed and shook him. Josef's bloody eyes opened slowly and then widened as the wailing sound of sirens and the roar of planes outside pummeled his ears.

153

Ludwik was dressed and out on Krakowskie Przedmiescie with his luggage in less than five minutes. Josef, with his luggage, was just a few minutes behind him. He wondered out loud if the sirens would give them and the citizens of Warsaw enough time to get to shelters. The two men knew Poland's long line of observation posts, manned by spotters throughout the country, would have relayed the air incursion immediately. If the planes were coming from the north or west, they would be over Warsaw very soon. If they were coming from the southwest, there would be more time to find shelter. The element of time depended on the reliability of communication between the posts and the respective bases charged with defending certain areas of the country. The fighters streaking north meant the raiders were coming from East Prussia. Not far at all from Warsaw.

"Low overcast," said Josef in a calm and measured voice. Looking upward, Ludwik saw that Warsaw was indeed covered by a large blanket of clouds. It would be hard for the enemy to find their targets.

"Let's hope it's still here when the Germans arrive," Ludwik replied.

"Who's covering Warsaw?" Josef asked.

"The Pursuit Brigade. Top notch pilots, not so top-notch planes. They'll have to get high to reach the bombers. Not sure what kind of fighter escort the Germans will bring. Probably 109s. They're awfully fast and really loaded."

People started to appear in the street. All were staring up at the sky. There was nothing to see but the clouds. The air raid sirens suddenly went silent and somewhere a loudspeaker proclaimed, "This is NOT a drill. Move to safety immediately. This is NOT a drill. Move to safety immediately."

Ludwik factored in the approximate speed of the bombers and the distance they had to travel from East Prussia to Warsaw and realized there were probably only a few minutes left before they arrived. Even with the overcast holding, it was still very unsafe to be outside. The Germans probably would have a good idea when they were over the city. They could still drop their bombs and create serious damage. Hustling back into the lobby, Ludwik saw the manager, Lucas Chimelewski, who knew him and the Pastula family well. Lucas was glad to see him. He said the basement had been converted into a bomb shelter and his orders were to get the guests down there as quickly as possible. Ludwik asked to have a radio brought down to the basement so they could listen to official updates on the attack.

Guests kept coming into the lobby. Some were half dressed. Some still in their bed clothes. Three carried suitcases; each one had clothes hanging out of them. Most of the women had managed to get dressed. A few wore long summer coats that covered their night clothes. Most of the children were still in their pajamas. Chimelewski directed a regally attired doorman to escort all of them down to the basement. They half stumbled and jostled their way down a corridor that led to the basement stairway. Ludwik asked Chimelewski if there was any water available in the basement. The manager said there were three sinks with taps. Ludwik told him to fill all the containers they could find with water. Just in case the bombing cut off the hotel's water supply. It was possible that people could become trapped in the basement. Water might mean the difference between life and death then. He said to fill the sinks also. Maybe even bring some bread or what had already been prepared for breakfast. Chimelewski rang the kitchen and repeated what Ludwik had just told him.

Ludwik asked if there were any flashlights, candles, matches or lamps in the basement; anything that could create light. Lucas said he didn't think so but believed there were some items in the desk and cabinets in his office that might be useful. Josef and Ludwik went through the

155

cabinets while Chimelewski searched the desk. Ludwik found a flashlight, some batteries, a doorman's whistle and a loaded revolver. Chimelewski grabbed the radio off his desk and retrieved a spare one kept in his clothes closet. He opened a wall safe and scooped everything in it out into a bag labeled, "THE Hotel Bristol." Josef discovered boxes of wooden matches, more batteries, another flashlight, a hammer, a screwdriver and a fat Christmas candle. Chimelewski said he was going to stay in the lobby with one radio and direct the guests to the hotel's basement. He said he would come when the bombs started falling. Ludwik took the other radio and warned him to stay away from windows. He started to tell him to make sure he was in position to get to the corridor that led to the basement when he was interrupted by a loud outburst of shouting from the lobby. Pandemonium had erupted out there. A dozen guests or so were yelling at each other in total hysteria. There was ushing and shoving going on at the hotel's entrance. Some people were trying to leave. Others stood in their way and screamed at them that it would be suicide if they were on the streets when the bombs fell. One of them started yelling that it was only a practice drill and that nothing was going to happen. Another group of people walked into the lobby demanding their breakfast.

When the crowd saw the two pilots come out of the office with the manager, they rushed them and demanded to know what was going on. Was this real? Was this a stupid ill-timed drill? Where was the wait staff? Had breakfast been cancelled? Were we at war? Chimelewski pointed at the two men in uniform and said, "Ask them." Ludwik smiled and waited for the hysteria to die down. Josef held a finger against his lips. When it was quiet, Ludwik told them the Germans were on the way. A woman started sobbing and someone whispered, "Oh, my God, what do we do now?" Ludwik told them that fighters had already left to intercept the Germans. He said he didn't know how the fighters were doing, but it was likely that some

156

German planes would be over Warsaw soon. He said the best thing to do now was to get to the basement quickly. It would be safe there. He added that there was no need to argue and fight with each other. The fight now was going to be with the invaders. He said they could do as they pleased but being in the streets or sitting here in the lobby at street level was extremely dangerous. He told them what he had advised Chimelewski to do concerning the windows. Then he and Josef left the lobby and went down into the basement with their personal bags and the articles taken from the office. They were quickly followed by most of the guests. A few decided to stay in the lobby with the manager. It was now close to seven AM.

The first sounds that came from the radio in the basement were the ending stanzas of the "Mazurek Dabrowskiego." The crowd of guests and staff that had assembled in the musty cellar stiffened with respect. As the anthem ended, sirens simultaneously blasted the "all clear" signal throughout the city. A spontaneous cheer erupted from the gathering. People hugged, danced and kissed each other as an air of relief swept through the basement. Ludwik and Josef made the sign of the cross and thanked God. The German planes had not reached Warsaw. Not one bomb had fallen on their great city. Reason enough to celebrate the moment.

The radio went silent. Ludwik turned up the volume hoping to get some information on the raid. All he could hear was a scratchy static. He shouted for quiet when the static ended, and someone began speaking. It was Stefon Starzynski, the mayor of Warsaw. He said the Germans had bombed some cities and attacked our air bases. He wanted everyone to know that our war planes had been moved earlier to secondary fields throughout the countryside and were operational. The air bases had been damaged, but the planes had not been touched. They had been in the air to meet the Germans. He proudly reported that an air attack on Warsaw had been turned back by the brave pilots of the Pursuit Brigade and many German bombers had been shot down. A loud cheer erupted in the basement. The mayor went on to say that while German forces were poised to cross the border in several places, the Polish Army was prepared to meet them. He asked the government workers in the city to report to work, stay calm and be strong. He urged the men and women of Warsaw not to abandon their beloved city; to stay and resist the temptation to flee into the countryside. He ended by saying Warsaw was safe for now and further updates on the military situation would be forthcoming on the radio and in the daily papers.

"It might be a good idea to get to your homes and tend to your families if you are not working," Ludwik said to the group huddled around the radio. A young man blurted back, "Why would we do that? Didn't you just hear the mayor say we turned back the Germans?"

Ludwik looked at him and said, "They will be back. And probably very soon. You should expect that. Be as prepared as you can when it happens. Stay away from open roads, bridges, railroads and airfields. Know where the shelters are."

"Let's get outside," Josef said.

Everyone quietly filed up the stairs. The celebration was over. The fact that the country was at war had sunk in. Germans WERE attacking Poland and life as they had known it was about to change.

Calls to Deblin went unanswered. Ludwik knew the base had probably been hit by the Germans. From the reports he had heard on the radio, it looked like the Germans were trying to cripple Poland's ability to defend itself from air attacks by going after the air bases. It had been a wise decision to move the warplanes away from the main bases. He wondered if the ground crews had made it to the secondary bases. They would be needed to maintain, repair and fuel the planes. And that brought up the question of the fuel depots.

Had they been hit? It was a vital question. Simply put, no fuel, no planes. No planes, no Poland.

"This has to mean war for the English and French. I wonder if they will attack Germany on the ground or in the air," Josef said.

Ludwik hoped it would be both. He knew opening a second front in the west would force the Germans to divide their forces. That would help. What Poland needed to do was keep the Germans at bay here until that happened.

"I hope my father can get to the mountains," Josef worried out loud.

Ludwik nodded. He thought about his family. There was nothing near the beet farm and Mazanki of military importance. That might rule out a bombing attack. His main concern was a rapid German advance on land. The farm wasn't that far from East Prussia. He also worried about the many ethnic Germans who farmed in the region. Some were very friendly. Some not so much. Some had accepted the German defeat and loss of land after World War I. Others harbored a deep resentment of the harsh terms imposed on Germany and would probably welcome a return to German authority.

The first thing the two men noticed as they walked out of the hotel was just how low the cloud cover over Warsaw was. Mother Nature had really extended a helping hand to the city. No doubt about that. There wasn't a bombsite made that could find a target through that blanket of clouds. It was one of the reasons why the Germans had failed to drop their bombs on the city. Another reason for their failure came bursting through the clouds with a whistling roar. Two PZLP 11 fighter planes of the Pursuit Brigade barrel-rolled their way across the sky in an impressive display of aviation excellence.

"God, those men are great pilots," said Josef.

"Among the best in the world," Ludwik quietly added.

The planes whizzed over the hotel heading for the Vistula and their secondary base somewhere on the other side. Somewhere on one of Poland's grassy, level plains.

Ludwik's attention was now drawn to movement on the avenue they stood on. A military procession was approaching. The lead cars moved by slowly. They were filled with high-ranking Army officers, their faces stone serious with purpose. Behind them came a convoy of trucks, motorcycles, horse cavalry, foot soldiers and even horse drawn carts filled with supplies. Ludwik assumed the move was designed to get them away from their barracks before the next bombing raid. They were headed west, probably through the suburb of Wola and into the countryside. Ludwik felt that the Germans had probably crossed the border by now. It was time to find out for sure.

"Are they across the border?" he shouted at an Army sergeant.

"They are. In the north, in the west and in the south. But not to worry my Navy friend. We will kick their ass when we get there."

Ludwik saluted the sergeant and wished him good luck. Things were beginning to move quickly now. It was time for them to pick up the hotel was filled with people including many foreign newsmen. Everyone was gathered around the two radios that Lucas had set up. Reports on the invasion were coming in. The Germans were claiming an attack by Polish infantry on one of their outposts had started everything and they were striking back to defend themselves. Gdynia, Kratowicz and Krakow had been bombed. No mention of damage or casualties was made. Early German incursions into Poland were being met with stiff and brave resistance from the Polish army. One report on the fighting claimed the Germans were being hurled back towards the border. That's when the news stopped. An announcement was made that the station was going to resume its regular morning program highlighting upcoming events in Warsaw. Josef wondered out loud if the people running the station had lost their minds. The country was at war, and they were discussing social events.

"It's the station's way of trying to keep everyone calm," someone said.

"I don't know about that. Look outside," Josef replied.

The avenue was filling with people. Many were running. Vehicles, horns blasting, sped by in both directions. It was chaos. Ludwik hoped they were going home. To be with their family. He turned his attention back to the radio. The "regular" show had been interrupted by a disturbing news update. All railroad lines heading into the city some distance away had been heavily damaged by planes in the early morning raid. Several trains had also come under attack. All railroad service in and out of Warsaw would be delayed. Ludwik knew that could take days. It meant they would have to get out of Warsaw another way. The first thing that he thought of was the lorry that had carried Bodil and her friends to Sopot. He asked Lucas if Viktor was still in the hotel. He said he had sent the young man home.

Many of the people that had been out on the street had made their way into the church of St. Joseph. Ludwik and Josef decided to join them. They went in and stood in the back of the packed basilica. The mass was quick. The sermon was more of a request than a related homily. It was short and to the point. The priest asked the worried faithful to pray for Warsaw and Poland, to join in the fight to defend their great city and to make sure their families were kept as safe as could be. He said the church doors and offices would always be open. Priests appeared in different sections of the church to administer communion. The end of the mass came with the blessing of the faithful. Everyone made the sign of the cross in return.

Ludwik crossed himself and asked Mary and Jesus to help him have the strength to get through whatever the future might bring.

Back at the hotel, Ludwik asked Lucas if they could keep what they had collected earlier that morning including the pistol. He thought there was a strong possibility they might have use for them in the coming days. Lucas said yes and then suggested they take some canned goods, utensils, pastries, tea, and coffee from the kitchen.

When their backpacks were filled, Lucas offered them a goodbye meal in the dining room. He said it was his way of doing something to help them. At least have something to eat on their way. Ludwik thanked him and said he had done enough. The diminutive manager tapped his head and said, "Ludwik Skoczylas and Josef Przyba; two names I will always remember. Free rooms the next time we meet. And please, call me Lucas."

Leaving the hotel, Ludwik said, "I think getting to the park and crossing the river to Praga might do us some good."

"Maybe find some trains running there?" Josef asked.

"Maybe. We'll probably have to head south from there for a train. Anything close to Warsaw probably has been hit."

"I'm ready to hike to Deblin if we have to," Josef said.

"We may wind up doing just that," Ludwik replied.

There were a few older adults wandering around in the park. The "all clear" siren had brought them out of hiding. The bridge across the Vistula into Praga, the eastern suburb of Warsaw, was crowded with vehicles. Only a few were coming into the city. The pedestrian-walk on the bridge looked open. The two men headed for it. Rounding a curve in the walkway leading to the bridge steps, they were surprised to find Franz and his long-legged girlfriend, Georgina.

162

She was posing as a happy, dutiful, young mother peering into a black baby carriage. She was wearing a black summer jacket. It was open, revealing a white silk blouse unbuttoned enough for any onlooker to notice her ample bosom. She was beautiful.

"Why are you out here, Franz?" Ludwik asked.

"I'm a painter."

"Are you aware that another attack could come at any time," Ludwik warned the young artist.

Ludwik worried about the young artist's brazen indifference to war. He seemed unshaken by the morning's turn of events. It also looked like he had convinced Georgina that everything was going to be fine. Obviously, he had no inkling of the power and danger of war. He was like that elder Jewish merchant in Old Town who had said, "Whatever happens would be "God's will." Ludwik was not a veteran of war, but he understood that kind of fatalistic logic was a death wish. He told Franz of their plans and invited him to join them. Franz refused. When Georgina heard Ludwik tell Franz he and Josef were going to Praga to try and find transportation to Deblin, she said Praga was where she and her sister, Wilfreda lived and that her sister's friend, Karl, who lived on the same street, had a car. She thought he might help them. She said Karl had been with them during this morning's air raid. He had escorted everyone down into the basement. She wasn't sure if Karl was still there, but they could go and see if he was. She gave Ludwik her address and said it was just a short walk from the Praga end of the bridge. She said her sister and Karl knew who they were. She had mentioned them as friends of the women that had come with Franz from Sopot. Ludwik said Deblin was seventy miles south of Warsaw. It would be a troublesome trip if the highways became congested with traffic. Georgina didn't think that it would be a big "bother" to Karl.

163

He had driven that way many times when visiting his family near Deblin. Ludwik thought to himself that it wouldn't be a big "bother," if it was going to be just a normal, weekend drive in the country. Any drive now would be dangerous; especially if it involved using the same roads that the Polish Army was traveling on. Ludwik thanked the beautiful young girl and told Franz to keep her safe.

Praga

"Nice of her to make that offer," Josef said.

"If we can't catch a train, asking for a ride from "Karl" or anyone else for that matter, would be worth a try," Ludwik said.

"I think a private car would be much safer than public transportation," Josef suggested.

Ludwik agreed and added, "Especially if one was forced off the highways and onto country roads."

Georgina was right. It only took fifteen minutes to get to her apartment once they crossed the bridge. It was located on Targowa Street, not far from Zabkowska Avenue, the main thoroughfare in Praga. There was a brass knocker on the door of number 3. It only took one rap to get a response. A man's voice asked who it was. Ludwik replied it was the two airmen who were friends of Georgina and Franz.

A tall, well-dressed man, somewhere in his late thirties or early forties opened the door and invited them in. He said Wilfreda was out shopping. He shook their hands and introduced himself. It was obvious the man was at home here. They sat in the small parlor just inside the door. Before he asked about the nature of their visit, Karl was anxious to find out what they knew about the invasion.

Was it serious? Was Poland's military ready? Would Poland get help from France and England and finally, did they think Poland would win.

Josef said it was VERY serious; the Polish military was ready to fight and with God's will, they would win. As for the French and English, he had no idea. Ludwik listened to the exchange while remaining silent as the two continued their discussion of the day's events. He could tell Karl was a patriot. That gave Ludwik some hope. When Karl asked what their plans were, Ludwik stepped in. He told him they needed to get to the air base at Deblin, but the train lines had been hit hard. No one knew when and if the trains would be running again. And that was what had brought them here. He said that Georgina mentioned we might be able to get a ride from him. Karl thought for a moment, then said it would be difficult to take the time off from his work. He would be needed in the city if bombs fell. Most people in his office had stayed home today but were expected to be back tomorrow. He didn't want to miss a second day.

"What about driving tonight?" Ludwik asked.

"That might be possible. I'd have to take Wilfreda with us though."

"One thing you should be aware of," Ludwik added. "It might be a little crowded on the main roads headed out of the city. There is a lot of traffic now. That will slow us. Coming back should be easier."

"I could drive east from here and then go south using the back roads to Deblin," Karl answered.

"You've been to Deblin before?" asked Josef.

"Yes. My family lives in Garwolin. It's not too far from Deblin. I could stop there to see them on my way back."

165

"Can you drive in the dark with just your running lights?" Ludwik asked.

"Why?"

"It would be a lot safer. The Germans will have their planes hunting for headlights to attack."

"I can see well at night and I know the backroads to my old home and from there to Deblin. There won't be much traffic on those roads. Let me show you. I have some maps in the desk. My only concern about driving you would be leaving Georgina here."

"She'll be with Franz," Josef said with more than a tiny hint of sarcasm. It didn't sound very comforting to Karl.

There was a small parking space open across the street from the apartment building. Wilfreda had no trouble squeezing Karl's five-year old Volvo into it. The car's back seat was filled with baskets of bread, pastries, meats, cheeses, jams and an assortment of fruits and vegetables. It was the most food she had ever bought at Goldman's. She had spent most of her time fighting traffic to get to the delicatessen and back. The streets were still jammed with vehicles. Most people had stayed home during the failed air raid, but when the "all clear" sounded, it seemed that every woman in Praga was out buying food. Normally, she used an old baby carriage she had found abandoned down by the river as her shopping cart, but Georgina and Franz had the taken it earlier. Franz wanted Georgina to pose with it. She wished the young man took the war seriously. He was treating it like it was a passing rainstorm. He was convinced that Poland would handle the brazen Germans quickly. Both he and Georgina were years younger than she and had not experienced what war could bring. She had been very young and Georgina just a baby during the struggle with the Russians that had followed the Great War. Those terrible times had cost her family both parents.

Father had died from an untreated, infected wound in one of those godless trenches. Mother had spent her last few years pining her life away after his death. It had been awful to watch her die from a broken heart. She and Georgina had become close after the passing of their mother. They lived a meager life on what money their mother had managed to save. They struggled through the early days of Poland's newly found independence when everyone was trying to find their way. Then, just as they began to understand how to do that, the dreadfully hard consequences of the Great Depression set in. They suffered but survived. Wilfreda worked hard for both of them. She did laundry, sewed clothes, polished leather, did grocery shopping for the ill and cared for children whose mothers were recovering from illness. She became known as "Mother Superior" by the women in Praga for how she raised her younger sister through those trying years. To the men of Praga, she was known as the "Goddess." She was that beautiful. There had always been a man in her life ever since her teenage years. Her beauty brought them early and often. They promised her everything; even things they didn't have and would never have. She saw through them all and never gave them what they wanted. Until Karl. He was different. He was a good friend to her and Georgina. Then he became her first and only lover. The reason she hadn't married him was Georgina. Wilfreda wanted her younger sister to find her place in life before she left to be with Karl. That was taking time. Georgina went from one affair to another. Franz was just the latest to sample her charms.

The three men rose to their feet as Wilfreda made her way through the door. Karl took the basket she carried and introduced the two men. Ludwik was immediately struck by her beauty. Her coal black hair was cut into bangs draped above two of the most beautiful violet eyes he had ever seen. Her full, ruby red lips completed the perfection. Ludwik thought he was looking at the most beautiful woman alive. Both Ludwik and Josef bowed and clicked their heels.

167

Ludwik introduced himself and said it was a pleasure to meet her. Josef followed with the same. Wilfreda smiled warmly at them. She admired their manners. She reciprocated by welcoming both men to her home. She thought Georgina's description of the two fit them perfectly. The taller, wavy haired one with the soft blue eyes had to be Ludwik and the other younger, slender one, had to be Josef. When she asked Karl to retrieve the baskets in the car, the two men asked permission to do that for her. She thanked them and said the baskets were in the black Volvo parked across the street from the oil truck.

The thick clouds that had covered Warsaw earlier in the day had disappeared. The sky was clear now, a beautiful day. Ludwik stopped in front of the oil truck. He looked across the river at Old Town, the heart and soul of Warsaw. So many good times there. His gaze shifted to the sky and that brought on an abrupt change in his mood. An icy uneasiness began gurgling gently in his stomach. He knew what that meant. It was anxiety and he knew that fear would follow. He had experienced this before; the last time years ago just before for his first parachute jump. This time it was the clear sky that brought on the anxiety. The German bombers would be back. No cloud cover to protect Warsaw now. The city lay bare in the bright sunlight. Easy pickings for a good bombardier.

Josef watched Ludwik staring into the sky across the river. His friend's body was rigid. He seemed to be in a trance. Josef understood. He had also taken note of the clear sky. A minute ago, he'd been thinking of nothing but the beautiful woman who had just walked into the apartment. Ludwik's stare at the sky changed that. He looked at his watch. It was four-twenty in the afternoon. He wished it was nighttime.

Ludwik saw the keys still in the ignition. Wilfreda had forgotten them. He put them in his jacket and grabbed the one basket on the floor. Josef had the two other baskets that were in the back seat.

As they crossed the street back to the apartment, they heard people calling their names. It was Georgina and Franz. They were pointing to the sky behind the apartment building. Ludwik waved to them and followed Josef inside. He started to ask where the baskets should be put but was drowned out by the roar of speeding planes overhead. Teacups and saucers rattled on the kitchen table. A picture frame fell off the wall and crashed to the floor. They all ran out into the street just in time to watch the tail end of the Pursuit Brigade pass over Warsaw. Another raid was on its way! The air raid sirens made it official. That's when Wilfreda and Karl realized that Georgina and Franz were just down the street from them. The sisters ran to each other and hugged.

The distant "pom, pom, pom" of anti-aircraft guns firing at the sky somewhere north of the city announced the arrival of the enemy aircraft. Almost immediately more guns opened up somewhere near Wola, the western suburb of Warsaw. A blanket of steel was being laid out in the sky by the Polish gunners. The enemy was close.

Ludwik told everyone that bombs were going to fall. He shouted for everyone to find cover. Karl, Franz and Josef hurried the women inside the apartment. Karl opened a trap door by the pantry and ushered Franz and the women down the stairs into a dirt basement.

Josef went back outside to be with Ludwik. Their eyes stayed fixed on the sky high beyond Warsaw. They waited for the bombers to appear and prayed their numbers had been depleted by the Pursuit Brigade. The rapid and distinctive sound of the Polish anti-aircraft guns grew in intensity and volume as more went into action. The bombers were approaching! They could hear them, the unmistakable drone of high-altitude planes. Scanning the sky with his eagle eyes, Ludwik spotted them. There were many. More than two dozen. Fighter planes were dueling all around them. A sudden burst of flame and a muffled explosion signaled the death of one of them.

169

Ludwik watched it fall in a ball of fire into one of the neighborhoods west of the city. He couldn't tell if it was German or Polish. There was no parachute. He prayed for the soul of the pilot if he was Polish and wished a trip to hell if he was German. It was the first death in combat he had witnessed. He knew there would be many more. On both sides.

The bombers had come with lots of fighter protection and had broken through the attacks of the Polish fighters. Their distant drone was now a strong hum as they began their bombing runs. Every anti-aircraft gun in the immediate area was now hurling as much steel as they could at them. Small, black puffs of flak covered the sky as the bombers advanced. There were so many of them!

Bombs began falling on the far side of the city. Their thudding "WHUMP, WHUMP, WHUMP............WHUMP, WHUMP" pattern of death and destruction shook the ground all the way across the river and into Praga. Ludwik watched the explosions walking their way towards the city center and Old Town. It was time to get off the street and find some cover. He and Josef grabbed their backpacks in the parlor along with Karl's maps and scrambled down into the basement. All four civilians were sitting in the dirt with their backs against the foundation. Their knees were drawn up to their chins. Ludwik put the maps inside his jacket and joined Josef and the others in the dirt. He knew the bridge Josef and he had walked across earlier from Old Town might well be a target of the Germans. The basement they sat in was just a few short blocks from that bridge. There was a fair chance the neighborhood would be hit.

The composition of the building's foundation they sat against was a major concern to Ludwik. It wasn't solid cement. It was just an assortment of large field stones that had been cemented together. Cracks had already appeared in it as the tremors from the bomb hits across the Vistula grew stronger and stronger.

170

The explosions were creeping closer to Praga as the first wave of bombers passed over Warsaw. Stones, shaken by the strong tremors, began edging their way out of the foundation. Part of the foundation to their left began crumbling onto the dirt floor. Clouds of dust flew across the basement, blinding and choking all of them. A huge explosion behind the building shook the foundation behind them. Dirt and rocks showered down on everyone. One of the larger stones fell on Georgina's back. Blood began streaming from the wound. The foundation began to swell like it was about to explode. Ludwik yelled for everyone to crawl over to the main support beam of the building. Georgina began screaming that they were all going to be buried alive. Blood pouring down her back, she ran up the stairs to escape. When she neared the top, she turned and screamed for her sister. Bombs were landing one after another now. Coming closer and closer. Everything was shaking. It seemed the whole ceiling above them was moving and sliding to one side. Franz, then Karl, started up the stairs to Georgina. Before the men could reach her, she was through the trap door and into the kitchen. Wilfreda raced up the stairs behind the men. All four disappeared from sight. Ludwik and Josef stayed by the main beam and hung on to it. Then the bomb hit. It exploded directly behind their building and blew its way right through to the street. Both Ludwik and Josef were stunned by the blast. Parts of the building, large and small, rocketed over their heads toward the street. The main beam was torn in half. The top half flew up and away with the rest of the building. Both men were pelted hard by stinging bits of stone, cement and dirt. A loud ringing in Ludwik's head crinkled up into his brain and started to squeeze the life out of it. He lost his hearing just before passing out.

When he opened his eyes, he was lying on his back in the dirt and looking straight up at the sky. The whole building overhead had disappeared. The two floors were now part of a huge pile of debris stacked on the street side of the basement and out into the street.

The ringing in his head had subsided, but he still couldn't hear anything. A movement above caught his eye. A small bird was circling the hole that had been the apartment building. He waited for it to come down and ask him how he felt. Then he remembered that birds couldn't talk. He had no idea why he would even think of such a thing. He told himself to get up and find Josef.

Josef had been watching Ludwik carefully. He had been sitting next to him for a good hour. He knew his motionless friend was still alive because of the mumbling conversation he seemed to be having with someone. When that stopped, his friend had opened his eyes and began blinking them rapidly like he had no idea where he was. Then he pointed up at the sky for a few seconds before sitting up and asking for him. Pieces of things that had been part of the two floors above lay piled high on the street side part of the basement. It was plain to see that if they had chosen to wait out the raid over there, they would be dead now. Just like they would be dead if they had gone up the stairs.

Josef put his arm around Ludwik and asked how he was. Ludwik pointed to his ears and shook his head. He had no hearing. Josef had a ringing, stinging headache, but he could still hear. Both men sat there covered with dust and a thousand tiny fragments of wood, cloth, stone and cement that had been blown into the basement by the blast.

The bombers were gone, but the anti-aircraft guns were still firing at something. There were sounds like sirens coming from the sky. German fighter planes whizzed overhead with machine guns blazing. They were strafing targets. Probably Army trucks caught on the bridge or alongside the river. Josef wondered if the bridge was still standing. People were shouting out in the street. A fire engine clanged somewhere off in the distance. A fog of black smoke drifted slowly over the exposed basement.

It was coming from the river and Warsaw. It carried a charred, musty smell with it. Josef got up and assisted Ludwik to his feet. Ludwik thanked him without hearing his own voice.

The stairwell had been destroyed. Pieces of it lie in a heap on the far side of the basement. Climbing out of the hole that the building had become would require a little ingenuity. They had been lucky. The blast had blown everything past them toward the street. The pile of debris now stacked on that side of the basement could be used to climb up to ground level. Josef shouted at Ludwik telling him about using the debris to get out. Ludwik turned and said, "That's what I was thinking." His hearing had returned. Each began making a "ladder" by pulling pull out pieces of the pile far enough to stand on and then repeating the process a little higher to form their own stairway up to ground level. Josef was pulling out some pieces of framing when he found her. He knew it was Georgina by the legs. Her body from the waist up was gone. He stared at those beautiful legs. There wasn't a mark on them. He began to mumble, "Just the legs, Ludwik, just the legs." He kept repeating the words until he was screaming them. Then he turned and vomited down onto the dirt floor of the basement, choking and screaming at the same time.

Ludwik watched his friend be sick and then helped him down. He covered Georgina's legs with a piece of tablecloth. He made the sign of the cross and left "her" there. He went back to the side of the pile he had come from and finished his stairway up to ground level. A stunned Josef sat immobilized in the dirt and watched him do it.

"There's nothing we can do for her now, Josef. She's with God. Get up and come with me," Ludwik yelled. He watched as Josef got up, looked at the tablecloth, and then make his way carefully up the pile of debris.

"They're all dead, aren't they?" Josef asked.

173

"Yes, the bomb hit while they were up in the kitchen. There was no way anyone could have survived that blast."

Both men were staggered by the scene that greeted them. Debris from the building had almost completely covered the oil truck that had been parked in front. Franz was part of the pile. He was wedged between the cab and the long tank behind it. On the other side of the street was the black Volvo that belonged to Karl. It was still upright. There was debris piled against it. Across the river, Warsaw was burning. The clear sky of an hour or so ago was now completely obscured by a thick black blanket of smoke that covered the entire city. Fires were burning everywhere.

It was difficult prying Franz's body loose from the tanker. Ludwik had to go to the street side of the cab and push the bloody, broken body back out the other side with both feet while he straddled the gap between the top of the cab and the tank. At the same time, Josef pulled down on the body's one free arm from the other side. It took some minutes of pushing and pulling to free the dead artist. Finally, the body just popped out toward Josef. He caught it in his arms, kicked aside some debris, and laid the young man down.

Franz had suffered a catastrophic head wound. His head had been split wide open across the top; ear to ear. Brain matter and blood covered his face and upper body. His shirt was shredded into pieces. They hung glued to his body by the blood that had poured out from the head wound and the countless cuts and slashes to his face. His eyes were open. They stared motionless through the blood and matter that had become part of the young man's face. Josef picked up a white laced doily that lay by the body and tried to clean the mess off Franz's face. He couldn't do it. His hand shook too much. Another hand appeared over Franz's lifeless eyes. It belonged to Ludwik. Spreading his fingers, he closed both of Franz's eyes in one gentle movement and then helped Josef to his feet.

Both men stood over the body. Ludwik prayed aloud for Franz's soul and asked God to forgive the young artist for any sins that he may have committed. Josef found a blanket and covered the body. Ludwik suggested he keep his feet uncovered so people would know a body was there. Ludwik wondered to himself how many other bodies would be found here in Praga and across the river in Warsaw. Glancing across the Vistula at the disaster that was Old Town, he knew it would be many.

They began searching through the wreckage for the bodies of Karl and Wilfreda. They started by uncovering the car. It didn't take long to clear the rubble off the side of the blast. No trace of them there. The interior of the car was littered with shattered glass. All windows, except for the windshield, had been smashed. Most of the blown-apart building had landed on the other side of the car. It lay in smoking piles on the grassy knoll that led down to the Vistula. It was obvious that the oil truck had deflected much of the blasted remains from the first floor of the building. Pieces, large and small, had glanced off the truck and gone flying over the car onto the knoll. Much of the first and second floors of the building was lying out there. The two men began pulling out parts of the debris small enough to handle. They kept away from anything that was smoking. Whenever they rested, they called out for Karl and Wilfreda. They never got an answer. There was little doubt in their minds that the two were dead, buried somewhere under the rubble, but they wanted to be sure. The fact that they had survived gave them some hope.

After two fruitless hours, they decided to stop. It had become hopeless. Both realized they would never find the two in that wreckage. They decided to look for anything that might be of value to them when they left. Starting from the far end of the knoll, Josef picked his way through the rubble back toward the car while Ludwik went back down into the basement to retrieve their backpacks.

He only found his. Josef found some cigarettes, two blankets and a pair of boots. He kept the cigarettes and blankets but left the boots. They were expensive boots. He hoped their owner had been away today. If he had, he hoped finding the boots would be a little something positive when he returned.

Ludwik's backpack had some clothes, a flashlight, some batteries, matches, a hammer, a screwdriver, some canned goods, tea bags, a length of rope and the loaded .38. He found a heavily wrapped loaf of bread in the rubble and compressed it enough to fit in the backpack. Josef carried the blankets over his shoulder. Both men walked over to the Volvo. Ludwik opened the driver's door and began picking up the glass that lay on the driver's side of the front seat and throwing it out. Josef asked him why he was bothering with the car. Ludwik took the keys out of his tunic pocket and jiggled them at his friend.

"Will it start?" Josef asked.

"Don't know. Let's try," replied Ludwik.

Josef had his doubts. "Let's have a cigarette while you try."

"Let me try and start the car first," Ludwik said.

The Volvo sprang to life immediately and began purring. A pleasant surprise. They let it run while they got every bit of glass, front and rear, out of the car. They sat on the cleaned up front seat and smoked their cigarettes. Finished with his, Ludwik put the car into gear and released the clutch slowly as he pressed gently down on the accelerator. The Volvo moved a few yards down the street. The car was drivable. Another surprise! Just as they stepped out of the car to clear some debris off the street, three planes appeared across the river heading directly toward them. They were Polish fighters. One was trailing smoke badly.

176

The other two seemed to be flying in support of it. There was no victory barrel rolling by the fighters this time. The city they had been sworn to protect was now in flames.

The farther the car went down Targowa Street, the less debris there was to move out of the way. It was amazing to see how little damage had been done to the street in general. In less than fifty yards or so from Wilfreda's apartment, the buildings were practically untouched. Only one bomb had hit Targowa Street. It was the one that had killed her and the three others. That was not the case with the street directly behind Targowa. That one had almost been obliterated. Turning onto Zabkowska Avenue, the two men encountered heavy traffic. It was hardly moving. Most of it was heading east; away from Warsaw. A few cars and trucks were moving in the opposite direction back toward the city. The dense, black cloud of smoke covering Warsaw also covered the bridge crossing the Vistula into Old Town. It was difficult to see if the bridge was still intact. Ludwik downshifted the Volvo, edged his way to the outside lane and went up on the sidewalk around the slow-moving traffic. He made a left turn on the first street he came to. Josef had Karl's maps on his lap. He quickly located the street on the map of Praga. From there, he directed Ludwik to the streets he felt would help avoid the mass of humanity that was on the move. Every effort was made to avoid traveling on a main avenue. Those would be all clogged and offer the enemy a great strafing opportunity. Ludwik thanked God that Karl had kept maps in Wilfreda's apartment. That had been a bit of good fortune. It would have been a lot easier if Karl was doing the driving tonight, but his maps would be enough to get them back to Deblin and into the war.

It took them an hour to get out of Praga. They found themselves on a one lane, dirt road that led through a pine forest and beyond to Wawer, their first checkpoint.

Both men agreed to keep the car off any main road for as long they could. They also agreed to travel through the night and stay away from railroad lines and any heavy traffic tomorrow. The first order of business now was to see if the headlights on the car were working. Ludwik waited until the darkness overtook them in the forest before putting them on. Only the driver side headlight cast a bright beam into the blackness. The other headlight was dead. Ludwik stopped the car and turned off the headlight. He shut the engine off and got out. Josef joined him. They needed that headlight to travel in the dark, especially here in the forest. They couldn't afford to run off the narrow road, hit a tree or drive into a ditch. If they lost the use of the car, getting to Deblin would become a lengthy chore. On the other hand, if they used the headlight, they would be running the risk of providing enemy planes with a target. Josef suggested dimming the headlight's beam by covering the headlight with mud. The map showed a small stream running through the forest just east of the road. It probably wasn't more than a hundred yards or so from where they stood. Besides getting some mud from the stream, they could both take a drink. They hadn't drunk anything since leaving Praga.

Ludwik took out the flashlight from his backpack, covered most of the light with one hand and stepped off the road into the trees. Josef followed. The space between the evergreens had very little underbrush. They moved quickly. It took five minutes to reach the stream. The water was moving fast. A good sign. Still pools of water could become stagnant and be unsafe to drink. The water was cool and refreshing. They drank their fill, scraped some mud off the shallow bank of the stream and carried it back to the car. It did the trick. They could see enough to stay on the road and not worry about being detected from the air. Josef figured they would get to Wawer soon after clearing the forest. It looked to be a short drive of four to six miles from there to Wesola, their second checkpoint.

The map showed a road on the other side of Wawer that led to another forest halfway between the two towns. They moved slowly out of the forest and into open farmland. The early moon cast enough reflected light on the road to allow Ludwik to shut off the headlight and drive slowly toward the small town.

Both men spotted the lights in the distance. At first, they thought it was oncoming traffic, but then realized the lights were not moving. They were coming from buildings in Wawer. Not many lights, but enough to cause a disaster. The lights were putting the town in serious danger. Not wanting to enter the lighted area, Ludwik parked the Volvo in the darkness of the country road. Josef ducked under a blanket and switched the flashlight on the map to search for a road that skirted the town and get them into the large forest east of it. There was none to be found. They would have to look for some inkling of a path that a farmer used and hope it led them to the forest. It was either that or chance driving the road they were on straight through the town. That was dangerous, but probably the fastest way to get to the forest. A farmer's path through a darkened field might be safer, but it could wind up at a dead end. They decided to risk driving the road.

As they reached the outskirts of the town, Ludwik turned the headlight on and stepped on the gas. The Volvo surged forward, picked up speed and zipped through the town quickly. Josef leaned out the windowless door and shouted at some startled people to "GET THOSE LIGHTS OFF NOW!" Once through the town, Ludwik slowed so they could spot the road that led to the forest.

The Farm

The moon-lit road was just wide enough to carry traffic in both directions. Ludwik kept the Volvo in the middle of the road and slowly made his way toward the looming outline of a large forest.

179

They passed several side roads that snaked their way across open fields on either side of them. The map showed that some of them wound their way back to Wawer while others went toward a few small hills off to the right. Josef said the map also indicated the presence of a military training area beyond the hills. He couldn't tell if any of the roads he saw on the map reached that area. Ludwik was sure the Germans would know about the military area. If they hadn't hit it yet, they probably would soon. Anyone living near, or traveling by that area, might become fair game for them. Even if they were civilians. After experiencing the massive bombing of non-military targets in Warsaw and the neighborhood in Praga, he wouldn't be surprised by what the Germans did. Right now, he hoped the bombing of civilian neighborhoods was the result of misses by German bombardiers going after military targets and the metropolitan transportation system.

The first part of the forest wasn't that dense. Still, the headlight was needed. They drove past several side roads as they moved into the heart of the woods. They passed stacks of logs, some more than ten feet high, along the way. Woodsmen had to be close by. They usually lived in cottages in the forest or on farms just outside the woods.

Ludwik pulled the car off to the side of the road and parked. Both he and Josef needed to relieve themselves. As soon as he cut the motor and stepped out onto the dark road, he heard the cries. Josef did also. They were distant and coming from somewhere off to their left. Both men stood in the silence of the dark forest and listened. The cries continued. They didn't seem to be moving closer or farther away. It was hard to gauge the distance from where they stood. Sound always seemed to travel farther at night. Ludwik's best guess was that whoever was yelling was at least a quarter mile or so from them. After relieving themselves, they decided to drive on and take the next side road on the left to get closer.

Josef stepped out in front of the headlight to block its dim beam and trotted ahead. Ludwik drove very slowly behind in first gear and kept his eyes on him. When Josef turned left, Ludwik was right behind him. Every few minutes, Josef would raise his hand to stop. Then he would walk ahead for a bit and listen to determine how close they were to the cries. He repeated the maneuver three times. After the third time, he returned to the car and signaled for Ludwik to cut the engine. Ludwik quickly turned the engine off and got out. He could hear the shouting clearly now. Pocketing the car keys, he continued on foot with Josef. There was some sort of clearing ahead. As they moved into it, they were greeted by the smell of smoke. It wasn't a clearing in the forest. It was the beginning of a large field that stretched far out to a stand of trees on the other side. There was a light flickering between the trees. It was a fire. The two pilots jogged quickly across the field. It had been freshly plowed. And that meant only one thing. They were on farmland. Ludwik had an instant flashback to his days as a youth working on the family farm. Mixing with the smell of freshly plowed soil and smoke from the fire was another odor; an unfamiliar one. Moving around the edge of the tree line and into another field, the fire came into full view. A small building was completely enveloped in flames. It was the smallest of three buildings. It looked to be a storage shed of some sort. Sparks from the blaze were shooting high into the air and cascading down onto a barn and house close by. It was just a matter of time before both caught fire. The framework of the burning structure suggested it had been a chicken coop. That explained the strange odor. Chickens were being roasted in the flames. There were five people passing water buckets back and forth in a line that stretched from a stone well in the barnyard to the burning coop. A man was at each end. One was cranking the buckets out of the well and the other hurling the water on the fire. A woman and two young girls were struggling to pass the buckets along the line. Ludwik could see their effort was a losing one. It was taking too long to pass the water.

181

The man at the well saw the two men running toward him from out of the shadows on the field. He waved them over. He was exhausted. Ludwik took his place while he moved into the line and replaced a young girl. He told her to take turns running the empty buckets back to Ludwik. Josef took the place of the other girl in line. The father shouted at her to go into the barn and close the hay loft door above the entrance and then bring out a shovel. The girl flew into the barn, closed and latched the door above the entrance and was back outside with the shovel in quick time. Her father told her to turn over any grass near the barn with the shovel before it caught fire. With five adults in the line now, the water buckets moved back and forth much faster. When the fire had been finally extinguished, the family fell to the ground; too tired to move. Ludwik kept drawing water from the well and Josef poured it on areas still smoking in the pile of wood that used to be the coop. The barn and house were safe.

After resting, the family got up, and huddled together in prayer. Ludwik and Josef joined them. The woman thanked God and the Blessed Lady for saving their house and barn and for sending the two strangers from the forest to help them.

The farmer said his farm had been attacked by a plane just before dark and while the house and barn had been hit by bullets, only the coop had caught fire. They had been trying to put the fire out for an hour before Ludwik and Josef came to help them. Ludwik said he was sorry about the loss of the coop and the chickens but was glad the flames hadn't reached the house and barn. The farmer's son, a tall, strapping boy named Max, said that some of the chickens had been let out of the coop just before the flames had spread across the entrance. He hoped to find them at first light.

The whole episode with the family brought on a sense of irony and guilt to Ludwik. Here he was helping strangers, by the name of Rubacha, fighting to save their farm and their very existence while his own family was experiencing God only knew what on the farm in Mazanki, a village that lay directly in the path of the German army.

The exhausted family gathered in the kitchen to finish the supper they had just begun when the attack occurred. The farmer insisted that the two men join them. Then he invited them to stay the night. Tired from the long and emotional day, both Ludwik and Josef accepted the offer.

Josef told the farmer they had a car parked in the forest. The farmer said it would be safe there. No one was in the forest at night. Ludwik asked if there were any Polish military in the area. The young boy, Max, said there was an artillery practice range not far from their farm and that a cousin of his had witnessed an attack on the barracks there today. He was also told that planes had attacked farms in the area and traffic of any sort on country roads. He said low flying fighter planes had killed people traveling on the roads and working in the fields.

The news that innocent civilians had been deliberately attacked and killed was very disturbing. It meant that the bombing of Old Town and Praga had not been an accident. Ludwik had studied this "total war" concept at the academy. It had been used by many armies in the history of warfare to hasten a victory. Its aim was to lessen the enemy's will to fight by creating an atmosphere of terror. It accomplished that by attacking and killing, without mercy, both military and civilian targets. And that included women and children. German historians called it "Schrecklichkeit." After listening to Ludwik's description of that tactic, Josef hoped that his father was on his way to the mountains.

After the meal, the farmer built a small fire in the fireplace to heat the kitchen where they would sleep. His wife gave them each a blanket to wrap themselves in. They were both asleep on the floor a minute after the family retreated to their rooms.

Ludwik dreamt about his family. It wasn't pleasant. They were all standing together by the barn watching two trucks approaching on the dirt road that led to the farm. Each was loaded with German infantry. The lead truck had a soldier manning a machine gun that stretched over the cab. It was pointing in their direction. His father and younger brothers stood fast as the trucks drew near. His mother was praying aloud to Mary, the Blessed Mother, to save them. His sisters were crying. One of the younger ones said she didn't want to die. That brought moans and cries from the other girls. The lead truck stopped just short of the barnyard. Soldiers began jumping off the back. The girls screamed and ran for the house. His father and brothers clenched their fists and took a step toward the truck. The soldiers stopped and aimed their rifles at them.

That woke Ludwik. He sat up and looked around. A little ray of light had made its way through the lone window in the kitchen. His family was not here. Just Josef lying beside him. On a farm belonging to a family called Rubacha that was far away from Mazanki. He asked Mary and Jesus to help his family. Then he told himself to get back to sleep. He needed the rest. They would be on their way soon. Yawning, he lay on his back, head on his rolled-up jacket and massaged his face firmly with both hands then slid the blanket up to his neck. The house was quiet. Still time for more sleep. He lay still and waited for it to come. Before it did, he thought he heard someone crying. It wasn't a dream. It was coming from outside. Someone was in distress. It sounded like a child. Possibly a young girl. Tossing the blanket aside, he rose and went to the door. He opened it slowly and stepped outside. A cold mist greeted him. It was thick. He could barely see the outline of the barn a few yards away. The crying was coming from somewhere off to its right. He closed the door quietly and called out softly into the mist asking if he could be of any help. The crying stopped.

He walked a few steps toward the barn and asked, "Where are you?" There was no answer at first. Then he thought he heard a voice, a soft voice that whispered, "I am with you." His entire body began to tingle, his arms prickling into little bumps. He felt warm. He moved toward the barn and the voice. Reaching the barn, he placed one hand on its front to help guide him through the fog. Keeping his hand on the barn, he walked slowly to its end and the open field beyond. The mist was very thick. Only the chirping of birds awakening in the forest beyond the field floated through the mist. Nothing else. The voice had gone silent. He stood there and listened for a few minutes, his eyes searching for any movement. There was nothing. He turned and retraced his steps back to the front of the barn. He sat on the lip of the well and faced the rising sun. It was going to be another warm day. He let the sun's rays warm his body. Walking through the mist had chilled him and he welcomed the warmth. He wondered what the day would bring after the mysterious encounter. He wondered if anyone else in the house had heard the moaning and crying. Yesterday had been a bad day. The boy had told him that farms had been attacked in this area and people had died. Very bad news! Thoughts of his family and the dream last night came to him. Maybe that had something to do with what he had heard or thought he had heard a few minutes ago.

Josef and Max came into the barnyard and approached Ludwik. The boy said he was heading out into the fields to look for chickens that had escaped the fire. Ludwik asked him if he had heard anyone outside the house in the last hour or so. Maybe a lady or a young girl. The youngster shook his head no. He said no one lived anywhere near the farm and they rarely had visitors. Only his aunt and uncle, along with his cousins, came to the house and that wasn't very often. And no one was ever around the house at night. Ludwik thanked him and wished him well on his search.

As the boy disappeared around the barn, Josef asked Ludwik what was going on. Ludwik explained what had taken place just a short time ago in the barnyard and beyond. Josef said he had heard Ludwik get up and go outside. He also heard him talking to someone, but thought it was the farmer. He never heard any of the crying and moaning. He said maybe the farmer and his wife had some idea of what it was all about. Maybe it was the farmer's wife herself out there looking for some of the lost chickens. Ludwik laughed and said he had a vivid imagination. Josef laughed in return and said he wasn't the one that was hearing voices.

A flurry of excited cackling exploded behind the barn. Max had found some chickens! The young man strolled into the barnyard with a triumphant smile on his face. There was a live chicken hanging upside down in each hand. The birds were flapping their wings and trying hard to peck at the boy's hands. He raised the birds in the air to show the men and then entered the barn. The men followed him in. They passed a horse, a cow and three goats. All were penned up in separate stalls. Max proudly lowered the chickens into an open wooden bar crate and secured its lid over them. He said there had to be others somewhere out in the fields or in the woods near the house. Ludwik congratulated Max on his find and told him he used to do the same kind of things on his farm when he was around the same age.

Max smiled and said he meant to tell Ludwik something that might be of help to him concerning voices in the night. He had heard his parents talking about a woman who supposedly walked the countryside at night looking for her husband. She lived in the forest somewhere between here and his uncle's farm. He suggested Ludwik talk to them before he left. Just then a chorus of cries for Max rang out. His siblings were looking for him.

They had come to help him in the search for chickens. He left the two men, gathered the small band of hunters together and led them out into the fields.

Breakfast was generous. Both men enjoyed a steaming bowl of porridge, an egg, and two slices of baked bread covered with butter and jam. The farmer's wife couldn't do enough for them. Ludwik asked if they had something they might use to carry water on their trip to Deblin. The farmer said he said he had an old canteen he kept under his bed. His wife went into the bedroom and brought it out. She cleaned it thoroughly, filled it with water and gave it to Ludwik.

Ludwik asked her and her husband if they had heard anything unusual outside the house earlier this morning. The farmer said he heard someone talking outside around dawn. He assumed it was Ludwik and Josef. Ludwik said it was just him. He was trying to find someone he thought he heard crying outside. He thought it might have been a woman. He said Max had mentioned they knew about a woman who came out of the forest at night looking for her husband. The wife said that was true. The gossip was her husband had been killed in a lumber accident a few years ago. She had been seen from time to time walking the fields around dawn with her dog. She always wore the same long, brown dress. Some said they were the same clothes she had worn on her wedding day. Rubacha said he had seen her tending sheep in the meadow by the river south of here, but that had been some time ago. He did not know her name. No one had ever approached her. Most stayed away because they thought the poor soul was possessed. Ludwik thanked them for the information. It made it seem likely she had been the one in the mist. It had been a strange occurrence especially when he thought he heard her say, "I am with you." Why would she have said that? Just the thought of it made his skin prickle. Just like it had earlier in the mist.

They said goodbye to the Rubachas and headed back across the field toward the forest. The children stood way off in the field and watched them go. They began waving goodbye. Ludwik and Josef waved back. Ludwik had a sudden urge to protect them. He wanted to yell for them to get out of the open; that there was death lurking in the morning sky. He quickly dismissed the thought. It was incomprehensible that innocent children, walking in a field looking for stray chickens, might be attacked. It was more likely that two men in uniform walking across the same field would be a target. He quickened his pace toward the woods.

Everything looked to be in order with the car. The blankets and backpack were undisturbed. Ludwik backed the Volvo down onto the main road in the forest and headed east toward Wesola, their second checkpoint. The gas gauge registered half full and with only sixty miles left to reach Deblin, fuel didn't seem to be a problem.

It was only a few miles to Wesola. The map indicated that once they left the cover of the forest, they would have to drive on roads completely out in the open past the town until they reached the village of Mrozy, some five miles further on. That could be dangerous if the Germans showed up. Josef suggested that he sit in the back and search the sky for any planes coming from behind. He could also check the sky on either side of the car while Ludwik drove and watched the sky in front. Ludwik agreed.

Just before the forest road ended and continued into open country, Ludwik pulled over to have another look at the map. He searched for anything that could be used for cover. He noticed there was a small stream running parallel to the road for some distance. That usually meant trees and other forms of vegetation along its banks. It might be possible to get in among them for cover. Satisfied with the option, he drove quickly into the open and accelerated down the road.

The road wasn't wide enough to handle two-way traffic or the lumbering trucks of the Polish Army. That was good. Being stuck in a military convoy was the last place Ludwik wanted to be. He wanted to stay on country roads and avoid the heavily traveled main roads. As Wesola came into view, Joseph spotted a plane off in the distance to their right and shouted for Ludwik to pull off the road and get to the small trees by the stream just a few yards from the road.

"Did you see it?" Josef asked.

"I didn't see anything," Ludwik said.

Josef suggested they sit still and listen for the plane.

They both lit a cigarette and waited. There was no sound of a plane, but they began to hear the bleating of sheep somewhere on the other side of the stream and beyond the crest of the hilly meadow. They were headed in their direction. The first sheep trotted over the crest of the hill. It was quickly followed by several others. Most of them were white with a few greyish-black ones mingled in. They spread out on the meadow across from them and began to graze. Ludwik immediately thought of Franz and his black and white baby carriages; his "checkerboard of life."

The Shepherdess

More movement on the crest caught their attention. A woman appeared. She stopped for a moment and then began making her way slowly down into the meadow. She stood among the dozen or so sheep and surveyed the area. She was too far away for Ludwik to see her face. She appeared to be very young. She was joined by a beautiful, brown shepherd that had come over the crest coaxing a stray sheep back into the flock. He was a large animal.

The dog and the woman seemed to blend together as one; her long brown robe matching the color of the dog's fur. He stared at them.

They both seemed to be looking back at him. That's when the tingling on his body began. The same sensation he had felt earlier this morning when he thought a voice in the mist had said, "I am with you."

"Are you alright?" Josef asked.

"I'm not sure." Ludwik said as he stared at the woman and dog. "I don't understand why my body feels like electricity is running through it. I had the same feeling this morning when I thought I heard someone crying outside the farmhouse."

"Is it that woman with the dog?" Josef asked.

"Why do you say that?" Ludwik said.

"Because you haven't stopped staring at her since she came over the hill and walked down into the meadow."

"I don't know. There's something I'm feeling."

Body still tingling, he watched the woman carefully. She moved about the meadow with a distinctive grace. Occasionally, she would look their way. There was a certain dignity about her. He had no desire to try and make contact with her. He just wanted to watch her move. She and the animals had become an integral part of a beautiful, pastoral scene.

"Did you hear that?" Josef asked.

"Hear what?" Ludwik answered.

"Listen," said Josef.

It was an airplane. The sheep heard it also. They stopped grazing and moved nervously back and forth in the meadow. The woman said something to the dog then turned and moved quickly up the hill.

The dog marshalled the sheep into a tight flock and got them moving up the hill after her.

"Here he comes!" shouted Josef.

The Messerschmitt was fifty feet off the ground and bearing down on the woman and her animals. The pilot opened fire just as the woman, dog and sheep disappeared over the crest of the hill. He streaked by the two airmen hidden in the trees and blasted away at the top of the hill with his cannon and machine guns. Ludwik and Josef watched him zoom over the crest, climb high into the sky and disappear into some clouds. They waited for him to turn back and make another run. Fortunately, he didn't. Just then an air raid siren went off in Wesola. Ludwik jerked his head toward the crest and took off up the hill. Josef was right behind him. They stayed close to the shrubs and reeds along the stream. As soon as they reached the crest, they spotted the lady. She was moving the small herd of sheep toward a stand of pine trees. It was a smart move on her part; wait out the plane under the cover of the trees. Just like they were doing. Ludwik wished he had his binoculars. He wanted a close-up view of the woman and her dog. He watched them move into the pines and slowly make their way out of sight. Then they were gone. And so was the tingling in his body. She was safe for now. The question was for how long? If all German pilots were like that pilot, she would never be safe. They waited ten minutes after the air raid sirens stopped.

"What man would try and kill a woman and her sheep?" Josef asked.

"One that makes love with devils and then becomes one himself," Ludwik answered.

"That makes it easy for me to kill him," Josef said.

"Yes, it does," Ludwik agreed.

The Artillery Range

Ludwik backed the Volvo out of the trees and onto the road. He headed for Wesola. It was past mid-morning now. They needed to get to Deblin sometime today. His mind wandered through the events of the past day and a half as he drove toward the town. Saying goodbye to Bodil early Thursday morning before dawn, the invasion on Friday, Praga on Friday afternoon, the horrible death of his new friends in the bombing, the fire on the Rubacha farm last night and now the vicious attack by a fighter plane on an innocent woman and her sheep. Poland's world had gone crazy! He prayed to Mary for the strength and courage to survive this early madness and for her protection so Josef and he could do something about it.

People were spilling out from the small church and milling around in front as Ludwik approached in the Volvo. Among them were three soldiers. They spotted Ludwik's uniform as he drove slowly by and shouted for him to stop. One of them, a sergeant, came over and asked Ludwik if he could help them. He said the truck he was driving earlier this morning had been attacked and destroyed by a German fighter. He and his two men had survived by leaping out of the vehicle and running for cover in the woods. They had walked the woods and country roads to Wesola hoping for a ride back to their base, but no one had volunteered to drive them. They didn't blame the villagers for refusing. Radio reports of repeated attacks by German planes on vehicles, railroads and bridges had made it very dangerous to drive.

Ludwik told him they were headed to Deblin. They were going to drive the forest roads into Mrozy first. The sergeant said Mrozy was only a few miles from the artillery range they were stationed at. They could walk to their barracks from the town. Ludwik told them to get in and keep their eyes open until they reached the forest.

Josef got out of the car and sat up front with Ludwik. The sergeant and two privates squeezed themselves into the back seat.

"What happened to your car?" the sergeant asked.

"Air raid on Warsaw. Concussion blew out the windows. Lots of dents, but the engine is fine," Ludwik answered.

"Was the city hit hard?" one of the privates asked.

"Yes, it was."

"Did the Germans attack your base on the range?" Josef asked.

"They did yesterday, and I wouldn't be surprised if they returned today. There were a lot of German planes around this morning. We met up with one on the way back to the base."

Josef told the soldiers about the attack on the woman and her sheep. They just shook their heads and silently cursed the Germans. One of the young privates said his mother and sister tended goats on their farm near the Carpathians south of Lwow. Josef turned to tell him that he and his father had spent many a day hiking and camping in that area, but stopped short when he caught sight of the tears running down the face of the fuzzy cheeked private.

Ludwik asked the sergeant what he knew about the first day of fighting.

"I heard yesterday, before we left, that our airfields were being attacked, but most of our planes were still operational. They had been moved earlier to secondary fields. Danzig apparently has been lost and other cities have been bombed. Casualties were high.

193

The Army is fighting attacks in the north, west and south by large numbers of tanks and infantry. It's not going to be easy for us."

"What was the meeting about in the church? Ludwik asked.

"An update on the war. They had a radio up in the loft. The news had us throwing back the Germans on all fronts and our fighters were punishing their bombers. A reporter from one of the fronts said that we were fighting with great courage and victory would be forthcoming. That was followed by a talk from a government official in Warsaw asking the government workers to stay and run the government. Not to leave. He also quoted the headline from the Warsaw Gazette that read, "To Arms United. We will Defeat the Enemy!" The whole radio spot was a lot different from the Army dispatches we got yesterday."

"We heard the same kind of reporting in Warsaw on Friday morning after the first air raid had failed on the city," Ludwik said.

The map showed the forest extending beyond Mrozy for some miles. The sergeant pinpointed the artillery range. If the forest roads were passable, they would be able to drive right by the outer limits of the range and let the artillery men exit there. It would mean they would have to back track to Mrozy if they wanted to stay in the forests. The other possibility was to leave the forest and drive them right onto the base and then take the main highway to Garwolin and pick up the country roads along the Wieprz River to Deblin.

The view from the forest was clear. Mrozy was untouched. It was quiet, but not without substantial activity around the train station. People were lined up on the platform. Dollies full of luggage stood waiting beside them. A steady stream of people was headed toward the station. They were pushing carts filled with luggage. Lots of luggage. They weren't going on a day trip. They were leaving for good. Ludwik remembered the little talk Josef and he had with Bodil

194

and her friends about making plans to get to safety if the Germans invaded. The words, "And where would I go?" from one of the friends rang loud and clear to him.

He could ask that same question to the people at the train station. He hoped they would have answers that made sense.

The three soldiers were glad to be back with their unit and grateful to the airmen for getting them there. They belonged to an artillery company that served as instructional cadre for artillery units that came to the range to practice firing their weapons. The barracks area had been strafed earlier that morning by fighters, but they had done little damage. The base was busy preparing for an expected second air raid either tonight or tomorrow. Ludwik asked the sergeant if he could get permission from his commanding officer to have them gas up the Volvo and maybe get a little food before they left. The sergeant left immediately to report in and make the request. He was back in a few minutes with his captain.

Returning their salute, the captain apologetically explained that he was under orders not to let anyone leave the base until further notice, but in the meantime, they would be treated as guests of his and could use his quarters to take a shower, change and relax on the base until 1800 hours when they could join him in the officers' mess for dinner. He said that Deblin was already under attack and maybe waiting here for a time would be wise. There were German planes everywhere. Ludwik respectfully disagreed but understood the order. He asked if they could be of any help. The captain said they already had by returning the three men. That their return would boost the morale at the base. Most of the men at the base had served with each other a long time. They were career artillery men. Like the sergeant was.

The three windows in the officer's mess were completely covered by blankets. They had been nailed into the window frames after the first attack. While that attack had been done during the daytime, nighttime raids could not be ruled out. Only candles were used to light the interior. The light was dim, but no one seemed to mind. The cabbage soup, ham, vegetables, baked bread and cakes were delicious.

Captain Nowicky gave Ludwik and Josef all the information he had on the progress of the war. It wasn't good. Air bases, cities, railroads, roads, communication centers and bridges had been under continuous assault by a seemingly never-ending parade of warplanes. Major damage had been done to the Polish infrastructure. Army bases like this one had been strafed but not bombed. More attacks were expected. All army divisions had been moved toward their defensive positions and were digging in to meet the enemy. His orders were to secure and hold this base. After today's brief attack, orders had been issued to set up machine gun emplacements around the base to protect any further strafing attacks. Ludwik asked if there was any news about the navy situation. Nowicky said he knew that most of the navy's small fleet had sailed for England sometime last week and that the naval air base at Puck had been hammered on Friday. Almost the entire squadron of sea planes had been caught in the open and destroyed. Naval recon planes on land had been flown out to a secondary field the day before the invasion started. He knew nothing about them. He said that radio reports out of Warsaw were reporting that Polish forces were inflicting heavy casualties on the Germans and had shot down many of their planes. The same reports never mentioned any casualties or planes lost on the Polish side. Ludwik guessed that meant casualties were high.

Discussing the Navy got Ludwik thinking about Bodil and her family. He wondered if they had made it to Sweden. It had only been a few days since they had said goodbye in Warsaw. Everything had changed since then. Life as he had known it, was gone. There would be very little long-term planning for a while. He would deal with the day as it unfolded and wouldn't worry about tomorrow until it arrived.

Nowicky excused himself and left to inspect the new gun emplacements before night set in. He said the weapons would only be effective against fighters coming in low to strafe the base. There would be no defense against bombers. They did not have the type of weapon that could reach them.

Ludwik and Josef returned to the captain's quarters and spent the next few hours looking over Karl's maps to decide on the safest route to Deblin. They both agreed to use the forest roads to get back to Mrozy, make a run through some open farmland to the next forest, get in there and drive to Garwolin. Once there, they would have two choices to get back to the base. One was to use the main road to Deblin. While that was the most direct and fastest way, it would probably not be the safest way. There was bound to be military and civilian traffic bunched up on it. The other choice was to follow the roads along the Wieprz River. They decided the river roads would be the safest. Josef marked the places on the map they would pass through. Most were small towns and villages except for Garwolin. It would be a trip of more than fifty miles. With the route and checkpoints agreed upon, the two men decided to make use of the sleeping bags that were stacked in a corner of the captain's quarters. It was getting late and they were tired. They needed to be rested and alert when they made their run "home."

It had been years since Ludwik had used a sleeping bag. The last time was with the Army on summer maneuvers before his first year as a cadet. He was surprised how comfortable and relaxed he felt as he burrowed deep into the warm confines of the bag. He didn't even feel the hard, wooden floor underneath. He prayed to Mary to safeguard his family and asked God to give him strength and courage. He closed his eyes as the warmth generated by his body heat in the bag brought him sleep. Both men had placed their bags on the floor so there was a clear path for the captain to get to his bunk.

197

It proved to be unnecessary. The captain never returned. The bunk remained impeccably made and undisturbed.

Daylight crept over the barracks and the artillery range. The range stretched its way out to a line of hills that served as the impact area for the thousands of shells that had been fired by the hundreds of Polish artillerymen who came here to practice their skill. Josef was up first. By the time Ludwik awoke, he had showered, shaved and dressed. He said he was going to gas up the Volvo and would be back in time for breakfast with him. Breakfast had started at 0600. It was now 0620. Ludwik said he would be ready by the time he returned. As Josef left, Ludwik closed his eyes and thanked God that his friend had come with him to Warsaw last weekend.

He was shaving when the sirens went off. There would be no breakfast on this day. This day would bring the Germans back in force to rain their pain on the area. Ludwik put his shirt and jacket on, grabbed his backpack, picked up Captain Nowicky's without thinking and raced outside to the base's assembly area. The Volvo was nowhere in sight. He decided to wait by the concrete base of a mounted WWI heavy artillery piece that had been used against the Soviets in the Polish-Soviet War. The decision to wait there would save his life.

They came out of the early sun that had risen to the top of the hills far up the range. No one saw them coming. They came directly down the range and headed straight for the barracks a scant two miles away. Ludwik dove behind the concrete base of the memorial as soon as he heard the cannons and machine guns open fire. The barracks in front of the assembly area seemed to explode. Lethal pieces of wood, steel and glass zipped through the air like bullets themselves and smashed into the memorial. Ludwik stayed crouched and safe behind the concrete base and watched the rooftop of the officer's quarters he had just left be blown off the building. Two fighters zoomed through the smoke and fire they had created and headed for what looked like a fuel depot spread along the base of a U-shaped row of hills. It was the only one way to attack the depot with planes not carrying bombs. They had to come straight down the range. The 109 fighters were met with a torrent of machine gun crossfire forcing them to split their tight formation; one peeling off to the right and the other to the left. Both climbed out of reach of the machine guns and reformed for another run. A higher run. This time the Polish gunners back up along the range were ready. As soon as the 109s began their run, the gunners opened up in advance and laid out a gauntlet of fire at alternating heights that the Germans would have to fly through. Both planes were hit. One of them staggered, dipped sideways, scraped a wingtip on a treetop and pin- wheeled its way into the ground exploding in a thunderous fireball. The other made it through and got to the fuel dump. Seconds later, a huge explosion rocked the earth. The German had hit his mark. Within a minute, a fire truck came storming into the smoky assembly area, horn blowing, bells clanging and charged through the smoke toward the fuel depot. It didn't slow an inch going by the burning wreckage of the 109. The flames from the fighter did not pose any added threat to the already burning buildings.

A loud screeching of tires came from somewhere in the cloud of smoke and fire behind the assembly area. A second later, a swerving, black Volvo bolted into the area. Josef had made it back! Ludwik jumped up and waved frantically at the car. Josef spotted him and wheeled over toward the monument. He bounced over pieces of barrack debris and stopped just short of where Ludwik stood. Smoke was now covering most of the entire area.

An ambulance, its horn and siren wailing, slowly made its way through the smoke and headed toward the blazing depot. It was followed by three men walking slowly behind. One of them spotted the Volvo and trotted over to it. He asked Ludwik and Josef if the

Volvo was theirs and if it was running. Ludwik said it was. The man said he had orders to have anyone with a vehicle help in the transporting of wounded to a medical tent being set up off the base proper. All drivers were to assemble in the woods a half mile up the range on its north side. Ludwik said they would comply. He jumped into the car and Josef slowly drove into the smoke and headed up range. Beeping the horn, he made his way carefully through piles of smoking rubble. He didn't want to run over any wounded or dead. In short order, they came across bodies of soldiers strewn across the wide area of the range where the artillery crews shot from. They got out of the car and checked to see if any of them were still alive. They were all dead. Back in the car, they continued on slowly up range. Visibility gradually improved. They could see dozens of soldiers slowly making their way toward them.

"They should be in the woods. Too wide open here," Ludwik said.

His words were prophetic. Three 109s suddenly popped over the crest of the hill up range and bore down on the men. It was a clever maneuver. Have the lone surviving plane from the first attack fly off. Let the Poles think the attack was over. Let them stagger into the open and then swoop back down for the kill. And kill they did. It was a massacre. The artillerymen were easy targets. They tried to run for the woods, but they never made it. The planes came down the range three across. They covered a wide swath of ground with heavy machine gun fire. The men were cut down like wheat in front of a spinning combine. The only thing that saved Ludwik and Josef was Ludwik's keen eyesight. He had spotted the three dots just under the sun streaking down range and yelled for Josef to get into the woods. Josef made a hard left turn and floored the accelerator. The Volvo bounced its way toward the pines. Just before nosing in, it was hit in the rear by bullets from the nearest Messerschmitt. Josef skidded his way over a carpet of pine needles between two pines. It was like driving on ice. There was a small clearing just beyond the line of pines and he made for it. Ludwik stopped him before he entered it. He told Josef to keep the car running while he checked the rear for damage. He returned quickly and said the car had been hit just above the rear tire. The tire had no entry marks. The damage had been limited to a few holes in the rear fender. Josef got out of the car and the two walked into the clearing to see if there were any paths or roads they could drive on. Only a narrow foot path led out from the clearing into the woods on the other side. There was nowhere to go. They decided to stay where they were until the planes left. When it was safe to do so, they would drive out of the forest and see what they could do to help. If they weren't needed, they could cross the range to the other side and find the road that would take them back to Mrozy and then on to Garwolin.

Death and Destruction

They waited for the "all clear" to stop before driving out onto the open range. Josef remarked that the men who had died should have waited for the "all clear" before making their way back to the base.

An ambulance and two trucks wobbled back and forth across the open area picking up the wounded. One of the trucks was being loaded with bodies and parts of bodies. It was a gruesome sight. They wouldn't be needed now. Plenty of help there. Josef pointed the Volvo toward the nearest machine gun position and the road behind it. It was a bit tricky driving through the smoke that still hung in the woods. The gun emplacement was empty. Josef drove past it slowly while Ludwik scanned the area for any wounded. It didn't look like the 109s had inflicted any damage there. The gun crew was probably out on the range looking for wounded or gathering the dead. The bodies would be brought to a common area and processed for burial. It would have to be done quickly. Another attack was always possible. The bodies would be identified, tagged and covered while a grave site was readied. Any personal belongings of the dead would be placed in the hands of their commanding officer. In the space of a few minutes, the artillery base had become a wasteland and many good men had died. Those charged with holding the base secure would have to move the survivors into the forest and await further orders. That would not include Ludwik and Josef. They wouldn't need permission to leave now. They could just go. Get to Deblin and see what was going on there. The artillerymen would remain at the base, reorganize and bury their dead.

Josef sighed and said, "I wonder where all our planes are?"

"Let's get to the base and find out," answered Ludwik.

The forest road was quiet. The drive was easy and without incident. The smell of smoke from the carnage inflicted on the small artillery base became fainter with each passing minute. The part of the forest they were in was thick with evergreens. They blanketed the sides of the narrow, dirt road. It was hard to see through them. Their size and numbers formed an almost tunnel-like, safe-haven for the Volvo as it moved between them. The sweet smell of pine sap and pine needles flowed through the windowless auto. It felt like nature itself was offering the two men a soothing respite from the violence and mayhem they had just left. Unfortunately, the peaceful interlude from reality ended before it could really be appreciated. It started with the smell of smoke once again. It wasn't like the smell of roasting chickens on the farm or the burning barracks on the artillery base. It was like the smell of Warsaw and Praga when they were burning. It was the smell that bombs made.

Mrozy was a fair-sized village. It had a church and a synagogue. There was a plaza with a fountain, some shops and a stable. A few dozen assorted buildings stood along a main street and a wide expanse of buildings were on its far side. Most were burning.

Some of the flames had crept to the outskirts of town and were slowly spreading toward the railroad tracks that led to a train station.

It was the station, or what was left of it, that had brought the bombers. They had flattened it and cut the tracks leading into it in several places. The rails lay blasted into jagged, useless pieces of steel jutting up into the air. There were bodies lying on the deserted main street. Ludwik and Josef watched a horse painfully drag a broken wagon that was on its side across a field. The animal was in obvious agony. It staggered on for a few more steps and then collapsed on its front legs. It stayed that way for a moment then rolled over on its side and lay motionless in the grass.

Josef backed the car a few yards into the cover of the forest. Both men got out, walked out to the entrance of the elevated wood line and peered down into the town. Flames and a cloud of thick, black smoke rose lazily into the sky. They scanned the area looking for people. Ludwik spotted them first. They were huddled in a cemetery on the far side of town. Most were sitting in small groups next to a low stone wall. No one was moving. They just sat there watching their town go up in flames. A stiff breeze began moving the cloud of black smoke up toward them and with it came a much stronger smell of what they had sensed on the forest road. There was no mistaking it now. Bombs had caused all this.

"Let's drive down and see what we can do. It should be safe. The Germans don't have anything else to destroy there," Ludwik said.

"Do we have any medical stuff?" Josef asked.

"Not in my backpack. Maybe in yours," Ludwik responded.

"I don't have a pack," Josef reminded his friend.

"I must have grabbed the captain's," said Ludwik.

"Just as well. It would have been blown up with the rest of his quarters. Take a look to see what he left us," Josef replied.

The backpack held shorts, undershirts, socks, a compass, cigarettes, a lighter, small binoculars and buried at the bottom, a basic survival first aid kit. A pang of guilt for taking another man's property stabbed at Ludwik as he inventoried the contents. Then he realized his innocent mistake had given them some items they could use. Josef was right. Better we had the backpack, he thought. It would have been burnt up if we didn't. He hoped it was a good sign of things to come.

Josef kept to the streets that were close to the edge of town. In some places, the intense heat from the fires forced him to drive off a street and into a field. As they neared the entrance to the cemetery, they passed a burning building that had a staircase leading down to the street. There was a body lying face down on the bottom steps. One arm was stretched out into the street. It looked to be the body of a man. Fire had burned most of the clothes off his body and taken his hair. It looked like he had tried to escape the burning building, but had only made it to the bottom of the stairs. His blackened and charred body was still smoking. Josef drove the Volvo off the street and into the beginning of a large alfalfa field that ran adjacent to the cemetery. Both men got out of the car and went to the body. Ludwik took hold of the man's wrists and eased him down the stairs. With Josef holding his boots, they carried him across the street and gently laid him on his back.

He had the face of a young man. Probably in his early twenties. He wore a wedding ring. Walking back to the car, they saw an old man shuffling through the iron gate of the cemetery. He stopped and shouted at them, "Why are you not fighting and killing the devils that are doing this?"

"We are on our way to do that," Ludwik answered.

"You are too late for us!" the old man cried.

His voice cracking, his wrinkled, weathered face contorted in agony, he continued, "Look at what they've done! That is my son you carried. He was in there trying to save his wife and child. He didn't know they were with us in the tomb. What do I tell her now?"

"Tell her the truth, but don't let her see the body," Ludwik answered.

"Would you take my son farther out into the field?" the old man asked.

"Of course," Ludwik said.

"What about his wife?" Josef asked.

The old man removed his cap and just stood there. Tears began to trickle down the craggy face he had earned over the years working the fields. "I will have him buried in the land he was raised on. His wife and son will know he died for them."

There had been more than a dozen women with children crammed into the hillside tomb. They came out slowly, one after the other. They stood in a line facing what was left of their town. No one said a word. Even the children seemed mesmerized by the sight; forgetting even to do what most children did once given the freedom of open space to run in. Men began to appear from all directions. They called for their wives and children. The calls jolted the children into motion. They raced towards their fathers screaming gleefully, "Papa …. Father!" Some women ran behind them, sobbing, relief covering their faces. Others blessed themselves as they walked into the open arms of their man. One woman stood quietly alone with her young son just outside the tomb. The boy was asking for his father. The woman didn't answer. She just stared across the street at the burning building that had been their church. She had told her husband to go to the blacksmith stable, leave the horse and carriage and meet her at the church.

When the planes came and the bombs started to fall, all women and children were rushed across the street to the cemetery and ushered into the tomb for safety. There she had prayed with all the other women that their husbands had found safety.

She saw the three men coming across the field toward the cemetery. One was her father-in-law. The other two were military men of some sort. As they came through the gate, the old man stopped, stared at her, took his hat off and slowly walked her way. The look on his face told her everything. Ludwik and Josef stood and watched the drama play itself out. People were hugging and kissing; praising God they still had a family. Never mind their town was no more. They would walk back through the fields to their farmhouses. For now, life would go on for them. Not so for the young woman now being consoled by the old man who had bravely swallowed his own pain to comfort her. The boy stood with his head pressed into his mother's hip and held onto her dress with both hands.

"Mother of God! Every day filled with misery," Josef said quietly. Ludwik stared at the young woman, now a widow, too soon a widow, nodded his head and started walking toward the Volvo. He thought of his family in Mazanki, especially his sisters. They were like the young woman here with her long, handmade dress, braided hair and colorful babushka. What was happening to them? The feeling of helplessness and anger raced through his veins once again. He asked Mary, Jesus and then God himself for help in trying to control his emotions.

"There's little for us to do here," Ludwik said.

"Can we leave them something?" Josef asked.

Ludwik nodded and said, "The captain's first aid kit might be of some help. A blanket for the old man to cover his son would be a good thing."

Josef took the first aid kit and blanket and placed them just inside the cemetery gate.

Ludwik brought out the maps and laid them out on the hood of the Volvo parked in the woods. He wanted to reacquaint himself with the area. He was also very hungry. The air raid on the base had stolen his breakfast. He emptied his pack on a bed of pine needles, took the loaf of bread he had found back in Praga and broke it in half. He examined the canned goods Chimelewski had given them in Warsaw. He chose the jam. The small tools they had taken from the hotel office made opening the can fairly easy. He punched a hole in the cover with the screwdriver, twisted a portion of the cover up and tore it off with a strong hand. He spread the jelly on the bread with the screwdriver and passed one half to Josef. Ludwik took small bites and chewed each one slowly as he scanned the map. He washed the bread down with water from the canteen the farmer's wife had given them.

"Do you realize the number of people that have given us what we have?" Ludwik asked Josef.

"I haven't thought about it. Been too busy trying to stay alive," Josef answered.

"Look around you," Ludwik suggested.

"The car from Karl," Josef said.

"And his maps," Ludwik added.

Josef took a moment and said, "The backpack from Captain Nowicky, the food and tools from the hotel manager, the canteen and water from the farmers……. We owe a lot to them all. God, how can we ever repay those good people?"

"By staying alive and fighting for them," Ludwik answered.

To Deblin

The trip to Garwolin was quiet. Not a sign of a plane all the way through the villages of Wezyczyn and Chromin. The traffic on the forest roads was very light. The only anxious time on the trip was when they had to drive out in the open for a mile or so behind a horse and wagon slowly making its way along the narrow road to Chromin. A few gentle taps on the car's horn went ignored by the farmer who just kept his horse plodding along like the day was no different than any of the other hundreds of days he had spent on this road. When Josef leaned hard on the horn to get the man's attention, the horse was reined over to the side of the road. Ludwik asked Josef to pull up alongside the wagon so he could speak to the farmer.

"Hello friend," Ludwik said to the man.

"Good day, soldier man," the farmer answered.

"It is not a good idea these days for any of us to travel so slowly out in the open," Ludwik offered.

The farmer leaned down toward Ludwik and asked him why it was not a good idea to be doing something that he had been doing for most of his life. Ludwik told him that Poland was at war and the enemy had many planes that were attacking everything that was moving in this part of Poland.

"Who are we fighting now?" the farmer asked.

"Germany."

The farmer smiled and said, "Didn't we defeat them the last time?"

"We did, but it's still very dangerous to be caught on the open road," Ludwik answered.

The farmer, a man of fifty or more years, smiled and said, "Yes, war is always dangerous. I've had my share. I did my fighting against the Germans and then the Russians after that. I will watch the skies. Thank you for the warning." With that, he saluted the two men and waved them ahead.

"Strong man," Josef said as he slowly passed the farmer.

"Yes, he is. I could see it in his eyes," Ludwik said as he searched the sky for the Germans. Josef pressed the accelerator down and sped for the safety of the woods and the road through them to Garwolin.

Ludwik scanned the town from the shade cast by the barn with Captain Nowicky's binoculars. Garwolin was much larger than the villages they had just passed through. The twin, white steeples of a Catholic Church reached high above everything. Just like they did in practically every town in Poland. The river Wieprz wound its way west past the town. According to Karl's map, it would merge with the river Vistula near the airbase at Deblin some thirty miles away. The plan was to follow the river to the village of Gonczyco, find a way to the forest around Stawy and get to Deblin from there.

There was a bridge near the center of town that crossed the Wieprz. It led to a tree lined dirt road that ran along the opposite bank. The trees would provide cover. They would have to drive into the center of town to find the street that led to the bridge. Once across the river, they could take the tree lined road and see how far it went. For some reason, the road was not on the map, but Ludwik figured it had to be of some importance or a bridge wouldn't have been built to get to it. And if it was important, it probably went for some distance.

Josef drove across the field and headed into Garwolin. They passed a dozen or so people, mostly elderly, walking in the direction of the church as they slowly drove through town. The windowless car and the two military men in it drew the attention of the pedestrians who stopped and waved to them as they passed. Someone shouted, "Poland lives forever!"

There were a few trucks and carriages parked along the street, but no vehicles were moving on any of the streets they passed. The town was strangely quiet. The only sounds came from the Volvo being geared down at every side street while Ludwik searched for the bridge. Suddenly, a line of bicyclists came out of a side street and whizzed by them. Their spinning wheels sounded like an angry swarm of bees as they gathered to attack an intruder menacing their hive. For a moment, a picture of German bombers being attacked by angry swarms of Polish fighters flashed through Ludwik's mind. He smiled as he pictured the bombers being shot out of the sky. They were halfway through Garwolin and the bridge hadn't been found. They could see the end of the main street they were on and the open road outside of town. The road would be dangerous. They had to find the bridge. Josef spotted an old woman drawing water from a well in a small plaza off to his left. He pulled over to ask her about the bridge. She only acknowledged his presence when her two full buckets had been tied to a hook on each end of a thick pole. She pointed ahead and muttered, "Berk." Then she squatted and set the pole onto her shoulders. Like a weightlifter. She stood up, steadied the pole and carried the water away. Not a drop fell from the buckets. Ludwik figured she was at least eighty years old. He admired her strength and grit and hoped the rest of Poland would be as strong as she was. He felt in his heart they would have to be.

Berk Street went straight out to the bridge. They were across the river quickly. Surprisingly, the road was semi-paved and went off in both directions along the river. Karl's map had to be an old one; not even a dirt road on it. There was a sign that read "Railroad Station" pointing in the direction they needed to go. It was not a welcome sign to them. The Germans had shown what they were up to already. They wanted to attack and disable Poland's infrastructure.

Hinder the movement of large numbers of troops and equipment. And that strategy made railroad stations a dangerous place to be.

"Let's take a look," Ludwik said.

Rounding a bend in the road, they saw the station about a half mile ahead. It was sitting in open flat land. They also saw that the road ended there. They would have to go back into town and use the main road to Deblin. And with the base already under attack according to Captain Nowicky, chances were good they would be seen. They had just crossed back over the bridge when the air raid sirens went off. Josef hit the accelerator and screeched the car around the corner onto the main road and sped toward the end of the town. People were out in the street running for whatever shelter they had.

The two Stukas ignored the town and the Volvo churning up clouds of dust as it sped down the dirt road out of town. They came screaming straight down out of the sky toward the railroad station. Each dropped their bombs before leveling off.

Fortunately, for Ludwik and Josef, the German pilots showed no interest in them as they banked back toward the burning station. They made three passes at the doomed station strafing it with cannon and machine gun fire.

"Remember what happened at the range," Ludwik said.

Josef remembered. The Germans had made it look like they had left, only to return when the soldiers had come out into the open to pick up survivors and treat the wounded. It had been terrible.

He drove off the road into a field and pulled up in the shade of a large barn. They sat there and waited. There was no trickery this time. The Stukas did not return. The "all clear" sounded. Ludwik looked back at Garwolin with the binoculars to see if anyone was out and about. He only saw a few. He asked Josef if he saw any people.

"Some on the road," Josef said.

A small group of men, women and children had appeared out of nowhere and were walking down the road toward the town. They were led by a soldier. Ludwik waved for the sergeant to bring the group over to the barn. The frightened faces of the women and children stirred the hearts of both men. The soldier shook their hands and said he was glad to see them. One of the women, recognizing the two men were pilots, asked them why they were out in a field in a car and not in planes shooting down Germans. Josef answered by saying they were not fighter pilots.

"And where are our fighter pilots?" The woman asked.

Josef had wondered about the same thing. All he could say was, "I do not know, but I am sure they are in the skies fighting for the motherland."

Like the old man in the cemetery, she said, "But not in these skies!" She was angry. Ludwik and Josef understood. She had a right to be angry. The sergeant was from the 15th Infantry Regiment stationed in the Deblin-Stawy area. He was from Garwolin and had been home on pass when the invasion began. All the people with him were family. He had taken them out into the countryside to set up a camouflaged encampment next to a small pond just a half-mile away. They had been there during the air attack on the railroad station. He had correctly figured the Germans would come for the station sooner or later and was worried they might attack the town itself. He wanted his family to have a place away from the town and station to hide in.

He had learned most of his regiment had left Deblin because of heavy air attacks on the airfield there. They had been moved to a position west of the Vistula to meet the oncoming Germans. A company of the 15th had been assigned to help guard the huge ammunition dump hidden in the Stawy forest.

He was going there as soon as he could. Ludwik asked him if there was a way to get to Stawy without taking the open main road. The sergeant said there were trails they could walk that had cover, but they were too narrow and rough to drive a car over. He said it was only twenty miles to Stawy from here if they drove the main road. He also said most people out here in the country would be staying home and not clogging up the road. No one was sure how the war was going and even if the Germans got close, there really wasn't any place for them to go. That made sense to Ludwik. He asked Josef what he thought about the main road. Josef smiled and said, "Let's do it."

Except for some men on bicycles, two trucks, and a few horse-drawn wagons, the road was clear of traffic and most importantly, the sky was empty. In less than an hour, they were in the forest. Deblin was only seven miles away now.

The gated roadblock was manned by a squad of Polish infantry from the 15th Regiment. A private stepped out in front of the gate and signaled for them to stop. He saluted and politely asked for their papers stating the reason they were here. Ludwik told him they were on their way back to the air base. They only had their I.D.'s and passes from Deblin to Warsaw. The private asked them to back the car into the small area just off the road and wait for the officer on duty to come and talk with them. He yelled for the private in the small shack just off the road to call for the captain.

Captain Beck didn't have good news for them. He said the air base at Deblin had been under attack for two days.

Much of the airstrip had been severely damaged. Most of the airmen, except for administrative personnel, the cadet pilots and their cadre, had been moved to secondary fields in anticipation of the attack. All operational planes had been flown out by their pilots. All training planes, including the light bombers Ludwik had been training on, had also been flown out by their instructors.

They were going to be outfitted with machine guns and used to support the Army on the ground. He said some of the barracks were still intact and cadets were sleeping in them after dark. They left the base early each morning for the cover of the forests. He said Deblin was being attacked as they spoke and advised them to wait until nightfall for a safe drive to the base. He also confirmed what Ludwik had suspected; the Germans were not making any distinction between military and civilian targets. It was total warfare. They were even machine-gunning Polish pilots who had parachuted from their planes.

Josef lit a cigarette, drew heavily on it, blew a pungent stream of smoke into the air and quietly murmured, "Bastards!"

"Have we had success against them in the air?" Ludwik asked.

"Reports say our pilots have done well, but they also say the Germans are many."

The captain wrote a pass for each pilot giving them permission to drive through the forest and past the huge ammunition depot that was hidden there. The depot was heavily guarded by infantry units. Josef drove the Volvo carefully, stopping at checkpoints to show their passes. Finally, they reached a checkpoint where no one was allowed to pass until nightfall. A long line of trucks stood quietly along the road there. They were loaded with ammunition. The drivers were lounging in the woods waiting for the sun to go down.

It would be much safer at night to deliver their cargo to the infantry, artillery and armor battalions squared off against the enemy.

"How would you like to drive one of those "bombs on wheels"? Josef said.

"I would if I had to, but I prefer the open sky and the room to maneuver," Ludwik answered.

"What do you think about our light bombers flying close support for the infantry?"

Ludwik shook his head and said, "Risky. Very risky. They should be bombing the German supply lines not flying fighter plane missions supporting the infantry. Our bombers are too slow for that. They can be shot down by machine gun fire from the ground. Even well-placed bullets from a rifle could bring them down. It's asking too much. It will be a waste of planes and men."

Ludwik checked the one working headlight to see if it was covered with enough mud to dim its light. Satisfied, he strode over toward the lead truck in the ammunition convoy. As he did, soldiers came out of the woods, got in their vehicles and started them up. Within a minute, the long line of vehicles was purring and ready to move out. Darkness was about to overtake the forest and the road beyond. The commander of the convoy, a young infantry major, answered Ludwik's question of when he could leave by saying it would be best for the Volvo to get a head start on the convoy. He didn't want to slow the two men down. Ludwik wished him luck and jogged back to the car. Josef put the car in gear and they quietly slipped out of the forest. The road was clear, clouds hid the moon and even with only one dim headlight, the Volvo was fast down the road to Deblin. They were at the base in thirty minutes.

215

Most of the fires on the base had been reduced to a smoky, thin haze by firefighters. The main gate, or what was left of it, was not manned by sentries. The Army barracks in the old fortress on the base had been hit hard. Air Force and Army personnel were wandering in from the forest and heading for a large canvas tent that had been hastily erected to serve as a mess hall. The enlisted men's mess had been destroyed. The officer's mess, once a magnificent dining hall, had been seriously damaged. A line of men, mess kits in hand, stood outside the tent and patiently waited for their first meal of the day. Amazingly, some of the barracks were still standing. Ludwik's barrack was one of them. He told Josef to let him off at the front door. He made his way into the darkened building with backpack on and shading the lens of his flashlight with one hand until he closed the door. Then he let the full beam light his way to and up the stairs. His room was on the second floor, first one on the left. It was as he had left it a few days ago when he went to meet Bodil and her friends in Warsaw. He thanked God the room was still in order. There were many things to be thankful for despite the mess he found himself part of. The room was one of them. A little thing. But a positive thing. The room had no windows. No need to worry about any light escaping into the sky and serving as a beacon for the Germans. He knew the entire base would be on alert and a blackout was in effect. He closed the door and pointed his flashlight at the desk and the mirror over it. There was a chain lamp on top of the desk. He walked over to it and gently pulled the chain down to see if the lamp worked. It didn't. He lay the flashlight on his bunk, propped it up on the pillow and pointed its beam at the mirror. The reflected light illuminated the small room. The desk draw held a manual and his notebook on the PZL 23B light bomber he had been training on. He went to his locker and began putting the manual and notebook in his backpack. He stopped, realizing he was finished here. There was a war on. He had to find out what his orders were. He knew his squadron had been attacked up north, all seaplanes destroyed, and

216

reconnaissance aircraft moved to the secondary base a few miles away. A knock on the door interrupted his thoughts. It was Josef and one of the training officers from the flight school. The officer told Ludwik to take what he needed and come with him for a meeting of all officers and pilots on the base. Ludwik crammed his backpack with a flight suit, two service blouses, a compass, flight gloves, flight helmet, fatigue jacket and pants, two service caps and a survival kit. He tied his flight boots together, slung them over his shoulder and followed the two men out.

The officer's dining hall was still intact, but only a shell of what it used to be. A bomb blast had opened a huge hole in one wall and shattered all the windows and beautiful glass chandeliers that had hung from the high ceiling. For many years the hall had served as an ornate ball room where many elegant socials had been held for the officers and cadets of the flight school. Now, it was nothing more than a glass littered, water stained, wrecked room. Ludwik thought it would be a long time, if ever, before the hall would resonate once again with a beautiful waltz and the swishing of a lady's full gown skimming the floor as she was whirled along in the arms of a white gloved gentleman of the Polish Air Force.

The briefing was quick and to the point.

1. France and England had declared war on Germany. That brought a rousing cheer from the men. The plan now was for the Army and Air Force to slow the German advance with a gradual defensive withdrawal until a western front was opened by France and England.
2. All personnel not operational nor assigned to a combat ready unit would withdraw south with the wounded to Lublin and wait for orders.
3. Pilots and cadets would move farther south closer to the Romanian border. They would wait for the arrival of

warplanes in Romania that had been promised by France and England. The pilots and certified cadets would then fly them back into Poland to press the fight against the Germans.

4. Everyone was reminded that many Polish citizens were of German ethnicity and their allegiance may have been compromised by the invasion.

5. Finally, there wouldn't be enough trucks for everyone. Many men would be on their own to find their way south. The destination for most was Lwow, close to Ukraine. All cadets and pilots would head for Stanislawow, near the Romanian border.

Hearing this, Josef checked his pockets to see if the car keys were still there. They were. He knew he not only had to worry about the Germans, he had to keep his eyes open for the Polish lads who were not too happy about taking a long walk. They might not be bashful about "borrowing" a car or two or anything they could get their hands on to drive.

Someone asked how the fighting was going. The briefing officer quietly said it was not going well. The German land forces were moving quickly, spearheaded by hundreds of fast, heavily armed tanks. Polish army units were being cut off and surrounded. There was a definite need for our Army to fall back into stronger defensive positions, consolidate their forces and stall the German offensive until the second front was opened. Warsaw was being defended well on the ground but had lost much of its air defense. He reminded everyone once again that their primary objective was to get safely south and wait for orders. The secondary objective was to get those new warplanes into Poland. He closed by reading a dispatch from Marshall Rydz-Smigly, Commander-in-Chief of the Polish military.

It read as follows: .... "The brave and courageous fight being put up by the Polish Air Force against the overwhelming numbers that the enemy has in the sky would be noted in Polish history as one of the country's most heroic episodes." The officer went on to say he knew all the men here would live up to that praise in the coming days.

An aide brought the men to attention. The briefing officer wished them God-speed and said he would see them soon. He saluted the men and went out into the night. The aide said food was waiting for them in the makeshift canvas tent. They would sit in a reserved part of the tent that had tables set up for them. No mess kits would be necessary. Someone shouted, "Our last meal, boys!! China and silverware provided. You find your own waitress!!!!"

The spontaneous outburst drew a roar of laughter from the tired and somber officers. Everyone enjoyed the moment. It felt good to laugh; especially now, in the face of all that was wrong. While the laughter only lasted a few seconds, it served to provide a sense of normalcy. When it ended, everyone quietly trudged their way out and headed for the mess tent. As each stepped through the doorway, they were greeted with the delicious aroma of sausage, potatoes, beets and kapusta that filled the tent. The smell of "eats" put a little "pop" in their step. Ludwik put his arm around Josef's neck, hugged him and said, "Germans be damned! We eat well tonight."

The Volvo had plenty of gas; enough to get beyond Lublin, their first checkpoint. Ludwik had marked out a route on the map of southern Poland that everyone had received during dinner. His plan remained the same. He would try to stay off the main roads if he could. Driving at night was preferred, but he wasn't sure if they would be leaving tonight. He would discuss it with Josef. The route he had chosen would take them through Lublin and Zamoscz, before reaching the rendezvous in Stanislawow. That would put them deep into southern Poland and close to their ally, Romania.

It would also take them near the San River and the village of Kurylowka where he had been born. He had relatives living there.

Ludwik and Josef were under no obligation to accompany any convoy that was being organized at the base because they had their own transportation. The first convoy to be sent off would carry the wounded. It would leave as soon as the trucks were loaded. Extra personnel had been assigned to ride with the medical staff to help in the care of the wounded men. Specific units had been assigned to ride the remainder of the trucks available. Units not assigned were on their own. Already, small groups of the non-assigned men were discussing ways and means of getting to their destinations. Some of them were talking about heading west to join up with the Army.

Others talked about pooling their funds to rent transportation like taxis. Maybe even buy a vehicle. Some considered riding trains. Ludwik knew he was fortunate. Thanks to Karl and a lot of good luck, he had transportation. He had maps and a good driver in Josef. Money was a problem. They didn't have much left. He and Josef had missed pay call last Thursday because they were in Warsaw. He wondered if he might still be able to get his pay now that he was back on base. He had learned at the meeting that all administrative personnel were still here. That meant the Paymaster had to be here. If he hadn't been killed. He would try to find him. He told Josef to stay around the area and keep his eyes and ears open for any word on the paymaster's whereabouts. He was going to check on the car and see if the Finance office was still standing. If it was, he would try and get their pay.

The Volvo had attracted some attention. There were two airmen in it. They were arguing with each other and never saw Ludwik approaching. Ludwik smiled to himself as he listened to them discussing the pros and cons of how to start the car.

"Can I be of some help to you," Ludwik said to the airman in the driver's seat. Surprised and a bit flustered, the young man said, "We wanted to see if it would start."

Ludwik opened the windowless door and gestured for him to step out. The other man got out his side and peered through the darkness over the roof at Ludwik. Ludwik motioned for him to come around to his side. The bare sleeves on their shirts revealed they had no rank yet. They were very young. They both stared at Ludwik's wings emblazoned on his tunic. That meant trouble for them.

"The car looked like it had been wrecked with all the windows blown out," the driver side airman said.

"Are we in trouble?" the other airman said.

"No," Ludwik answered. "We are at war and Poland needs you to fight. Besides, I didn't see the car moving or hear the engine running. No law about sitting in a car."

Ludwik asked them what unit they were from. The rider side airman told him they belonged to the Quartermaster supply unit. He said they were heading there for the night when they spotted the car. He added they had not been assigned any transportation out of Deblin and thought maybe the car could be started and used.

"Isn't the Quartermaster building next to the Finance Offices. The Paymaster's office?"

"Yes, it is, sir."

"Are both offices standing?"

"Yes, they are, sir."

That was good news. If the paymaster had survived the bombing, he might be found in his office. It was worth the try.

The three made their way past the barracks area and headed for the Quartermaster and Finance offices. The two young airmen man left Ludwik at the Quartermaster's office. Ludwik walked to the Paymaster's office and climbed the short steps onto the porch that covered the front of the building. It was dark inside. He peered through a side window for some sign of life. He was rewarded by seeing a red glow pulsating in the dark. Someone was smoking a cigarette in there. Ludwik knocked on the window and waited for an answer.

"Identify yourself," the smoker said to the faceless figure in the window.

"Navy pilot, Skoczylas, training unit, light bombers, reconnaissance," Ludwik answered.

"What do you want?"

"I haven't been paid this month."

"What did you say?" the cigarette holder said.

"I said I haven't been paid this month."

Laughter erupted from inside.

"Only a Navy man would have the balls to come here at night and ask for money. Especially with a war going on."

"Yes, sir. Especially with a war going on," Ludwik answered.

"Meet me at the front door," the man ordered.

The smoker was the Assistant Paymaster. He was a young officer. A very young officer. He told Ludwik that all absent personnel on payday had their money returned and that it was stored in a safe. He needed to see Ludwk's I.D. and check it against his files.

222

That done, he asked Ludwik to hold the tiny flashlight he had brought out of his pocket so he could dial the combination on the safe. After dialing in the first number, he spun the dial in the opposite direction for the second number, but the dial stuck before the number was reached. He spun the dial back towards the first number and tried again. Again, the dial stuck. Ludwik asked him if the second number had been changed. The officer said it hadn't. Ludwik said he was a certified locksmith as well as being a mechanical engineer. He had worked on safes at the Technical University of Warsaw as part of his training. He said he might be able to help. The young officer accepted. Ludwik knew that the dial on this model always clicked inward under pressure and locked. It would only move back to the first number. The young officer had obviously pushed inward too hard. All Ludwik had to do was pull the dial out from the safe's surface until he heard the click that meant it was free to spin both ways. He explained to the officer what he was about to do. After the click, he spun the dial back and told the officer to spin the numbers without pressing on the dial. Within seconds it was done. A minute later, Ludwik had his pay envelope.

"Was there anyone else with you on pass?"

"Josef Przyba. He's in navigator training. Bombers."

"Is he with you now?"

"Yes, we're leaving with the convoy tomorrow. We have a car."

"The convoy is not going to leave tomorrow. It will leave on Tuesday."

"Is that official?" Ludwik asked.

"Yes, the extra transportation was hit hard this afternoon. Several trucks were lost. More will be coming, but they won't get here until tomorrow night," the young officer responded.

"Any chance Josef can come here for his pay?"

"I owe you for the safe. Bring him here. Don't let anyone know what you are up to. Tap an SOS on the window so I know it's you. And if you would, my ignorance concerning the safe is between you and me."

Ludwik and Josef were back in twenty minutes. Five minutes later Josef had his pay, and they were on their way to the car in front of the barracks.

"How did you arrange all of this?" Josef asked.

"I went to University," a smiling Ludwik answered.

"What time is the convoy leaving?" Josef asked.

"It's not leaving until Tuesday. They don't have enough trucks. I think we should catch a little sleep and then leave before dawn." Josef agreed. He was tired.

All buildings still standing were crammed with men for the short night of sleep. Breakfast was to be served between 0300 and 0430 hours. That meant most would probably be sleeping five hours or less. All personnel had to be off the base by 0445 and into bunkers that had been dug out in the fields and woods adjoining the base. Any pilots and aircraft ground crew members left would leave just before dawn on the few remaining trucks still on base. Personnel that had private transportation were to leave when ready. They were to get to the designated rendezvous areas as soon as possible. Someone had brought a bus on base from either Deblin or one of the other towns nearby. It was going to be used to transport cadets from the flying school to a point past Stanislawow and not very far from the Romanian border.

Ludwik's room was small. His bunk had a double mattress. One would be used by Josef. It was made even smaller with the addition of three cadets that had been using the room. They spread out on the floor around the bed. Josef was at the foot of the bed on the mattress. No one was sleeping. A conversation had developed between the three cadets that centered on the possibility of leaving the base to join Army units.

Two wanted to leave with the cadets going south. The other argued there would be no bombers to fly among the planes arriving in Romania. He had heard all the planes were fighters. He said it would be a waste to sit and wait there for nothing; it would be better to fight the Germans now. He didn't want to be that far away from the fight. The other two cadets argued that they had to fight with what they had been trained to fight with. Ludwik interrupted the discussion by saying they had orders to obey. And orders were orders. And in addition to orders, he would enjoy getting as much sleep as he could.

"And what about our families?" the lone dissenter interjected.

"We all have families. We all want to be with them. To protect them. We just need to have faith that God will take care of them until we can defeat the Germans," Ludwik counseled.

"We can't help anyone if we don't get enough sleep," Josef cut in.

"I'm leaving in the morning to fight with the Army. You can turn me in if you want. I'll be gone," the dissenter said.

"No one will turn you in," one of the other two trainees said.

"Goodnight gentlemen, time for sleep," Ludwik ordered.

Only the whispers of men talking on the floor outside in the hallway interrupted the quiet that had settled in the room. Ludwik wondered if those men were weighing the option of leaving to fight with the Army. It wouldn't be a surprise to learn that some would do just that. They wouldn't be deserters if they did. They would be patriots. Not running from a fight. Running to one. He just hoped the majority, especially the pilots, would follow orders and wait for another day to fight. Everyone wanted to fight. Ludwik knew that sooner or later they would all be fighting, and pilots would be crucial to Poland's effort to maintain its freedom. Josef began to snore. A sure sign to sleep now before the roaring began. He needed to sleep. He thanked God for his life and asked Him for help. Josef's snoring ceased. Ludwik smiled and told God that was a good start. He dreamt of the farm children waving goodbye in the field and the black and white carriages of Warsaw.

The showers didn't work, but there was water available from the taps along the long sink that covered one wall of the latrine. Both Ludwik and Josef had been up before most and had made their way over the snoring bodies in the hallway with Ludwik's flashlight. They carried a fresh change of clothes with them. Josef had Captain Nowicky's clothes. They were a bit of a loose fit but comfortable enough. They washed their bodies as best they could with the light from the flashlight. Both took some extra time to shampoo the grime and filth of the past three days off their skulls. That felt especially refreshing. They dressed in the latrine, returned to the room, packed their dirty clothes into the backpacks, stepped around the two remaining trainees who were still fast asleep and left for breakfast.

Breakfast was disappointing. Nothing like the sumptuous dinner they were treated to last night. The only thing hot was the coffee and that came without sugar. The main topic of conversation centered around the cadet that had left the room last night to join the Army. They were among the first to leave the mess hall.

Ludwik stopped for a moment to light his cigarette. He cupped his hands to cover the flame from the match. Josef pointed toward the darkness that was the woods and wondered out loud if the enemy could see the flame. Ludwik said yes. He then suggested it would be a good thing if they got used to being very careful. That it wouldn't surprise him if the Germans dropped some paratroops behind our lines. He said they also had to remember what they had heard in the briefing about ethnic Germans in Poland. That some are friendly. Some are not.

To the Border

Ludwik thought about his Jewish friend Kramer in Old Town and the struggle he must be having trying to convince his parents to leave Warsaw before it was too late. He knew if his parents refused, Kramer would never leave them. Good man, he thought.

Josef drove. There was lots of movement on the base. Most of it centered on foot traffic to and from the mess hall. There were still no sentries at the gate when they crossed the base perimeter. They passed by the town Deblin and headed for the river Vistula. They entered an open two-lane road along the river that led to Golab, a small town about four miles away. The one light of the Volvo was sufficient for driving and was enough for the oncoming convoy of trucks headed for the base to see them. That was a surprise. The trucks were not expected to arrive at the base until tonight. Someone had taken care of the transportation issue very well.

They were well past Golab and nearing Pulawy at first light. Josef sped down the open road taking advantage of the daylight. They wanted to get through the town and drive alongside the large concentration of woods that ran parallel to the Vistula until they reached Konskowole, some six miles away. There was no traffic on the road. The only sign of life were three men in a field that ran alongside the Vistula. They were cutting flat the tall grass that would become the hay for their livestock this winter. Ludwik admired the well-coordinated rhythm of the swinging hand scythes. The men worked as a team as they cut their way across the field. He was surprised when one of them stopped and broke the synchronized teamwork. He watched the man throw his scythe to the ground and run toward the river. The other two men stopped their cutting and looked behind them at the sky. A second later, they were both running for the river. Ludwik stiffened. It had to be planes!

He yelled for Josef to stop the car, take the keys and follow him. They ran into the field and dove into the tall grass. Both lay on their stomachs and propped themselves up on their elbows to watch the planes advance. They flew directly over them. Headed in the direction of Deblin. Ludwik rolled over on his back to get a better look. There were twelve Heinkel medium bombers and a protective cover of six M109s. He knew the bombers carried a heavy payload of bombs and the damage they could inflict with them. Suddenly, the 109s broke formation and accelerated up into the sky. Ludwik saw their target. Three Polish fighters were diving down at the bombers. The PZL-11 fighters went right by the German fighters and into the heart of the bomber formation. Within seconds, two Heinkels were sent spiraling out of the sky. Ludwik and Josef watched in awe as the bombers crashed and exploded up the river on the other bank. There were no parachutes. No survivors.

Once through the formation, the Polish fighters split up and circled back to attack again. One streaked upward toward the rear of the Heinkels and the other two nosed up toward the formation's underbelly. The lone Polish pilot attacking from behind the bombers never made it. He was met by two 109s that had circled back and dropped behind the formation to counter any second attack by the Poles. The Pole was hit, wobbled awkwardly and began to trail smoke. Then it exploded. Ludwik and Josef watched the smoking pieces of the plane scatter across the sky and fall like rain into the Vistula. Ludwik made the sign of the cross and thanked the pilot for his courage. The two remaining Polish fighters were cut off by the other four 109s before they could reach the bombers. Both fighters dove toward the ground, split up and went into evasive maneuvering. Each had a 109 on their tail. The Polish pilots wheeled away from each other, climbed straight up, nosed over and dropped behind their pursuers to a few feet above the ground to evade the much faster German planes. It was a brilliant maneuver.

It kept them safe from the devastating firepower of the German fighters. They stayed just above the ground and sped away from their pursuers. The 109s broke off their attack and climbed to rejoin the other four fighters and the bombers. Ludwik and Josef stood up and watched them move out of sight. They began their walk back to the Volvo. Before they reached the car, they were startled to see, the two Polish fighters returning.

They were streaking just above the ground in the direction the Germans had gone. They weren't finished with their fight.

The tremors under their feet told them the bombers were dropping their payload on the target. Probably Deblin. While it had been good to see there were still Polish fighters in the sky, it hurt to watch how overmatched they were. It seemed even the bombers were faster than the Polish fighters. The Polish pilots had shown lots of courage and skill in their attack and evasive retreat. The plan to get to the border and pick up the more advanced fighter planes in Romania was absolutely essential now. With those new fighters coupled with the skill of the Polish pilots, the war in the air would be a lot different. The question of numbers would remain. Would they get enough planes to keep the Germans at bay until a western front was opened?

Putting those thoughts aside, Ludwik urged Josef to speed up the drive to Pulawy in case more German planes showed up looking to wreak havoc on the open roads.

With his eyes fixed on the sky, Ludwik wondered how the two remaining Polish pilots had made out. They had to know what they were up against. The German bombers were by now high over the PZL-11's ceiling. It would be impossible for the Polish planes to reach them. They would have to be lucky to get at any of them. It had to be very frustrating for them not to be able to make the enemy pay more. They had surprised the Germans at first by lying in wait above the attacking formation and its cover. The surprise had turned into two kills. The Germans would not make that mistake again. They would come in much higher the next time. Ludwik had known about the huge differences in aircraft capability between his country and the Germans before today. To see it play out firsthand only cemented the dread in him that Poland was outclassed and certainly outnumbered in the sky by superior German aircraft. He wasn't concerned about the quality of pilots Poland had, just the machines they flew.

He had already seen the skill of Polish pilots in the skies over Warsaw and here today. They were excellent but he realized how difficult it was going to be if they didn't get those new fighters from Romania.

"What are you thinking, my friend?" said Josef as he shifted down to make the sharp turn toward Pulawy.

"We have to make it to Stanislawow, Josef," Ludwik replied.

"Traveling on these open roads in daylight is going to make that difficult," Josef said.

Pulawy

The Volvo raced quickly up and over a small incline. Pulawy came into view straight ahead. It was about a mile away. Josef let the car slow to a stop. There was something about the town that didn't look right. Something was going on outside the town. Ludwik had Josef pull over to the side and pulled out the binoculars for a closer look. He saw two cars, a truck, a few bicyclists, three horse drawn wagons and many people on foot. They were pulling carts filled with bundles of housewares and clothing. Some men were carrying huge sacks on their backs. Three abandoned cars sat in the adjoining fields just off the road. An overturned limousine was in a ditch. One of its front tires was missing.

A burnt-out truck sat sideways in the middle of the road. The two cars, now joined by a hearse, were easing their way around the truck and the people on foot. It looked like the whole town was leaving. He shifted the binoculars to the town itself. Many buildings had been damaged. Piles of rubble lay in the streets. People were working on removing some of it. Probably looking for survivors. There was no doubt about what had happened. They had been hit by an air raid.

"I didn't know Pulawy had a military base," Josef said.

"It doesn't," Ludwik responded.

"Where do you think the people are going?" Josef asked.

"South. To where I couldn't guess," Ludwik answered.

"They're retreating. Like us. Not a pleasant sight," Josef sighed.

A bridge crossing the Vistula into Pulawy was still intact. Ludwik wondered how long it would stand. Any bridge crossing the Vistula would be critical to an invader.

He hoped if it ever came to it, the Army or Air Force would destroy all bridges crossing the Vistula and other rivers to delay any advance made by the Germans.

A large docking facility on the river lay untouched. There were railroad tracks leading into the town. Ludwik couldn't see the station, but knew it must have been the main target of the Germans. The town looked to be a major hub of transportation with the port on the river, the bridge and the railroad.

"I didn't hear any air raid sirens," Josef said.

"They've been bombed already. Probably yesterday," Ludwik observed. "Hopefully, we can get through without too much of a delay."

"We have a visitor," Josef said. He pointed past Ludwik toward the river. Ludwik turned and saw a man approaching. He was tall, well dressed and bearded. He wore a black overcoat and sported a broad brimmed hat. He was carrying a small black bag in one hand and using a long walking stick with the other. He was having some difficulty making his way across the field. He looked to be a professional of some sort. Certainly not a farmer. He waved the stick at them, took a few more steps toward the car and then collapsed. Ludwik got out of the car and ran to him. The man saw him coming and tried to stand to greet him. He managed a weak smile and apologized for not being able to greet Ludwik properly. His name was Johan Sikora. He was a doctor and was returning home from Kurow, a small village about ten miles east of Pulawy. He had gone there Friday night with his brother to deliver a baby. The delivery had been complicated and had taken most of the night to complete. They were returning to Pulawy early Saturday morning knowing that Poland had been invaded and were very anxious to get home. A few miles from Pulawy they ran into a caravan-like exodus of people streaming out of the town and clogging up the road. They were so busy dodging vehicles and pedestrians they never saw the planes drop out of the sky and come down over the road. He said they didn't even know what the commotion on the road was until the car was hit. In an instant, it was in flames and off the road in a field. He said his brother was unconscious and bleeding heavily from a head wound. He had been hit himself in one of his legs. He said he got his brother out of the car and dragged him across the field to a small stream and then hopped and crawled his way back to the car to retrieve his medical bag. On the way back to his brother, a huge explosion behind him knocked him to his knees. He saw a man flying through the air like he had been shot out of a cannon land in the field only a few feet away from him. The man wasn't bleeding but had been knocked unconscious by the blast. His own head was ringing from the blast, and he momentarily forgot where he was. Then he saw his brother and the blood seeping from his head wound. He staggered over to him and quickly wrapped the wound with a dressing pad and gauze to stop the bleeding. Then he elevated his feet up into a small bush to prevent shock. That done, he stumbled back to the other man and dragged him to the stream. There wasn't much he could do for him. He was unconscious but breathing. He said he knew his main job was to make sure his brother's bleeding was kept under control.

Suddenly, the doctor began shaking and slurring his words. He seemed to be on the verge of passing out. Both Ludwik and Josef got hold of him and dragged him to the car. Ludwik propped his back against a rear tire. Josef poured a little water on his face and made him a drink from their canteen. Ludwik wasn't comfortable sitting out in the open like this, but he didn't have much choice at the moment. The doctor was becoming a little delirious. He kept mumbling about his brother and the unconscious man he had dragged to the stream. Josef gave him a little more water and that seemed to bring him around.

"Why are so many people leaving town?" Ludwik asked.

The doctor said most of the people leaving were Jews. He said the man he dragged to the creek had regained consciousness and told him that. The man said he was one of them and was in the last group of Jews leaving Pulawy. He was on his way to catch up with his family when the bomb exploded. He said their rabbi had told everyone to leave. That Jews were being shot on the spot by the Germans. That the Germans were defeating our army quite easily and gobbling up lots of territory. Then he told everyone to pack up whatever they could and go east to put as much distance between them and the advancing Germans. Many left, including his family. Some remained. One was his brother. He had stayed to try and convince him to leave, but he had refused. He left then and was on his way to rejoin his family when the planes came.

The doctor stopped at that point. He seemed to realize that he was talking too much about something that wasn't that important anymore. He needed to be with his family. He began to shake and said, "I tried to do my best for my brother. I loved him." Then he broke down and began to sob. Ludwik and Josef knew then his brother was dead. The doctor regained his composure and said it wasn't long after the man left to rejoin his family that his brother had died. He said there wasn't much he could have done for him.

All he could do was just hold his dear brother in his lap and pray for him. When he died, he had no choice but to leave him there and try to get back to his family in Pulawy as fast as he could. Once there, his wife who was a nurse, could take care of his wound and then get some help to bring his brother home. That was the last thing he remembered before passing out.

"That was Saturday. It's Monday morning, now. What happened to Sunday?" Josef asked.

"I woke up next to my brother sometime this morning. I had been unconscious all that time. I took his overcoat off and covered him with it. Then I left. It was dark. I cut across the road and went through the fields toward the backside of Pulawy. I did not want to be on that road when daylight came. My leg was throbbing, and I knew it had become infected. It was difficult for me to walk. My plan was to get to where you are now. Then I could walk into town using the fields beside it. Then I saw you."

It took a few painful minutes to load the doctor into the front seat beside Josef. Ludwik got in the back. The doctor's home was near the end of the bridge that crossed the Vistula. That was a good thing. The area around the bridge had been left untouched. That included the doctor's home.

It was a small cottage a few hundred feet from the river. A field stone chimney on its left side was puffing a thin trail of smoke into the air. People were home and now, so was the doctor. Josef drove up the short driveway and parked a few feet from the cottage's front door. As Ludwik got out to help the doctor, he spotted a set of white curtains being parted in a window off to the chimney side of the cottage. The anxious face of a pretty young woman appeared in the open window and stared at him. He caught her eye and smiled. She did not return in kind. Her suspicion changed to euphoria as soon as Ludwik opened the car door, and the doctor gingerly swung his feet onto the driveway. A scream of joy laced with relief exploded from the woman. She was out of the cottage and beside the Volvo in seconds. Ludwik stepped aside as she leaned into the car to kiss and hug her husband. With Ludwik's help, she managed to get him on his feet. He hugged his wife and asked for the children. She turned and called for them to come. All three stormed from the cottage screaming, "Papa, Papa, Papa!" The doctor gathered them in his arms and pulled them close. He kissed each one on the head and then had them face Ludwik and Josef and said, "My children. My wife. My family. Thank you for bringing me home. Please, let me introduce them to you. This is Hugo, my oldest. He is ten. He wants to be a doctor. This is Sebastian. He is eight. He wants to be Hugo's assistant. And this is Lila. She is six and wants to be a doll maker. And this lovely lady is my wife, Stephanie, the love of my life. I do not know your names."

"I am Ludwik Skoczylas, and this is my friend, Josef Przyba. We are pilots."

The two boys came forward and shook their hands. Lila curtsied and smiled at them. The wife thanked them for her husband. She asked the two pilots to bring her husband into the back yard where there was a small garden and a picnic table with benches. She asked them if they could stay and help her treat her husband's wound. And if they did, it would be her honor to feed them. They agreed.

"Good," she said. "Now please go inside and wash your hands thoroughly. Use the sink in the kitchen. After you are done, I will do the same. We must be careful about infection."

While washing his hands, Josef remarked that the woman was strong. Ludwik said that was a plus; this was not a time for weakness. Finished washing, they stepped outside to watch the doctor.

Cleansed, the wife came out with a medical bag and a towel that covered a scalpel and forceps. Both instruments had been cleaned with an antiseptic from the medical bag. She moved with confidence and purpose. She had Josef and Ludwik help her husband to the picnic table and lie him belly down, on it. She gave Josef scissors and directed him to cut the pant leg off at the knee to expose the piece of shrapnel lodged in the doctor's calf. Then she asked both men to hold her husband down when she began the extraction.

The doctor advised his wife to make an inch incision close to one side of the shrapnel, have one of the men limit the loss of blood by blotting the flow with heavy compresses while she used the forceps to wiggle the shrapnel free. She said she understood. She handed him the towel to bite on and began. She made the incision close to the imbedded piece of metal and had Ludwik apply a compress to limit the loss of blood while she gently wiggled the metal out with the forceps. The doctor somehow managed the excruciating pain that must have caused. His body stiffened slightly through the entire procedure. It stiffened even more so after the metal was extracted and the antiseptic applied. That also caused a violent, muffled scream into the towel by the man. The wife covered the wound with compresses and had Ludwik wrap them in place with gauze and tape. When Ludwik was done, Josef helped the doctor up into a sitting position. The woman called for Hugo to bring the whiskey. The boy jogged out from the kitchen with the bottle and proudly handed it to his father. It was his part in the operation and he played it proudly.

Ludwik admired and respected both the doctor's courage and the skill his wife had shown during the procedure. He had winched with every wiggle of the forceps on the shrapnel. So had Josef. He could only imagine how painful that had to be. After Ludwik and Josef carried the doctor to his bed, they asked the wife for permission to change their clothes before they left. She had Hugo bring them their backpacks and show them to his room.

The clean fatigues felt good. Ludwik was glad to have his boots on. Returning to the doctor's bedside, Ludwik asked him if he knew a way out of Pulawy that would avoid the center of town. The doctor said there were two ways. One would bring them near the road where his brother and others had been killed. The other would take them through the woods on the far side of town. He had his wife draw a map under his direction that showed the two ways from their home. After she handed the maps to Ludwik, she said that her husband was in need of rest and it might be best if they left soon. She apologized for not feeding them and asked if they would accept some food to take. Ludwik said no apology was necessary and yes, they would accept the food.

The doctor protested. He wanted the men to stay and be fed. Josef thought he was being polite beyond reason. And then his wife told her husband exactly that. Ludwik told the doctor they had to be on their way. That every minute counted. The wounded man managed a weak smile and said protein was what they would be needing.

His wife smiled at her husband, always the doctor, went into the kitchen and brought back a few smoked sausages and some fresh bread. After handshakes, thanks and goodbyes had been exchanged, they left the family and went outside to the car. Just before they got in, they were stopped by Hugo. The young lad wanted to know if they were going to kill the man that had killed his uncle and hurt his father. He said if they weren't, he would do it when he grew up. Ludwik took the thin youngster's hands in his and told him the best thing to do now was to help his mother care for his father and be a big brother to the other two children. He told the boy that one day that German pilot would meet his end. The youngster said he hoped that day would come soon. Josef patted him on the shoulder and said it probably would.

Josef started the engine and let it run for a few minutes. He looked at Ludwik and said, "Ten years old. Already so filled with hate." He slipped the Volvo into gear and slowly made his way down to the dirt road along the river. He was on it for less than a mile before it left the river and made its way across a large expanse of farmland. The quilt-like patchwork of greens, browns and honeyed yellows on both sides of the road were beautiful to behold. Ludwik willed himself to take his eyes off the sky for a few moments every now and then to enjoy the color.

"It pains me to think we might lose all this," Ludwik said.

"It's an awful possibility," Josef answered.

Everything changed when the country road ended at the main road outside of Pulawy very near the area where the Jewish exodus from the town had been attacked by the planes. Men were everywhere. Some were near the pavement collecting the bodies of those that had been killed in the attack. Others were spread out in the fields on both sides of the road searching for bodies of those that had died there. They watched as men carried the dead to horse drawn wagons and carefully stack their bodies like bales of hay on the open, flat wagons. Some of the bodies were of small children…..little boys and little girls; not unlike the three they had just left at the doctor's home.

A burnt-out truck, pieces of carts and wagons, a disabled limo and a few dead horses had been cleared from the road to make room for the makeshift hearses. It was the artillery range all over again. This time with civilians. It was a clear sign to Ludwik that driving the open main roads had to be a last resort. He had Josef turn the car around and head back to the river to follow the doctor's map that led them into a forest and far away from the open road. It was quiet in the forest. Good road. Good cover. Unfortunately, the forest wasn't as large as they hoped for.

There was plenty of daylight left when they reached the end of it with nothing but open road as far as they could see. Ludwik took out his map and spread it out on the hood and tried to find another way. There wasn't one. They had no choice. It had to be the open road. He noted there were a few villages between where they were now and Lublin; a distance of twenty miles.

They might offer a place to hide. He also noted there was nothing in those twenty miles of any military significance; no bridges, no rail lines. That meant their only real worry would be an unlucky encounter with fighters who might use the Volvo for target practice.

"We could wait for nightfall," Josef suggested.

"Too much time wasted," Ludwik reluctantly answered.

Josef suggested they camouflage the Volvo a little more before making the run. Maybe a little wavy smear of mud on the hood and roof and place a few pieces of brush into each of the four window wells. Ludwik told him to do the mud. He would cut the brush. It took an hour.

The camouflaged Volvo, looking more like an over-sized porcupine, crept out of the forest and made its way down the dirt road and onto the main road that led to Lublin. Traffic was very light; mostly tractors and horse drawn wagons from the local farms. In fifteen minutes, they were in the village of Konskowole. Noting the gas gauge read less than a half tank, they stopped at the one inn on the main street and asked if gas was available anywhere. They were surprised to learn the Army had a small gas depot hidden under nets a few miles down the road and out in a field. The information was good but at the same time, troubling. It meant that Army vehicles would be on the road or in the area. And that meant targets for the Germans.

The depot was easy to see from the road. Almost invisible from the sky. It wasn't big. Three gas trucks and a small shack. Camouflage nets were strung over the top of everything and stretched down to the ground on two sides. One side was left open for entrance, the opposite side for exit. Very well done. The sergeant in charge was glad to help.

The village of Kurow was crowded with people. Josef had to slow considerably to avoid an excited crowd gathered in the town's small square. Many were Jews from Pulawy. Some wanted to return home. Others wanted to stay. And some, obviously the locals, wanted them all out of their village. The scene was chaotic, rife with anger, anxiety and fear. The German plan of terror was working in Kurow.

A few miles out of town, they ran into a slow-moving convoy. It wasn't big; three medium trucks filled with Polish airmen and headed in the same direction as them. They were greeted with cheers as they passed. Most of the passengers were enlisted men; probably ground crews and support personnel. Ludwik and Josef laughed at the rowdy comments that rained down on them as they went by each truck. The men in the first truck they passed wanted to know, "who shit on the car?" The second truck had an airman who leaned over the side and screamed, "It's a secret weapon!" The men in the lead truck all stood up and blew them silent kisses with no insulting remarks. Ludwik and Josef knew the silent gesture probably meant the commander of the small convoy was sitting next to the driver.

"Good to see a little humor," Josef remarked.

"Good to hear it also," Ludwik responded.

Five miles from Lublin they approached the remnants of a convoy that had been attacked. It had been headed in the opposite direction they were going. There were more than a dozen trucks littered on and off the road. Most were troop carriers. Many had been destroyed. There were a few still intact. Ludwik knew that five-gallon gas cans were sometimes strapped to a truck's undercarriage just past the rear axle. He told Josef to pull over behind one of the trucks not totally destroyed to see if it had any gas cans. He got out for a closer look. There weren't any there. He walked slowly ahead to see if any of the others had them. He spotted one truck, virtually untouched except

241

for a missing rear wheel. The carriage above the missing wheel and tire had collapsed and was resting on the road at a small angle that lifted its opposite side a few feet off the ground. He walked around to the opposite side, knelt and peered under the carriage. There were three gas cans strapped to the under carriage just past the rear axle. The farthest two were less than two feet above the road. He would have to crawl under the carriage to reach them. He waved Josef up to help. The nearest can was easily reached. Ludwik unbuckled it and slid it back to Josef. He would have to crawl under the truck a bit to reach the other two. It would be dangerous, but fifteen gallons of gas would come in handy down the road.

Ludwik cut the straps of the nearest can with his survival knife and slid the can out to Josef. He freed the last can and began to drag it out himself as he wormed his way away from the truck. He was stopped by a wide-eyed Josef scrambling on his belly to join him. Ludwik knew it had to be a plane. It was. It roared over them and streaked down the road.

"Did he see you?" Ludwik asked. Josef said he didn't think so. He had spotted the fighter coming down to make his run a long way off and thought he had enough time to get out of sight. Both men curled their legs up to their chest and waited. There wasn't anything they could do but hope and pray the German hadn't seen Josef. They waited for ten minutes. The plane never returned. Both men crawled from under the truck and scanned the sky. No planes. The German had missed Josef and apparently had decided there was nothing on the road worth wasting his ammunition on.

Not even the beat-up looking Volvo sitting sideways on the road amidst all the trucks. Ludwik took note of how the Volvo was parked and complimented Josef for making it look like it was part of the wreckage. As they loaded the gas cans onto the back seat floor, Josef said, "I wonder if the convoy we passed escaped. That plane may have come the same way."

"They were far behind us. They may have turned off the road before the plane found them," Ludwik replied.

They were just a few miles away from Lublin when they heard the faint sound of air raid sirens coming from that direction. Ludwik nudged Josef and told him to get off the main road and find something that might give them some cover. He knew there wasn't much time. Josef floored the gas pedal and the Volvo streaked ahead. A weathered wooden sign off to his right caught his attention. It read, "Private Way." Josef slipped off the road onto a small pathway and headed for whatever private place the sign meant.

The pathway widened somewhat as it made its way alongside a fenced in apple orchard that was strung out on the side of a small hill. Ludwik spotted a gate and told Josef to stop there. He said they were going to hide in the orchard. He jumped out of the car and swung the gate open. Josef drove in and followed Ludwik into the orchard. He ran three rows deep and pointed to a space between two of the apple trees. Josef slowly wedged the Volvo into the small space, got out and helped Ludwik pull the branches in the window wells out and place them on the roof, hood and trunk. Satisfied with the cover, both men grabbed their backpacks and ran uphill away from the car. They didn't want to be near it in case some German pilot got lucky and spotted it. They found a tree with thick layers of apple-laden branches to hide under and wait out what they thought might be an incoming air raid on Lublin.

The Pencil

Josef relaxed and lit a cigarette. He sat back against the skinny, gnarled trunk of the old tree and watched the smoke from his cigarette drift slowly up into the branches above. It seemed to hang in the upper parts for a time before a warm breeze sent it on its way. Just like he and Ludwik had had been doing he thought. Hanging around, waiting for whatever came along to put them in gear. Then hanging around some more. Like now. He marveled at how good they were getting at using everything nature gave them to run, hide and stay alive. It was good to be alive of course, but he wondered how long it would be before they stopped running and hiding and did some fighting. For the first time, he began to question if they were doing the right thing. He thought of the young cadet in the barracks at Deblin who had left to join the infantry and fight. He had to believe there were many others like him. They were probably fighting Germans now as he sat here hiding. He hoped that would change when they reached the rendezvous.

He tried to remember where that was, but he was too tired to think anymore. He crushed the cigarette out, rolled over to one side and tried to nap. He thought of his father in Krakow and wondered if he had left the city and gone to the mountains. He would be safe there. As old as he was, the man was in great shape and knew the outdoors better than most.

Ludwik tried to focus the binoculars on the sky around Lublin. Nothing to see. He looked at the land around the city. It was wide open with one main road headed into the city. He decided to move to a higher point on the hill for a better view. Maybe get a good look at the city itself. He turned to tell Josef he was moving up the crest but was greeted by a healthy snore from his friend. He wasn't surprised. Driving a car under these stressful conditions could exhaust anyone. Best to leave him alone and let him sleep.

He scratched out an arrow in the ground with his knife to let his friend know in what direction he had gone. Then he rose and walked quietly through the orchard toward the highest point of the hill.

The only sounds he heard on the way were the intermittent snores from Josef behind him and the muffled wail of sirens far off in the distance before him. Kind of a poetic metaphor. Back there was Josef, now a secure individual, deep in sleep and oblivious to danger. Ahead, somewhere far over the hill were frightened families, wide-eyed and fearful, death possibly just a few minutes away. The metaphor was stark. Peace and bedlam. Poland, before and after. He recalled reading a passage somewhere that had proclaimed, "Sometimes it takes the sadness that comes from a time of madness, surely to remind us that a heaven is there, waiting to be shared." As he neared the high point, he wondered if Poland's "sadness" from suffering was going to be anything like what Jesus had to endure before God brought Him home.

The last row of apple trees lined the crest up to the high point of the hill and then down the other side. He could see Lublin off in the distance. It was large. It covered a wide area of land. Not as big as Warsaw, but impressive none the less. The binoculars were excellent. Lublin was very hilly in sections. There was a medieval castle on one of the hills. It overlooked the city proper. It reminded him of the much smaller castle near his home in Mazanki. Near the castle was an extraordinarily beautiful cathedral. Its Gothic spire reached high into the sky. He wondered if it would be spared when the Germans bombed the city. It was not likely. Early reports had consistently shown there was very little concern about what their bombs landed on and even less concern for the civilian population that was affected.

Most Germans were Christians. Even Hitler was a Catholic; just like himself and most Poles. He shook his head thinking of that sad excuse for a human being attending a mass. And from what he had learned about the Nazi Reich, he knew compassion and forgiveness were not part of their vocabulary.

It looked like Lublin was a highly structured city in its layout, not unlike Warsaw. It looked to be laid out in geometric grids that contained small streets, plazas and grand avenues all leading to a large plaza, like Old Town in Warsaw. It was a city planned for efficient movement and living. There was very little traffic on the streets. Everyone was probably inside whatever air raid shelter they could find. He thought of the crowded basement in the Hotel Bristol in Warsaw where he and Josef had waited for the bombs to drop. He knew from that experience and later in Praga, where bombs had dropped, how that kind of wait could create anxiety and a paralyzing fear. He knew if the Germans were acquainted with the geometric grid system in Lublin or had pictures of Lublin's grids, it would be a disaster for the city. German bomber command would simply assign specific grids for several planes to bomb. This "grid bombing" technique would make for an efficient and deadly bombing attack. It would help to insure maximum damage over a short period of time. Very few bombs would be wasted and depending on the number of bombers sent, it would be possible to destroy most of the city in a few raids and hopefully destroy the will of the people to carry the fight back against them. Surely one of their primary goals was to do exactly that. Make the civilian population suffer. Create the pressure to surrender by inducing a "sadness that comes from an unrelenting avalanche of madness."

Ludwik wondered if the French and English would actually bomb German cities in retaliation. He wasn't sure they would take the risk of killing civilians. Bombing strategic targets in and around a city to hurt the German war effort certainly was a legitimate strategy. The killing of innocents to impose one's will on another was something different. That was disturbing to Ludwik. He hoped he wouldn't be asked to be part of anything like that. He would have to wait and see. At the moment, Germany was calling the shots. Nothing had been heard from the French and English and he had no idea if the Polish

Air Force had the strength to retaliate in kind on German cities or if they would. He had high hopes that bombers would be available in the bridgehead to attack German supply lines, troop concentrations and their bases in both Poland and Germany.

Ludwik shifted the binoculars from the city to the sky. As he focused on a large formation of clouds, the air raid sirens abruptly stopped and the "all-clear" signal went off. He hung the binocular straps around his neck and let the binoculars rest on his chest. No air raid today! Good for Lublin. Good for him and Josef. When the all-clear siren stopped, he sat down in the grass, lit a cigarette and relaxed. It was quiet here.

A warm breeze blew briskly past him and moved down through the open field below. It rippled the grass like a fast-moving wave heading for the beach. He enjoyed the soothing, warm air and the comforting whisper it made as it continued down the hillside and onto the road that led to Lublin. It was pure nature. Not spoiled by man. He didn't want to hear anything made by man just now. He needed to hear and feel God's voice. He closed his eyes and listened to Him speak in the breeze. It was perfect. Just God, nature and him. The lit end of the cigarette burned down between his fingers, the heat jarring him awake from his moment with God. He twisted the spent cigarette into the ground and made sure no grass had been singed enough to flame. It was time to get back on the road.

Josef was still lying motionless under the tree. He was sound asleep. Ludwik decided to let him rest a little longer. He would take the time to get a little practice with the binoculars before he woke him. He brought the binoculars up to his eyes and scanned the sky in the relaxed, measured pattern of movement he had been taught in flight school without binoculars. He could hear his instructor saying, "Find them FIRST before they find YOU!" If he was flying, he would just have his eyes to use, but he was on the ground now. With help.

His careful scanning of the sky turned up nothing but a few birds, probably eagles or hawks riding a thermal as they looked for prey. He kept the binoculars trained on the sky testing his arms for the strength needed to hold that position. He dropped his arms briefly to give his eyes a break from his search of the sky. Binoculars back up, he concentrated on the intermittent clouds that drifted across the sky as the Earth rotated away from them. A slight movement of something just disappearing into one of the clouds caught his eye. He shifted the binoculars to observe the other side of the cloud to see if anything exited there. He dropped his elbows directly under his hands to steady them. He waited. Then he heard something. A familiar sound. A faint drone of an engine. Far above him. There WAS a plane up there. Somewhere in the clouds. Maybe the cloud he had the binoculars trained on. It probably was a friendly. The "all clear" wouldn't have been sounded if it wasn't. Then he saw it. But just for a moment. It was black and very long. It slipped from the cloud he was watching into a short stretch of clouds nearby and then emerged out of them as it flew toward Lublin. That's when the air raid sirens sounded again. Ludwik brought his binoculars to bear on the plane and zoomed in for a closer look. It wasn't Polish! The black swastika bordered in white proved that. Somehow the plane had evaded detection by Polish spotters. It was a strange looking aircraft. It had a very long, very thin fuselage and looked to have another cockpit mounted on its right wing. It had twin tails mounted on an elongated horizontal stabilizer. Ludwik was sure he had seen a plane like this one before. Then he remembered. He had studied it while learning to fly the Air Force's light reconnaissance plane. It was a Dornier photo reconnaissance plane unique to the German Luftwaffe. It was called the "Pencil" because of its long, narrow fuselage. It had a crew of four.

Its mission was to photograph potential targets and bring back the photos for study on how the target could be bombed. The potential target here was obviously Lublin.

The anti-aircraft guns outside the city opened fire at the fast approaching "Pencil." It sounded like a thousand guns had gone into action against the lone intruder. No Polish fighters rose to meet it. It was far above their reach. It was going to be the job of the gunners on the ground to knock it from the sky. It wasn't going to be easy to do that. They would have to be experts in their craft or very lucky to score a hit on the highflyer. There was no evasive maneuvering on the part of the pilot. He was using altitude as his defense. The gunners on the ground and the people scurrying to shelters had no idea the plane was only taking pictures.

The noise from the guns reverberated across the miles of flat farmland and up into the orchard. The sky over Lublin was filled with puffy, black splotches of flak that were desperately searching for the thin skin of the Dornier. The sudden eruption of the fireworks in the sky and the wailing of sirens, distant as they were, snapped Josef out of his sleep and onto his feet.

"What's happening?" he shouted as he ran to Ludwik.

"Recon plane taking pictures of the city," Ludwik answered.

"One plane?"

"Take a look." Ludwik handed Josef the binoculars and pointed to the flak filled sky.

Josef picked up the plane immediately. "What the hell is that?" he asked.

"It's called the "Pencil," a recon plane with lots of cameras."

"Hey!" Josef yelled, "It just took a hit!"

Ludwik looked toward the city and saw smoke trailing high above it. Josef kept the binoculars fixed on the smoking aircraft. Flames were spreading out along the wings. The plane was dying.

"He's in big trouble," Josef calmly reported.

"Any parachutes?" Ludwik asked.

"Not yet. Wait. There's one!"

"Only one?" Ludwik asked.

"Yes, just the one," Josef answered.

Ludwik searched the sky over the city. The parachute was barely visible. Only the eagle eyes that he possessed could see it from this distance. It was drifting straight down into the city.

The flaming "Pencil" was now beyond the city and losing altitude. It was much easier to follow because of the thick black and white smoke that poured out from it.

"Another chute!" Josef yelled just as the plane exploded.

"One for us," he said as he watched pieces of the plane fall on the countryside.

"Just two chutes?" Ludwik asked.

"I only saw two. How many in the crew?" Josef asked.

"Four. Time to get moving," Ludwik said.

"Through the city?" Josef questioned.

Ludwik nodded. "Through the city. There won't be a raid today. They'll be waiting for the pictures."

"Good. I'm sick of hiding in the woods."

"The woods have been good to us," Ludwik reminded him.

"Sooner or later, we'll run out of woods," Josef cautioned.

Ludwik said their biggest concern now was to remember the three cans of gasoline in the car and how ironic it would be to escape the bombings in Warsaw and Praga plus the strafing at the artillery field only to blow themselves up by lighting a cigarette.

Josef laughed and said, "You're right. No medals for that."

"Let's get through the city," Ludwik urged.

In less than twenty minutes they were making their way through the city. There seemed to be some sort of celebration happening on the street they were on. Large groups of men were yelling and smiling. Some were holding mugs of beer.

They were all over the place. One young man, standing on the sidewalk and watching the crowd, was called over to the car by Ludwik and asked what was going on. The young man said they were celebrating the downing of the German plane and the capture of an airman that had parachuted from it. He said this avenue was the very one the German had landed on. Ludwik asked what had happened to him. The young man said he had been taken by the local police. He said they had probably saved the German's life by getting to him first before the crowd got their hands on him. They put him, parachute and all, into a police wagon and whisked him away. Word was he was going to be brought to an Army unit just outside the city. Ludwik asked about the other parachutist. The man had no idea there had been another one. He said there was no one here that did.

As soon as they made it out of the city and moved into the countryside, they saw several Army vehicles fanning out in earnest across the field and roads. They were all heading east. They had not missed the second parachutist. And now, the hunt was on for him.

It was going to be mostly an open road trip with several scattered small patches of woods and a few villages along the way. The town of Zamosc was the next checkpoint on Ludwik's map. Night was still a few hours away. It wouldn't pay to become complacent about day travel because the "pencil" had been shot down. A bombing raid might not be in the cards for a while, but the threat of fighters strafing targets everywhere was.

Revenge

There wasn't much traffic on the road. A few Army vehicles zipped by heading back toward Lublin and an occasional tractor lumbered off onto one of the many side country roads. They were five miles out from Lublin when they were stopped by an Army roadblock. They sat third in line behind a car and a horse-drawn hay wagon. Three soldiers were busy examining the papers of two men outside the car while another soldier watched two others stab their rifle bayonets repeatedly into the stack of hay on the wagon.

"Looking for the German," Ludwik said to Josef. "He must have come down in this area."

"His plane or what's left of it can't be too far away then," Josef added.

"How long after you saw the parachute open did the plane explode?" asked Ludwik.

"No more than three seconds. He's probably dead."

A sergeant approached the Volvo and saluted the two officers. He asked them to please step out of the car and take out their identification papers. He said it was just procedure. Two young privates with automatic weapons appeared behind the Volvo and eyed Ludwik and Josef intently. The sergeant said his orders were to check ALL persons stopped and to search each vehicle thoroughly. He said they were looking for Germans. The word "Germans" got Ludwik's attention. He asked how many Germans they were looking for. The sergeant said he wasn't sure. He knew there was at least one airman from the plane shot down and an unknown number of German saboteurs that had been dropped into this area last night. One of the saboteurs had already been captured. He was carrying explosives and dressed in a Polish Army uniform. He also spoke perfect Polish.

Satisfied with their papers and the search of the Volvo, the sergeant said they were free to move on as soon as the hay wagon had been cleared. He reminded them, with respect, to be cautious of strangers and to keep their eyes open. The stabbing of the hay pile was completed without drawing any German blood. The farmer climbed back onto his seat, flicked the reins and brought his horse back to life. Josef waited until there was room and then spurted past and flew down the road.

"What do you think?" Josef asked.

"I don't think we'll find Germans out on the open road in daylight. If they're around, they'll be up in the woods somewhere waiting for dark. Then they'll do their work. I figure the only thing out here to blow up or cut are the phone lines."

Josef nodded in agreement and accelerated down the road; eager to cover as much ground as he could before darkness arrived.

He hadn't driven far before they came to another road block; this time on the other side of the road. The soldiers on their side were signaling for them to slow as they went by. They wanted to get a good look at them. It was obvious they had heard from the other roadblock who was coming.

"We have to be very careful from here on out my friend," Ludwik said. "The war is moving closer to us. It's not just airplanes now. It's also men."

As they approached the village of Janowek, Josef suggested they stop and eat. Ludwik was hesitant, but when he saw there were no military targets for the Luftwaffe in the area, he agreed. A hot meal and a glass of beer or two sounded good to him. And Zamosc was still reachable before night fell.

The entrance to the inn was through twin ten-foot-high doors. Each was fastened to the doorway by four, very thick iron hinges. The door on the right had an iron handle located about waist high for most men. It was so well balanced it swung open with only a gentle pull from Ludwik. He was impressed with how easy it was to open such a door. He thought whoever had built and installed these doors knew what he was doing. He remembered how hard it always was to open the barn doors back home on the farm. He made a mental note that if he ever got back home, he would suggest to his father to add hinges like these.

The inn was crowded with men. The haze of cigarette and pipe smoke was thick. There was some sort of meeting going on. One man stood in front of an empty stone fireplace. He was facing a group of twelve men seated at tables in front of him. A large pitcher of beer sat on each table. There was a heated discussion going on between several of the men. Lots of yelling and cursing. It ended as soon as Ludwik and Josef walked in.

The abrupt silence did not go unnoticed by the two pilots. They knew their presence was the cause of it. They stood there for a moment, not knowing what to do. The impasse was quickly broken by the man standing in front. He walked toward them with a welcoming smile. He proudly introduced himself as the builder and owner of the finest inn south of Warsaw. He said with much enthusiasm that he was happy to welcome two members of our "proud and brave military." On que, with a polite, "Na drowia," all the men raised their glasses to salute the two newcomers. The owner led them to a table up front, had two beers brought in and invited them to join in the discussion. He said an opinion from the military would be a welcome help in solving a problem they had.

Josef said he didn't know how they could contribute anything about a local issue unless it had to do with a widowed woman who was looking for some companionship. He laughed at his attempt to make a joke and hoped it would lighten the mood in the room. It didn't. It was met with an uncomfortable silence and some shuffling of bodies and feet. No one was smiling. The owner approached Josef and said, "Actually, we were talking about a widow who had just become one today. We have the man who killed her husband. The discussion was about what to do with him. Your input as airmen would be most welcome."

"Why is that?" Ludwik asked.

"Because he is a German!" someone shouted.

Both Ludwik and Josef were stunned. They had the parachutist! Ludwik gathered himself and asked where the man was.

"Downstairs in the wine cellar with the other rats!" another voice shouted.

"What happened, sir?" Ludwik asked the owner.

"He was hiding in woods near the dead man's farm when the dogs caught his scent. They made a commotion. That drew the farmer and two of his workers. They went into the woods to investigate. They found a parachute and quickly after that, the German. He had crawled into a woodsman's lean-to for cover. When they went to grab him, he shot the farmer dead. The workers jumped on the lean-to and collapsed it on him. That knocked him unconscious. They tied him with their belts. One stayed to guard him with the German's pistol, the other came to us for help. And so, here we are. Your thoughts?"

"He's a prisoner of war now," Ludwik said.

He's our prisoner," a man shouted. "He's a murderer like the rest of the animals that are killing our people."

"So, there is our dilemma," the owner put in. "What do we do with this man? He showed no mercy to Krasinski. Shot him like he was a wild boar. A few here would like to hang him."

"He might have some information we can use," Josef counseled.

The owner nodded his head and said, "I understand that, but we're not going to do anything right now. I would like you to consider our dilemma after you eat. You did stop here to eat, didn't you? You eat while we continue our little debate. We'll talk when you finish."

"I would like to see the prisoner," Ludwik said.

"After you eat. He's locked away and I have the keys."

The food was excellent; schnitzel, a potato salad and kapusta. Ludwik and Josef didn't waste much time eating. They wanted to see the German. From the conversation they overheard while eating, it appeared the majority, including the owner, named Piotr, wanted the prisoner turned over to the military. Three men were opposed.

They wanted revenge. The owner tried to do his best to mediate the arguments. He didn't want any more violence. He wanted to keep tempers in check until Ludwik and Josef had a chance to talk to everyone. When their meal was finished, Ludwik asked to see the prisoner then bring him upstairs for questioning. He asked if anyone spoke German. One man said he did. He agreed to translate. Piotr asked the men if they approved bringing the German upstairs. All but the three looking for revenge did.

The narrow, cob-webbed, stone wine cellar was cold and very dark. In a side room, Piotr's flashlight beam caught a large rat disappearing into a dark hole near the lifeless looking body of the German lying on the dirt floor. He was gagged and bound hand and foot with two wide leather belts. He stirred when the beam of light shifted to his face. Then his eyes opened wide with fear. Ludwik and Josef picked him up and carried him out into the main cellar and sat him in the light on the bottom step of the stairs. Ludwik took the oily rag out of his mouth and asked Piotr if he would bring some water down for the man to drink. An angry chorus of voices followed the owner into the kitchen and back to the stairs. They wanted to know if the airmen were going to take "their" prisoner. Piotr assured them no decision had been made.

The German was young. Somewhere in his early twenties. He looked very frail in his torn and filthy uniform. There were pilot wings stitched onto his flight jacket. Ludwik knew this man would have lots of useful information the Polish Command would love to have.

The pilot spoke no Polish. Ludwik knew some German, but not enough to conduct a conversation of any length. He would have to convince the men upstairs, with the help of the one who would translate, that this man was a valuable source of information and needed to be questioned by the military. The young pilot saw the pilot wings on Ludwik's fatigue jacket.

A glimmer of hope sprang into his eyes. He knew the civilians wanted to kill him. Ludwik tipped the cup of water into his mouth and had him drink. That brought the man's eyes to life even more. Finished drinking, he looked at Ludwik and said, "danke." Ludwik and Josef lifted him off the stairs and carried him up into the dining hall. They sat him on a chair next to the fireplace. All eyes in the room were fixed on the German; the man that had killed their friend and neighbor. It was too much for one of them. He leapt to his feet and charged the bound prisoner. Piotr stepped in front of him with his rather large bulk and blocked his way. Holding the irate farmer in place he said, "Let the officers talk to you. To all of us."

Ludwik took a step forward and watched the man return to his table. He asked everyone to let reason dictate their action. He said the prisoner would be punished. He would be placed in a proper jail or camp after he had been interrogated. He said a German pilot, like this one, was privy to important information that would go a long way in defending this part of Poland. He asked if any of them knew how the war was really going. He said he wasn't sure himself and he was in the military. He asked if anyone knew that German saboteurs had been parachuted into this region who spoke perfect Polish and if they also knew why this man was flying over this area without dropping bombs. He said the German had information on these matters and many others. And this was the reason he should be kept alive as a prisoner of war. Before he could say another word, the sound of a table being scraped loudly across the wooden floor caught everyone's attention. A man slowly stood up behind the table. He was huge. All eyes went to him. Ludwik didn't remember him being there before. He was a new arrival. The man walked slowly to the side of the tables and turned toward Ludwik at the front. Keeping his eyes on Ludwik, he slowly walked toward him. No one made a move to stop him. Not even Piotr, himself a large individual. Ludwik had the feeling that everyone in the room knew this man and feared him.

The big man stopped a few feet in front of Ludwik. Ludwik stood his ground and waited. The big man looked Ludwik straight in the eye and asked in a very polite and calm manner, "And if this man killed your brother?"

Before Ludwik could answer, the big man pulled a revolver out of his coat pocket and aimed it directly at him. Ludwik didn't move. Everyone in the room froze.

"I am Felix Krasinski. This German killed my brother. I will show you what this brother will do." In one swift movement, he turned the gun on the prisoner and aimed at his head.

The German screamed, "Bitte, nein, nein, meine mutter, bitte!"

The bullet entered the side of his head next to the right eye. He was dead before the chair and his body hit the floor. The big man looked coldly at Ludwik and Josef and said, "He will not be the last German I kill. They may kill me someday, but before they do, they will pay for this war and my brother's death." Then he turned and quietly walked back to the tall doors, opened one and stepped out into the night.

Everyone was stunned by the killing and the nonchalance of the big man. No one said a word. They just stood there and stared at the stream of dark, red blood that ran along the floor and spilled down onto the stairway that led to the cellar. Piotr broke the silence and suggested quietly they bury the German. He looked to Ludwik and Josef for approval. Ludwik nodded and said they should strip the man of all his clothing except for his undergarments. The clothes and anything they found in them should be brought to the Army for inspection. They had experts who knew how to extract information from the least bit of clothing. Josef added it might be a good idea to examine the lean-to in the woods for anything the German may have hidden there. He said anything they found, including the parachute, should be brought to the Army.

"How do we explain the German's death?" Piotr asked.

"That would be up to you," Ludwik answered.

They drove in silence for a half hour in the dark. Both men were using the quiet to process what had happened. Then Josef broke the silence.

"What are your thoughts on all of this, Ludwik?"

"Believe it or not, I was thinking how young that pilot was and how quickly his life ended. I will never forget his cries for his mother."

"What did he say?" Josef asked.

He said, "Please, no, no. My Mother, please."

"Dear God," Josef sighed. "Let this war be short. Let our friends from France and England get into it."

Ludwik agreed and added, "It might take them a while. Just get those planes into Romania. That'll be a good start."

Five miles from Zamosc, they nearly rear-ended an Army truck in the darkness. It was the end vehicle in a convoy. Josef tried to pass it and the others ahead of him but was cut off by the truck driver who moved over to block his effort.

"We're going to have to be patient," Ludwik observed. "I don't think the Germans will pick up the convoy in the darkness, but if being here looks to be dangerous, we can always pull over and let them go on."

The one muddied headlight of the Volvo was a bit brighter than the running lights of the truck in front of them. That was encouraging. It would be hard to see them from the air. The first time the convoy slowed to make a right turn in a bend of the road, Ludwik leaned out the window to count the number of trucks by watching their brake lights. After a few bends to the right, he estimated there were some twelve trucks in the convoy. He cautioned Josef to maintain a good distance from the truck in front of them and keep his eyes open. A few miles down the road, the truck in front of them braked to make a sharp turn. Ludwik spotted the Army scouts that were directing them. They were waving lens covered flashlights. When the scouts caught sight of the Volvo, they jumped in front of it with their automatic weapons aimed directly at them. Shouts of "HALT" rang out. One scout put the nose of his machine pistol a foot away from Josef's head and screamed for him to stop or die! Josef stopped the car right there.

"What the hell are you two doing at the back of this convoy?" the corporal with the machine pistol asked. Someone else yelled, "Get them out of the damn car!"

Showing their I.D.s, they explained they were heading for the Romanian border. That satisfied the scout commander who had driven back to the main road to see what was going on. He asked Ludwik where their rendezvous point was. Ludwik said Stanislawow via Lwow. The commander said his convoy would be bringing airmen arriving on their own to Lwow where they would be trucked to one of the temporary bases near the border. He said he had no idea where those bases were at the moment. His job was to get as many men as he could to Lwow. The lieutenant recommended they drive past Zamosc tonight and get to Lubelski, some fifteen miles farther south. The town was close to a huge forest that had a road running through it. He suggested they take that road to avoid the mass movement of troops that was coming north on the main roads. He said there were villages along the road where they could get a good night's rest and some decent food. When Josef asked how the fighting was going, the lieutenant replied, "Not well." Ludwik asked if the Polish forces had slowed the German progress.

The commander smiled weakly and said, "If you consider holding them to thirty miles a day slow, then you might say we are holding them."

"How about our planes?" Ludwik asked.

"I haven't seen many. Have you?" the lieutenant shot back.

Ludwik shook his head no then said, "Good luck getting our pilots and ground crews to the bridgehead." He shook hands with the scout as Josef put the Volvo into gear and began to drive off.

"Remember to get off the road at Lubelski," the scout shouted.

Ludwik and Josef had never been to Zamosc. Both had flown over it during their training at Deblin and knew what it looked like thousands of feet over it during the day. The September moon, now clear of an overcast sky, gave them a fairly good view of the blacked-out city. It was similar in many respects to Warsaw and Lublin. It had a definite "renaissance" feel. It had an Old Town surrounded by tenements which stood on arcades of stone arches that one could drive into and out of the square. Like Warsaw, it had an open area reserved for dining and dancing, but tonight it was empty. No tables, no candles, no music.

The Old Man

Civilian traffic was being separated from military traffic in the square. The Volvo and its two passengers were marshalled out of the square via one of the many archways and sent on its way out of the city. As they left, a message describing the black Volvo with one muddied headlight and two pilots in it was radioed ahead to the remaining checkpoints in the city to facilitate their passage. Three more checkpoints later, Ludwik and Josef were out of Zamosc.

In short order, they passed, without incident, the towns of Kalinowice, Jatutov, Labunki and Krynice. Turning right at Tarmawata Lubelski, they entered the forest road recommended by the scout and headed toward the village of Pasieki. It was now late in the evening. They discussed their options for the night as they drove slowly through the woods. After passing Pasieki and a few more small villages, they decided it might be best to get some sleep in a place that had an inn. They stopped in the small village of Rozaniecka. There were a few dim lights visible. No one was about. They parked the Volvo in the small plaza in the center and got out to look for an inn. There were none. Coming back to the car, they saw an old man sitting on a bench in front of a small store. He was staring at them. They went over and asked him if there was a place to stay in the village. He said no, but there was a cottage in the woods not far away. It was owned by a family from Warsaw. They came for the summer only and had left a few weeks ago. His nephew, Demietrius, had been hired by the family to be the caretaker in their absence. Unfortunately, he had died last week. The old man suggested they sleep in the cottage. He would give them directions. Josef and Ludwik were surprised by the offer. They were curious as to why the man would do this for them. Josef asked him.

"I am old. I cannot fight. You are both young. You can fight. And you must. It is the least I can do for Poland."

The key was exactly where the old man said it would be. Taped flat under the bird feeder standing in front of the large bay window. They entered the cottage and lit the candle the old man said would be on the first table to the right in the short entrance way. The cottage was bigger than they expected. It was clean, roomy and well furnished. Up to date appliances sat in a large kitchen. There was a radio. Each of the four rooms had expensive wooden floors. The bathroom had a large tub and shower. Blue and white tiles covered its walls from floor to ceiling.

A huge, stone fireplace serviced both the long parlor that had the bay window and what had to be the master bedroom on the other side of it. Whoever owned this place had to be extremely wealthy.

"If I were the owners, I would do my best to get out of Warsaw and get down here," Josef said to Ludwik.

"I hope they can. This place is far enough away from targets the Luftwaffe might attack," Ludwik offered.

"It might even be far enough away to sit out the war," Josef wished out loud. Ludwik reminded him that the scout had said the Germans had made great gains into Poland already. And if that were true, they would be here soon. That grim reminder tempered Josef's wish.

The cottage was cold. Ludwik closed the drapes across the bay window, opened the flue in the fireplace, and covered the long andirons with a pile of kindling from the kindling box. The kindling was dry and burst into a bright flame quickly. The split logs placed on the andirons ignited quickly as well. The crackling blaze grew in size and warmth and brought life into the cottage. Ludwik went into the master bedroom to see if the bed had a duvet. It did. Feeling uncomfortable about sleeping in someone's bed, he had Josef help him carry the heavy duvet into the parlor. It was unlike any of the ones that he had slept under growing up on the farm in Mazanki. Those were handmade ones filled with goose down and chicken feathers, mostly chicken feathers. He remembered being pierced in the buttocks one night by a sturdy quill. This duvet was store bought and filled with goose down. They placed it atop the thick carpet rug in front of the fireplace. It was big enough for both to get under and enjoy its warmth. They unlaced their boots, stripped down to their undergarments and socks and folded their fatigues neatly alongside their boots that were within an arm's reach of the duvet. The warmth and sweet smell of the heavy duvet and the soothing, gentle popping of the logs burning was a beautiful thing. It had been another long day. Good to be off one's feet. For a few minutes before sleeping, Ludwik forgot about the war and why he was here, in a stranger's home, in the middle of a forest he had never been to before. He knew he would be up in a few hours but didn't care about that or anything else. He was glad to be here. To be warm. To be safe. To be thankful. And to remember there was always something to be thankful for, no matter the situation. Just recognize it for what it was. Analyze the reasons for it. Then do what you can in the time that you have to deal with it.

His watch read 03:30 A.M. He had slept for four hours. The fire had almost gone out. Slipping out from under the duvet, Ludwik went to the stack of split logs next to the fireplace, brought two back and put them on the andirons.

He stoked the warm remnants from the earlier fire and coaxed a small flame out of them. It curled its way up hungrily toward the fresh logs. After adding a little kindling under the logs, he had a full blaze going that heated the parlor once again. Satisfied, he put his pants on and lit the candle he had used to explore the cottage. He went into the kitchen and looked at the radio. It was a battery run American Philco, one that was called a "farm radio." He turned the volume knob down all the way then switched the radio on. Turning it around, he saw the glow of the tubes through the perforations in the back cover. It was working. Turning the volume up slowly, he heard the scratchy static all radios made as one dialed his way to a voice. He wished there was one broadcasting now but knew there was no chance for that at this hour. Radio stations wouldn't be transmitting until after dawn. That made him think that sleeping here the rest of the night and staying the day tomorrow might be a good idea. He could listen to the radio and find out how the war was going. He'd have time to check out the condition of the car. It would also be a complete day of rest for both of them. With luck, they might be able to drive all the way to Stanislawow

265

tomorrow night. The more he thought about it, the more sense it made. He looked back into the parlor to see if Josef had come out of hibernation. All he could see was the back of his head. He was having a good sleep.

He was glad that Josef and he were together. "Two heads are better than one," the saying went. Sleeping long tonight and resting tomorrow was the smart thing to do. He turned off the radio, blew out the candle and walked back to the fireplace. He would talk with Josef in the morning about an extended stay and see how he felt about it. Josef was very happy to stay the day and rest up for the final leg to the bridgehead tonight. He took charge of getting a fire going in the wood burning, iron stove while Ludwik searched the kitchen pantry for food. It was full. The old man's nephew had stocked up enough food for the fall and well into the winter. There would not be any problem eating today. There were two crates of packaged food items on the floor of the pantry. One shelf above the floor along a wall held several tins of coffee, tea, sugar and flour. A second shelf held boxes of English biscuits, assorted Polish candies, spices and several jars of jam. Josef found jars of butter, eggs, radishes, potatoes, carrots and a dozen jars of canned peaches in the American General Electric refrigerator. All in good condition. Ludwik prepared breakfast. He boiled six eggs, cut each in half, scooped out the solid egg yolk, mixed in a little mustard and a few spices until the yoke turned into a yellow, brownish paste. He refilled the twelve empty egg halves with the sharp-tasting yoke and sprinkled each with a trace of paprika. Josef made the coffee very strong. Both men drank it black. Josef added half a tea spoon of sugar. They ate slowly, enjoying each morsel of the stuffed eggs. They were especially tasty. Josef was impressed by Ludwik's touch with the eggs. This was going to be good, he thought; a leisurely breakfast, a cigarette or two, maybe a nice lunch and an afternoon with a nap and no pressure of having to get somewhere. "Potato pancakes for lunch," said Ludwik.

"Sounds good to me," Josef chimed in. "Maybe we can crack open a little chocolate for dessert. Maybe have some of those expensive English biscuits stacked in the pantry."

Ludwik barely heard the chocolate and biscuit suggestion from Josef. His mind had wandered in another direction. He was thinking it might be a good idea to leave a note of thanks to the owners with some money to pay for the night's stay and the food they were taking. He asked Josef what he thought about the idea.

"That might get the old man in trouble," Josef offered.

"You're probably right. Just felt it would be nice to show our gratitude."

Josef agreed. They had gotten a great night's sleep, raided the pantry and refrigerator for breakfast and lunch, had a nice hideaway for the day that kept them off the roads with the Army convoys and the ever-present German Luftwaffe. They had much to be grateful for.

"Maybe the right thing to do would be to leave some money with the old man," Josef suggested.

"Good thought, my friend. We'll try to find him on the way out."

Breakfast had been good. Josef loved the eggs. He said they were almost like the way his father made them every Easter. Ludwik poured a second cup of coffee and took it outside. Josef joined him. There was a bench in front of the woods off to the side of the cottage. They couldn't see the forest road from there. And that meant anyone on the road would not be able to see the cottage. It was a comfortable feeling to be out of sight. Today was a day to enjoy the sun and the silence of the woods.

"I am going to enjoy this day," Ludwik said.

Josef got the message. His friend needed some space. He got up and went inside the cottage to try and find some news on the radio.

The clear sound of the "Mazurek Dabrowskiego" from the radio brought Ludwik to his feet in front of the bench. He stood at attention without thinking. When he realized where he was, he relaxed, but continued to stand as the anthem played. The recording was a mellow rendition of his country's proud and historic past. It fit perfectly into the quiet forest setting and the relaxed mood he was experiencing. He had always been moved by the stirring, patriotic words of the anthem. Especially the verse that was so appropriate for the day:

"Poland has not yet perished, so long as we live

What the alien force has taken from us

We shall retrieve with a saber."

He mouthed the words in silence as he listened to them drift from the cottage into the woods. They were strong words; words that gave him a sense of pride, patriotism, honor and duty. He thought back to the day when he first began to feel like a patriot. It had come on his first day at the Naval Academy. He remembered standing at attention with his fellow plebes on the school's parade ground and watching the "colors" brought down for the evening by an honor guard. He remembered how the flag landed in their hands just as the bugler finished; how precise and professional they were in wrapping the white and red of their country. So impressive! Each man moving with care and respect for the flag and what it represented. The pride he felt in being Polish was never greater than that moment. He knew then, as he did now, that he would die for his country if he had to.

As the anthem ended, an announcement was made that an update on the war was about to be given. Ludwik quickly made his way into the cottage to hear it. Josef was leaning on the counter by the radio and listening intently. Someone from the mayor's office in Warsaw began by saying Polish forces were heavily engaged with the enemy all along the western front and they were inflicting heavy casualties on the German attackers. He said a few cities, including Warsaw, had been bombed, but the damage had been minimal. He closed his battle report on by saying the military garrison on the Hel peninsula was bravely holding out against a very large German force that was attacking them from both sea and land. He asked the civilian population to hold fast in their homes and not jam the roads and hinder the movement of our military. He urged all able-bodied men to volunteer to help build anti-tank barricades in the suburbs of Warsaw and in Warsaw proper. He said the government had been in contact with the French and English governments and that military action by them against the Germans would be forthcoming soon. He proudly stated the Polish government was still running and all government officials were still in Warsaw. He urged all Poles to remain steadfast in their defense of Warsaw and other parts of the country. He finished the broadcast by asking everyone to stay tuned to the station for future updates. The station then cut to a loud, marching rendition of the "Mazurek Dabrowskiego." When the anthem ended, so did the broadcast.

"I don't think they are reporting all the facts," Ludwik said. "I really would like to know what the casualties are and how the air force is doing."

"And just how far away the Germans are," Josef said.

Ludwik gave the Volvo a thorough going over from front to back to make sure it was ready for the next leg. He checked the oil and battery, looked for any loose wires in the engine, checked all the clamps and hoses, felt the tires including the spare, worked the windshield wiper and added a little water to the radiator.

After a discussion with Josef, Ludwik decided to clean off the mud on the working headlight and create the appearance of a lone motorcyclist zipping down the highway in the dark and hopefully becoming an unworthy target for a German pilot.

While Ludwik worked on the Volvo, Josef foraged the pantry for the ingredients and tools for the potato pancake lunch/supper. It took both an hour to wash and grate the potatoes into thin strings before adding them to the chopped onions, butter and flour. A little water and a firm mixing gave Ludwik the pasty mix he needed to knead them into the pancakes he would fry in the skillets Josef had found tucked away behind a curtain at the end of the pantry. While Ludwik did the mixing, Josef restarted a fire in the stove. Butter was melted in a large skillet and the salted potato/onion mix was spooned out into it forming the first of a dozen good sized potato pancakes. Josef ate the first three hot out of the skillet, switched places with Ludwik and flipped the next three to him. What was left of the mix was tuned into smaller pancakes and stored in the ice box for their supper; a nice addition to the fancy chocolates and English biscuits Josef had successfully lobbied for.

After cleaning everything they had used, they made sure the fireplace ashes were completely dead, returned the duvet to the master bedroom and put everything back where they had found them. They saved the key for last. It would be taped under the bird feeder just before they left. The rest of the afternoon was spent taking turns enjoying a cleansing bath, washing some clothes in the sink and drying them in the sun. They kept the radio on all afternoon hoping to hear an update on the war but heard nothing but static all afternoon. Hours later, when the forest started to come alive with the sounds of approaching night, they ate the rest of Ludwik's pancakes and a few of the English biscuits. The key was carefully taped under the bird feeder, and they were off to the village before full night arrived. They had an old man to thank.

He wasn't on the bench in front of the small store. A few women carrying water walked slowly by the Volvo on their way to wherever they lived. Two men came out of the store, sat on its front steps and lit their pipes. Ludwik leaned out the window and asked if they knew the old man whose nephew was the former caretaker of the cottage in the woods owned by the family from Warsaw. Both men laughed. One said there was only one cottage in the woods, and it wasn't owned by a family from Warsaw. Ludwik said he had been told that by an old man in front of the store last night. He described the man to them. One of them chuckled and said the old man was the owner of the cottage and that he came into town occasionally to talk with some of his deceased wife's friends when they came to draw water. He had been doing that for some time now.

"Another mystery. Like the voice in the mist and the woman in the meadow with her dog and sheep," Josef said.

Ludwik got out of the car and walked over to the two men. He asked them to thank the old man for giving them a night's stay in the cottage. The men looked at each other in surprise. They both knew the old man never let anyone near his place. They told Ludwik that.

When they passed the road that led to the cottage, Ludwik said, "I wonder why that old man let us use the cottage and never let anyone else come near it."

"He said he wanted us to rest and be ready to fight," Josef said.

Ludwik said nothing. He was trying to piece together what the past few days had brought and what they might mean. They had been strange: the old man and his offer, the execution of the German pilot, a voice in the mist saying, "I am with you," watching a plane try to kill a shepherdess for no good reason and the tingling sensations he had experienced with the voice and the shepherdess in the meadow.

He was beginning to think they were not alone on this trip, that someone, something was with them.

"We have been very lucky on this trip. I'm beginning to think that someone is watching over us. Just think about how fortunate we have been," he said to Josef.

Josef wasn't sure if Ludwik was jesting or serious. They had over a hundred and fifty miles to go with only one headlight. He had to pay attention to his driving. He didn't respond to Ludwik's thoughts but didn't dismiss them either. He didn't have the faith and reverence for his religion like his friend did. He wasn't sure if anyone in heaven ever heard any of his prayers. And yet, he did remember praying hard that the damaged Volvo would hold together. And so far, it had.

Stanislawow

It took more than five hours to drive the one hundred and fifty miles to Stanislawow. Traffic was light in their direction; heavy going the opposite way. Lots of trucks loaded with infantry headed north toward Lublin. Ludwik wondered if it was just going to be the Air Force in their part of the bridgehead. He knew if there was a large Army contingent there, it might mean the Germans were close. He couldn't worry about that right now. If things went well, he would be one of the pilots being sent into Romania to fly a plane back into Poland. The two shipments of warplanes were supposed to be the first of many sent by the two allies. He figured the planes would be on their way soon. At least, he hoped so.

Stanislawow was blacked out. Nothing to see from their perch on the hilly road. They had been traveling up and down hills for the past hour. It seemed the whole area leading into town was hilly and heavily forested. It was two thirty in the morning. They were tired.

"Let's get into the woods and sleep until morning. I don't want to be driving anywhere near our men in the dark. The guards will be jumpy about those Polish speaking German paratroopers being dropped behind the lines. And we don't know the password for tonight. Better we wait," Ludwik counseled.

"Good idea. We can drive into town early and see if we can find any of our friends who fly airplanes," Josef added.

"My guess is our men will be set up outside the town somewhere in one of the forests. We'll eat the biscuits in the morning and then drive in and find them," Ludwik said.

Josef took the one blanket for cover. He stretched out on the front seat as best he could, the car keys safely tucked away in his field jacket. Ludwik unrolled his dress jacket for his blanket. He slept on the back seat. Both men were up before dawn. They ate the chocolate laden English biscuits and waited for the sun.

The town looked peaceful enough. It was situated before one of the many foothills of the Carpathian Mountains that loomed majestically far off to the south. Beyond the mountains was Romania. And somewhere in Romania there were the airfields that the French and English planes would be brought to. Ludwik began to feel excited. They were nearing the place where he might finally be able to do something for his country. His time to contribute was close now. He thought about Bodil's last words when she left him in Warsaw, "Be strong. Fly for us and our Poland. And may God be with you."

Their first task was to look for military personnel in the town or ask someone from the town if they knew the whereabouts of any military. As it turned out, they had no problem finding them. They were everywhere. A mess hall of sorts had been set up on a narrow, cobblestoned alley between a store and a hotel. A line of soldiers was shuffling, half asleep, down the alley toward their breakfast.

273

The smell of strong coffee, baked bread and porridge was enough of an inducement to park the Volvo and join the line. They had no mess kits, but a plate, fork and cup were foraged from the hotel's kitchen for each of them. In between eating and enjoying their hot coffee, they learned from the men that all arriving airmen were being sent to airfields south of town. They said they had only been here for a few days and that Ludwik and Josef were the first two pilots that had arrived. The private collecting the plates, cups and utensils used by Ludwik and Josef said his platoon leader had invited them to join him in the hotel dining room for a briefing on the day's agenda.

Lieutenant Zdzislaw greeted Ludwik and Josef with a smart salute and firm handshake. Learning their names, the tall, baby-faced lieutenant introduced them to three other junior officers finishing their breakfast coffee. All three stood in respect for the two airmen. They came forward and shook each man's hand and welcomed them to the "Romanian bridgehead." The officers looked at Ludwik and Josef with interest. They were the first two airmen they had seen since reporting to Stanislawow. Their assignment was to get pilots like them, their crews, and ground maintenance personnel, safely to airfields near the Romanian border. All other Air Force personnel were going to airfields and supply depots closer to Stanislawow to help the Army prepare defensive positions. Some would be assigned to help in the delivery of fuel and ammunition. Others would help in the construction of field hospitals.

Zdzislaw said the number of Air Force personnel on their way to the bridgehead was in the thousands. That hit Ludwik hard. It meant the war was not going well for the Polish Air Force. The somber moment was interrupted by a sergeant and private entering the dining room. The sergeant had maps and a dispatch. The private had fresh coffee.

Zdzislaw read the dispatch aloud. It said a convoy of trucks was expected to arrive around 1500 hours today. In it were maintenance crews, reserve pilots, support groups, medical people and their wounded. He said the priority was to have the wounded moved to field hospitals ASAP so they could be properly treated. He said the reserve pilots in the convoy were bomber pilots. They had not been put into action up north because there were no planes for them to fly. Along with bomber crews and ground maintenance personnel, they were to be escorted to an airfield close to the Romanian border. He suggested Ludwik and Josef join that convoy. He also said that cadet flyers from Deblin were expected to be trucked here in the next few days. Some would report to the same field as Ludwik and Josef were going to. Others would be joining instructors from the many civilian flying schools in the southern part of Poland at a different airfield. Instructors and some of their students would probably be trickling in on their own. Like Ludwik and Josef had. Ludwik asked the officers where the airfields were located. Zdzislaw said airfields were being set up south and east of the city. It had taken some time to find areas that had enough flat land to handle the landings and takeoffs. He said all airfields were on grass and next to woods. Tents would be erected in the woods for the men and space in the woods was being created for vehicles. Planes were to be left out in the open under camouflage netting. One of the other junior officers said one airfield was located east of the Dniester River. His battalion was setting up defensive positions near there. Another airfield was south of Stanislawow, close to the mountains.

That was the one the first convoy would be sent to. He said Army units had been set north to reinforce the outer perimeter of the bridgehead. That line was located south and east of the San River. It would serve as the first line of defense for the bridgehead area. Zdzislaw ended the meeting by giving the two pilots directions to the convoy assembly area and told them to wait there for their convoy.

Romanian Border

Ludwik and Josef enjoyed another cup of coffee and spent some time familiarizing themselves with the map of southern Poland. Its detail was much better than the Deblin map and Karl's old one; God rest his soul.

There were eight trucks and four cars, including theirs, in the convoy. Two Army scout cars led the vehicles on what was supposed to be a relativity short trip south toward the mountains and a grass airfield that had been set up next to one of the hundreds of small forests that dotted the land there.

There were very few farms along the way. Ludwik could only guess that this was a region with poor soil. The land was flat; good for planes to land and take off on. It was beautiful country. Josef said it reminded him of the area close to the mountains south of Krakow. The same area that he and his father had spent so much time hiking, fishing and hunting in. He said that sub-Carpathian Poland had the potential to be a great tourist attraction; that many resorts, retreats and spas had been built there. Some were high in the mountains. Others were in the passes that connected Poland to Hungary and Romania. He hoped the airfield they were headed to would be close to a pass that led to Romania. He said the passes into Hungary were not very auto friendly.

Their conversation shifted to the three dozen reserve pilots in the convoy. With the arrival of the Deblin convoy in a few more days, the number of pilots and trained cadets would be over a hundred. They hoped the number of planes arriving in Romania would match or exceed the number of pilots and crews waiting along the border for them. That would guarantee them an assignment and finally get them into the action.

It was a bright, sunny day. The convoy had been on the road for an hour. The mountains stood majestically on the horizon. Waiting for them. Ludwik studied the notes he had made while reading Lieutenant's Zdzislaw's map. Romania wasn't on it. No idea where the planes would be. They might be somewhere near the ports where they were to be unloaded or a spot close to the border with Poland. He was musing the possibilities when the Heinkel zoomed over the convoy. It wasn't firing its weapons. The scouts leading the convoy split off in opposite directions across fields and sped toward wooded areas. Ludwik knew the Volvo would never make it. He yelled for Josef to pull off the road and run for it. He grabbed both backpacks and bolted out of the car running as fast as he could into some tall grass. Josef was somewhere on the other side of the road. Men were running into the fields from their vehicles all along the convoy. The scout cars had disappeared.

The Heinkel's pilot came back over the road and began dropping leaflets on the vehicles. He finished his pass, gained altitude and flew off. Ludwik sat in the field and thanked God and the Blessed Mother for their good fortune. The plane could have done some serious damage to the small convoy of trucks and cars. It was obviously on a propaganda mission. Ludwik guessed the crew had probably dropped leaflets on Stanislawow and happened onto their convoy by chance while doing some reconnaissance. It was a chilly reminder that there was no safe place in Poland whatsoever now. The Luftwaffe was everywhere.

Ludwik watched the men run back to their vehicles from both sides of the road. He spotted Josef approaching the Volvo. He watched him pat the hood, look up at the sky and blow a kiss toward the heavens. Ludwik liked his sense of gratitude. It was well placed. He made a quick scan of the sky before running back to the car. It was empty. No artillery range trick today. Both Ludwik and Josef scooped up as many leaflets as they could before jumping into the car.

Men were climbing back into their vehicles with a lot of energy; everyone very anxious to be on their way. No one wanted to be sitting out in the open any longer than they had to. Everyone knew their position must have been radioed back to German command, wherever that was and a flight of fighters was probably on the way. The two scout vehicles were back on the road. One took off to look for any other possible trouble ahead on their route. The other waited for the trucks and cars to reload. That done, the convoy departed and sped down the road.

Josef asked Ludwik what was on the leaflets. Ludwik said it had to be some sort of propaganda, but he didn't want to read anything yet. He was keeping his eyes open for planes. He said he thought the field had to be close. If it wasn't, the scouts would have them hiding in the woods in anticipation of an air attack. He was right. A few minutes later, the convoy slowed, turned off the road and lumbered across a wide, flat, grassy field toward a wood line. Josef said this had to be the temporary field. It was perfect for takeoffs and landings. As they neared the woods, Ludwik saw two planes off to his right under camouflaged netting. They were civilian sport flyers. A hundred yards out from the woods, a large section of netting in the wood line was suddenly hoisted in the air allowing all vehicles to enter a clearing among the trees. After the last car had entered, the netting was dropped back down, and the convoy effectively disappeared from sight. All vehicles were quickly covered with netting to avoid detection from the air.

The message was predictable on the leaflets. They all read, "The most important thing about war is to survive it. Continue your hopeless resistance and you will DIE. Surrender and you will LIVE!" Josef laughed and said he needed to take a shit. He grabbed a few of the leaflets and told Ludwik he was going to enjoy wiping his ass with them.

The number of men scattered among the trees had to be close to a hundred. Most were Air Force personnel. Some were Army. The soldiers were from the same battalion as the scouts. They were going to provide security for the area. The only vehicles in the woods were the twelve from the convoy plus a water wagon, two supply trucks and a communication trailer. Ludwik later learned that a fuel depot had been started a half mile or so down the wood line to their left and an ammunition depot begun about the same distance away to their right. Tents for the men to sleep in had been erected in the woods just beyond the clearing. There would be no cots for the time being. Each man was given a blanket and was responsible for making themselves comfortable with whatever nature gave them. A large mess tent, covered by netting, had been set up under the trees a short distance from the clearing. Airmen and soldiers alike were digging a large latrine in the woods some fifty yards away from the tents. Other men, including officers, were digging slit trenches around both the mess tent and the sleeping tents. Ludwik and Josef were assigned to help there.

Food preparation and serving was handled by the cooks that had arrived with the supply trucks earlier. A serving line table had been set up inside the mess tent. Anyone not having a mess kit was issued one. There were no chairs or benches to sit on. All men were ordered to stay in the general area for an informational briefing at 1930 hours. The status of the war and their role here at the makeshift airfield would be the main topics.

At supper, Ludwik and Josef joined a group of reserve pilots that had been trucked in a few days earlier from their base outside of Krakow. Josef was understandably upset by their opinion that the city his father was living in was about to be overrun. Chow was over by 1900 hours. The informational briefing lasted thirty minutes. An air force major conducted the briefing. He detailed the following:

279

1. All personnel restricted to camp unless otherwise ordered.
2. Each man assigned to a numbered tent.
3. A list of tent occupants to be compiled.
4. Morning muster at 0615 hrs. Ranking officer/enlisted man to conduct tent roll call.
5. Count reported to camp commander at 0630 hrs.
6. Breakfast served from 0630 to 0730 hrs.
7. Duties for day posted at each tent. (Scouts to handle security)
8. Daily password to change every day. "Kapusta" for tonight.
9. Lunch 1200 hrs. Supper 1700 hrs. daily.
10. Tents to observe nightly blackouts.
11. All personnel in tents by 2300 hours.

Each tent held thirty men. Ludwik and Josef were assigned to tent 1. The briefing major was the ranking member in their tent. All personnel in tents 1 and 2 were either pilots, navigators or bombardiers. Tent 3 was for enlisted men. All three were in the woods closest to the mess tent. When needed, other tents would be erected deeper in the woods behind them.

The major had the senior members of the three tents assemble outside of Tent 1 to assign supervision. He assigned a senior ranking officer along with a senior ranking enlisted man to each tent. They would be responsible for that tent. He said additional tents would be erected based on need and the number of personnel that arrived in future days. He said, if possible, keeping individual units and their commanders intact would be a priority. Someone asked for an update on the war. The major said Warsaw was being threatened and under siege and that the Polish High Command, along with the national government, had left the city and were somewhere in this area close to the border. That brought an outcry of disbelief from the men.

Angry voices began shouting. The loudest one demanded to know who was going to defend the citizens in the city.

"The Army is in position to do that. And the mayor has organized elements of the city population to erect obstacles in the streets and dig trenches for the Army to use," answered the major.

"And what about the commanders in the field?" someone asked. "If the Germans cut our communications, how will they get to know what the High Command has ordered if they are not in the same area?"

"It sounds like our leaders are not that optimistic about defeating the Germans," a young navigator shouted.

The major waited for the din of anger and disappointment to ebb. When it did, he said, "You all know what the strategy is. We get the warplanes from France and England in enough time to bring the battle to the enemy. The French and English attack the Germans in the west and we have a war in which the Germans have to fight on two fronts. We establish superiority in the air and get in a good position to do serious damage. We are a part of this plan. Let's focus on doing our part and not worry about things that we cannot control." He finished by reporting that forward elements of the German army were still some distance from the Romanian bridgehead and were not expected to arrive there any time soon. And when and if they did, our forces would be ready for them. With that, he dismissed everyone with a reminder to execute their duty as good officers and leaders of men.

The first week at the hidden camp and airfield saw hundreds of Polish airmen arrive and then moved east toward established airbases in the Lwow area. Others were sent to temporary airfields like theirs somewhere along the border. A few hundred or so stayed with them. Most were enlisted men who had been stationed at Deblin.

They came by bicycle, horseback, buses, rented taxis and privately owned cars. A few had arrived in an old hearse.

News came that the Germans were pounding Warsaw with artillery and air raids every day and there were no Polish planes left to defend the capitol. That made the delay in delivery of the sorely needed warplanes even more excruciating. The Luftwaffe had total command of the skies and every Polish unit on the ground was at the mercy of their heavy bombers, Stuka dive bombers and fighters.

Everyone knew the Army was fighting hard all over the country, but without any support from the depleted Air Force, they were being pushed back almost daily to the east. There were reports of courageous battles still being fought by encircled Poles at the Modelin Fortress north of Warsaw and on the Hel peninsula in Danzig. The story of those brave souls bolstered the spirit of the bored and impatient airmen awaiting their turn to fight the Germans. With no word on the arrival of the promised aircraft and time running out, the Polish Command decided to send two hundred pilots and a large technical staff across the border into Romania to speed up getting the planes into Poland.

Unfortunately, they were stopped at the border because the Romanian government was in the process of deciding if they were going to break their alliance with Poland and become a neutral country. And if they did, all Polish forces crossing the border would be arrested and held in internment camps. In the meantime, Ludwik was spending his time at the airfield working with a group of men who were mechanics. He had drawn their interest while tuning up the Volvo. They were impressed by his workmanship on the car. They became more impressed with his ability to disassemble and reassemble parts of autos, bicycles, trucks, compasses, airplane engines and any other mechanical item, big or small, without error. His reputation spread to the commanding officer at the field.

He immediately put Ludwik in charge of a motor pool of sorts that was tasked with maintaining and servicing vehicles, planes and equipment. Ludwik immediately requested the services of Josef who had been assigned the unenviable task of overseeing the installation and emptying of large latrine barrels, a very boring and messy detail. Fortunately, the camp had not seen a significant increase in the number of men, so the barrels were only half filled and not ready to be dumped. Josef was quickly relieved of the dumping duty and transferred to do all necessary paperwork for the motor pool.

Ludwik also repaired personal items like watches and other jewelry brought to him by some of the men. He usually refused payment for the work, but sometimes did accept tokens of appreciation. Some of the items he accepted were needles, thread, a compass that he fixed, many packs of cigarettes, extra jewelry and several pairs of socks. One day, a week into his work at the motor pool, a familiar face showed up. He was driving a scout car. He was looking for the navy pilot who could fix "anything." His name was Lieutenant Pelcz, the commander of the scouts that had escorted the convoy to the airfield. The same one who had told Ludwik to take the forest road at Lubelski. He recognized Ludwik immediately. He saluted him and asked if he had taken his suggestion. Ludwik said they had and thanked him for making it.

"You can thank me by fixing the steering column on this wretched machine," the smiling lieutenant replied.

It took Ludwik and two of his mechanics an hour to take care of the steering problem. When Pelcz returned, he was surprised to find the scout jeep good as new. He said it was his turn to be thankful. He asked Ludwik if he needed anything. Ludwik said he could use some windows and a headlight for the Volvo. Pelcz said he would do his best to find them in his travels but wasn't sure if there would be enough time.

Then he walked over to Ludwik and said, "I just came back from your commanding officer, my friend. I had to bring him some very bad information."

"What is it?" Ludwik asked.

Pelcz hesitated a moment then said, "The planes are not coming. Romania has refused them entry. They have turned their backs on us for fear of angering the Germans."

Ludwik was stunned. He knew what that meant. It was a disaster for Poland. Pelcz knew it too. Ludwik asked what the orders were. Pelcz could only say what his were. He was to continue with his reconnaissance and await further orders. He said he didn't believe anything was going to happen in this area for a while.

Ludwik watched him drive across the field and disappear in the woods on the other side. He told Josef the news over a cup of coffee. Josef shook his head in dismay. Like Ludwik, he knew what that meant.

"What happens now?" was his only response.

"We wait," Ludwik sighed. "We may end up with the Army. In the meantime, we wait. We just wait."

A feeling of despair descended on the airfield as the news spread that Romania was no longer in Poland's corner. The question of "what happens now," was further intensified when other news came that there was a Russian buildup on the Ukrainian border. Some of the Polish airmen thought the large Russian presence might be helpful. They thought if the Germans got too close to Ukraine, the Russians would attack them and that would help Poland. Ludwik knew that thought had absolutely no merit. He reminded everyone, especially the young, enlisted men, of the war between Poland and Russia after

WWI when the Poles defeated the Russians, that the Russians would be in no hurry to help them. He also reminded them that the Russians had signed a non-aggression pact with Nazi Germany just a short time ago. He saw the buildup on the border as a real threat to Poland.

Lieutenant Pelcz returned two days later. He brought with him four windows from a wrecked car and several head lamps he had scavenged from other wrecks.

"We're even, my friend," he told Ludwik. "Get the car fixed right away. You may be needing it sooner than you think."

"What's the news, lieutenant?" asked Ludwik.

"Doesn't look good. We're taking a beating. I don't know how much more time we have left."

"And the Russians?"

"Intelligence thinks an attack could come from them soon. We have about eight to ten thousand airmen and soldiers along the border. None of them are really equipped to fight off an attack. I will be on that border tomorrow. My orders are to report what areas along the border in my sector are showing the largest increases in Russian deployment."

The Volvo had new windows and a new headlight by noon the next day. All windows could be opened and closed. No replacement glass was available for the rear window. Josef asked what would happen to the car if they had to leave. Ludwik thought if the opportunity arose, they might be able to sell it.

"Who's going to buy it?" Josef asked.

"Someone is always looking for a bargain," Ludwik answered.

Breakfast was exceptionally bad the next morning. Everything served was cold. The only thing hot was the coffee. The day did not get any better after breakfast. A few minutes after breakfast hour ended, an emergency muster of all personnel was called. The major had an announcement.

"Evacuate With All Speed"

"The Soviet Army has launched a major offensive against us. The High Command is flying out of Poland and setting up a provisional government in Paris. The order for us is to "EVACUATE WITH ALL SPEED!" and get into Romania as soon as we can. By any and all means. All personnel should have gear packed and ready to move in one hour. It is less than twenty miles to the border. Cross it immediately and form up with any unit and be ready to be taken to an internment camp. That's international law. We would have to do the same if they came into our country under similar circumstances. Be advised that all personal items you carry may be confiscated by the Romanians. The first thing they will look to take will be weapons, money, cars, bicycles, and personal items such as watches and other jewelry. Those of you with transportation may leave as soon as you're ready. Hope to see you in Romania. God speed."

The road was packed solid with thousands of soldiers and civilians all headed south. The news had traveled fast. It was less than three miles to the border now. Ludwik, Josef and the three officers that had joined them sat quietly in the Volvo as it crawled its way forward. One of the men, a married man, had been reduced to tears as he lamented the fact that he was about to leave his family behind. In the last few minutes, he had decided to go back and try to reach them. They lived in a village near the San River. He said if he couldn't make it home, he would join an army unit and fight the Germans with them. Ludwik said it was possible that the Germans were already there. That didn't faze the man. He said he had to try.

One of the other men, stirred by his friend's anguish, said he would go with him. He asked Ludwik if he would sell the Volvo. He said they were an easy walk to the border now and the Romanians would probably confiscate the car anyway. The idea appealed to Ludwik. He wasn't anxious to take money from the two, but he knew the officer who volunteered to go with the married man came from a very wealthy shipping family near Gdansk and could afford it. And he thought the money might come in handy if the need arose with the authorities in Romania. It could also buy transportation, food, clothes and favors. He asked Josef what he thought. Josef liked the logic of it all. And on top of that, he wasn't sure about being interned. Ludwik was glad to hear him say that. He had misgivings about internment also. Crossing the border at another point away from the convoy might buy them some time to see what was happening to the men in the convoy. The third officer had no problem walking the three miles to the border. He was anxious to get out of the slow-moving traffic. It was decided. They would sell the car.

Josef turned the Volvo around. Ludwik was paid a generous sum. More than the car was probably worth. They wished the new owner good luck and watched the Volvo speed back into Poland. Then they left the convoy and headed south across a field toward a long wood line that fronted an extensive area of thick forest. Ludwik did not want to remain in the convoy. Something told him to find out what this "internment" looked like before agreeing to become part of it They had only walked for a few minutes when Ludwik stopped and turned to look back at the Polish countryside. He wondered if he would ever see it again.

There was more than a thick forest behind the wood line. A swift moving stream was between them and the forest on the other side. Ludwik knew they hadn't walked the three miles that would put them at the border. They were still in Poland. He took out the binoculars and took a long look up and down the stream.

There was no human activity, but there was a small walking bridge that crossed the water some three hundred yards downstream. They made their way quickly to the bridge. Ludwik wasn't sure if Romania was on the other side of it. It didn't seem likely. They had been a few miles from the border when they left the car. He decided to wait awhile and survey the area with his binoculars. See it there was any activity up and down the stream. He asked Josef and the new man to keep their eyes and ears open. After a few minutes of seeing no activity or hearing anything, they decided to cross the old, rickety bridge. They found what looked to be a hiking trail and followed it into the thick forest and toward Romania. The trail was marked with faded yellow paint on trees and a sign in Polish stating, "You are three miles from Romania."

Part Three

The Odyssey of a Polish Patriot

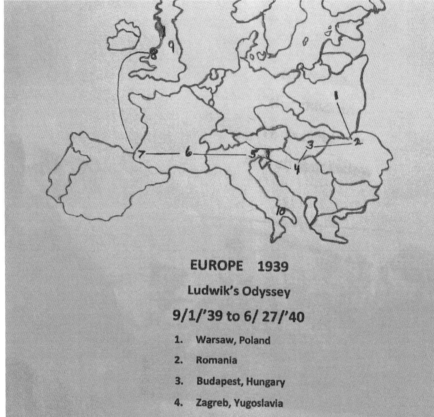

EUROPE   1939

Ludwik's Odyssey

9/1/'39 to 6/ 27/'40

1. Warsaw, Poland
2. Romania
3. Budapest, Hungary
4. Zagreb, Yugoslavia
5. Udine, Italy
6. Lyon, France

   (l-6 with Josef)

7. St. Jean de Luz, France
8. Liverpool, England

---

9. Carlisle, England   (home)
10. Campo Casale, Italy (Special Duties base)

Bednarz was impressed with Ludwik's detailed account of his experience during the first few weeks of the war. He had taken enough notes to swell the pilot's file by several pages. He decided to take the rest of the day off to write some of his thoughts and impressions of those first weeks. He asked if Ludwik would be willing to continue his story at 0900 hours tomorrow. Ludwik said he looked forward to it.

Hide and Seek

Bednarz had the coffee ready the next morning. He was happy to hear that Ludwik had slept all night with the one sleeping pill. No dreams.

"So, you and two others crossed into Romania on your own. Start there."

Ludwik said when they left the convoy, they cut across a field and headed south toward a forest. No one tried to stop them. They crossed a stream and walked undetected for an hour through the forest without any sign of being in Romania. It wasn't until they crossed a road on the other side of the forest and saw a wooden crucifix with a sign overhead that read, "Isus Hristos," that they knew they were across the border. They went into a line of trees past the crucifix and rested. There were questions to be answered. Had they made the right choice crossing on their own? Might the internment camps still be an option? Could the Romanians be trusted? Ludwik and Josef thought not. Hadn't they already let Poland down? Albert, the other officer who had joined them, wasn't so sure. He had begun to change his mind about going it alone thinking it might be best for them to join up with the troops crossing the border. Safety in numbers he speculated. Ludwik suggested they get to the main border crossing, find some cover, and see what was happening to the Polish troops once they crossed into Romania.

He figured the crossing was probably five miles or less to the west of where they were. He suggested they use the cover of the forest they had come through for as long as it would take them. All three blessed themselves as they passed the crucifix and jogged back across the road into the forest. They were only a few feet in when they heard a truck coming. They sprinted deeper into the woods and hit the ground behind a large pine, lifted a ground sweeping branch up enough to get a good view of the road and still not be seen.

The truck was carrying several brown-clad soldiers standing in the open back and hanging on to the sideboards. They were all singing, laughing and jabbing long sabers and rifles high into the air. They were very drunk. The three pilots crouched a little lower in the pine needles and watched the truck rattle by and go out of sight. They looked at each other and knew that surrendering to drunken Romanian soldiers like those would not be a good idea. Neutral or not, those Romanians looked very dangerous; especially the ones waving those long swords.

"Those men would take everything we had and then some," Josef said.

"Totally dangerous individuals," Albert calmly responded. The sight of them convinced him that safety in numbers was the way to go.

Ludwik knew they would stand little chance if it came to a fight. The only weapons they had were the all-purpose Swiss knife in his survival kit and the .38 he took from the Hotel Bristol. His survival training began to kick in.

"I think it would be a good idea if we move quietly from now on. Let's use hand signals when moving and be very quiet when we have to stop. I'll lead. Ten-yard intervals. Alfred second. Josef, the trailer. Eyes and ears wide open."

They moved deeper into the woods and walked quietly for a half hour. Not a word was spoken. Ludwik looked for a safe spot to stop. When he saw the clearing through the trees, he raised a clenched right fist in the air; the signal to stop. He turned and put a finger to his lips. No talking. They dropped to one knee and listened. Nothing there. Ludwik stood and pointed a finger ahead. He led the two men between two heavy Swiss pines into a very tiny clearing in the middle of a huge stand of pines.

Their conversation was kept to a whisper. Ludwik thought it might be a good idea to hide most of their money in case they were captured. He suggested they put a small amount of money in their pockets to make it look like that was all they had and hide the rest. He slit the lining inside his jacket with the Swiss knife, took out a needle and some thread from his backpack and placed most of his money into the lining. Then he sewed the slit back up. He did the same for Josef. Taking off one of his boots, he slit a three-inch cut into the bottom of the heel with the knife, pried the cut up, wedged a small stone under it to keep it that way while he scraped out a hollow with the knife. He rolled five of the higher valued bills into cigarette long cylinders and packed them into the hollow. He popped the stone out and watched that portion of the heel slowly ease its way back into place. After rubbing dirt on the heel, the cut was barely discernible. He did the same to one of Josef's boots. Albert declined the slits in his boot and field jacket. He was anxious to move on.

The cutting and sewing took more than an hour. Josef and Albert sat quietly watching Ludwik do his magic. Josef knew he was watching a very talented man. He had seen him fix cars, repair jewelry, iron and cook. He knew this farmer from Mazanki could do just about anything. And beyond that, he was smart and a real leader.

"Where did you learn to use a needle and knife like that?" Albert whispered.

293

"On a farm," Ludwik answered.

Ludwik and Josef shared a cigarette over an area they had cleared of pine needles. No need to start a fire. The two smokers were careful to exhale their smoke toward the ground then disperse it by waving their caps to kill any aroma it might carry through the woods. Finished, Josef field stripped the cigarette, spread the tobacco bits on the ground, made sure there were no embers and covered the cleared area with pine needles.

Ludwik took the point again and they set off to find the border crossing. He picked a very faint and narrow path that meandered through the heavy pines almost to the end of the forest. They knew they were going in the right direction when they began to hear engines revving and horns blowing somewhere ahead off in the distance. Ludwik said they would go as far as the forest provided cover and hopefully find a spot to observe what the noise was all about. He had little doubt that it was coming from their trucks, but he needed to know why.

They found their spot under another ground scraping pine at the edge of the forest. Josef and Albert carefully lifted a bough a few inches off the ground while Ludwik crawled forward under it to take a look with his binoculars. The first thing he saw was a Romanian army patrol walking through an open field toward a barricaded road and a narrow bridge that crossed a small river. Several uniformed men stood on the Romanian side of the bridge. They looked to be police. There was no sign of the drunken, saber wielding soldiers anywhere. On the other side of the river was the convoy. Men were out of the vehicles and milling around in small groups. No one was being allowed to cross the river. Every now and then an impatient truck driver leaned on his horn, obviously upset with the lowered gate on their side of the bridge and the reluctance of the Romanian police to lift it. It seemed the Romanians were waiting for orders.

He watched as one of the Romanian policemen walked across the bridge toward the Polish side. Several Polish officers were standing there. The Romanian stopped short of the gate and saluted them. One of the Poles came over to him. They stood there for several minutes talking and gesturing. Finally, the Romanian stepped back, saluted the officer and returned to the Romanian side. The Polish officers walked back to the stalled convoy and gathered the officers. Shortly after that, men began jumping out of the trucks and joined others already on the ground. They all started walking toward the forest next to the river. That brought dozens of Romanian soldiers out from the woods off to Ludwik's right some three hundred yards away. The drunken saber-waving individuals were among them. They had been hiding there all the time. They moved toward Ludwik's position to cut the Poles off from crossing the river. Ludwik backed away and told the other two they had company on the way. They jogged back through the forest until they reached the road the Romanian saber men had come on. Crossing it in the open was out of the question now. There were too many Romanians around. They would have to go back where they came from and find a place in the forest to hide. And do it quickly.

Ludwik spotted the huge boulders first. They were piled high at the base of a small cliff just a few feet behind a thick stand of pines. Squeezing themselves between the pines and the boulders, they made their way toward the center of the boulder pile. Just past the center they found a cave-like opening between two huge boulders. It was about five feet high and deep enough room for the three to fit in comfortably with their backpacks. They would not be visible to anyone standing on top of the boulders or walking in front of the thick stand of pines. With darkness approaching, they would be invisible. Ludwik took first watch. Albert was too keyed up and not able to sleep. Josef was asleep in minutes. As soon as he started to snore, Ludwik shook him awake and glared at him.

Josef grimaced, nodded his understanding and went back to sleep. He remained quiet until Ludwik woke him to take the second watch. Darkness had fallen. Ludwik stretched out and joined Albert in sleep. Within a few minutes, Josef's head began nodding. His dozing was interrupted by cursing Romanian soldiers passing in front of the pines, their flashlight beams sweeping the forest from side to side. Josef held his breath and prayed his friends would remain silent in their sleep.

It was pitch black when Josef woke Albert. Albert whispered to Josef that he couldn't see a thing. Josef whispered back saying that meant the Romanians couldn't see a thing also. Albert relaxed. He thought about his two friends that had bought the Volvo and gone back into Poland. He could have gone with them, but he knew better. His family lived in Danzig. That was the first city the Germans had taken. He stared into the darkness and tried to focus on his family; on the street near the busy center of the city where their house was. He could picture the streetcars rumbling their way past the house, a line of cars stopped in traffic and bike riders weaving their way around them. He decided to shut his eyes and listen. The forest was silent. Then there was something. It was faint. Far away. He began to think he was dreaming. It sounded like the traffic on his street. Engines revving. Horns beeping. It sounded like a celebration. Ludwik was up. He listened for a few seconds and knew.

"What is it?" Albert whispered.

It's our brothers joining us in Romania," Ludwik replied.

"Let's go see," a wide awake and alert Josef said.

Ludwik cautioned, "Let's do it quietly. We don't know how the police or soldiers are going to react if they see us on this side of the border."

It was a moonless night. They made their way carefully in the darkness back to the main road. There was no conversation. They moved quietly on the road toward the sounds of commotion. Five paces between each man and a steady stride. One of the great things about the night was how far sound traveled and how easy it was to know vehicles were approaching. Any lights were a dead giveaway. Any sound of oncoming traffic or lights from either direction was their cue to get off the road and into the forest for cover.

Josef was the last man in line. His job was to glance behind every so often to check for lights coming on the road or flashlights being carried on and off the road. Only once did they have to duck into the forest for cover.

The roar of engines and bouncing streams of light on the other side of the hill they were walking by told them they were close to the crossing. They left the road and walked up the hill into a stand of large pines. It was close to the spot they had been earlier in the day, watching the stalemate at the bridge. They watched one vehicle after another cross the bridge, follow the road over another hill, and disappear. The night sky was lit up on the other side of that hill. It was obvious the convoy was stopping there. That's when Albert announced he wanted to join the convoy. He said he felt safer in a larger group. Ludwik understood. He said they would walk with him for a bit and see him off. They went halfway down the hill in a meadow with Albert, then watched him run in the faint light thrown by the vehicles crossing the bridge. He disappeared into a spot of darkness in the meadow, then reappeared along the road some distance from the bridge. He ran alongside a truck and jumped on the running board passenger side. As soon as the truck and Albert disappeared over the hill, Ludwik and Josef retreated back up the meadow and went down through the woods to the road they had come on. They worked their way around the patch of woods the soldiers had hidden in earlier in the day and headed for the hill where trucks were lighting up the sky on the other side. Josef estimated it was less than a mile away. As they neared the lights, they left the road and made their way up another hilly meadow to get a look at the other side. They found a good spot to watch the action below. Trucks coming over the hill by the river were being directed into a field by men with flashlights. There were many vehicles parked there. Ludwik could make out four lines of trucks and cars. They stretched far out into a darkened field. There had to be two dozen of them in each line. The ones they could see clearly were empty. Then headlights from the trucks farthest down the front line went on. That's when Ludwik saw the men. They were standing in formation. He watched nervously when the front rank raised their arms to the side as uniformed men approached them. It was like watching ants swarm over a pile of sugar and breadcrumbs. It was disturbing. Weapons and other items were taken from the Poles and stacked off to one side. Backpacks were returned after a quick search. Once the search was completed, the men were escorted off into the darkness and the next line of Poles stepped forward for the same procedure. Ludwik saw Polish officers observing the searches with their Romanian counterparts. He decided he had seen enough. He motioned for Josef to follow him back to the dark side of the hill.

Josef was the first to speak. "I don't like what I saw," he said.

Ludwik nodded, "I don't either, but I would be interested...... He stopped in mid- sentence and put a hand over his mouth. It was the signal for silence. Neither moved. Ludwik pointed at the dark meadow below. They both peered out into the darkness. A soft breeze gently rippled over the meadow and up toward them. It carried only the faint sound of trucks maneuvering on the river road. Nothing else. Ludwik's eyes moved slowly across the meadow from left to right and then back the other way; never stopping too long at any one spot. He knew if he did, his mind would trick him into seeing movement. And that would be a mistake.

He might think someone was there while that person was somewhere else. Somewhere close to them. Real close. And yet, there was a spot out there in the darkness his eyes always came back to. He let them remain on that spot for a few seconds longer than usual, but never picked up any movement. Finally, he broke the silence with a whispered, "I thought I heard something moving out there." Suddenly a voice came from the very spot in the meadow that Ludwik's eyes had constantly returned to. The voice was deep, calm, steady. It spoke in Polish. "I am not armed. I am your friend. May I advance?" Ludwik cleared the fright out of his throat, regained his composure and said, "Advance."

A man rose out of the grass not twenty yards from them. He was big. And he wasn't alone. Alongside him was a very large dog. Both approached them very slowly. They stopped five yards away. The big man raised both arms high into the air and said, "There is nothing to fear from me or my little friend. My name is Constantin Lupu."

"Are you Polish?" Josef asked.

Constantin Lupu

"No. I am Romanian. Decebel, my friend here, caught your scent in another meadow and led me to you. I watched one of you leave and head down toward the trucks. It was then I realized that you two and all those crossing the river had to be Polish. Radio reports earlier today had informed the Romanian people that their old ally, Poland, was on the brink of defeat and to expect refugees at our border soon. I became curious why only one of you had gone to join the convoy. I decided to follow you two to see what you were up to. You made a wise move in staying away from the woods near the bridge. There is a detachment of soldiers bivouacked there. I wouldn't have followed you through those woods. Too risky. I was a bit behind you when you went up the hill on the meadow side.

I could hear you talking in the wood line. That's when Decibel startled some small animal near us. I knew the animal's jump through the high grass had caught your attention when you abruptly stopped talking. I pushed Decibel down into a prone position beside me and we lay still in the grass. I could feel someone's eyes scanning the dark and settling directly on me. I waited for trouble, but it didn't come. I am thankful for that. And you should be also. Decibel doesn't take kindly to any threat. I heard your concern about joining your comrades. I thought you were making an intelligent observation. I happen to agree with you. You have reason to be nervous about internment. It will not be a pleasant experience. I think I can help you. With your permission of course."

Lupu was a large landowner of means. His house reflected it. He had many important friends in the Romanian government. That made him privy to high level information. He knew his country would eventually declare neutrality to curry favor with Germany. He spoke Polish well. His sister had married a Pole and lived on Poland's Baltic coast for a long time before moving to England. He had picked up the language from them on his frequent visits to see his sister. He told Ludwik and Josef that he despised Hitler and his "Third Reich." He had seen firsthand the dramatic and fanatical change that had overtaken some of his German friends as they touted the future of Germany under Hitler. He said the Romanian authorities would take everything from the Poles crossing their border including trucks, cars, weapons and anything else of value. There were no plans to harm Poles that came across the border, but they would be putting them into camps that any dog would refuse to enter. Nothing more than hellholes. Some in areas filled with mosquitoes and malaria. He said they would not give the internees a decent meal unless they were bribed. And even with a bribe, you wouldn't get much more than a few apples and a cup of weak coffee. He said that most internees would probably be sleeping on the ground with only a small blanket.

300

He suggested they get out of Romania quickly and again politely asked if they would accept his help. Ludwik said they would accept any help that came their way but was curious as to why he was so generous to complete strangers. Lupu replied it was for Poland, Romania's traditional ally, his sister, and an intense hatred of Adolph Hitler. He said it would be good for them to get a head start. That in a week or so, the countryside would be filled with escaping Poles and who knew how many corrupt Romanian authorities chasing them.

"What about security at the camps?" Josef asked.

"The guards are poor. The camp commandants are greedy. Both steal and look for easy money. If you have money and I'm sure you have some, they will look the other way if you pay. On the other hand, the common folks you come across in the countryside are generally good hearted and the people of means in the larger towns will be sympathetic to you and all Poles who have been driven out of Poland. The ties between our two countries are good. Our history with you is long. I don't know if it will last. It is best for you to get out of Romania as soon as you can. You will stay here and rest up. I will take any money you have and exchange it for our lei. I will also get you some clothes and good maps to use."

"What about trains?" Ludwik asked.

"You may wish to ride trains. That may be a little risky without papers. Not impossible, but a little risky. You can try to get to Bucharest and get some false papers from your embassy. That might put you on a ship headed to Greece, Cyprus, Africa, or France. Maybe even England."

"How do you know this?" Josef asked.

"I have friends. They have anticipated this. They are not without influence. They come here to hunt, hike and cheat on their wives.

They bring their mistresses here. They drink, fuck and talk. I hear it all. Some of them were here last month. They knew my sister had married a Pole. They like her and don't care for the Germans. They told me to warn her to get out of Poland. I'm sorry to say the Germans and Russians are going to take your country. The Russians will have Vilnius soon and Lwow, excluding some divine intervention, will fall within a week. The invaders are too strong for your forces now. Your leaders know this. That is why they ordered you to get out and live to fight another day."

"You paint a dismal picture, Mr. Lupu," Ludwik said.

"I only deal with the facts, my Polish friend."

"Did your friends know the Russians would invade?" Ludwik asked.

Lupu thought for a moment and said, "Your government had every indication they were coming. My friends did also. Everyone here hoped they would stay out of Poland, but the non-aggression pact they signed with that devil in Berlin was a clear sign they were going to be involved in some way. Now we know. It will be interesting to see what Stalin and Hitler have in store for your country."

Ludwik nodded and said, "I have a feeling that your country may have some problems with them also."

"The Germans have been here for some time," Lupu replied.

"How so?" asked Josef.

"Their Gestapo has sent agents into our country. Especially into Bucharest. They will be watching every move your forces and others make in Romania. Especially in the internment camps. I'm sure Hitler will pressure our government to keep all of you safely tucked away until they come for you. When that happens, they will come for us also. I will have disappeared by then."

"Will the Gestapo be in the countryside?" Ludwik asked.

"They will be watching the train stations, especially the ones to and from Bucharest. They will also ride the trains. That's why I said traveling by train might be a bit risky. I recommend a hike west through the passes in the mountains and then go by train to the border of Hungary. The farther away you are from Bucharest, the safer it will be for you to ride trains."

The guest room was like the ones in the mountain resorts of Poland that Josef had stayed in with his father on some of their hiking trips. Trophy heads of prized animals hunted and killed by Lupu, and his friends hung on the room's walls. A fully antlered head of a stag hung partly over the bed. The head of a giant bear and wolf glared menacingly down at them from two of the other walls. The room was a miniature hunting lodge.

"I wonder if they have a head of one of those mistresses mounted somewhere in this place," said Josef.

"Funny man. We need to talk. This is moving a little too fast for comfort," Ludwik said.

The discussion went on for over an hour. It revolved around Lupu and his believability. Could they trust this seemingly honest and well-informed man? What about his suggestion they head west over the Carpathians and into Hungary instead of going to Bucharest and the embassy? The idea of taking a train to Bucharest had some appeal. If they could reach the embassy, they might be able to get papers that would help them in their travel out of Romania. On the other hand, the thought of the German Gestapo hanging around train stations and riding trains was concerning. It wouldn't be easy picking them out in a crowd. Ludwik didn't believe the Germans had any authority to stop and hold anyone in a neutral country, but Lupu had said the authorities were corrupt.

The Germans might just arrange a Romanian arrest of them with a little bribery. Josef like the idea of hiking their way through the mountains then boarding a train into Hungary. He said he thought they could make it on their own. The only thing that worried him was the long trip to Hungary and beyond without papers.

Lupu's man servant, Andrei, woke them up with a gentle rap on the door. He said breakfast would be served in the dining area at seven and Mr. Lupu would be joining them at that time. He said to bring their backpacks with them.

Lupu had already left the house at dawn on his daily morning walk with Decebel. Normally they walked through the forest before returning home. But not today. Today, he would make a visit to the bridge and see if he could find out what was happening to the Poles that had crossed the border last night.

There were two guards on duty at the bridge. A sergeant sat on a pegged stool just inside the lowered gate on the Romanian side. His long rifle was set upright against the gate. His chin was resting on his chest. He was obviously dozing. The other sentry, a private, was leaning on the gate and gazing across the river into Poland. His rifle was slung over his shoulder. Both were startled by Lupu's shout of greeting as he approached. The sergeant grabbed his rifle and turned to face the visitor. He relaxed when he saw who it was. He had met and talked with this man before. He had orders to treat him with respect and courtesy because he was known to have contacts at the highest levels of government. He could make trouble if he wanted to. He told the private he knew the man and not to be concerned; he was a friendly and a man not to be disrespected. After a friendly exchange about the day and weather, Lupu asked in a casual and unassuming manner, what all the noise and fuss was about last night. At first, the sergeant told him everything he already knew. What he wanted to hear came next.

The sergeant said all Polish military would be trucked to internment camps in Cernauti and Focsani and all civilian refugees were going to being interned in camps south of here. He added that more soldiers would be arriving in a few days to increase surveillance on the border and help process the Polish military crossing into the country. He said that nearly five hundred Polish airmen and soldiers had crossed here last night. Many more at spots all along the border. He said there was going to be an increase of Romanian patrols in the countryside up to three miles inside the border. He said they had reports that small groups of Poles had crossed on their own last night. Some had crossed near here. The additional patrols would be looking for them. He said some Polish planes, all sport flyers, had landed in Romania yesterday. Their pilots had been interned and the planes confiscated. Lupu thanked the two for updating him on the goings on. He handed them a pack of expensive French cigarettes and headed home. He needed to talk with his two guests.

At breakfast, Ludwik told Lupu they had decided not to go to Bucharest on the trains. They were going try for the Hungarian border overland. Lupu nodded in agreement and said, "I have learned there will be an increase in patrols along the entire border soon. Maybe even tonight. Some will be up to three miles inside the border. They will be looking for you and some of your friends. You will need to always stay at least five miles from the border. You should travel at night and sleep during the day.

Once the border ends with Poland, you should be fine. If they do catch you, make sure you remember that most of the police and military will be open to taking a bribe. It's a cultural habit that comes from living in a very poor country. The authorities will be looking for men in uniform. Some of our less-desirable citizens will be also. They will turn you in for a cigarette. I suggest you stay out of large towns and any city. The countryside is your best bet. People there will be more sympathetic to you and your country's problems.

Many will not even be aware of what is happening in Poland. Now, let's talk about clothes, money and supplies. You cannot travel in your military clothes. You will need civilian clothes. Preferably things that Romanians wear. You want to look like one of the natives. It will help to throw off any unwanted attention. Caps are a necessity. They must be large enough to pull down over your eyes to feign sleep. Especially on trains. Try not to sit together and avoid unnecessary conversation with each other if you can. Anticipate being separated and have a plan to reunite. If you have a choice of sitting next to a man or a woman, choose the woman. The authorities might think you are a Romanian couple and not bother you for papers or ask questions."

Ludwik and Josef cut the zloty out of their jackets, pried the rest out from their boots and gave it to Lupu. He gave them a quick lesson in the value of the lei he handed them in exchange. After that, he told them to go with Andrei to find some clothes. He asked and got permission to inventory their backpacks and see if they had the proper items for a long hike. Especially a hike in the mountains.

Andrei was much more than a gentleman's manservant. That became immediately apparent when he opened the door of a huge walk-in closet in his quarters. The mountain gear and equipment hanging in there was first rate. Josef, a hiker and climber himself, had never seen anything like it. He knew this was a man that had spent some serious time in the outdoors. The gun rack on the opposite wall caught Ludwik's eye. It was no less spectacular. It was stacked with an impressive array of rifles and handguns. Only a hunter of means would ever be able to afford such a collection. Andrei explained in broken Polish that everything in the closet belonged to the guests that visited Lupu. He told them to take anything they wanted. They wouldn't be missed by the rich and influential people that came here to vacation and frolic. He said to make sure to include cold weather items like winter gloves, heavy socks, and long underwear.

Ludwik found hiking pants, sweaters, jackets, gloves, long underwear, a cap and hiking boots that fit him perfectly. Josef had trouble finding clothes and boots his size but settled for high quality clothes and boots that were a tad larger than he normally wore. Both men brought the clothes and boots down to the dining room. They found Lupu looking at their backpack items he had spread out on the wooden floor.

"Your packs are not that large and with your "new" clothes, there may not be enough room. I believe it would be wise to discard anything that would identify you as Polish military. That will give you room in your "new" backpacks for your "new" clothes and certainly increase your chances of going unnoticed. Word has come to me that our government is being pushed hard by the Germans to keep Poles in the internment camps. If you make it to Hungary, you will be put in a camp there, but I believe you will not stay in them for long and it won't be anything like internment here. If I were you, I would make every effort to get to your embassy in Budapest. They will help you. The International Red Cross and the Catholic Church operate without any interference from the Hungarian government. I am sure you will be welcomed at both places. There is a group in Hungary known as the "Iron Cross." They may cause you some problems. They don't care for "outsiders," especially Jewish ones. We have a pollical group in Romania called the "Iron Guard," but they won't trouble you in the mountains or rural areas. They tend to cluster in Bucharest and other cities to demonstrate their politics. Your main concern will be to avoid the police and military. If they do find you out, remember to bribe them. If they want more than money, offer them articles like this Swiss knife you carry." He picked the knife up and flipped it to Andrei. The mountain man inspected it closely and said he wouldn't trade the knife for anything; that it could save a man's life a dozen ways.

Ludwik and Josef looked at their possessions: two flashlights, several batteries, matches, a canteen, a hammer, a screwdriver, a survival kit, ten packs of cigarettes, 10 feet of rope, uniforms and shoes, military socks, one blanket, assorted jewelry, two compasses, the knife and the revolver.

Ludwik knew that Lupu was right. Anything that identified them as military had to go. Even his aviator watch. Everything else was safe and compact enough to get in the larger backpacks that Lupu had brought in for them. And there was enough space left to include the new clothing they had brought down.

Lupu left the dining room with Andrei while they split their possessions and began packing the backpacks. He returned shortly with a proposal. "Andrei and I have a proposition for you. Andrei has made many trips into the mountains. He has family in the mountains you have to cross. He has been planning a visit to them soon. He said he might as well go now and take you with him. It won't be an easy hike, but I guarantee you no one will know you are up there. He will get you over the mountains and make arrangements to put you on a train to the Hungarian border. From there, you will be on your own. He will show you how to hide in plain sight and teach you some valuable evasive maneuvers when you are by yourselves. Would you be interested in going with him?"

Ludwik and Josef looked at each other. And then at Andrei. It was a generous offer. Having a guide to help them evade the authorities and get out of the country safely was a good thing. They both said, "Yes!"

"Then it's settled. You will stay here tonight. You will leave with Andrei before dawn. He will push you. If you are not up to it, he will leave you to fend for yourself. Agreed?"

"Agreed," answered Ludwik.

308

Lupu said they would be sleeping outdoors for the most part so he would be giving each of them a good sleeping bag; much better than what the Polish military issued. He said Andrei would teach them how to roll and rope it to their packs. He gave them a map of northern Romania and said that after breakfast, he and Andrei would sit with them and show them the route they were going to take. He said if for any reason they were stopped, Andrei would say he was your guide and was taking you on a hunt. He will have a document bearing the signature of a good friend of mine in the government. It will guarantee you safe passage to the mountains. He finished by saying they did not have to hide the fact they were Polish, but they did have to hide the fact they were Polish military.

Breakfast included strong, black coffee, slices of cold ham, hard boiled eggs, bread and a flaky, apple tort. After the table was cleared, Lupu spread the map out on it and had Andrei finger his way across it to show them their route. Lupu made each one finger the same route and then instructed Andrei to give them a weapon to prove they were hunters.

Both Ludwik and Josef were given similar rifles to carry. The weapons would not be loaded. Andrei showed them how the bolt action, scoped rifles were loaded and fired, how to sling the weapon and adjust the scope. He had them begin practicing what he had shown them. The practice session didn't last long. It was interrupted by the sound of vehicles wheeling up the driveway toward the house. Andrei had both men grab their loaded backpacks and follow him into the walk-in closet in his quarters. He went to a bureau at the end of the closet and moved it away from the wall. He slid open a panel in the wall and motioned for the two to get in with their backpacks and sleeping bags. He told them to be silent. Then he slid the panel back into place and moved the bureau back against the wall.

They stayed in the crawl space for a half hour before Andrei came back and let them out. He said they had been visited by three policemen who wanted to assure Mr. Lupu that he would be safe from any of the Polish unfortunates crossing the border into Romania. They also wanted to know if he had seen or heard anything unusual last night near his home.

"I don't trust them," Lupu said as the four entered the dining room. "They hardly ever show their face up here."

"Will they be back?" Josef asked.

"No, but they may be watching the house for a while."

Andrei laughed. "Decebel will tell us if they're around. He can smell those unwashed characters a mile away."

Lupu laughed at that and said, "Still, I think it would be wise to leave the area at least two hours before dawn. One should never underestimate the possibility of trouble. Something brought them to the house."

Lupu asked Andrei to check all doors. Then he commanded Decebel to "guard!" The big dog trotted into the kitchen and settled comfortably on his haunches in front of a low window facing the woods by the driveway.

Lupu spread the map out on the dining table and asked Andrei to explain to the two Poles why he was taking them the way he showed them earlier. Andrei said the Prislop Pass through the Rodna Mountains was best. Plenty of cover there and a cabin that had been built by his stepfather. He said the trip would take one, maybe two days to reach the cabin. It was always stocked with food, but he thought it would be wise to take a little extra with them. Just in case. He said they would spend one night in the cabin.

The next day they would hike to the town of Borsa. He would buy train tickets for them to Satu Mare on the Hungarian border. From there they would be on their own crossing into Hungary. He advised them not to be caught in Hungary close to the Romanian border. That might mean being sent back to Romania.

Lupu summarized the plan, "So, my two friends, you will be escorted by a good man for the first fifty miles. He will take leave of you at Borsa. The train ride from there to Satu Mare is around a hundred miles. Treat that ride as the most dangerous part of your trip. Find yourself a woman to sit next to if you can. Be alert at every stop for anyone that looks suspicious. And don't forget to lower your cap. Sitting in a crowded car would be best. You won't stand out so much. You will need to be asleep right after nightfall tonight. Keep the curtains closed in your room. Do not put any lights on. Take a shower. You may not have a chance for one for some time unless you use one of the waterfalls or streams in the mountains. They're clean, but ice cold."

Ludwik and Josef went into the windowless library to relax and smoke. Andrei went to the kitchen to prepare lunch. Lupu left to take another walk with the dog and reconnoiter the area.

"What do you think, Ludwik?" Josef asked.

"I'm nervous, but excited to be on our way," Ludwik answered. "I am a little concerned about not having anything on me that proves I'm a Polish pilot. When we get to France, I want to show them who I am."

"I hadn't thought about that," said Josef. "Anything we can do?"

"Get the eagle off your cap before it's burned or buried by Lupu. The "gapa" will prove we're pilots. I'm going to put mine in the heel of my other boot. I can do yours also if you like."

311

"I'll do mine myself," Josef said.

Andrei came into the library just as Josef finished. He asked him what they were doing. Josef displayed the boot's bottom and explained. Andrei asked to see the boots. He said hiding something in the heel of a boot wasn't that original and easy to detect. It only took a quick glance by him to see the cuts that had been made in each boot. He said he could seal the hollow tight and cover the cutline with a mixture of hot tar and dirt. That would keep what they were hiding secure until the boot was cut open. He took the boots and told them to follow him.

The cellar resembled a small supply depot. Andrei pointed to the far wall and told them to pick out some canned goods from the well-stocked shelves there while he took care of the boots. He said to take about five pounds each, bring them upstairs and put them in their backpacks. He said to spread the cans out and place undergarments between them; that metal on metal produced sound. And the sound of metal in the wilderness was a dead giveaway.

Most of the canned and packaged goods came from countries like England, France and the United States. Brown bread, biscuits and candy were scooped up first. That was followed by several small packets of jelly, peanut butter, sugar and coffee. Small cans of beans, soups, fruits and vegetables completed their haul. Andrei told them to also take a small pot, a Swiss Army knife, a small ax, a canteen, some fish line and hooks and some sewing material. He said they should be able to survive at least a month with what they had and another three weeks without any food. Lack of water was different. Three to five days without water could kill them. He reminded them that everything they had gathered could also be used as bribes, but not to offer everything at once. He thought it was a good idea to sew money into their clothing, but to make sure they had enough in their pockets to purchase items or bribe someone.

Andrei brought the boots up to Lupu and asked him to inspect them to see if there was anything out of the ordinary that caught his eye. Lupu shook his head no. Satisfied with his work, Andrei told him what he had done. Lupu slapped him on the back and asked whose idea it was to do that. Andrei said it was Ludwik's.

"Yes, the man with the eyes," Lupu responded. "I know it was his eyes in the meadow last night that were on me as I crawled toward them in the dark. I could feel them. He interests me. There is something unusual about him. In another time, I would make it my business to see how well he fared in the mountains. You can tell me when you get back."

Supper was served in the windowless library. It was regal; rice, fried peppers, buttered mashed potatoes, smoked sausage and two glasses of merlot imported from France. Coffee, fruitcake and cigarettes ended the evening meal on a high note. Ludwik appreciated the life the two kind Romanians led and their willingness to share it with them. Lupu shook their hands before retiring and wished them well. He said he would not see them again.

Everything was checked and double checked in Andrei's quarters. The food had been divided evenly and placed in the two backpacks. All extra clothes had been rolled tightly and placed in the backpacks also. Each sleeping bag had been compressed into a small roll and adeptly tied onto the backpacks. All three men had a canteen filled with water. Every bit of Polish military clothing had been burned. Ludwik's aviator watch was now in Lupu's possession. They took a shower and went to bed. No lights. Their odyssey to France would begin a few hours after midnight and promised to be long and challenging. Both men were ready for the hike and felt very comfortable being in the hands of Andrei.

Andrei

At three A.M., Lupu turned on the lamp posts outside the front door and stepped out into the light with Decebel. He let the big dog find one of his favorite spots to relieve himself. By the time he began his walk with the dog down the driveway, Andrei, Josef and Ludwik had made their way quietly out the back door of Andrei's quarters and into a row of pines some fifty yards away. They watched Lupu and Decebel make their way toward the forest. The dog's behavior told Andrei that nothing was amiss. If someone was out there watching from the forest, he would have let everyone know. They saw Lupu disappear into the darkness at the end of the driveway then listened intently for a few minutes. Satisfied there was no threat, they turned and slipped silently through the trees and entered one of the numerous hilly meadows surrounding Lupu's home. They moved without a sound through the moist, ankle-deep grass and wild flowers that covered the ground. Andrei had proved he was a master in preparing for a silent journey in the wilderness before the two men had left his quarters to retire for the night. Canteens had been carefully wrapped with black tape to cover their reflective surfaces and had been secured tightly to their belts. Anything metallic in their backpacks had been separated by clothing to prevent any clinking. He showed them how to cuff and tie their pants just above the ankles so no pant edge would catch and snap any bush bottom or dead branch that would give away their position.

The three men moved as one. Andrei was at point, leading the way effortlessly. Josef trekked five yards behind; his eyes glued to Andrei's back. Ludwik served as the trailer some fifteen yards behind Josef. Lupu had tipped off Andrei to Ludwik's exceptional night vision. Andrei knew that a trail man with that kind of vision would be able to see what was on their flanks long before he did. It was his job to concentrate on what was in front of them and lead the way.

The password for the entire trip was "Decebel."

Andrei seemed to have lights in his eyes. There were no miss-steps or hesitation in his stride. He was definitely in his element. Ludwik and Josef found the pace tolerable. Both were in good shape and confident that the man leading them knew what he was doing.

Andrei felt it wouldn't be much longer before they would be out of range of any Army patrols that Lupu said might be operating along the border. All he had to do was stay more than three miles away from any point on the border. While that information had come from bridge guards, not necessarily the best source of intelligence, it was to be respected. If true, it probably meant no patrols would be near the mountains, his ultimate destination. Still, these were unusual times, and it would pay to stay alert; no matter what area they were in. For now, he would keep to the country and avoid populated areas. No sense in taking unnecessary chances. Lupu had been right in creating a diversion by walking the dog so early in the morning. The visit by the police had been unusual and suspicious enough to warrant devising a distraction. They had both learned in the Great War to try and keep a few steps ahead of trouble.

Andrei knew most of the farmers and landowners on both sides of the route they were going to use. They were good, decent and friendly folks and wouldn't be alarmed at hunters walking through their land and by their farms. Especially if he was guiding them. He saw the break beginning between the clouds and knew they would be walking in moonlight shortly. He stopped and waited for the two to reach him. He explained what was about to happen. He said they had to cross a road in the moonlight. He would show them how it was done. He said once they made it through the woods on the other side of the road, they would be on land belonging to people he knew. People he could count on for accurate information.

The maneuver was simple. Tuck the rifle vertically close to your chest and roll across the road on your elbows. Keep the end of the barrel away from your head and keep your hands away from the trigger. When Josef finished his roll, Andrei was already waiting at the entrance to the trail he wanted to use. As soon as Ludwik joined them, they set off into the dense forest. The trail was narrow with brush and trees on each side. The deeper they advanced into the woods, the darker it became. Every now and then a sliver of moonlight penetrated the dense cover and gave the men a dim view of the trail. When drifting clouds obscured the moon, the darkness returned. Only familiarity with the trail and the instinct of a mountain man kept Andrei on track. Josef could barely make out Andrei's form in front of him. The dark seemed to swallow everything. It was worse for Ludwik. He was too far back. From time to time, he would lose sight of Josef and had to depend on the very faint sound of his friend's footsteps to guide him. Every time the sounds stopped, he had to stop, hold his breath and listen. That worked twice. After his third stop, he lost contact. He waited to see if they would come back for him. When they didn't, he moved on. He knew the approximate width of the trail so by holding his rifle horizontally across his body and extending his arms straight out, he could use both ends of the weapon to make contact with anything on each side. If contact was made with something on one end, he would move a little to the opposite side. It was slow going, but he made steady progress. Eventually, he walked into a clearing. There were two openings in it that suggested the beginning of a trail. He went to each one and listened. He heard nothing. He moved ten paces into one and listened. Nothing again. He took out his compass. It showed the trail he was on was headed west; the same direction they had been going. He decided to stay on that trail, trust the compass reading and use his keen eyesight to stay out of trouble.

316

The trail was wider than the one they had used on the other side of the clearing. It was easy going for a while. The forest had thinned out somewhat and that allowed a fair amount of moonlight to help him make his way. That changed when the trail began to slope downward. The farther down he went, the darker the forest became. It felt like he was in a tunnel. Hardly able to see what was in front of him, he slowed and moved deliberately. His steps became measured; uncertain. And there was something else. He began to feel that he was not alone. He sensed that someone or something was nearby. He stopped and looked back up the trail and the dim light at the top. Nothing there. He turned back to the blackness and listened intently. That's when he heard it. Breathing! It was unmistakable! And now, movement off to his left. Coming his way. He froze. Then slowly, very carefully, he swung the rifle toward the presence in the blackness and waited. Whatever or whoever it was had stopped. Ludwik had had enough. He was going to attack. He took a strong stride to his left and jabbed the barrel of the rifle straight ahead like he had a bayonet on it and uttered a short, "Haaa!!!" Something made a snort and crashed away through the woods. Ludwik jumped back at the noise, his heart pumping. It took a few seconds to realize he was safe. Or was he? He wondered if anyone had heard the commotion. Almost on cue, he heard someone coming down the "tunnel" toward him. He could see the outline of two men in the dim moonlight at the top moving toward him. He recognized the forms immediately. It was Andrei and Josef. He gave a short whistle to let them know he was there.

"What happened to you?" Josef asked quietly.

"Too far behind and just a little too dark," Ludwik answered.

"You did well in the dark," Andrei said.

"I was lost," Ludwik answered.

"Lost, but going in the right direction," Andrei responded.

Dawn uncovered the spectacular countryside they were crossing. Andrei assured them they were in friendly territory now and far from the Polish border. He said they would be visiting friends today. They could see for miles. Off in the distance were the Rodna Mountains. Tucked away somewhere in their beautiful, green folds was the Prislop Pass, their destination for the day. Dozens of the iconic Romanian cone shaped haystacks covered the landscape on both sides of the narrow country road. They looked like an architect had built them. The farmhouses they passed were colorfully painted in reds, whites, blacks and browns. Each of them was bordered in front by an intricately woven, wooden fence. It was Romania at its finest. Most impressive were the people; adults and children alike. All were friendly. No one asked questions. They just smiled, waved and went about their business. Ludwik was intrigued by the lack of machinery in the area. Oxen, horses, carts, and wagons dominated the roads.

"Beautiful country," Josef said.

"God's country," Andrei responded.

"How far will we travel?" Ludwik asked him.

"Thirty miles today. Twenty miles tomorrow. We sleep in the mountains tonight."

The pace was reasonable. Andrei knew the two aviators were in fairly good condition, but the day had turned quite warm. He didn't want to make the trip a forced march. He needed them to be well rested. The last ten miles of the trip would test their endurance and strength. That's when they would be hiking the mountain trail up to the cabin. He gave them a break every hour for ten minutes, had them remove their backpacks and take their drink. His plan was to get a good rest at the farm, eat, check all gear and get to the cabin before nightfall.

318

The farm was large. It could have been the Skoczylas farm back home in Poland. The farmhouse was at the end of a long dirt road that wound its way through an apple orchard. It was surrounded by several barns, coops and a large pen. A jumbled stone wall ran alongside the road and ended at the entrance to the farm courtyard. There wasn't a statue of the Madonna by the farmhouse, but there was a magnificent, hand painted, wooden replica of Jesus on the Cross in the orchard. Andrei said the folks on this farm were like family to him.

Grigore Antovich was in his eighties. He and his wife of fifty years stayed on the farm and tended to their garden and barnyard livestock. Their three sons tended the orchard and a large flock of sheep. Grigore had found Andrei, a boy of fifteen then, wandering high in the mountains many years ago. He was filthy, emaciated and half naked; barely alive. He wore a wolf skin for a coat. And a deer skin for a poncho. He had fled to the mountains to escape thieves who had killed his parents. Andrei had killed one of them in the fight that took his parent's lives but was forced to flee by the killers. Wanting revenge, they pursued him for two days into the mountains, but gave up the chase when a winter snowstorm began burying the entire range. They retreated from the storm believing the boy would never make it off the mountain alive. But he had. By chance, Andrei had stumbled upon a cabin just before the full force of the storm hit. It was the cabin that Grigore and his sons had built to use when they were hunting. It had enough in it to keep one alive for some time. It had tools, blankets, traps, an axe, fishing poles and several hunting knives. There was a pantry that held a small barrel of flour and several containers of sugar, tea and coffee. Best of all, it had a fireplace and plenty of firewood. There were weeks when he couldn't leave the cabin because of the brutal cold and huge drifts of snow that almost buried the entire building. He dug a pathway outside and carried snow back inside to melt for his drinking needs.

319

The flour lasted for two months. When it ran out, he was forced outside to find food. The only protection he had from the cold was the stretched skin of a deer nailed onto a wall. He cut holes in it for his head and arms and used it as a coat over the rags his clothes had become. He buried traps in the snow where he saw the tracks of animals. Whenever he caught one, he killed it with the axe. After he skinned it, he would cut off a foot and use it as bait to trap bigger game. That's how he came to be wearing the wolf skin when Grigore found him. He brought Andrei to the farm and took care of him. After listening to his story, he decided to have the boy stay with him and help work the farm; a hired hand at first, then as an adopted son. Five years later, a wealthy Constantin Lupu came to his farm looking for a guide to help him hunt in the mountains. Grigore recommended Andrei. The two spent a week in Grigore's cabin. They hiked, hunted and fished. By the time they returned to the farm, Lupu had convinced Andrei to go with him and work as his all-around man on his estate by the Polish border. Grigore gave his blessings to Andrei and made sure the young man knew he would always be considered a part of the Antovich family.

The barking of the two old dogs woke Grigore from his nap on the front porch that overlooked the orchards and the roadway in to the farm. Someone was coming. He didn't have to wait long before three men turned the corner of the roadway and began walking toward the house. He recognized Andrei immediately. Always in front. It was good to see him coming "home" once again. The other two men had rifles slung over their shoulders and followed Andrei in single file. They looked to be military of some sort. He stood up and waved. Andrei waved backed. The two dogs were straining to leave the porch, but had been trained not to move unless ordered. Grigore looked at his old four-legged friends. They knew who was coming. He said, "Go!" and they were gone. He smiled as he watched the two retired sheep dogs race toward their old friend.

He hadn't seen them so excited in months. Andrei knelt on one knee to greet them. Both vied hard for his attention. Grigore's wife, Anna, came out on the porch and watched.

"That has to be Andrei," she said. "I'll put some coffee on and see what's in the ice box."

"Down," Grigore shouted. The two dogs immediately dropped prone on the ground and watched anxiously as the old man and Andrei met and hugged in front of the porch. They growled softly as the other two men stepped forward to shake Grigore's hand. As soon as their master had shaken each man's hand, they relaxed.

"Are you hunting, my son?" Grigore asked Andrei.

"No. But my two young friends are," Andrei answered.

"So, what is it they hunt in this part of the world?" Grigore asked him.

"Their freedom," Andrei answered.

Grigore had been following the news on the radio concerning the war and how it was unfolding. He asked Andrei to translate what he had heard to the two Poles. He was sad to report that Warsaw's days of freedom were about to end. The Soviets had taken most of southeastern Poland and were looking to hook up with the German forces driving toward them. He was extremely disappointed in the French and English for not opening a second front on Germany's western border and he apologized to the two Poles for his country's decision to go neutral. He understood why his government had done so. The Russians were all over the Romanian border and Germany was closing fast to join them. He told Andrei that Romania would not be able stay out of the war for long.

He put a hand on Andrei's shoulder and said, "The hunting in the mountains all these years will come in handy when our time comes."

There was some good news. Grigore had heard reports that thousands of Polish airmen and soldiers had made it across the border. And while they had been sent to internment camps, some had already escaped and were on their way to Bucharest. A few had already reached the Polish embassy. It was his guess that identification papers, passports and money was going to be put in their hands so they could get out of the country. When Andrei asked how that would happen, Grigore said that the ports on the Black Sea would be filled with ships ready to take them. After relaying the conversation to the two pilots, Josef asked if any men might come this way. Andrei laughed and said it wasn't likely, but it was the way he would choose. No submarines in the mountains.

The four men sat quietly while Anna piled the eggs, bread and cheese on the kitchen table in front of them. They ate their fill, careful not to overeat. There was a ten-mile hike awaiting them.

To the Mountains

They stayed for two hours. Ludwik and Josef thanked the two elderly Romanians for their hospitality and left ahead of Andrei. They walked down the roadway a bit to give their guide a little private time with his adopted parents. They picked a few apples and squeezed them into their packs while Andrei finished his goodbyes.

Grigore had some parting words for his adopted son, "The wolves are many this year. They are not particular. Do not worry about others in the mountains. There is no one there. One thing more. Do the young Poles speak our language?"

"They do not," Andrei answered.

"Then teach them a few words; a few sentences that might help them in their travels. You have learned much Polish from Constantin, yes?"

Andrei made sure the two men understood what the next few days were going to be as they walked toward the mountains and the cabin high in the pass. They would stay the night and be on their way to Borsa in the morning. It would take most of the day to get there. They would wait for him in a forest near the town while he bought the train tickets to Satu Mare. From Satu Mare on, they would be on their own and in God's hands. But before all that happened, he had something for them to learn that might be of use. He told them to keep walking and to listen carefully, then repeat what he said. He began with "Buna." (Hello) They repeated it. He went on. "Buna dimineota." (Good morning.) "Buna ziva." (Good afternoon.) "Buna seara." (Good evening.) The lesson went on with other common phrases for an hour. It ended with simple sentences like, "Eu sunt Poloneza." (I am Polish.) and "Eu am bani." (I have money.)

The cabin had been improved over the years. It was no longer drafty. All cracks between the logs that served as the walls had been sealed permanently with tar and small stones. An outhouse had been erected just off to one side of the cabin. A loft had been constructed above the stone fireplace on the back wall. It was large enough to sleep two adults. Two huge, thick, bear skins laid out on the floor of the loft were used as beds. Heat from the fireplace, rising directly up into the loft, made it comfortable even during the coldest winter nights.

Pack mules had brought up a bevy of materials including a heavy chest, full sofa, a kindling stove, two cabinets and a wash tub. The chest was loaded with blankets, clothes and utensils that stayed in the cabin all year round. The sofa was situated in front of the fireplace.

It served as Andrei's bed. He had been sleeping on it for years. U shaped iron braces had been forged and nailed into the wall on both sides of the door and onto the door itself. They held a heavy four by four piece of lumber dropped by rope across the door at night for added security. It would take an elephant to pry the door open. Cordwood and kindling were stacked six feet high on both sides of the fireplace and along another wall. The stove, wash tub and cabinets, stocked with canned goods, covered the remaining wall. A table and two benches behind the sofa served as the dining area. The cabin was a far cry from the building that had saved Andrei years ago.

Ludwik and Josef selected "pork and beans" cans and some salted venison hung on a wall Andrei enjoyed a tomato soup with onions. As night closed in, the heat from the fireplace and the long trek of the day, put both Ludwik and Josef up into the loft early for a well-earned night's sleep. Andrei lay out on the sofa to enjoy the fire.

The howling came from somewhere deep in the forest. It woke Ludwik. The darkness in the cabin made the animal's cry seem a little more menacing than it really was. It was a not so gentle reminder of the situation he and Josef were now part of; strangers in a foreign land, sleeping on a bearskin in a loft, in a mountain cabin far away from home and totally dependent on another man. To Josef, the wolf's cry was nothing more than a minor disturbance. He rolled over once in the loft, grunted, and resumed snoring in defiance of the mournful intrusion. To Andrei, the howling was a chilling throwback to his battle with the wolf he had found caught in his trap that near fatal winter long ago. The weakened animal had fought him off for over an hour before the ax finally crushed its skull. He wondered if this wolf, somewhere out there in the forest, had come seeking revenge. He smiled at the thought. He knew the only wolves he had to worry about were the two-legged ones; the ones that would be on him and his fellow countrymen soon.

Putting that aside, he concentrated on the day ahead and how he would get these two young men out of Romania.

By noon of the next day, the three had made it through the pass and down onto the flat plain that extended west toward Borsa. Andrei had them practicing the Romanian phrases and sentences he had taught them. He was impressed with their intelligence and ability. Even their newly learned Romanian accent was good. He encouraged them to exchange greetings and make small talk with some of the peasant farmers they passed. Andrei said the trick in conversing in a foreign language was to initiate and control a conversation with questions that had one-word answers. Like yes and no. They did well with his suggestion. The people didn't seem to think they were foreigners.

During one of their rest periods, Andrei pointed to the triangular shaped haystacks that were spread out in the field before them. Each had to be close to fifteen feet high. He said a framework of tree limbs and branches underneath supported the huge bulk of dried grass piled on it. He said a man, maybe even two, could burrow into the base of one and avoid spending a cold night in the open. He laughingly said many a farmer's daughter had lost her virginity in the interior of a haystack; his point being it was obviously a good place to hide; night or day.

"Me and a young beauty in the middle of a haystack would be something," Josef said. He flashed a bright smile.

"Be careful about what you wish for," Andrei said. "All your "young beauties" might have a husband, boyfriend, father, grandfather, or brother. If any of those men caught you in the act, they would kill you."

Ludwik smiled at the warning. Josef's smile had disappeared.

325

Andrei continued, "You will be on your own soon. Take what I say now for whatever it's worth." Ludwik and Josef nodded.

"Know what is always going on about you. Take nothing for granted. Be very careful of who you trust. Don't be hasty. Take your time. If possible, make sure when one of you sleeps, the other is awake. Stay away from places where you stick out as strangers. Try not to get injured. Constantin told me you have first aid material. That's good. Treat each other's injuries. Stay away from hospitals. They report to the authorities. And don't get caught screwing someone's wife."

"How about a single, mature, and not so "young and beautiful" woman?" Josef asked.

Andrei laughed and said, "For those, you have my permission."

The rest of the trek was uneventful. They saw very few people on the road. Most were working the fields. A few motor vehicles and horse pulled wagons went by. Their drivers hardly looked at them.

Andrei's objective was to reach the small bridge with a crucifix bolted to its railing. It was only a few miles to Borsa from there. He would leave the road after the bridge and follow the stream that flowed under it up into the forest and the waterfall. There was a clearing in the woods at the top of the falls. From there it was a short walk downhill to the train station on the outskirts of the town. If anyone was looking for strangers, they would be watching the roads, not the forest. The two pilots would wait for him while he went down to the station and bought the tickets. Constantin had told him that two trains left Borsa every day: one late in the morning and one late in the afternoon. The afternoon train was the one he had to get the two men on. That's when the constables in Borsa would be home eating supper. There was a good chance that no police would be around at that time.

He would tell the two men to check the station just in case and if a constable was there, to avoid him at all costs before boarding.

Both Ludwik and Josef crossed themselves as they passed the crucifix on the bridge. Ludwik always had a sense of sorrow tempered with hope when he looked at Jesus hanging on the cross. This time was different. He felt a surge of strength, not sorrow, race through his body. It was as if the Lord had whispered, "Stay strong. I am with you," as he passed by.

The roar of the waterfall was deafening. Andrei motioned to the path near it and pointed to himself and then up. He pointed at them and waved his hand down. He was going up first. They were to wait. He went up the near vertical trail like a mountain goat. They watched him disappear over the top. In a few minutes, he reappeared holding a few coils of rope. He flung the rope down and motioned for them to come up one at a time. The spray from the falls made the going slippery, but the rope and Andrei's strength made it easy for them.

It was a quick walk through the forest up top to the clearing that looked down at Borsa. It was about a mile from where they were to a lumber yard on the outskirts of the picturesque, country village. A careful view of the yard with binoculars showed there was no one about. Andrei pointed out the train station to Ludwik and told him to keep an eye on it while he went there for the tickets. He said he would be back in an hour.

He was back before the hour was up. The train was expected at the station within the next two hours. He said it would be best to wait here for a while then go the station just before the train arrived; get on it immediately and if possible, find seats in the car at the rear of the train. If they encountered trouble for any reason, they could exit the rear of the train and jump to safety. He said the train went to Baia Mare, some fifty miles away. They would have to change trains there.

327

The second train would take them to Satu Mare. It would arrive just before dark. It was only a few miles from the Hungarian border. From Satu Mare, they could use the cover of darkness to walk the tracks across the border. He suggested they walk in Hungary for a few hours before finding a place to sleep. Tomorrow, they should find a bank and exchange their lei for Hungarian pengo. He said the tickets he bought were a gift from Constantin and he didn't need their thanks; just the rifles. He suggested they go and wash in the stream leading to the falls and fill their canteens. They did that. When they returned, the rifles were gone. And so was Andrei. They were on their own again. The last few days with Andrei had been good. They didn't have to do much thinking. They just played "follow the leader." And now, tickets tucked away, they were two train rides from Hungary. After that would come Yugoslavia, northern Italy and France. Then, they would get in the fight.

No one paid them any attention as they walked through the small station and onto the track platform. The train was a local. There were only three passenger cars behind the engine and coal car. A few passengers had already boarded. Many were still saying their goodbyes. Everything looked normal. There were no suspicious looking characters anywhere. And most importantly, there were no policemen.

Sisters

Ludwik and Josef walked toward the last passenger car. There was a group of women exchanging goodbyes with two other women near the car's steps. As they neared the group, the two women left and dragged their suitcases over to the steps. The first one had difficulty lifting her bag up the stairs and into the car. She couldn't do it. Ludwik wondered how she had managed to get it this far. She was small, slim, well dressed and pretty. Without thinking, he stepped forward, took the bag from her and carried it onto the train.

Then he reached down and gave her his hand and assisted her up the stairs. His actions brought an approving whisper from the ladies on the platform. Not to be outdone, Josef took the other woman's bag and followed suit. That brought some excited remarks from the ladies. Ludwik could see from the reaction of the two on the train, the remarks had been bawdy. Both seemed to relish the flavor of the words. Their hearty laughs told Ludwik they were well experienced in the world. The two waved their goodbyes to their friends as the train pulled away from the platform and then turned their attention to Ludwik and Josef. They thanked them for their kindness. Ludwik and Josef didn't understand a word they were saying. Then with more words they didn't understand, they invited them to join them. Ludwik and Josef stood there smiling and tried to be polite. The woman that Ludwik had helped realized they were foreigners. That interested her. Looking directly at Ludwik, she patted the seat next to her and moved over slightly. The other woman pointed to the seat next to her and motioned Josef to come and sit there.

Ludwik remembered Lupu's advice about sitting with a woman to create the appearance they were a couple. There had already been enough Romanian spoken by the women to leave the impression to anyone nearby that the two men understood what they were saying. Their Romanian clothes, caps, and rolled sleeping bags further enhanced the appearance they were natives. Ludwik thought it might be a good thing to accept the invitation but was concerned they would somehow give away the fact they were foreigners. He would try out Andrei's lessons in using the native language to keep their identity quiet. He drew the attention of the lady next to him by putting a finger across his lips and whispering softly "Numele meu este Ludwik. Eu sunt Poloneza. (My name is Ludwik. I am Polish.) She put a finger across her lips and nodded yes to let Ludwik know she would keep his secret. Then she pointed to Josef. Ludwik said, "Josef, Poloneza."

Moving closer to Ludwik, she said, "Numele meu este Tannsha Bourean." She pointed to Josef's friend and said, "Byanka Bourean." Then she reached across to her sister and quietly told her that the two men were Polish, and they didn't want anyone to know that. She had heard that many Polish military had escaped into Romania and were being put into internment camps by the Romanian government. She was guessing these two men had escaped from one of them. Byanka understood. She asked what Josef's name was. She said that "Josef" was welcome to stay with her if he needed to hide. Tannsha sat back next to Ludwik, looked at him and said to her sister, "I wouldn't mind having a handsome man in my bed tonight either."

Ten minutes after the train had departed Borsa, the conductor came into the car. He smiled at the two couples playing some sort of hand signal game with each other. He greeted them with a polite, "buna seara," (good evening.) Both couples answered simultaneously in kind. That brought an outburst of laughter from the two ladies. The conductor smiled again and asked for their tickets. Ludwik and Josef hesitated and waited for a response from the two women. When they handed their tickets to the man, they reached for theirs.

The "hand game" continued for some time. The universal signals by hand to exchange information about each other went well. There were no other passengers seated in a way to observe them so the hand signals went on unabated. In ten minutes, they all knew how old each other was, if they were married or not and what their destinations were. How to say "yes, no, maybe" was answered by the women with head and body moves along with the spoken Romanian word. Both sisters were older than Ludwik and Josef. Tannsha was thirty. Byanka was twenty-eight. They were not married and lived with each other near the train station in Baia Mare. It was hard for Ludwik to ignore Tannsha's obvious charms. She was very good looking, had a happy personality and was not bashful about pressing her well-endowed body against his in the tight confines of the seat.

330

He knew the main goal for tonight was to get across the border and out of Romania. He told himself to keep that in mind. But while he was this close to the lady, he decided to enjoy her company. He noticed that Josef wasn't having any difficulty enjoying the company of his seatmate. She was full of life.

It was late afternoon when they reached the outskirts of Baia Mare. People were about. Horse drawn carriages and a few automobiles could be seen on the streets beyond the buildings they passed. The train began to slow as it approached the station. Ludwik stepped over Tannsha's feet and opened the window. He wanted to take a look ahead at the platform. His heart almost stopped when he saw the police coming out of the station and onto the platform. He took Tannsha's hand and pulled her to the window to have a look. He said, "nu buna." (No good) She understood. She told her sister there might be trouble for their two friends at the station. There were police on the platform.

As the train came to a stop, a man burst his way into their car from the one in front of them. He sprinted to the back, opened the door and jumped out onto the tracks. Two policemen raced by on the platform. One had a gun drawn. Nobody moved in the car. Shouts came from outside the car. Tannsha and Byanka slid down in their seats and motioned for the two men to do the same. They stayed in that position until the conductor walked into the car and told them it was time to exit the train and leave the station. He said no would be allowed in the station the rest of the night. He said this train was going to remain here. The police needed to search it. If there were any passengers that were supposed to go to Satu Mare, they would have to wait until tomorrow to do so. He apologized for the disruption.

331

Tannsha motioned for Ludwik to take her bag down. Then she tapped him on the chest and indicated that they should exit the train together. Ludwik understood. Byanka did the same with Josef.

There were police in the station. They didn't give Ludwik and Josef a second glance. They just stared at the two beautiful sisters as the foursome made their way through the station to the exit. The two couples walked arm in arm down the street. They walked for a few minutes to a park on the town's outskirts and found a secluded bench in the shadow of a large elm. Ludwik and Josef sat and watched Tannsha explain what was going on with her clever sign language along with a few words she had heard the two men use. She asked for Ludwik's ticket by showing him hers. When he produced it, she said, "Nu seara." (Not evening) Ludwik told Josef, "No train tonight." Remembering Andrei's words, he asked her, "Buna dimineota?" (Good in the morning?) She shrugged her shoulders and lifted her hands. She wasn't sure about a train in the morning.

"Hotel? Josef asked Tannsha. She and Byanka laughed. Byanka said, "Nu!"

Tannsha folded her hands together on one side of her head. She leaned her head against her hands and closed her eyes. She then pointed to Josef and Byanka and smiled. She did the same for Ludwik and her. It was unmistakable. They were being offered a night in bed with two very attractive women. Josef pointed to his empty ring finger and then at Byanka's. He wanted to be sure she wasn't married. He didn't want to be party to an adulterous act. And he didn't want any unpleasant surprises.

The sisters lived in the small village of Recea. It was a two mile walk from the park. Their home was a stone cottage. There was a small bungalow next to it. Tannsha kissed her sister goodnight, smiled at Josef and led Ludwik into the bungalow that served as her studio.

Inside, she lit a candle and led him past several covered easels to a bed opposite a small fireplace. She gave Ludwik some matches and motioned for him to start a fire. By the time the first flame flickered up from the kindling, she was under the covers; naked, and waiting.

It was the first time in a long while that Ludwik was able to think about something else beside the war and the events that had led him and Josef to this village in Romania. He relaxed and let the lady take the lead in her quest for pleasure. When she was finished, they rested in each other's arms for a few minutes. Then Ludwik rolled her over, walked to the fire side of the bed, gently dragged her to him, lifted her hips and mounted her for more.

When dawn broke, Tannsha dressed and slipped out of the bungalow while Ludwik slept. She unchained her bike and rode back to the train station in Baia Mare. There was a friend that worked mornings cleaning the facilities there. She would know if the police were still about or if they were planning to return. She would also know if the trains were going to resume their usual schedule. It would be important for her Polish lover and his companion to have that information. She wanted them to stay and hoped they would but knew they had somewhere to be and it wasn't anywhere in Romania.

Her friend said the police did not catch the man who had jumped off the train. He was wanted for bank robbery and murder and was considered to be very dangerous. The police had searched every inch of the train looking for any bank money he might have hidden on it. They finished their work after midnight and would not be back today. She said two trains would be going to Satu Mare today; an express at ten o'clock this morning and a slower, local one that would leave at four this afternoon. Ludwik was still asleep when Tannsha returned. She added some wood to the fire. She wanted the bungalow warm when Ludwik woke. For now, she would let him sleep. He had earned his rest.

She went to the cottage and made ready the kitchen for breakfast. The sound of heavy snoring coming from the bedroom brought a smile to her face. She knew what her sister could do to a man once she got him in bed. She was small but strong and insatiable.

Tannsha got the message across to Ludwik and Josef about the train schedule. The morning one was an express to Satu Mare, arriving at 11:00 A.M. The other train, a much slower local, would arrive at Satu Mare, at 7:00 P.M, an hour before dark. She made sure they understood there would not be any policemen at the station today. They were all in the countryside looking for the fugitive.

Ludwik and Josef decided to take the local train. They felt if they had to jump to avoid trouble, it would be best to be on a train that would slow to make stops. In addition, they did not want to spend much time in Satu Mare. With no papers to show authorities on either side of the border, they felt it was to their advantage to arrive late in the day, avoid contact until dark and then find a way across the border.

After breakfast, they excused themselves to study their map. They settled on the idea of crossing the Somes River into Hungary and then finding a train headed west they could hop or chance buying a seat on. They decided to get into Hungary first and then decide what to do.

Most of the day was spent in and out of bed with the women, taking naps, playing cards and helping to prepare food. Leaving late in the afternoon, all four walked to the station. They arrived at 5:40. The 6:00 local was just pulling in. Tannsha's friend had been right. There were no policemen at the station. The two couples said their goodbyes with affectionate hugs and kisses. It was good theatre. Anyone watching them had to think the women were saying goodbye to their husbands.

Just before the train left Baia Mare, Ludwik and Josef boarded the last car and sat in the last row on each side of the aisle. Ludwik checked the door behind them that led to the back platform outside. When he found the door locked, he picked the lock with his knife. He wanted the door open in case they had to make a quick exit. It only took a few seconds to pick the lock; less time than it had to open the safe back in Deblin. Josef was amazed how quick Ludwik was.

"You would have made a great thief," Josef said quietly.

"Maybe in your eyes, but not in the eyes of God. Remember the 7th commandment?" Ludwik answered.

"I do, but what if you could steal something that would get you to France quickly and in the fight against the Germans"

"Then I would do it and ask forgiveness later."

"I believe God would forgive you," Josef responded.

They paid close attention to everything the train passed, exchanging quiet, verbal notes on places they might be able to use for cover or a rendezvous point if they had to leave the train quickly. Every time the local began to slow for a stop at one of the small villages, they made sure they looked ahead to see who was on the platform and around the station. Eyes and ears were on full alert for anything out of the ordinary. Everyone that boarded the train came under their scrutiny. Thankfully, no one looked out of the ordinary to them. They were mostly worker or farmer types. None seemed to be from the merchant or government class. Their clothes indicated that. Most of them rode from one village to the next. Only a few remained on the train after the stop before Satu Mare. Ludwik enjoyed the late afternoon view of the countryside as the train chugged its way toward Satu Mare. Everything was bright in the full sun of early autumn.

The fields were green, gold and a fallowed dark brown, the ponds, streams and rivers beautiful shades of blue. Complimenting those colors were the multi-colored autumn leaves of the forests off in the distance.

The diversified brilliance of color absolutely defined God's creativity to Ludwik. He saw it all as a gift to man, God's greatest creation. Romania was a beautiful country. Very much like his Poland. It pained him to think about Poland's pastoral countryside being ground into mud and dust by tanks and the boots of a million men trying to kill each other. So different from what he was seeing here. He reminded himself that it was going to take patience to regain what was being lost in Poland. He recalled a survival training instructor at Puck referring to an old Chinese proverb that seemed appropriate for both Poland's recovery and this journey; "A journey of a thousand miles begins with a single step."

Only a dozen or so people had boarded their car between Baia Mare and Satu Mare. None of them had shown any interest in the two young men in the back row, one on each side of the aisle. What they didn't realize was the two were watching every move they made. As the train approached Satu Mare, both men became alert. Josef opened the window on his side and poked his head out to see what was ahead. Ludwik did likewise on his side. The first thing Josef saw was a small flock of sheep high on a hillside. They were tended by a young woman in a brown robe. There was a large dog by her side. There was something familiar about her. He called Ludwik over to have a look. As the train approached her and the animals, she turned and looked down at them from the hill. Her gaze was steady and fixed. She smiled and waved to them as the train slowly slid by. Josef smiled and waved back to her. Ludwik just stared. Every inch of skin on his body was prickling. Just like it had in Poland when the shepherdess and her dog tending their sheep had narrowly escaped a strafing Messerschmitt.

This woman and her dog were striking in similarity to the woman and dog in Poland. It had to be an unusual coincidence or a sign of some sort. His prickling skin convinced him it was the latter. Josef knew better to question Ludwik when it came to matters like this. The man's faith was a powerful force. He was sure he felt things that most people didn't. He knew he didn't.

They didn't want to chance buying train tickets and having to show papers they didn't have when they reached the border. They decided to cross the border by following the Somes River at night, then hop a train heading west across Hungary as soon as they could.

Haystacks and Trains

It was almost dark when they dug the fire hole in the woods next to the river. They filled it with twigs, pine needles and dry leaves for kindling. Josef chopped some brittle branches from a dead tree and shaved off some thin pieces with the small ax Lupu had given them. He fanned the kindling in the bottom of the two-foot hole until it burst into flame. Then he added some small pieces of the brittle branches. When the flames grew strong, they wedged three pieces of a sturdy branch across the hole to form a grate and set two cans of tomato soup on them. It took a while for the soup to warm. When it was ready, Josef put his gloves on and opened the cans with the finger can opener from the survival kit. After finishing the soup, they put out the fire and buried the cans in the hole. They waited for night to set in then went down to the river and followed it toward the border. An hour later they were in Hungary.

It took two hours of walking on the tracks that crossed the border before they were certain they were headed west. West to Budapest. Ludwik checked his compass frequently and Josef doubled checked that by using the North Star for reference.

The objective was to get to a city that had banks. They needed to change their lei for pengo and buy tickets to Budapest. Their maps did not show any towns or cities of any size that might have banks in the rural flat land of east Hungary. They all seemed to be farther west. All they could do now was to keep walking westward and hope for that slow moving train. Not having to cross any borders to get to Budapest meant that official papers would not be necessary. All they would have to do was ride a train to the city and get to the embassy.

As midnight approached, the two men began to tire. Breaks came a little more often. It became apparent that chances for a freight train to come chugging by at this late hour were slim. And when a misty, light rain began to fall, it convinced them that it would be best to find a place quickly where they could stay dry and get some sleep, a place not far from the tracks. Just in case that freight train did come.

A half hour later, the tracks led them through an open field that was dotted by numerous haystacks off to their left. They were similar to the ones they had seen in the Romanian countryside with Andrei. He had told them it was possible to crawl into the base of one and find an empty space in the middle. A good place to hide or sleep. They picked one closest to the tracks reasoning that if a train did come while they slept, the rumbling and tremors from it would wake them in time to get out, roll their bags onto the back packs and make a run for the train as it went by. If they slept through the night, it would not be a bad thing. Sleep and rest were always necessary. It was going to be a long trip riding and hiding until they felt it was safe enough to become paid passengers. And if that meant they would have to hide tomorrow and wait for nightfall, then so be it.

Before the tunneling into the haystack began, they walked the tracks ahead to make sure there would be no surprises in the morning should they sleep through the night. The first hundred yards or so, there was nothing but open meadow on both sides of the tracks.

As they moved farther ahead, Ludwik could make out the faint outline of some kind of high structure that loomed directly above the tracks. He guessed correctly it was part of a long trestle that spanned a river. The trestle was wooden. It rose high above the tracks on both sides of the bridge. It was hard to determine its length over the river because of the darkness, but Ludwik thought it to be substantial. The sides of the trestle rose some twenty feet above the tracks. It formed a tunnel-like cover over the bridge. The sides were open, crisscrossing lengths of four- by-four wooden planks; easy to climb. Just before the top of the trestle was a narrow, walking platform that ran parallel to the tracks. It was a perfect place for a person to hide on. All one would have to do was wait until the engine passed, step down on the inside of the sidewall and jump onto the roof of a boxcar or into an open flat car. The speed of the train would be the determining factor in deciding if such a jump was safe. Ludwik and Josef discussed the possibility of attempting such a jump on the way back to the haystacks. They realized that making a jump like that would have to be made in daylight. And they would need a flat, railroad car that was open with room in it to stay out of sight. And for that, they would need some luck.

Ludwik tunneled into the base of the giant haystack by pushing the hay inward and to the sides. Josef stood watch outside. After five feet of hay had been moved, Ludwik found the empty space he had been hoping for. It was a good three feet high. Josef quickly crawled in after him. Feeling with their hands in the darkness, they found there was enough room for both of them. Josef turned back into the "tunnel", crawled to its entrance and slowly backed his way into the interior while replacing the hay that had been pushed aside. Ludwik was inside his sleeping bag by the time he finished. He listened to the peaceful drum of rain pelting down on the haystack. He marveled at the ingenuity that had gone into the haystack's design. It was perfectly dry inside. It was something any engineer would appreciate.

Josef, safely tucked away in his bag, asked Ludwik if he knew anything about the haystack's purpose. Ludwik quietly answered, "It keeps most of the hay from being soaked and rotting. If the cattle don't have hay to eat, they die. And eventually so will the farmer and his family."

Satisfied, Josef silently prayed for the safety of his father and Poland. He thanked God, Jesus and Mary for this day and all his days. He asked them to give him the strength and courage to go on and be worthy of God's promise of eternal life. Then he thanked Ludwik for the prayer he had just said. It was one that was good for a lifetime.

The rain was constant that night, but never interrupted the sleep of the two men. The structure of the haystack was sound. The best engineers from the best technical universities couldn't have designed it better. Its shape and construction funneled the rain water down its sloping sides and into a shallow drainage ditch that was cut to carry it away from the base. Only a few inches on the sides of the haystack's exterior were penetrated by the rain. Nothing that a good day in the sun couldn't dry.

It wasn't the first glimmer of light that woke Ludwik. It was the soft, trotting footsteps outside in the meadow. They kept circling the haystack. Every now and then they would stop. Almost as if the animal they belonged to was listening; waiting for a sound that would confirm what its nose had told it. Ludwik held his breath and didn't move. He thanked God that Josef was still as a stone and buried deep in his bag. When he heard the whining and excited panting begin, he knew it was a dog. And that meant the dog's owner wouldn't be far away. Probably the farmer who worked this land. He gently nudged Josef's bag. His head popped out and looked at him.

Ludwik tapped a finger across his own mouth. He tapped his right ear and pointed to the side of the haystack. Josef nodded his head.

The dog's pace and low whine had quickened. He was getting very excited. Then a voice from far off in the meadow silenced him.

"Villam!!" "Villam!!" "Gyere ide!" "Gyere ide!"

And just like that, the dog was gone. His master had called him and saved the day for the two tenants in the haystack. Ludwik and Josef quickly rolled and tied their sleeping bags to their backpacks. They dug their way out on the side of the haystack away from the direction the voice had come from. Peeking around the edge of the haystack, they saw a man far off in the meadow walking with their four-legged visitor toward a small, white cottage. Chickens patrolled the dirt yard in front of it. A few ducks and geese slowly pedaled their way around a small, greenish pond. The smoke curling out from the chimney drifted its way up the meadow and over the haystacks. It carried with it the smell of breakfast. When the cottage door closed behind the man and his dog, Ludwik and Josef made their way up to the tracks. Making sure to keep the haystack between them and the cottage, they walked straight up and over the tracks, down the grade of earth on the other side and made their way to the bridge. When they got there, they went down the embankment to the river and got under the bridge. The river was wide. It stretched some two hundred yards across to the opposite bank. They stripped to the waist and washed their head and upper body with the cold, river water. Even without soap, they felt cleansed and refreshed. They dressed and remained out of sight under the bridge. Breakfast was biscuits, chocolate and a long drink from their canteens. They shared a cigarette and discussed their next move. There were three options. One, they could walk the tracks west and make it look like they were hikers and hop a train if one came by. Two, they could walk to a town or village near the tracks and hope there was a bank there to exchange their Romanian lei and then try to buy train tickets. Three, they could wait here for a slow- moving train, climb up the trestle onto the platform and jump on the train as it passed underneath.

341

Their biggest concern was getting caught here, close to the Romanian border, and being sent back to Romania and interned by the authorities. They decided to wait for a train. Even if it took all day.

It was early afternoon when they heard the familiar chugging of a train engine far off in the distance. It was coming their way. Ludwik scrambled up the bank and climbed the side of the trestle where the platform was. He could see by the smoke puffs from the engine that the train was not moving very fast. A closer look with his binoculars showed it was a freight train. The black, coal burning engine was pulling a long line of box cars with a few flat cars mingled in. He told Josef to bring the backpacks and climb up to him. Their ride was approaching.

Lying flat on his stomach with the binoculars, Ludwik detailed the train's lineup to Josef: eight boxcars behind the engine and coal car, two open flat cars, loaded with lumber and no sides, three more box cars, two flat cars loaded with hay with sides, five more box cars and a caboose. The boxcars were not an option; no place to hide in daylight and jumping onto lumber with no place to hide was also out of the question. Their best bet were the two flat cars carrying bales of hay. They had sides they could hide behind.

As the train approached the bridge, it began to slow. When the engine and coal car rolled by underneath them, the two got up and climbed down the trestle through the black smoke and waited for the hay-carrying flat cars. As soon as they spotted the bales of hay in the first open car, they made ready to jump by going down to the next level of boards and leaning out over the train as it passed underneath. Ludwik jumped as the front part of the second hay car passed him. Josef leapt a second later. The hay bales weren't that soft. They had been compressed tightly and there wasn't much give when they landed. They rolled across the hay to the far side. Ludwik's backpack cushioned the collision with the sideboard. Josef wasn't that lucky.

342

He rolled head over heels into the sideboard slamming his left ankle down on top of it. He lay there writhing in pain. Ludwik crawled over to him, unlaced his boot and took it off. Thankfully, there wasn't any break. There was a little blood oozing from some scraped skin just above the ankle and a very colorful bruise blossoming in the same area. Josef put the boot back on without lacing it up. They crawled over the hay bales to the other side where the sideboards were a little higher. They took off their backpacks and sat back against the sideboards, their heads a foot or so below the top of the boards. For the moment, they were safely out of sight from anyone on the ground.

It only took a few minutes to realize they could be seen by someone on ground higher than the train or on an overpass the train went under. Ludwik thought he had seen space between the hay bales and the sideboard on the other side after he had made his jump. He crawled across and saw there was a foot-long gap between the hay and the side of the car. He took his knife and cut away the edge of the hay and saw there was open space all the way down to the floor. He signaled for Josef to crawl over. Using their knives, they cut their way down through three levels of hay bales until they were standing on the floor of the flat car. They cut enough hay away from the bottom bales to stretch their legs out when sitting with their back to the sideboard. They dispersed the cut hay along the floor toward both ends of the car. Ludwik then reached up and wiggled three bales of hay out from the top level over to the sideboard. That put them out of sight from anyone above and would give them some cover if rain came.

"Saved by a pile of hay again," Josef said as he patted a bale.

"Your landing wasn't jump school perfect," Ludwik chuckled.

343

That brought on some quiet conversation about their parachute training, the dry land practice, the tower jumps and the balloon drops. Both admitted they almost wet their pants before their first jump. Josef said he almost forgot where the toggle was.

"What did you think after the chute opened?" Ludwik asked.

Josef smiled and said, "I didn't think. I just thanked God."

They spent the next few hours sprawled out on the floor catching up on the sleep they missed last night in the haystack. The train's whistle ended that. The engineer was announcing the train's arrival at some place. Josef tied his boot loosely, put on his backpack and stood up beside Ludwik who was peering through a crack in the sidewall.

Debrechen

The sign read, "DEBRECHEN" in large black letters. It was above a large, barn-like building. When the train stopped, Ludwik moved a few feet down the car to another crack and saw what looked like several buildings next to the "barn." They were in a city. Someone blew a whistle and the train jolted forward. It moved ahead very slowly, switched onto another track and gradually rolled to a stop. Through the crack he watched a man walk toward the train headed for the engine. Soon after that, he heard a clanging of metal and someone yelling that was obviously the signal to move out as the engine cranked up and began to slowly puff away from the line of freight cars it had delivered. The freight cars now sat motionless on the track. Muted sounds of activity could be heard off in the distance somewhere behind them. That meant people. And that could mean trouble. The question now was were they far enough away from the border that they could risk buying tickets to Budapest or should they remain hidden from people a while longer.

Ludwik reasoned a city like Debrechen would have many banks and there was plenty of time to reach one before they closed. Josef said he wasn't sure about his ankle. Ludwik decided to have a better look at the surroundings. He reached up and slowly moved one of the overhead bales back to where it had been. Working his way up the bales, he grabbed the top of the sideboard and pulled himself up to peek over the edge. What he saw surprised him. They were in the middle of a large railyard. Long lines of boxcars were everywhere. One was directly in front of him. And on the other side of that line were buildings; buildings that people lived in. That's where the sound of activity was coming from. Sounds of a city. Much clearer now in the open air. He slid back down onto the floor of the flat car. He cupped his hands for Josef to get a boost up and have a look for himself. He was only there for a few seconds.

"A man saw me!" Josef blurted out.

"Where is he?" Ludwik asked.

"He took off running toward some buildings on the other side of us."

Ludwik scrambled up for a look and saw a man enter a building on the far side of the yard. He came out with another man and pointed directly at them. It was time to leave.

Josef handed the backpacks up to Ludwik then took his hand for help in climbing up. Staying low and out of sight, they dropped the backpacks to the ground, climbed over the side and slid down to trackside. Ludwik threw his pack on and climbed over a coupling connecting two boxcars on the track in front of him. On the other side of the boxcars were two empty tracks and the city.

Josef lay on the ground for a moment. He had aggravated his bruised ankle. It was pulsing pain quite hard.

Before he got up, he peeked under the flat car and saw three men holding shovels headed their way. One was the man who had spotted him. He stumbled to the boxcars with his backpack, threw it over the coupling to Ludwik and scrambled under it to the other side.

There was nothing but the empty tracks between them and a street lined with high tenement houses that ran parallel to the railyard. There were children playing tag in the back of one of the tenements. A few others were walking up the empty tracks toward them hopping on and off the rails trying to balance themselves. They were too busy playing to notice them or if they had noticed, they didn't seem to care.

Josef threw on his backpack, and they began crossing the empty tracks toward the tenements. They didn't run but moved with energy toward a tenement that did not have any children outside.

The banging on the flat car by the three men with their shovels echoed off the tenement buildings and stopped the children from their games. That's when they saw Ludwik and Josef making their way across the tracks. They stood still and watched them with interest. One of the little ones waved to them. Ludwik waved back. Then the little one and his friends ran across the tracks to peek under the boxcars to see what all the commotion was about. The banging on the flat car was now being accompanied by yelling.

"They think we're still under the hay," Josef said.

"That's good, but let's get out of the railyard before they climb into the car and see we're gone," Ludwik responded.

By the time they cleared the railyard and got to the street, Josef was hobbling. There was a large garden with a gazebo in its rear just across the street. They walked slowly through the garden area and took a seat on a bench in the gazebo.

Ludwik didn't think the railroad men would continue their search out of the railyard. He was right. No one appeared between the tenements. They were safe. At least for the time being.

It was early afternoon. Debrechen was a very large city. Ludwik felt the best thing to do was to stay in plain sight and try not to attract attention. He felt being on the streets, blending in with lots of people would be safe. The neighborhood garden they were sitting in was not that kind of place. It was too local, part of a neighborhood community. They were definite strangers here. Plus, who knew how many people in the tenements had seen them make their way across the railyard and into the garden. No, it was just a matter of time before they were confronted by someone in the community or worse yet, the police. Once again, it was time to move on.

They left the gazebo and headed out of the railyard neighborhood. Josef still had a slight bobble in his step, but walking was manageable. He suggested after they found a bank, they find out where the railroad station was. Ludwik thought it couldn't be too far from the railyard they had just left. He said they should keep their eyes open for street signs that might help them. They agreed to walk until they reached a part of the city that was a commercial center. It was still early in the afternoon and barring closure for lunch, everything was probably open.

When they saw the wide avenue flanked by trees and grand buildings, they knew they were in the right area. There were hundreds of people walking on shady promenades that ran between the trees and buildings on both sides of the avenue. A steady volume of automobiles and carriages slowly made their way headed in both directions. A bright red tram clanged its way past them on the track in the center of the avenue. It was a big change from the mountains, rivers and forests they had tip-toed through the past three plus weeks.

347

They joined a bustling throng of pedestrians that were working their way in and out of several cafes, a library, a government looking building, a museum, several shops and businesses and a beautiful stone building with a title carved out in marble that read, "MAGYAR NEMZETI BANK." They had found their bank.

They sat near some young people, likely college students, who were sitting on the wide, marble steps that led up to the entrance of the bank. Without attracting attention, Ludwik took off his backpack and jacket. He folded the jacket across his lap, slipped his knife out of the backpack and slit open the lining of the jacket that held the Romanian lei. Josef did the same. They decided to leave the money in the boots. Money secured, they went up the steps and entered the bank lobby. Before entering the area used for transactions, they walked around the lobby and looked at the notices posted on the walls for information that might help them exchange the lei without attracting too much attention. They weren't sure if they understood the rate of exchange between the two currencies, but decided whatever it was, it had to be done.

The teller greeted them with a smile and a few words of welcome. Ludwik guessed correctly the young man was asking him how he could be of help. He returned the smile and placed a stack of lei in front of him and said, "pengo." The teller smiled at the mispronunciation of the word and knew immediately he was dealing with two foreigners, most likely Romanian. He was fluent in that language and began speaking to them in Romanian. His first two words were the only words Ludwik understood. He had learned them from Andrei on their trip through the mountains. "Buna ziva" meant "good afternoon." Ludwik was impressed with the teller's friendliness and decided to find out just how friendly he could be. When the teller had finished his words, Ludwik used the Romanian greeting in response then pushed the stack of lei toward the young man and said, "pengo."

348

He pointed toward the teller's draw where the "pengo" was and pulled his hand back and put it into his jacket pocket. The move confused the teller.

"They want to exchange the lei. Get to it, please." The voice of authority came from a man sitting behind a desk off to the side of the teller's station. His words jump-started the young teller into action. Ludwik nodded his thanks to the well-dressed gentleman who had risen from his chair and was heading toward him. "I recognized your accent," the bank official said in Polish. He shook hands with both men and welcomed them into his bank.

Jan Zaicek was the bank manager. He had worked as a bank investment consultant and manager during the hard days of the Depression in Europe. His banking skills and aptitude for languages had made him a valued asset to banks in Poland, Romania and now in Hungary. He had worked for Bank Polski in Warsaw for three years. His apartment there was just a few blocks from Old Town. As soon as he heard Ludwik's accent, he knew he was Polish. He wanted to greet him personally and see if there was a chance to chat with him and his friend concerning the war. See if they had any information about his old haunts near Old Town. He invited them to have lunch with him. Ludwik said they needed to buy train tickets to Budapest and get to the Polish Embassy on official business. Zaicek said there were plenty of trains going there at all hours and if they boarded one now, the embassy would be closed by the time they got there. Ludwik was suspicious at first but was impressed by the man's willingness to help and his friendly invitation.

Zaicek ordered lunch for both men at the sidewalk café next to the bank. He was deeply saddened by Ludwik's description of the horrific, indiscriminate bombing of Warsaw and his old neighborhood. He was sickened to hear their eyewitness accounts of the bombs that fell on Praga and the death of their friends.

349

He shook his head in disbelief over their stories of the slaughter of innocents in the city and on the country roads. He suspected the two men were military and were part of the force that had left Poland to get to France. He thought it was smart they try to reach Budapest. There was a good chance they could get papers there. He had heard that Poles had crossed into Hungary over the mountains and had been sent to internment camps along the border. He wasn't sure how long they would be kept there. The best bet for these men was to get to the embassy. He had friends in Budapest, one, that might be able to help them.

Zaicek said Hungary was on the side of Poland. President Horthy had even denied Hitler the use of northern Hungary to move his troops into position to attack Poland. He had publicly stated the reason for his refusal was the long-standing respected Hungarian-Polish friendship.

"That's good to hear," Josef said.

Ludwik was interested in knowing why Polish soldiers that came across the mountains in the north would have trouble getting to France. Zaicek said there were some sections of the country that were in the political hands of individuals and organizations like the "Iron Cross" that were not friendly to refugees, especially Jewish ones.

"That's NOT good to hear," Josef added.

"What do you recommend?" Ludwik asked Zaicek.

"First, let me say I believe you two are military. Do you deny this?"

Ludwik studied the man. If this man was trouble, they were already finished with their travel. If he wasn't, he might be of some help.

He decided to find out and said, "I do not deny that."

Zaicek smiled and said, "Good. I understand your reluctance to be interned. Stay overnight here. I can set you up in a hotel near the train station. Take a train into Budapest in the morning. They leave every two hours starting at seven. When you get to the city, someone will meet you at the station. He will help you. The embassy will get you papers to get you into France. Not as military though. Maybe as a tradesman, gardener, student, professor. Maybe even as a priest. Do you have identification?

"We do. Now, who are you, our "banker friend?" asked Ludwik.

"You answered your own question with those two words," Zaicek said.

It was a five-minute ride to the Grand Hotel. Zaicek paid the driver, took the men inside and arranged for a room. He insisted on paying and told them to use the money saved for a good meal here. He asked for and received a copy of the hotel's dining room menu from the front desk. Circling his favorite choice on it, he gave the menu to Josef and said it was the best meal here. Before leaving, he suggested they take the nine o'clock train in the morning. It was a semi-express with only a few stops. That would leave them with plenty of time to get to the embassy and begin the process of obtaining paperwork that would get them into France.

Zaicek had done well. The room was immaculate. Everything was brand new. The bed covers, walls, rugs and curtains were a beautiful blend of greens, blues and browns. There was a peaceful, earthy quality about the place. Enhancing that feeling was the warm sunshine that poured through the two windows overlooking the tree lined avenue in front of the hotel. Most of the traffic passing the hotel was pedestrian. Men and women casually strolled up and down the tree lined promenades that ran parallel to the avenue. Ludwik drank it all in. It was so much like his beloved Warsaw.

He wondered what the city looked like now after the bombing and shelling. He wondered if Debrechen and all the cities in Hungary would suffer a similar fate down the road. He hoped not.

The bath area, tiled in black and white, was better than the Hotel Bristol's in Warsaw. That was saying something. Ludwik lingered a long time in the relaxing, warm water of the large, porcelain tub. He closed his eyes and thought of how his life had changed so much in less than a month. He thought of the almost daily struggle to hide and survive while making their way out of Poland and Romania. He thought of all the men and women he and Josef had come across in their travel. So many good people.

Refreshed after their baths and a short nap, both men emptied their backpacks and spread the contents out on their beds. All clothing was unrolled and put into two piles: one clean and one unclean. Ludwik filled the tub halfway, dumped his unclean clothes in it and began scrubbing away with the hotel soap. When he finished, he wrung out each item and laid them on the carpeted floor in the sunlight to dry. Josef followed suit. After laying his clothes next to Ludwik's on the floor, he asked how they were going to get their clothes fully dried before morning. Ludwik pulled out an ironing board and iron from the closet. He said he would press all their clothes and hang them in the closet before they called it a night.

The meal was fantastic. Zaicek knew what he was talking about when he had circled the number 3 on the menu. The three-course meal began with a stew called "porkolt." That was followed by the main course of deliciously spiced stuffed cabbages called "toltott." The meal was topped off by a dessert made of sponge cake filled with rich chocolate sauce topped with a touch of whipped cream. It was called "somloi galuska." Josef made a point of keeping the menu. He said if he ever had another chance to order a meal in Hungary, it would be this one.

The dining room stayed virtually empty throughout the meal. Ludwik and Josef didn't care what the reason was for that. They had picked out a table off in a corner to avoid being overheard talking in Polish. Ludwik said it probably wouldn't matter, but one never knew for sure. Zaicek had said there were elements in the population that didn't take kindly to foreigners. It was best to be cautious. That was the reason he decided not to tell Zaicek about the pilot wings hidden in their boots when he was asked if they had any identification on them. He felt there was no need to reveal everything to anyone.

Breakfast was hectic. Many people crowded the tables in the dining room. There wasn't a seat open. Long lines of well-dressed people shuffled along two buffet tables piling food onto their plates. Not wanting to be close to so many strangers and possibly being pushed into a conversation, both Ludwik and Josef buttered four small croissants each, poured strong coffee into their cups and made their way back to the room. It was seven thirty. The sun was shining in a cloudless sky. A great day to travel.

The walk to the train station was uneventful and quite relaxing. They arrived at 8:45. The plan was to take the 9 o'clock train as Zaicek had suggested. The fare for the ride was posted outside the ticket seller's window. The destinations were easy to read. The Polish word for Budapest was spelled almost the same as the Hungarian spelling. The only difference was the Polish version had a "z" after the "s." The pronunciation was just about the same. The cost of the fare was a different matter. It was written in words not numbers.

The ticket seller never even looked up when Ludwik said, "Budapest." He just announced the price. Ludwik passed him a five pengo note, not sure if it was too much or too little. He got the ticket and four small coins in change. Josef followed suit and both went out to board the train. There were three trains in the station.

353

They followed the posted signs that read "Budapest." They boarded the last passenger car and went directly to the back and sat together in the last row. They read their tickets carefully and determined the train would arrive in Budapest at 11:30. Several miles out of Debrechen, the conductor punched their tickets. All they had to do now was wait for Budapest, detrain with a crowd into the city and find the Polish Embassy before it closed for the day.

The train meandered its way across a seemingly never ending plain. It swayed its way over rivers and whistled at every small town it approached. It never seemed to be in a hurry. Once again, the countryside intrigued Ludwik. It was mostly farmland. It could have easily been mistaken for Poland or Romania. The people looked the same. Country folks: people of the land, trying to make a living. Trying to take what nature and a strong back would give them. He thought of his family and the work it took to run a farm; the sugar beet fields, the orchards, the gardens, the livestock, the house, the barn, the fences and so much more. He thought of the young children out in the field back in Poland looking for lost chickens. He remembered the fear he felt for them as they waved goodbye standing innocently out in the open, not realizing that death could arrive at any moment from the sky. And how that was no different for his own family in Mazanki.

The first stop was at a small town called Kaba. Only a few men boarded. They were dressed like businessmen and carried briefcases. They reminded him of Zaicek, their new banker friend in Debrechen. That gave him an idea. If Zaicek knew Polish because he had worked in Warsaw, there had to be others like him in Budapest. They might even be Polish. If they were, they could get a lot of information from them about the city, especially the location of the Polish embassy. He tapped Josef's leg.

354

"How would you go about finding out if a man or woman was Polish in Hungary without asking them?" Ludwik asked.

"Their clothes. Listening to see if they spoke Polish," Josef suggested.

Ludwik responded, "Clothes no. Listening yes. If we keep our ears open, we might find someone that is Polish or can speak Polish to help us."

The stops at Skolnok and Cegled lasted a little bit longer. Both places were big. Many passengers boarded at Cegled. Most were young children of school age. It looked to be a field trip of some sort to the capitol of their country. Apart from two men that had joined Ludwik and Josef in the rear and a man and woman leading the children, the rest of the seats were filled by youngsters. The noise and commotion raised by them trying to outshout each other made it impossible to hear anything else.

The two men across the aisle from Ludwik were smiling at the din created by the youngsters. They knew this was going to be a "grin and bear it" exercise for some time. As the train lurched forward, the man that had come with the children stood up in front of the bedlam and demanded "silence" by extending an arm high into the air. He held it there until the last two boys yelling at each other saw him and stopped. The man's female companion then stood up and touched her lips. The car became silent. One could hear the sounds of the train as it wobbled and creaked its way over the tracks toward Budapest. The woman caught the eye of all four men in the rear. They watched her give the students the signal to be quiet. She was beautiful; tall, slender and very well proportioned. Her long, blond hair covered one side of her face and came to rest over one of her large breasts. The hair complimented her black dress and the tiny, yellow flowers printed on it.

Ludwik heard one of the two men across the aisle say to the other, "Mein Gott, sie ist schon!" The words froze him. He had heard those words before. It was at an airshow in Germany. A German in a group of German sport pilots had spotted Bodil walking across the tarmac toward her father, brother and him. Ludwik had felt amused then by the words that meant, "My God, she is beautiful." He wasn't amused now. He turned to Josef and quietly said, "Our friends across the aisle are German."

Budapest

The rest of the trip to Budapest was spent feigning a nap by lowering their flat caps over their eyes to insure there was no eye contact with the two Germans. Ludwik didn't think the Germans could cause them trouble, but one never knew for sure. In any event, a confrontation that might lead to something worse in front of all the children was out of the question. Better to relax and avoid trouble.

When the train entered the Keleti station, the children became energized once again. The massive size of the structure with its glass cathedral-like ceiling was impressive. The children were completely overwhelmed by it all. They were on their feet, noses pressed hard to the windows, shouting and pointing at every new thing that came into view. Their chaperones didn't bother to curb the outburst of enthusiasm. They waited for the hiss of the engine to confirm a full stop before the arm was raised again for silence. Then they filed, two by two, off the train and onto the platform. They were followed by the two Germans. Ludwik and Josef fiddled with their backpacks until the car was empty. Then they stepped off the train and followed the children toward the exit. It was slow-going. There had to be close to two hundred school children jamming up the entrance to the station. The two Germans and a few other adults stood quietly behind them patiently waiting to move into the station.

Ludwik and Josef kept an eye on the two Germans. They were being greeted by a man and had moved away from the children. Ludwik wondered if the man was a business acquaintance and more importantly, if their business was political. They walked by them and followed the tail end of the children into the station. They moved through the station and out the main entrance into a large, triangular shaped plaza that was filled with trees, statues and benches. They choose a bench off the main walkway and sat to get their bearings.

"So, what do you think of our city?" a voice behind them asked in Polish. Ludwik and Josef turned to look at the source of the voice. A middle-aged gentleman dressed impeccably in a belted, tweed jacket, white shirt, brown tie and matching brown fedora stood there waiting for an answer. He was close enough to reach out and touch.

"It is beautiful," Josef answered.

"And who are you?" Ludwik asked.

"A good friend of Zaicek. He called me early this morning and said you would be coming in on the 9 o'clock train. He described what you were wearing and the color of your backpacks."

"How did he know what we were wearing?"

"He watched you leave the hotel. He wasn't sure if you would take his advice about the 9 o'clock. Allow me to introduce myself. I am Itsvah Puskas. I am an owner of a jewelry store not too far from the embassy. Zaicek asked me to help you with any information that you might need. Like how to get to the embassy for example. I took the liberty of writing the directions from this plaza with a few other items that may be of use." With that he handed Josef a map of the city with the directions to the embassy. "Polish Embassy" was spelled out on the map. He said chances were very good they would be interned in the city and probably would not have to face total confinement.

"How would you know all that?" Ludwik asked.

"Let's just say that many of my customers have friends who talk a lot."

"Zaicek, too?" Ludwik asked.

"Only since the heathens invaded our country."

Puskas gave them an emergency password they had to use to gain immediate entrance to the embassy. No questions asked. He said it was necessary for the time being. There was concern that Polish speaking Germans might try to wiggle in and come out of the embassy with information that might be detrimental to any plans the embassy had to aid Polish military personnel. He said they could also see him at his jewelry store if they had questions or a problem. It was only a few blocks from the embassy. It was called the "Ekszer-Haz." He said never to come together and if there were other people in the store, they were to come to him, and only him, and ask in Hungarian, "Is this watch worth anything?" He would reply, "Let's take a look at it." Then they would go into the repair room at the back of the store and talk. He said there were two broken watches in the black bag he had foot-pushed under their bench. They were to be used as an excuse to visit him. He said not to make a habit of visiting. People would probably be watching them.

It was an easy walk to the embassy. They turned right on Rottenbiller, another right on Varoslegeti, and walked up to the modest, two storied embassy that had a sign over the front door that read, "Polska Ambasada" It was then Ludwik realized while he knew the password to get in the embassy, he didn't know how to say, "Is this watch worth anything?" in Hungarian. A sign in Polish instructing visitors to please ring the doorbell and wait for someone to answer was on the door. Ludwik rang twice. A distinctive electric buzz was heard on the other side of the door.

There was no immediate response. A minute passed and no one came. Josef said there was a man across the street sitting at a table at a sidewalk café taking pictures of them. Ludwik pulled his cap down closer to his eyes and told Josef to turn his back to the street.

When the door opened, they were greeted with a warm smile and a few words in Hungarian by an attractive young woman. She was either asking them why they were here or how could she help them. Ludwik quietly said, "Czarna Madonna." Her beautiful, brown eyes went wide. It was the first time she had heard the password used. It was only to be used by Polish military needing assistance. She let them in.

"I am so happy to see you here. Please, come with me," she said.

They followed her up a staircase leading to a balcony that circled the entire second floor. She went directly across the stairs to a large door and tapped on it twice. A booming, "What is it?" came from behind the door.

"Two of our men have arrived."

That was met with silence. Then a quieter voice said, "Bring them in."

The portly, mustachioed ambassador stood up behind his desk and welcomed Ludwik and Josef to Budapest. He eyed them carefully before asking them for identification. Ludwik asked for permission to use his knife to get their pilot's wings. The ambassador hesitated at the strange request. He nodded for the woman to leave. When she did, he gave Ludwik permission to use the knife. Ludwik told him they were ordered to get rid of anything that would identify them as Polish military. The ambassador said he knew that, but he had to ask. It wasn't enough that they knew the password. They could still be German agents. He said they were all over Budapest now.

They would be looking for Polish military refugees. Ludwik said there was an agent across the street who took pictures of them. The ambassador wasn't surprised by that. He said everyone who worked in the embassy, including himself, had been followed from time to time.

Ambassador Bogalowski watched as Ludwik and Josef each took a boot off. He watched Ludwik pry open a well-hidden slit in the heel of his boot. "Clever lads," he thought to himself.

Both metallic wings lay side by side on the ambassador's mahogany desk. He stared at them carefully. He was intrigued by Ludwik's wings. The diving eagle with a wreath in his beak was interesting.

"What branch of service do you fly in?" he asked Ludwik.

"I am a navy pilot," Ludwik answered.

"How did you come to be with your Air Force friend?"

Ludwik told him he and Josef had met in Deblin and had become friends. They had gone to Warsaw together on pass a few times. They were in the city for a long weekend with friends when the war began.

The ambassador laid out a map of Poland on the desk and asked Ludwik to show him the route they had taken to get here. He was particularly interested in knowing how the Romanian officials had treated the Polish crossing their border. Ludwik gave him Lupu's description of the harsh treatment they could expect in the internment camps and that many of the police and government officials were corrupt and were always looking to extort what they could from people under their jurisdiction.

"You won't find that here," the ambassador said. "The Hungarian government, with very few exceptions, will treat you fairly. There is even a plan being considered to pay refugees a weekly stipend for as long as they stay in the country. I don't believe you will be here for long. And you should also know that very few of the Hungarian people approve of Germany's actions. The Hungarian government realizes that many Poles escaping Poland will come here. We have had assurances from the top levels of government that military refugees will be treated with respect while they are here. As for the embassy, we will begin processing the necessary paperwork you will need to travel to France or England."

He went on to describe Hungary's official and unofficial positions on the issue of military refugees. The official position, according to international law, was to arrest and intern all military refugees that entered a neutral country. The unofficial version was to arrest, intern and then look the other way when the Poles escaped. He said he had worked out an agreement with the Hungarian officials responsible for the Polish refugees coming across the border and the ones already here. The agreement included a certain amount of money that would pass hands. Josef interrupted him and asked if it would be possible to leave his father's name with the embassy in the hope that if he had made it across the Carpathians from Krakow, he might be notified. The ambassador agreed to do so. He said to give his father's name to the young woman who would be interviewing him today. He said the purpose of the interview was to garner information the embassy would need to create travel papers. He added they were trying to recruit people in Hungary or refugees that had talent in creating false documents to work with the embassy. He said the Red Cross, Catholic Church and something called the "Polish Relief Agency" were all planning to help with the refugee issue. He finished by saying the embassy could use men like themselves to help process the expected flood of military refugees. He asked them to consider the offer. Then he buzzed for one of his aides to come and collect the two pilots. As they were leaving, he turned and looked out the window at Budapest and said, "We must always keep our faith."

361

The same young woman who had brought them to the ambassador's office led the way down two flights of stairs to the basement. On one side of the windowless room were two long, flat tables loaded with rolled parchment and assorted stacks of paper. Another table held scissors, razors, knives, assorted brushes and two typewriters. On the opposite side of the basement were two desks with chairs front and back, flood lights, three large screens with three standing cameras facing each screen and a chair in front of each screen. The entire basement had been converted into a passport and travel paper manufacturing center. Behind the two desks was a door that led to another room. The woman explained it was their darkroom where the necessary photos would be developed. She introduced herself as "Bella," and said she was going to interview Josef. Ludwik would be interviewed by her co-worker who was working at the moment in the darkroom behind the door.

Minutes later, a woman came out of the darkroom, greeted Bella and Josef then came over to Ludwik. He rose to meet her, politely took her hand, kissed it, clicked his heels and introduced himself. It was the way he had been taught to greet a woman at the Academy. Taken aback by the polite and respectful gesture, the flustered young woman blushed and asked Ludwik to sit in the chair in front of her desk. She was movie-star beautiful. Not very tall, but well proportioned. Her classic Slavic, high cheekbones supported two, very large brown eyes. Her jet-black hair was pulled straight back over her head and tied neatly into a bun in back. Her name was Basha. She was a native of Budapest. She spoke Hungarian, Polish and German. Her job, like Bella's, was to interview Polish military and determine what fake vocation best suited them for their travel papers to France. An appropriate destination and purpose for traveling to France would be connected to their "vocation." The questions were basic, name, date of birth, height, weight, color of eyes, rank, military status, religion, education, marital status, etc. etc.

362

Basha was impressed with Ludwik. Not only was he a pilot, he was also an educated gentleman who knew how to act like one. He was also very handsome. She was particularly taken by his piercing, light blue eyes and gentle voice. She also noticed that he stared at her throughout the interview. He never looked away. Embassy regulations specified not to encourage any social relationship with a refugee, military or civilian. Get the information, get the papers filled out and get them on their way. The sooner the better. At the end of the interview and picture taking, if any interviewer thought the refugee had the right potential, they could ask him/her if they would be interested in helping to process the hundreds of refugees that were expected to come to Budapest soon. The interview and picture taking ended, she began the request for help.

"Mr. Skoczylas, thank you for your information. Before we select an appropriate profession for you, I would like to discuss an opportunity you may want to consider. The embassy has authorized me to ask certain refugees if they would have any interest in helping the embassy or one of our consulates, with the processing of refugees. I think you would be helpful to us. And if you chose to volunteer, certain monetary considerations would be made. As for the time you spend with us in Budapest, you will receive an additional weekly stipend from the Hungarian government. Would you be interested? If so, I will answer any questions you may have."

Ludwik gazed into her dark, brown eyes for a long moment. He wanted to ask her if she was married, did she have a man-friend and was she available for dating. Instead, he asked, "How long would I be here if I decided to help? Where would I live? Would I be interned while I worked here? How about my friend, Josef?"

"A lot would depend on how the war progressed. If Hungary is threatened and our borders become fragile, then that would be the time you leave. Your friend will be offered a position here also.

I am not sure about your internment status and where that would be. I believe it will be in the city somewhere."

"I see. What profession have you chosen for me?" Ludwik asked.

She said it basically would have to be connected to his education. She went over his answers from the interview to see how it might figure into the profession that would be listed on his travel papers. She felt his degree in mechanical engineering made the profession of locksmith an ideal choice. She took out a manual that listed all types of French industries and fingered the section locating locksmithing and safes. There was a Fichet Company that manufactured safes in the town of Oust-Marest. She decided the company needed a new head of the security locks division. She would award the "position" to Ludwik.

Because of his age and slim, youthful looks, Basha advised Bella to list Josef as a student at the Sorbonne in Paris. She agreed. As far as when the two would be on their way, Basha told them it would depend on the "papers" being readied, their internment situation, and how long they might stay working for the embassy. Bella said if the two men agreed to help them, the embassy would work out an agreement with the authorities to have them interned in the city and be allowed to come to the embassy to work. She said her government was willing to do what they could to help their Polish friends. She said it would be wise for them to accept the offer to work here. It would get them out of internment every day, and when their papers were ready, they could strike out for France.

When she had finished, Ludwik turned to Basha and asked if it would be possible to stay in the embassy. Basha said it no, that the embassy had agreed with the Hungarian government to follow international law, which stated that refugees must be arrested and interned when entering a neutral country.

After that, her government had promised to look the other way while "escapes" were made. She said all Polish military would be interned at Hungarian military posts and that they could expect fair treatment. Ludwik said he hoped the Hungarian government would keep their word. He did not want to be arrested and put into a cell. Basha said that would not happen. They would have some freedom to move about. All they had to do was obey the country's laws. If they didn't, a cell was very likely and more importantly, that sort of behavior might affect the Hungarian governments willingness to aid military refugees.

Finished with a call to the local police to come and arrest the two men, Basha warned them that German agents were probably outside waiting to see what had developed with them. She said they would be followed when they left, and they should be prepared to be followed whenever they were away from their place of internment. She felt they would be interned somewhere in the city. Perhaps the Citadel across the river. She cautioned them about striking up a conversation with anyone that spoke Polish. She said to be sure they were Polish. Then she asked if they could trust her and the people they had met so far in the embassy. Both men nodded their heads. Basha nodded back and said, "Then I suggest you both leave at least half of your money with us for a while. One cannot be totally sure you will be treated with the respect you deserve from all Hungarians."

Ludwik asked how they would get the money back. She said the money would be returned when they had their papers. She asked if there were any other questions. Ludwik said he had one. He wanted to know how to say, "Is this watch worth anything?" in Hungarian. Basha gave him a puzzled look but didn't ask why he needed to know. She verbalized the sentence in Hungarian then wrote each word out phonetically.

Before she gave Ludwik the paper with the words, she advised him to memorize its contents and then get rid of the paper before the authorities became interested in what it meant.

Josef thought the embassy holding their money for safekeeping was a good idea. Ludwik agreed. They gave Basha more than half of their money. They made no mention of the lei in their boots. She said the money would be placed in a safe. Then she led them up to the lobby to wait for the police.

The two arresting officers were polite in performing their duties. Their job was to officially "arrest" the two Polish servicemen and transport them to the Army. They searched both men for weapons and examined the contents of their backpacks. They confiscated two knives, the Hotel Bristol revolver and the small ax from the packs.

Basha asked the officers if the men were going to be interned in the city. The sergeant in charge of the detail said they were being brought across the river and turned over to the military at the Citadella. He said they would be officially interned today after being interviewed by the Army and would spend the rest of the day learning how internment was going to work. Basha relayed the information to Ludwik and Josef. She said the Citadella was about a half-hour walk from here. She gave Ludwik a card. On it was her name and phone number at the embassy. As Ludwik and Josef were being escorted to the front door, she said to call her by the end of the week. She also said for them to keep their eyes open for men near the entrance of the embassy that looked suspicious and try to remember what they looked like. It would come in handy later if they were out and about.

The police vehicle was a fairly new Peugeot sedan. It had been modified to satisfy police requirements for security and safety. The back seat was separated from the front by a wire mesh screen. The rear doors, normally locked from the outside to prevent an escape, were left unlocked by the sergeant out of respect for his passengers. The backpacks and suitcases were loaded into the trunk. The sergeant told them to relax, smoke if they wanted, and to enjoy the short ride across the river and up the hill to the Citadella. Ludwik and Josef did not understand a word the polite sergeant said but felt at ease because of his friendly demeanor.

Josef noticed the man right away. He saw him get up from his seat at the outdoor café as they got in the car. Once they were in the back seat, he tapped Ludwik on the arm and said, "Bet that guy is one of the ones your lady friend told us to look out for." He jerked a thumb at the man standing across the street in front of the café. He was well dressed; brown tweed, double breasted jacket, matching brown slacks and brown shoes. He wore dark, horn-rimmed glasses. His hair was a very distinctive light blonde. He was young…. and obvious. He couldn't keep his eyes off the Peugeot. When the car drove off, he hopped into a black sedan that had just pulled up to the curb. The sedan quickly moved after the Peugeot and kept it in sight three cars behind. All five vehicles stayed in a single line as they moved toward downtown and the Danube River. Ludwik made mental notes of the drive; straight down Varosligeti onto Kiraly, left onto Karoly, right onto Kossum, across the Danube over the Erzsebet Bridge, past a park and up a steep hill toward the castle-like Citadella. His concentration stopped when the driver suddenly pulled off the road and let the black sedan pass. The sergeant pointed at the car and said, "Gestapo." He shook his head and made the motion of slitting someone's throat.

The Peugeot was greeted at the gate by a sentry that came to the sergeant's side of the car and exchanged some words with him. The young man, a Hungarian Army private, looked into the back seat at Ludwik and Josef, stepped back and saluted them. It was an unexpected friendly gesture. The gate opened and the car slowly made its way into a large courtyard.

367

The Citadella

The sergeant hopped out and motioned for Ludwik and Josef to get out. He pointed to the ground they were standing on and said, "Citadella." Then he pointed outside the gate and said, "Gellert" making a motion with one hand and pointing a finger downward. Ludwik correctly deduced that "Gellert" was the hill the "Citadella" sat on. They were escorted into a large office by the sergeant and presented to a young, Hungarian Army officer. Three enlisted men, who looked to be part of his clerical staff, sat staring at them. The tall, smartly uniformed officer rose to greet his new "guests." He said a few words to the sergeant, clicked his heels, and shook the man's hand. When the sergeant left, the major turned to Ludwik and Josef and pointed to the two chairs in front of his desk for them to sit on. He spoke to them slowly, stopping from time to time to allow one of his men to translate into Polish what he had said. His name was Major Seles and he was commander there. He wanted to welcome the two Polish officers and hoped they would find everything here to be satisfactory. He knew they probably understood that military refugees arriving in a neutral country were bound, by international law, to surrender all weapons and be interned for of a time that would be determined by the government. He said the Hungarian government and military viewed the Polish as their brothers and would respect the kinship that had developed over the years between the two peoples. He added that he was personally upset by the German invasion and was sympathetic to the plight of the Polish people. The major continued his official welcome by saying the two Poles would be asked to help him properly document their entrance into internment. There were questions they would be required to answer and when that was done, the rules of internment would be explained. When that was finished, they would be brought to their quarters.

On the way there, they would be shown the mess hall. And after the evening meal, there would be a briefing there on the war in Poland.

The questions were very similar to the ones that the embassy had asked. And like the ambassador had done, the major asked if they could prove they were pilots. Ludwik said their wings were in their backpacks. He made no mention of hiding them in their boots prior to reaching the Polish embassy. The major asked if they would kindly retrieve them and place them on his desk. Like the ambassador, the major was curious about Ludwik being a naval officer and asked how they had managed the trip from Poland to Budapest. Ludwik began to realize that being a Navy pilot was going to be a source of interest and a reason for questioning from here on out. He explained, through the interpreter, he was in Warsaw with Josef when the war began. He outlined their trip from Warsaw to Budapest. He was wary of revealing any names of the people that had helped them. Especially here in Hungary. Josef caught on to that and when asked to give his version of their odyssey, he too, made a point of not revealing any names.

The rules of internment at the Citadella were straightforward. They were expected to answer roll call at 0700 hours every morning in the courtyard. Breakfast would follow at 0715 hours. Any business the Hungarian Army had with them would usually be conducted after breakfast. Lunch would be held from 1200 to 1300 hours daily. Afternoons would be open for any Polish officer to leave the Citadella and go into the city at their own expense. If the military authorities did not have business with them after breakfast, they would be free to leave by mid-morning. They would not be required to return for supper. They could eat at their own expense in the city. Unless given explicit permission to return the next day by 1200 hours, they were expected to be in their rooms by 2200 hours every evening. No weapons of any sort were to be brought into the Citadella and all civilian laws were to be obeyed.

They would be given a pass today they must always carry on their person. In addition to the pass, they would be receiving a government stipend equal to the average pay a Hungarian worker made in a week. The major said he did not know how long the government would continue this practice, but he did have the understanding that as long as a Polish refugee was in Hungary, he or she would receive that stipend. And then he said something very revealing. He repeated, very slowly, the words, "as long as a Polish refugee was in Hungary." The major asked if they understood what he was saying. Both Ludwik and Josef said they understood "everything" that he had said.

The young interpreter, a sergeant, showed Ludwik and Josef the mess hall where they would eat and then escorted them to their quarters in the part of the Citadella that had been reserved for officers. They were asked to report to the dining area at 1800 hours for dinner. The dinner would be followed by a briefing updating the war's progress. That would begin at 1915 hours. It would be held at the far end of the mess hall that held a podium and several rows of chairs. He said they were the first two Polish military refugees that had come to the Citadella, but more were expected to arrive soon.

Their quarters consisted of one good sized room that held a bunk bed, writing table, two chairs, a lamp, a closet and a large window that overlooked the Danube and the part of the city across it called "Pest." The latrine and showers were located at the end of the hall. There were ten rooms on each side of the hall. Only the two end rooms, one of them theirs, had a window. All rooms were furnished the same. The sergeant explained that there were three other areas in the Citadella set up to house internees. He said the fortress would probably hold between one and two hundred men. Most, if not all, internees being sent here, were supposed to be Polish officers. He said there would be no bed check at night and no guards posted in their area. "Lights out" was at 2200 hours.

370

They were free to visit other internees when they arrived, but had to be in their room before 2200 hours. He finished by saying no doors would be locked. He then clicked his heels and left.

Ludwik gazed out the second-floor window and tried to retrace their trip from the embassy to their new "home." He had a good idea where the embassy was. He thought if it weren't for a few tall buildings in the city, he would be able to see it from here. He felt good about the events of the day; meeting Basha, having his "escape" papers being prepared, the politeness of every Hungarian individual they had met, the beautiful Warsaw-like city of Budapest and the very pleasant internment arrangements here at the old fortress. He thought about the offer to stay in Budapest and help the embassy facilitate the movement of his comrades to France. He wondered if that would be the more patriotic thing to do. It wouldn't be flying, but it might be a good thing to help his country get back into the fight. He would ask the jeweler, Puskas, for his opinion on the matter. He had the distinct feeling the man had an important role in whatever plan the Polish Embassy had to move their men out of Hungary and into France.

Josef had already claimed the top bunk. Ludwik stood looking out at the city. It was quiet in the room. He was enjoying the moment, but had something on his mind he needed to share with his friend.

"The major made it pretty clear that he thought we wouldn't be here long enough to really enjoy this view."

"I know. That's good," Josef answered.

Ludwik continued, "Did your lady at the embassy ask if you were interested in staying in Hungary to help with the processing of our people?"

371

"She did," Josef answered. He went on, "I might be interested in doing that if it would be helpful in getting our men into the fight. I also wouldn't mind being here a little longer to see if my father somehow made it over the mountains into Hungary. I know the embassy would probably have his name if he did."

Ludwik nodded and said, "That's a good thought. I wouldn't be opposed to staying here and helping, but before deciding, I need to know if France is in the fight. If they are, then I'm for leaving. If not, then helping here might be best. I'm going to ask the major tonight what he knows about France's efforts up to this point. Then I'm going to ask my friend at the embassy to give us an update on the same question."

"By "my friend," do you mean that little beauty called Basha?"

"Yes. You know we're not leaving until the travel papers are done. Until that time, I'm going to try and enjoy myself a little. I'm hoping she can help me with that."

Josef chuckled and said, "Can't blame you. Budapest and Basha beats walking over mountains with Andrei and hiding in haystacks."

There were several Hungarian soldiers already seated and eating in the mess hall. The major and his small staff of clerks and interpreters sat at one table. Two sergeants and four young privates were eating at another. Three men, dressed in white aprons and caps, dropped food onto trays held out by another dozen soldiers shuffling slowly along a serving line in front of a massive kitchen area. Ludwik wondered how many men were stationed in the Citadella. He figured most of them were probably part of a guard force that was going to be responsible for all Polish military refugees being interned here. The major saw them hesitating at the entrance and waved them over to his table. One of the interpreters, a young sergeant, said the major would like them to join him.

He said because there were no other Poles in the Citadella now, it was decided to use only one mess hall. He added when the internee population grew, this mess hall would be for them. The Hungarian detachment assigned to the Citadella would be eating in their own mess hall.

The food was good. The main item was a goulash that featured meat, potatoes, some green vegetables and a healthy portion of a crescent shaped bread called "kifi." Ludwik and Josef watched the men eat to see if there was a "right" way to eat in Hungary. Ludwik noticed there were no prayers said. Men just dove into their meal. A spoonful of goulash was followed by a bite of heavily buttered "kifi." Some dunked their buttered bread into the goulash first, soaking it thoroughly before consuming it. There was very little conversation between the men. They were here to eat. The interpreter said most of the conversations between the men took place over dessert and coffee. He said the major would brief them here at this table tonight. There was no need to use the podium. They were the only internees in the Citadella.

The coffee was strong. Ludwik took it black. Josef piled the cream and sugar in. The dessert was something called "grundel." It was a tasty concoction consisting of ground walnuts and raisins soaked in rum and rolled into a chocolate topped crepe. The major had the interpreter warn them not to get used to this quality of dessert once they began eating with their fellow internees. He said, with respect, that the internee menu would differ somewhat from the regular one offered in the Hungarian mess. Ludwik said if it was close to what they had eaten today, he would be most grateful. Josef, remembering the days on the run, couldn't agree more.

The major tried to put the news of the war in the most favorable light he could concerning the plight of the Polish military and Poland itself. He would not however, exaggerate that point.

He had said while Germany and the Soviet Union had scored major successes against the surrounded Polish forces, there was still heavy resistance being put up in and around Warsaw and at the Romanian bridgehead. He said encircled Polish armored units in the south had broken out and escaped into the Carpathian Mountains. A few hundred of them had crossed the border into eastern Hungary. They brought civilians along with them. The Hungarian government was going to intern them in camps along that part of the border. He had also heard Polish pilots and ground service crews from the Polish Air Force might be sent here to Budapest. He thought there was a push to get the airmen out of Hungary as quickly as possible. Word had it that General Sikorski, head of the Polish Air Force, was going to be named Commander-in-Chief of all Polish forces in exile soon. He said that Sikorski and a large contingent of Polish officers were heading to Paris to set up a government-in-exile. Their immediate task was to get as many of their men out of Romania and Hungary and into France as soon as possible.

Ludwik's first question was about casualties. The major said he had no exact numbers to give, but his understanding was that thousands of lives had been lost in the fighting on all sides. The German Luftwaffe had complete control of the air and was bombing targets at will. Reports from the German end of the conflict maintained that hundreds of thousands of Polish prisoners had been taken. Similar reports were being made by the Soviets. He was concerned those reports might unfortunately be true. He said the Polish Embassy would have more information on the matter.

Josef asked what was being done with the Polish civilians escaping into Hungary across the Carpathians. The major thought they were probably going to be placed in separate internment camps until the government decided their future. He said there was a certain animosity among some in the Hungarian government and military toward people of the Jewish faith.

374

He hinted that Polish Jews escaping into Hungary might not be treated with the same respect as the others. Ludwik thought about his Jewish friends in Old Town. He hoped they had gotten out. He thought about Bodil and her family. Had they been able to make it to Sweden? And what about his own family? His mother, father, brothers and sisters, aunts, uncles and cousins. Would he ever see any of them again?

"Any other questions?" the major asked.

"Just one," Ludwik said, "What are the French and English doing about their declarations of war against the Germans?" The major finished his coffee and said, "I'm afraid the answer is…nothing."

The first night in their quarters at the Citadella went by very well. Everything about the room was good. There was plenty of space. The door was unlocked and the bunks comfortable. Lights went off at 2200 hours. Josef climbed the iron ladder hooked onto the top bunk and sat with his back to the wall looking out the window at Budapest. Ludwik walked over to the window for a look. He marveled at the lights in the city. If Paris was THE "City of Lights," this city had to be a close second. Far below, the Danube seemed to dance and come alive as it shimmered in the reflection of the lights that bordered its walkways, boat launches and bridges. The golden hue cast on the dark water coupled with the brilliant yellow and white spotlighted buildings, basilicas and castle like structures blended into what some might call a masterpiece in light.

"I wonder if Franz had ever seen anything like this," Ludwik said. He thought about the young artist. He wished the young man had lived long enough to finish his "black and white Warsaw," then came here to this place to paint this view. He stared at the lights along the Danube for some time trying to compare their beauty with Warsaw's Vistula and its lights.

He said to Joseph that he would like to walk along the Danube some night, have dinner and wine with a beautiful woman and then make love with her in a room that had a view like this.

"A beautiful thought to sleep on," Josef answered.

Ludwik dreamt about Bodil, his girl from Sopot, Basha, the embassy Hungarian with the beautiful eyes. And the shepherdess, the lady that made his skin tingle. He was flying, dancing and laughing with all three. It was good; being alive and loving life. And having life love him back.

Breakfast was familiar. Definitely military and nothing like the meal they had enjoyed last night. The sparse spread featured eggs, a small chunk of ham, bread, butter, jam and coffee. They sat with the major and his interpreter again. The major suggested they exercise in the courtyard then return to their quarters and try the showers. After that he would like them to report to his office. He had an interest in discussing their journey from Poland. He said they would have the option to eat lunch here and leave with their passes for the city or just leave with their passes and eat in the city. He reminded them they had to return before 2200 hours tonight. If they returned for supper, they would not be allowed out a second time.

They circled the courtyard ten times. Ludwik estimated the distance covered was about two miles. The exercise felt good. Almost necessary. The showers were not hot, but warm enough to linger under until the water ran cold. It was nothing like the hot tub and shower in Debrechen but good enough to start the day with.

Josef thought it might be good to buy some clothes for winter. Ludwik agreed and said maybe his "friend" at the embassy would help them find the right shops to bargain at today. They both agreed, for the time being, to keep the lei in their boots.

376

"What about staying in Budapest?" Josef asked.

"I'm not sure yet. I'd like to visit our jeweler friend and find out what he knows about France getting into the war. After we meet with the major, why don't you go to the embassy, get our money and see what they know about France getting into the war. I'll meet you at 1300 at the café across the street there."

"What if the Germans are there?" Josef asked.

"Let them take their notes. We'll eat," Ludwik said.

The meeting with the major lasted an hour. Josef left the Citadella first. Better to have someone tail him to the embassy rather than follow Ludwik to the jeweler. Both Ludwik and Josef suspected the jeweler might be working for the Polish government in some capacity and it would not be good to draw attention to him.

After Josef left, Ludwik spent an hour disassembling and examining the jeweler's broken watches he had given them to use as an excuse to visit his store. He saw that one watch was missing a click spring and two winding pinions. The other watch was a total loss. He set about repairing the one needing some parts. He removed the winding pinions and a spring from the other watch and positioned them into the watch he was fixing. The difficult part of the transfer was that he had to pressure the spring into a size that allowed its insertion into the watch's movement. He accomplished the intricate work with a needle and a screwdriver from his backpack. It took him an hour to finish. When it was done, he had one watch in good working order and another to be used for spare parts. He decided to take both with him. He thought the working watch might be valuable enough for the jeweler to sell. If it wasn't, then he would keep it for himself. He had two and a half hours to meet with the jeweler and then join Josef at the café.

The German kept a small group of people between himself and Josef as they all made their way down through the hillside park toward the Erzsebet Bridge. His standing orders were to follow any "strangers" that left the Citadella on foot or call in the license plate and description of any vehicle that left the Citadella with people he did not recognize. The young man he was following was someone he hadn't seen before. He had studied a file for weeks containing the photos of all the Hungarian soldiers and civilians that worked at the Citadella. He knew the man some twenty yards in front of the group he was following, was not one of them. It was possible he was one of the two men that had left the Polish Embassy in the custody of the police yesterday.

Ludwik had no idea if Josef had been followed or not. He made sure he took his time sauntering down the hill through the park. It was eleven thirty. Plenty of time. He stopped occasionally at a bench to smoke and watch for anyone that looked suspicious. He made sure to memorize the people that passed him where he was sitting. He knew if he saw them again in his walk, there was a good chance they were agents. It was strange playing this game. In Poland, people were killing the enemy when they saw them. He remembered the young German with the light blond hair and glasses from yesterday. He had not been alone. There was at least one other person in the car that had picked him up. He had no idea what the driver or anyone else in the car looked like. The police sergeant knew the car belonged to the Germans. He had even said they were "gestapo." It was obvious that cloak and dagger games were being played here in Budapest.

When he crossed the Erzsebet Bridge, he went into the first coffee house he came to. He sat at a small table facing a window and the street. He ordered coffee in his native Polish. The waiter didn't hesitate. He was back within a minute with a small pot. Ludwik poured himself a cup and relaxed. The only time his eyes left the window was when he poured the coffee.

He finished the pot in five minutes. He sat back in his chair, lit a cigarette and waited. No one had come into the café after him and no one in the street passing by worried him. He paid his bill, left a coin and headed for the jeweler.

Basha let Josef into the embassy with the same friendly smile she had the day before. He said he had questions about what France and England were up to and the embassy's offer for them to work here. He also asked for their money. They needed to buy clothes. And finally, could someone in the embassy help them with the shopping. Basha answered all his questions quickly. She had no idea what was happening with the French and English, but Josef could speak to her supervisor about that. As for the two men working for the embassy, a meeting could be set up to explain how that would work. She would get their money immediately and she would see if someone could help them shop for clothes. And, by the way, where was Ludwik today? Josef said he didn't know, but he was meeting him at one o'clock at the café across the street. He asked her if she would like to join them. She said she was very busy but would think about it.

The supervisor's answer to Josef's question about the French and English was the same one he had heard from the major at the Citadella. There had been no indication of a western front being established by them. The English were mobilizing for war on the home front and the British Expeditionary Force was still waiting for orders in northern France. There had been some propaganda leaflet drops done by the Royal Air Force on towns in western Germany but there had been no bombing raids. The French efforts to mobilize along the Maginot Line was proceeding, but the word was their government lacked any real resolve to fight. Josef asked the diplomat's opinion on what country might be the one that would welcome Poland's government-in-exile's offer to help begin the fight with Germany. He said it still was too early to tell, but sources of his seemed to think it would be the English.

They were very busy getting ready to fight. The French were not. He added the planes were better in England and while the Royal Air Force might resist the idea of accepting foreign pilots into their ranks, they would be more accepting than the French. He told Josef he would find that out when he got to France. Josef asked him what their plan was for getting all the men to France from here. The supervisor said they were planning two options: one by boat from Yugoslavia to Marseilles on the Mediterranean, the other overland through Yugoslavia and northern Italy into France. He encouraged Josef to look for an opportunity in England once he got to France. Josef thanked him for the information and left. He stopped at Basha's desk on the way out and reminded her that he and Ludwik would be across the street having lunch at 1 o'clock. She said to say hello to Ludwik and went back to her work.

Ekzer-Haz

Ludwik wasn't sure if the jeweler's store was before or after the embassy. He wasn't even sure if it was on the same street. He remembered Puskas saying his place was a few blocks from the embassy. As he reached the intersection of Kiraly and Izabella, he saw it. The sign featured three diamond engagement rings on a flat marque with the words "Ekszer-Haz" beautifully scripted through the three bands.

Puskas was in the showroom with a well-dressed, elderly woman and a female employee. The woman was looking at a selection of expensive wrist watches in a glass showcase. Puskas and the sales lady stood behind the showcase, hands clasped behind their backs, waiting patiently for the woman to select one of the watches. When Puskas saw Ludwik enter the store, he said something to the employee and went to greet him. There were no other people in the store.

"May I help you, sir?" Puskas asked.

"Is this watch worth anything?" Ludwik asked in good Hungarian.

Impressed, Puskas said, "Let's take a look at it."

Ludwik followed the jeweler into a backroom workshop.

"So soon you come here," Puskas said quietly.

"I needed some information from a reliable source," Ludwik responded.

"And I am a reliable source?"

"I thought you might be."

"Go on," an alerted Puskas directed.

"My friend and I have been asked to stay in Budapest and work at the embassy to help process our men out of here and into France. I need to know if you have any information about France and England getting actively involved in the war. If they are, then I will leave as soon as possible. If they are not, then helping the effort here might be a good option."

Puskas replied he was happy to hear they had been interned at the Citadella. He said they would be treated well there, but he didn't know how long that would last. He said the German Embassy was demanding the Hungarian government keep all internees under a close watch and to make sure they stayed in place. He said most of the soldiers from the Polish Army that had come across the border were going to be interned in the Miskoics military areas north and northwest of Budapest. And that Polish Air Force personnel would be sent to Jolsva in the same area and to a place called Nagy-Kata, east of Budapest. He added that others were going to be sent here to the Citadella and a place in the Lake Balaton region west of Budapest.

Puskas paused to look at a small, yellow light blinking on the wall behind the workbench. He said someone had entered the store and he had to leave and see if he was needed.

It was a woman who said she would like to browse for a while and look at some earrings and bracelets. Her accent troubled him. And the fact that she had arrived shortly after Ludwik made him suspicious. Puskas told her he had a customer out back and would be with her in a few minutes. He returned to Ludwik and said he only had a few minutes to give him. He said the French were dragging their feet and it did not look like a western front was imminent. He warned Ludwik that unless he was a fighter pilot, there was a good chance he would be placed into the French Army as an infantryman or into a service battalion trucking supplies to the troops. He didn't trust the French to treat the Poles with much respect. And they didn't seem to be that anxious to get into a fight with the Germans. He said Ludwik's chances of getting to England from France had some merit, but he would have to have money to accomplish that. As of now, there was some hope that Poles could make it all the way from here to England. It wasn't likely, but not impossible. The Polish command wanted their men to get to France where Sikorski was. Some would be getting papers here to help them do that. Most would be on their own getting to France. He asked Ludwik if that helped him. Ludwik said it did. He said the major in charge of the Citadella had pretty much said the same things.

"Will you be staying a while in Budapest then?" Puskas asked.

"I think I will. And by the way, here is your watch."

Puskas stared at it. It was working. He was amazed. He was impressed by this Polish pilot. He gave it back to Ludwik and told him it was his.

Part Four

BASHA

Basha & Ludwik

Josef was early. There was only one table available outside. He took it and motioned to the waiter that another setting would be necessary. There was something familiar about this table. Glancing across the street at the embassy, he realized it was the same table the German had sat at yesterday. Without thinking, he glanced down the street to see if the car that followed them was there. It wasn't. But the German was. He was sitting on a bench that faced the embassy some twenty yards down the street from the café. His distinctive light, almost white, blonde hair and glasses gave him away. Josef knew he wasn't reading the newspaper he held in front of him. He was either watching the embassy or had followed him here. Probably the latter he thought. He sat unserved for the next ten minutes. It was getting close to one o'clock. Then he saw Basha waiting to cross the street. She waved to him. He waved back. That's when the waiter appeared. He was holding a menu. Obviously tired of waiting for Josef's guest to arrive. Before he had a chance to order, Basha arrived and said she would do the ordering if he didn't mind. Josef stood to greet her. He pulled out the other chair, seated her and said it would be an honor for her to order. The waiter clicked his heels and left. Josef was delighted. Another friendly voice speaking for him. It was getting to be a habit.

"It's one o'clock and I don't see your handsome friend," she said.

"He'll be here. Ludwik is always on time."

Ludwik watched the two from inside the café. He had been watching the German on the bench for some time; deciding what to do. The appearance of Basha made it easy. He stepped outside and went directly to them. He stopped in front of the lady, clicked his heels and said, "What a pleasant surprise. May I join you?"

A chair was brought out to the table along with the three glasses of wine. Ludwik was impressed with Basha doing the ordering.

386

Lunch was good. Basha ordered everything. She tried to keep the Polish palate in mind by ordering the "toltott kaposzta" a rich, stuffed cabbage of ground meat, rice and sour cream. She followed that with a dessert called "Dobas torta," a delicious chocolate and cream sponge cake. The conversation between the three was in Polish with a smattering of Hungarian terms that Basha thought might be helpful to the two Poles for as long as they stayed in the city. She taught them words like, "szia" (see-ya) "hello", "koszonom szepen" (kuh suh num, say pen) "thank you." She said they could each practice saying "thank you" to her for doing all the ordering.

Smiling at Josef, Basha passed an envelope under the table to Ludwik. It held money she had missed in the safe earlier when Josef was in the embassy. She said to keep it hidden. Ludwik stuffed it behind his belt and out of sight under his jacket. Basha said they had enough money to live comfortably for a while. She said the embassy was working on the business of the weekly stipend that the Hungarian government was offering each refugee. While it wasn't enough to support a lifestyle that included trips to the opera every night and dining in the finer restaurants in the city, it was enough to get along and not go hungry.

"I may have been followed by the gentleman sitting on the bench behind you down the street," Josef said to Basha.

Without looking, Basha said, "That is Willie. He sits there or here at the café almost every day. His job is to watch the embassy or follow whoever he is told to follow."

"How do you know that?" Ludwik asked.

"Willie told me. We had dinner on a few occasions. He likes the opera and so do I. I enjoyed his company. He is a nice young man."

"And now?" Ludwik asked.

"And now, he is a German, and I am working in the Polish embassy. Nothing more to say after that."

Miss Zulick sipped the last of her wine. She pushed the empty glass toward Ludwik, looked him in the eye and said, "If you decide to stay and help us with the processing, I can promise you "wine" that you have never tasted." The invitation was unmistakable. Josef nearly fell off his seat. He excused himself and headed for the men's room. Ludwik reached across the table, took Basha's hands into his own, kissed each one and said, "I would like to taste that wine."

She wanted him to sweep the table clean, come behind her, kick the chair away and bend her over onto the table. She wanted to feel her dress piled up on her back, her panties ripped down and away from her ankles. She wanted to spread her legs and feel his manhood penetrate her with deep and repeated thrusts. She knew that Ludwik wanted her too. She could see it in those pale, blue eyes. It was hard to believe she had known this man for less than a day and could feel like this. It was a wonder. She knew the war would take him. Probably soon. War was ugly, but if not for the war, there would be no Ludwik Skoczylas. It was totally ironic; a feeling so good coming from something so awful. She pulled her hands away and glanced down the street at Willie. She knew he hadn't missed the romantic exchange. He was trained not to miss any detail like that.

When Josef returned, he said he was surprised to see the both of them still there. Ignoring the comment, Basha said, "Let's talk clothes and your stay in Budapest." She recommended that each man buy clothes that fit his status listed on the travel papers. Ludwik's clothes would have to be more of a gentleman's attire seeing that he would be "in charge" of a division of a prominent security company in France. Josef's clothes would not have to be that impressive. An aspiring "student" would not be expected to dress that way. Informal, recreational garb would be best.

388

She said the upcoming weekend would be a good time to get the shopping done. She told them to meet her inside St. Stephen's church on Saturday morning at 9 o'clock. It was located two blocks west of the embassy on Andrassy Street. She said to sit in a pew together and she would find them.

As she prepared to leave, she mentioned it would be good if they could tell her in a day or so if they were interested in working for the embassy. She said they would be needing help soon. There were dozens of Polish airmen and soldiers already in the country and some, mostly officers, would be sent here for internment in the city.

"Would we be working at the embassy?" Ludwik asked.

"Possibly. There are other places in the city that are getting organized in the hopes of helping move men into France."

"From what I've heard, France doesn't seem to be in a hurry to fight," Ludwik said.

"I heard the same thing today when I was at the embassy," Josef added.

"Will that affect your decision to leave or stay?" Basha asked.

"I think it will. Josef and I will discuss it and have an answer for you Saturday. I'm leaning toward staying awhile," Ludwik said.

Basha smiled. She had heard the words she hoped for.

Six Polish Army officers arrived at the Citadella on Friday. Ludwik and Josef met with them after they had been assigned quarters on their floor. They were part of a Polish tank unit that had broken through a German encirclement south of Krakow and had escaped by making their way over the mountains bordering eastern Hungary. The unit was interned in a camp just south of that point.

While there, they heard of efforts in Budapest to help move Polish troops into France and join the French Army. That prompted them to leave the camp two nights ago and board a train to Budapest last night. The "escape" was made possible by bribing the guards to look the other way when they left. The six expected more men to leave the camp soon.

All six believed that Poland's surrender was now inevitable. They were fighting on two fronts against forces that had superior manpower and complete control of the air. Their supply lines of ammunition and fuel had been cut early in the fighting and communication between units was almost non-existent. They said the Army fought hard, but there never seemed to be a cohesive plan of battle other than retreat to the Romanian bridgehead and wait for a second front to open. They were headed to the bridgehead when they were cut off by a Russian force. Their only hope was the mountains. They met a few civilians from Krakow who knew the way over them. They were the ones that had guided them safely across the border into Hungary.

Josef perked up when he heard that bit of news. He asked if they knew the names of the guides or could give a description of them. No one knew their names, but the description of one of them seemed to fit his father. Josef asked what had happened to them. One officer, a tank commander, said they had gone back over the mountains to help other Poles trying to escape.

Encouraged by the possibility that his father might have been one of the mountain guides, Josef decided to stay in Budapest, work for the embassy and hope that his father would eventually make it into Hungary. Maybe even with his two sisters. Ludwik had already made up his mind to stay until word came from the embassy that the fight was indeed on by England AND France. Then he would leave for France and join the fight in any way he could.

St. Stephen's was a monument to Hungarian architecture and Christian ornateness. The church looked down on a large stone square that spread its way out to the street. Identical bell towers rose majestically on both sides of the basilica. Inside, the blues and browns of the tiled floor blended smoothly with the red and gold tapestries hanging eloquently from the pillars and walls. Statues of the Holy Family and the church's patron saint, St. Stephen, looked down upon the rows of pews. Ludwik and Josef sat quietly in a pew before a beautifully sculptured, marble image of the Holy Mother and said prayers for their families, friends and country.

Basha arrived with company. Fellow employee, Bella and a well-dressed man were with her. She introduced her older brother, Hugo, to the two Poles. They shook hands with him and exchanged a "hello" in Hungarian. Basha had the whole day organized. Bella would take Josef and help him with his purchases. She and Hugo would take care of Ludwik. And tonight, they would all have dinner.

Hugo's apartment was on the top floor of an apartment building. It was close to St. Stephen's. Basha had said there was a surprise for Ludwik there. Hugo took them into his bedroom, opened a large closet door and told Ludwik to help himself. Ludwik looked incredulously at Basha. She laughed and said, "Do it."

Everything fit him. Basha thought it would. She knew her brother and Ludwik were both close to six feet in height, slim in the waist and about the same weight. And she knew that her brother had more clothes than he really needed. When she asked Hugo if he would help Ludwik with some clothes, he was more than glad to oblige. Ludwik took two dress pants, a sport coat that matched each, two dress shirts, two ties, a belt, four pairs of dress socks, one pair of shoes, two sweaters, a scarf and a very expensive overcoat. Hugo brought out a travel bag and some caps. Ludwik picked a black cap to match the overcoat.

When it was done, Ludwik told Basha he didn't know how to thank Hugo. Basha translated that to Hugo. He said thanks were not necessary. And he hoped the clothes would help Ludwik get to a place where he would be able to fight for his country. Before he left, he said in broken Polish, "Fly for Poland and may God be with you."

His words went straight to Ludwik's heart. He had heard something similar not that long ago. Bodil had practically said the same thing to him when they parted company in Warsaw just before the invasion. Ludwik answered with a warm, "koszonom szepen." The Hungarian "thank you" startled Hugo. He gave Ludwik a strong hug, clicked his heels, kissed his sister and left the apartment.

Basha watched Ludwik roll his new clothing in military fashion and pack it carefully in the travel bag. There was enough space left to fold the sport coat and overcoat in half and place them on top of the other items. After closing the bag, he went to Basha, cupped her face in his hands and kissed her gently on the lips. She reached up, cupped his face in her hands and returned his kiss with another. She put her head on his chest and asked him if he would like to see her apartment. He hugged her firmly and said yes.

They spent the first two hours in bed. Only sheer exhaustion stopped them. When Ludwik woke, he was laying naked across a naked Basha, mid-section to mid-section. The smell of sweat and sex hung in the bedroom air. Slowly, very quietly, he lifted himself off her body, covered her gently with a blanket and went into the shower.

Basha was making coffee and sandwiches when he stepped into the parlor. He changed quickly and joined her at the table. Each was as ravenous with the food as they had been with their lovemaking.

"More?" Basha teased.

"Enough for now," Ludwik answered.

392

They both laughed. Life was a little better now. The world, such as it was, had been forgotten the past few hours. It was time to come back to it and discuss the future. Basha suggested that Ludwik leave some clothes in her apartment. She thought someone in the Citadella, Hungarian or Polish, might be tempted to steal them. Ludwik agreed.

The conversation switched to her brother. Ludwik wanted to know how he could afford to give away so many fine clothes. Basha said he owned a restaurant and a men's clothing store in the city. She said the only reason Josef wasn't included in the clothes giveaway was that he needed "student appropriate" items that her brother didn't have.

Ludwik asked her if Bella was going to be as "giving" to Josef as she had been with him. She said, "You'll have to ask him that."

He then asked her if she knew how he and Josef would get permission from the authorities to work at helping the refugees. She said the embassy would handle that.

"What about the travel papers?" Ludwik asked.

"They will stay the same. You will still be traveling to Paris and your "new job." We will put in the appropriate dates just before you leave."

Ludwik said, "You know I will leave when the time comes."

"I understand that. Do you understand that your time here will be spent fighting the Germans in another way?"

Ludwik nodded. He wanted to fly against the Germans but would have to wait until that was possible. Until then, he would help his country as much as he could here in Budapest.

Hugo's restaurant was crowded. A table had been reserved for the four of them. Dinner was delightful. Ludwik and Josef insisted on paying the bill, but before it was presented, Hugo had it reduced by half. He knew they wouldn't recognize the difference right now.

The two couples enjoyed an after-dinner stroll on the river walk. They watched the boats casually make their way under the brilliantly lighted "chain bridge" that spanned the Danube. Basha pointed out the illuminated Citadella atop Gellert Hill and the Castle District, all on the Buda side of the river. She proudly pointed to the country's magnificent Parliament building just up the river on their side; the Pest side. Ludwik said Budapest was like Paris on the Seine and Warsaw on the Vistula. Basha surprised and delighted Josef and Bella with a kiss on Ludwik's lips for the compliment.

There wasn't enough time to revisit Basha's apartment. Ludwik wanted to, but they had to make it back to the Citadella before "lights out." It had been a wonderful day. God had been good to them. Once again.

The first three months in Budapest were busy. It was December now and very cold. The fighting in Poland had ended in early October. The country had been carved up into two large sections by the Germans and Russians. Danzig and most of western Poland was now under Nazi Germany's rule while the eastern half of the country was in Russia's hands. Poland's government in exile was still in Paris. General Sikorski was now Commander-in-Chief of all Polish armed forces in exile. Much of Poland's military was now in prison camps that stretched from Germany to the gulags of the Soviet Union. A substantial number of the Polish Army had gone underground and formed partisan groups in the forests that dotted Poland's landscape. Many others had returned to civilian life to avoid capture. They hid their weapons and stockpiled ammunition in caves or buried them underground in their fields, forests and mountains.

Thousands of Polish soldiers and airmen had escaped from Romania by sea and had been sent to ports along the Mediterranean that stretched from the Middle East to Africa. From there they had sailed to southern France. Some men had taken the overland route through Hungary, Yugoslavia and Italy to get to France.

Most of the refugees that had arrived in Hungary the past month were civilians. They were helped by the Red Cross, the Catholic Church and organizations like the Hungarian & Polish Affairs Committee as well as the Polish Embassy. They were given housing, medical aid and some employment. A very sympathetic and co-operative Hungarian government and people allowed Polish leaders to set up schools for children and young adults of all ages. Those without a job were given temporary financial assistance before finding work on their own.

Initially, Ludwik and Josef worked in the embassy itself and dealt strictly with Polish military refugees and some of their family members. Later, they were moved to an adjacent building doing the same thing. Many Polish soldiers and airmen had used bribes to "escape" internment camps in Hungary and Romania. Those in Hungary came to Budapest looking for help. While the Hungarian government went about its own business, the embassy was busy helping the Polish military get out of the country with fake documents and a little money. As time went by however, the Germans, realizing what was happening, began applying pressure on the Hungarian government to keep the Poles in internment camps.

By the end of November, hundreds of soldiers and airmen had made their way from Hungary into Yugoslavia. Once there, they traveled south to the city of Split on the Adriatic coast and booked passage by ship to northern Africa and southern France. Others went overland by train or other means across Yugoslavia, thru northern Italy and into France.

One of Ludwik's jobs was to pass on information to the men and some family members, concerning the political situations in Yugoslavia and Italy. He relied on information from the embassy and Puskas, the jeweler. He and Puskas had become good friends. They always met secretly and out of sight from the likes of Willie, the German agent. One bit of information that Puskas had passed on to the embassy through Ludwik, was how dramatic the number of German agents had increased in the city. It was becoming obvious that Hitler was extremely upset with the Hungarian government's willingness to accept Polish military refugees into its country and its unwillingness to strictly enforce their internment.

It had been more than four months since Ludwik had flown an airplane of any sort. While his lifetime passion for flying had been tempered by the fortunes of war, he had found other places to focus that passion on. One was the movement of Polish airmen into France. He had learned his job of facilitating that process quickly and had made suggestions that made the process more efficient. His suggestion of combining the records of all agencies involved in listing Polish airmen into a central bank of information was hailed as a major step in efficiency. He also suggested that all Polish airmen and soldiers interviewed should be able to describe in detail the history of their training, from enlistment to flight or service school. The intent of that was to make sure German agents were not infiltrating their ranks to garner information on the movement of men out of Hungary. One German agent's body had already been discovered floating in Lake Balaton, some seventy miles southwest of Budapest.

Another place to focus his passion was in the arms of his lover and constant companion, Basha. He had worked out a deal with Major Seles at the Citadella to stay in the city Friday and Saturday nights. In return, he offered to pay the major half of the stipend he was receiving from the Hungarian government and promised to return to the Citadella by Sunday evening.

Seles had refused the money but insisted Ludwik be back on Sunday and attend informational meetings on Friday. Josef left the embassy to work for the Council for the Aid of Polish Refugees that had been organized in October. He wanted to be in a position where information concerning incoming Polish civilians was firsthand. Not a day went by without him checking for his family's name on the lists shared by all civilian relief organizations in the country.

Ludwik's weekday evenings after work were spent at Basha's apartment. Dinner was always a mix of Hungarian and Polish dishes. Conversation was about the day's events, the latest news each had heard and what they might do on the weekend. After that, their lovemaking would begin. It was always good. It never waned in intensity and always ended in time for Ludwik to return to the Citadella.

Fridays and Saturdays usually included the company of Josef and Bella. Hugo's restaurant, the opera, cafes, dance halls and the always beautiful lights of a Budapest night along the Danube were the favorite haunts of the foursome. They all offered an escape from the rigors of work with refugees who had brought with them the misery of the human condition and the ongoing tragedy that had created it.

Sundays were reserved for prayer and Basha's family. St. Stephens was their favorite place of worship. Ludwik had surprised Basha early on by his seriousness for prayer and his reverence for Mary, the Blessed Mother. The Zulick family had never been as faithful and devoted to the church as he was.

From the church, it was a short stroll up Andrassy Street past the Opera House to Nagymezo Street and the small apartment of Basha's parents. There was never any question from her parents concerning her relationship with Ludwik. They had long ago decided to let their two children live their lives as they saw fit.

Ludwik was a bit surprised by that attitude. It was just the opposite of the way his parents had raised his family. Strictness and discipline had been the order of the day back in Poland. Here, with the Zulicks, openness and individualism had been fostered early. Both Basha and Hugo, in addition to being well educated, had been given free rein to live their lives as they saw fit.

Basha's parents had been impressed by Ludwik the first time he came for dinner. What they didn't know was that Basha had given him a course in traditional Hungarian manners and customs. He had taken his shoes off before entering their apartment, brought a box of chocolates as a gift, introduced himself using his last name first, waited to eat until the father had begun, put his fork and knife on the right side of the plate when he had finished and drank all the alcohol he was offered. He also made sure not to criticize anything Hungarian and never talked about himself unless he was asked.

The Zulicks had always felt Hungary and Poland shared a common history of culture and friendship. They were acutely sympathetic to the Polish people and what had happened to them. They were educated and very up to date on the political events that were unfolding around the world and in particular, their country. So were their children.

On one Sunday, some weeks after Ludwik's first visit, Hugo, his father, Hugo Sr. and Ludwik retired to the library for a brandy and smoke after dinner. A minute later, a hidden door, part of the floor to ceiling bookcase, opened and Puskas, the jeweler, walked into the room. He greeted Ludwik and said he was asked to come and translate for Mr. Zulick, a good customer of his and a man that had provided valuable political information to him over the years. Basha's father was going to pass on some information today and he wanted Ludwik to hear it.

398

The elder Zulick did all the talking. Puskas translated. Hugo and Ludwik listened. The information was sobering; Ludwik was in danger because of his relationship with Basha. Plans were in the making to have Ludwik arrested and imprisoned to embarrass the Zulick family. He said the time in Hungary for all Polish military was coming to an end and Ludwik needed to consider leaving as soon as possible.

Puskas knew Hugo Zulick Sr. was well connected politically and was truly sympathetic to the Poles. He did wonder, however, if Ludwik's relationship with his daughter was the real reason for this gathering. He asked him if the meeting was personal. Zulick said it was. He had been told by a friend that a member of the German embassy had asked him if he knew that a daughter of a prominent Hungarian family, working in the Polish embassy, was cohabitating with a Polish refugee who some believed was involved in criminal activities. The friend had seen Basha at the Opera House more than once with a Polish gentleman. The friend knew that Basha worked in the Polish embassy and deduced she was the one the German was "gossiping" about. Zulick went on to say that the Hungarian government was beginning to waver on its kind treatment of Polish military refugees; especially the ones that were suspected of "criminal" activity. He was concerned that his daughter might be implicated in a charge, real or not, of aiding and abetting a criminal. He continued by saying the government was under increasing pressure internally by opportunistic, political forces and externally by a looming German threat. It all meant that his daughter was now walking in harm's way.

After hearing the translation, Ludwik said he appreciated Mr. Zulick's concern. He told him he was not involved in any criminal activity. Zulick answered by saying his political enemies, influenced by the Germans, did not care about the truth and were only looking for the Hungarian government and political opponents like himself, to bend a knee to Germany.

Ludwik asked if there was anything the Hungarian government was considering that would indicate it was bending a knee. Zulick said a law was in the works that would state no man under the age of forty-five would be allowed to leave the country. Puskas added that most Polish military internees in Hungary had left the internment camps and were either already out of the country or in cities looking for help to get out. The number of those still in cities was considerable. Pro-Nazi politicians were aware of this and were waging a well-funded campaign to instill the fear of invasion and retribution by the Germans because of those numbers. That fear was enhanced by demands from the Nazis to either stop the flow of Polish military exiting the country or suffer severe consequences for not doing so. He said the number of refugees coming into Hungary had been reduced to a trickle. The borders had been effectively sealed by the Romanians along their border with Hungary and the Russians had done the same along the Polish border.

Ludwik was aware that time was running out for him. He had been warned that he might be arrested on some trumped-up charges by the police. And now the Hungarian government was discussing a bill that would make it illegal for any man under forty-five to leave the country. The barriers to freedom were growing greater every day.

Back at the Citadella, Ludwik told Josef the bad news. Josef just shook his head and said he had bad news also. The mountain passes from Poland into Hungary had been shut down by a record snowfall and the entire border was suffering from one of the coldest winters on record. That meant his father had to remain in Poland.

At a briefing in the Citadella the next day, Major Seles warned the remaining Poles that when the "under 45" bill became law, they would not be allowed out of the Citadella. He advised all of them to get out of the country quickly. He said he would not stop anyone from leaving, but not to make it obvious they were.

400

He hoped they understood. The major's warning would not be the only one Ludwik received that day. A second warning came in the belfry of one of the majestic bell towers of St. Stephen's Church. The landing in the belfry was one of Ludwik's and Basha's favorite places in Budapest. Well worth the climb up the narrow, spiral staircase that ended on the belfry with its spectacular view of the city and the revered Danube. They had spent many an extended lunch hour alone up there admiring the view and discussing whatever two lovers discussed. Sometimes they played a game of guessing who the echoing footsteps approaching the belfry on the staircase belonged to. Man or woman? Young or old? Height and weight? Ludwik almost always got it right, but today, he was wrong. Very wrong. He guessed the footsteps approaching belonged to a young woman, one that was slight and moved patiently with steps hardly discernible. Basha said it was a young man wearing dress shoes whose steps seemed measured and deliberate. Today, she was correct.

The white-blond haired young man stepped out onto the landing and removed his spectacles. He pulled a handkerchief from his winter coat and wiped them very carefully as he eyed Ludwik and Basha. It was Willie from the German embassy. Ludwik and Basha stared at him not knowing what to expect. Willie asked Basha to translate. Facing Ludwik, he said, "I am not a German agent. I work at the embassy and sometimes I am ordered to follow people and report their activities. I know that you are not a criminal and not a threat to any of us here in Budapest. We know you help in the movement of your comrades out of the country. Personally, I admire your efforts. You could have left a long time ago. But you haven't. I know that Basha is one of the reasons you are still here. But neither she, nor her father or brother, will be able to help you in a few days. You will be arrested early Sunday morning at Basha's apartment or on the way back to the Citadella Sunday evening.

"On what charges?" Ludwik asked.

401

"Counterfeiting Hungarian money," Willie answered.

"Why are you telling us this?" Basha asked.

"You know my family left Germany when Hitler came to power. They are now in the United States. I stayed to serve my country. Just like your Polish friend here stayed to serve his country. I respect that. You and your family treated me well when I was seeing you. The war has changed everything. I do not care to see you, or your family dragged into the mess that will be made by some in your government over your relationship with this Polish airman. There are men that do not care for your father's political views and your cohabitation with a "criminal." They will make an example of you and your family and put a stain on your family's reputation."

He brought his attention back to Ludwik, "Do not go to Basha's place Saturday night. Find a place to stay undercover. Stay away from the embassy on Saturday. You need to leave the country. You will have to smuggle yourself out. Whatever travel papers you have will not be any good in Hungary. You will be wanted as a fugitive from justice and will be arrested and taken into custody. Do you understand what I have told you?" Ludwik nodded. The German turned to Basha, clicked his heels, bowed and left.

Ludwik lit a cigarette and walked over to the edge of the belfry and watched for Willie to exit the church. He wanted to see if the German met with anyone or got into the car that had followed him and Josef to the Citadella on that first day some months ago. He watched Willie walk alone up Androssy Street until he was out of sight. The man had seemed genuine. But he was still the enemy.

"What do you think, Basha?"   Ludwik asked.

"Our family has been hearing things like this recently. Lots of bad things. I believe Willie. Father has too many enemies.

I think you have done all you can for your country here. It is too dangerous for you now. We will have your papers updated today."

Ludwik held her close, kissed her gently and said he would check this out. He felt if this was true, he and Josef would have to leave this week. Not wait. Willie was probably right about his fake travel papers. The Budapest police would have him in handcuffs without even asking for his papers. He suggested Basha go to her parent's home and relay what she had just heard from Willie. See what she could find out. He would ring her at three o'clock.

Puskas was not surprised. Rumors had been flying ever since the meeting at the Zulick home. His sources had confirmed some of them. He knew the Hungarian government was going to pass the law keeping every man under the age of forty-five in the country. It would be the beginning of the end of life in Budapest as he knew it. He also knew that every foreigner, especially the Poles, would have to be very careful in the days ahead. Idle conversation with any stranger was out of the question. Even discussions with trusted friends had to be discreet and away from treacherous ears. He knew the trumped-up charges against Ludwik was a way to get at Hugo Zulick, Sr. Someone had a score to settle with him for his liberal political views and at the same time, make points with the new pro-German government candidates that looked to be the favorites in the upcoming Parliamentary elections. A public trial of Ludwik would be a disaster for the Zulick family and sully the reputation of the leading proponent of anti-German sentiment in Budapest. He also knew there would be no trial if there was no Ludwik. Time had run out for the patriotic Pole and his friend. They had to leave quickly. He would make arrangements. It would take a few phone calls to get everything moving. With any luck, the two Poles would be out of the city and on their way out of the country in a few days. He had done this before to save one of his men. He explained to Ludwik what his plan was. He said Josef will go back to the Citadella Thursday after work.

403

As usual. He was to pack all essential clothing and materials for both of you and wait for a taxi to pick him up at eight o'clock that night. An arrangement will be made to compensate Major Seles to make sure the guards do not interfere. Josef will be dropped off at St. Elizabeth Church. From there he would go to Bella's and stay the night. Major Seles will be made aware of that. The luggage will be taken to a barge docked in the shadows under the Erzsebet Bridge. The captain of the barge had done work for him in the past and was very reliable. He went on, "I want you to make plans for dinner around seven at Hugo's restaurant Friday evening for you, Basha, Josef and Bella. After dinner, you two couples will take a walk to the bridge where the barge is. You and Josef will board the barge. The women will leave with two of my men that have been waiting there. They will be wearing similar dark topcoats and caps that you and Josef will be wearing. The two "couples" will walk down the river walk to the next bridge. A cab will be waiting. They will be driven to Bella's place. Bella and her "man" will exit the cab and enter the building. She will go up to her apartment. He will leave the building out the rear and disappear. The same pattern will be repeated at Basha's place. If anyone has been following them, they will have to assume both men are with their women for the weekend. Basha and Bella can do what they please on Saturday. While the police are waiting to spring their surprise early Sunday morning or late Sunday night, you and Josef will be well on your way out of the country."

"How will the women be made aware of this plan?" Ludwik asked.

"You will tell them. It would be best to wait a while before you do. You don't want them to worry the rest of the week. Try to stay normal. Keep your eyes and ears open. Just keep the timing right and wear those dark clothes. It's very important. And one other thing. If for some reason the authorities come to the embassy looking for you, remember you have immunity while you are inside the embassy.

Basha will let me know and we will get you out of there and hide you until Friday night. Then we will get you and Josef on the barge."

"And Josef this week?" Ludwik asked.

"They won't bother him. It's you they want. He should do what he usually does during the week. But he must get to the church with the luggage and then stay with Bella. And the same goes for you. Everything is as usual. Not to worry. Just go about your business. If you don't hear from me then everything is all set. I will see you at Hugo's Friday night."

"Who are the other men involved in this plan?" Ludwik prompted.

"Your friends. That's all you need to know."

"Thank you for helping us," Ludwik said.

"You can thank my banker friend in Debrechen for bringing you two to our attention. We are not many in Hungary, but we do what we can for Poland. Before the Germans come, and they will come, we will be gone from here."

"Where will you go?" Ludwik asked.

"Not France. Probably England. Maybe America."

Ludwik nodded, shook the "jewelers" hand and left to see Josef.

Josef was sitting with a Jewish family that had somehow made it across the border from Romania. The couple had two small girls with them. They had left Poland when the Russians invaded from the east. They had crossed the border into Romania with thousands of others and were sent to an internment camp. They were there for some time before realizing they were being discriminated against by the authorities because they were Jewish. They used some personal jewelry to bribe their way to Bucharest and the Polish Embassy.

They were told to wait. The embassy's priority was to help move as many Polish soldiers and airmen out of Romania as they could before they began to help Polish civilians. When they discovered that anti-Jewish discrimination existed in Bucharest also, they decided to leave Romania without help and come to Budapest. Josef explained to them that unfortunately, they had come to Hungary at a time when pro-Fascist legislators had begun passing anti-Semitic laws making the future for Jews in Hungary questionable. After his warning, he made arrangements for them to stay with a Jewish family in the city until they found work and could support themselves. He sent them out with some money and directions to the home of the host family. He called the host family and alerted them about the family on the way to their home. Josef watched them shuffle out into the street and thought about the rabbi back in Poland leading his people away from Pulawy only to be massacred on the road by German planes. He thought of Kramer Rubenstein, the tailor from Warsaw's Old Town, and how certain Kramer was that if the Germans attacked and were victorious, it would be the end for Jews in Poland. He feared that Kramer might be right. He had heard some of Hitler's racist rants in newsreels. And now those same rants were making headway here in Hungary.

Josef sat quietly while Ludwik ran through the plan outlined by Puskas. Ludwik emphasized the fact that the police were going to arrest him, not anyone else. Josef reminded Ludwik of their pact to stay together all the way to France. He would be going with him. Ludwik hugged him. Josef smiled and said he did have plans to be with Bella Friday night anyway. He would call her and tell her he needed to be with her Thursday night, stay there Friday and have dinner with her at Hugo's Friday night. Ludwik reminded Josef to pack all the winter clothes he had in his suitcase and backpack and bring them along with his sleeping bag to the church Thursday night. Leave everything else.

Josef understood. He would pack their suitcases Thursday after work and add to their backpacks items that would be useful in the woods and mountains. That would include two hunting knives he had bought and hid in the Citadella. Then he would wait for the taxi. Ludwik nodded his approval. He gripped Josef's shoulder and said, "We've been spoiled here. It's time we get closer to a place where we can get in the air and fight."

Josef agreed, "I think we have done well in Hungary, but you are right. It is time to move on. I just wish my father had made it to Budapest. I'm afraid I will never see him again"

Ludwik felt his pain and said "We all want to know what has happened to our families. When your father does make it here, our friends will take good care of him. I plan to call Basha whenever possible. She will have an eye out for him. So will Bella and your contacts in the center."

Josef smiled and said, "This is true. He's probably holed up in the mountains somewhere. He won't try the pass until spring."

At 3:00 o'clock, Ludwik rang Basha from his workstation. She was worried. Her father had been very upset over the news that Ludwik was to be arrested this weekend. He was furious that his political enemies were trying to use their relationship to embarrass him and the family and to discredit his opposition to the fascist leaning moves of the government. He was worried about the family's future in a Hungary run by a sympathetic pro-German, anti-Semitic Parliament. He was now faced with making a difficult decision; stay and fight the change of government or leave with the family while they could. He said the family's predicament now was no different than what the Jews had faced in Germany when Hitler came to power. She wasn't sure what her father might do.

Ludwik understood and told Basha plans were in the making for him and Josef to disappear. That would give her father some time to make his decision. He said he hoped that if it looked certain the government was going to change, her father wouldn't be that proud. He would get the family out of harm's way. He told Basha it might not be wise to go to her apartment Thursday night. The police might change their mind about a Sunday morning arrest and come for him that night or Friday morning. Basha said they could stay at Hugo's apartment Thursday night. Ludwik agreed. He told her to have all his winter clothes sent to Hugo's Thursday morning and have Hugo home to accept them. And to make sure the overcoat and black cap was included. Basha asked him if Friday was going to be their last day together. He hesitated a moment then said, "I'm afraid it might, my love."

The cab passed through the unattended gate of the Citadella at 8 o'clock sharp. It circled the courtyard and pulled up to the door that led to the barracks area of the old fort. Josef stepped quickly outside with the suitcases and backpacks. The driver jumped out, opened the trunk and was back behind the wheel before the first suitcase landed inside. Seconds later, the backpacks had been retrieved and loaded in with the suitcases. The driver told Josef to get in the back seat and put on the Hungarian officer's hat that was there.

The cab rolled slowly rolled back through the open, unattended gate. As soon as the cab made it outside the wall, two sentries stepped from the guardhouse and closed the gate. The whole process took less than two minutes. Major Seles watched the transfer from the window of his darkened office. It had been a quick and professional piece of work. Someone in the city, probably the same man he had dealt with a few days ago, had called him and said the money in the package left earlier at the gate for him was for leaving the gate guards inside the guardhouse at eight with the gate open. The man, probably a Polish agent, was already aware of what was happening in Hungary.

His government's politics had taken a turn. It wouldn't be long before all refugees would be placed under the umbrella of suspicion and any Polish military personnel still in internment camps would be put under lock and key. And they wouldn't be the only ones targeted by the government. Already, Jewish members of the Hungarian military, distinguished or not, were being drummed out of the Army and placed into labor battalions where they would no longer be allowed to carry weapons. His country was changing. All the latent anti-Semitism in Hungary had been driven to the surface by this wave of Nazi influence.

The cab driver spoke perfect Polish. He reminded Josef about the plans for Friday night. Without taking his eyes off the street, he flipped an envelope into the back seat. He said it was Yugoslavian dinara and he was to split it with the other pilot. He pulled his hat down to the bridge of his nose and drove across the Erzsebet Bridge into Pest. Josef never got a good look at him and when he tried to ask a question, he was told to go through the door the car stopped at. And to leave the hat.

Ludwik had arranged with the major to stay in the city Thursday night. The major didn't seem to mind. Thought it was a good idea. Basha had asked Hugo if they could stay in his apartment that night. Without asking why, Hugo said yes and that he would stay at the restaurant.

Basha warmed up the large bowl of goulash that Hugo had left in the refrigerator. The warm bits of meat and vegetables, flavored with strong pepper was the perfect meal for the cold Thursday evening. When the meat and vegetables were gone, she brought out a small plate of sliced, buttered, hard bread for dipping into the warm, goulash stock left in the bowl, a delicious twist to a tasty meal.

They each took a glass of brandy into the dining room and toasted each other. Ludwik thanked Basha for all she had done. She thanked him for coming into her life. They both knew tomorrow would be their last day together. Finished with her brandy, Basha got up, turned off the lights and asked Ludwik to join her at the window. They looked down at the spectacle of lights that was Budapest. Ludwik said, "I remember saying that I would love to be with a woman in a place with a view like this." Basha slipped an arm around his waist, placed her free hand on his chest and let it trail slowly down toward his belt. She stood up on her toes, nipped his ear and whispered, "And here is that woman."

Ludwik rang Puskas early the next morning and said he wasn't at Basha's apartment but was with her at Hugo's place. Puskas said that was a good thing. He didn't think the police, or the Germans were watching anyone else in Basha's family, but they may have very well been watching her place. He said to stay out of sight until it got dark then take a cab to the restaurant. He said he would be in the restaurant with a "friend" to keep an eye out for trouble. He said to have Basha call Bella and have her go to the embassy, tell her superiors Basha was sick then fill in the proper dates on the two sets of travel papers and stamp them to prove passage into Hungary.

After breakfast, Basha called Bella to take care of the travel papers for the two men and to bring Ludwik's papers to Hugo's restaurant along with Josef for dinner tonight; seven sharp and don't be late. Then she called Hugo to make the reservation.

"Are you finished?" Ludwik called from the bedroom.

It was mid-afternoon when they woke. They took a hot shower together. It quickly turned lukewarm and then cold. Basha cursed her brother. Ludwik playfully held her in the stream of cold water and laughed while she yelled curses and absurdities at him.

He relented and changed places with her. He took the cold without flinching and held her at arms-length. Then he took her in his arms and kissed her. The heat from her body more than made up for the cold water flaying his broad back and backside. They dried each other with towels and went to bed for the last time. The lovemaking was slow. There was no urgency. Just an unspoken wish that it would last forever.

The Escape

Basha was impressed with the quick planning that had been made by the unknown Polish agent. She knew from her embassy work that Poland had operatives working in the country. She also knew they watched her people as well. That never bothered her. They had a job to do just like she had a job to do. And in these times, she was glad to see that people like Ludwik had friends who could help. And those friends, she knew now, had become her friends.

She liked the plan. The two railroad stations in Budapest were always watched carefully. Police would already have pictures of Ludwik and her. Maybe even of Josef and Bella. If anyone of them attempted to board a train this weekend in Budapest, they would be detained at the very least. Ludwik would be arrested. Leaving the country by barge under the cover of darkness was a good idea. She knew the authorities at the Citadella didn't expect Ludwik back until Sunday night. No problem there. Hopefully by that time, the two men would be out of the country.

There was a small church a few blocks from the restaurant. Ludwik said he needed to stop there for a few minutes. Basha had gone to mass with Ludwik every Sunday for some time now and knew how religious he was; how devoted he was to Mary, the Blessed Mother. At times, she had even felt a tinge of jealousy toward Mary because of the reverence she was shown by him.

411

She had never known anyone who was that deeply committed to his faith like Ludwik. She knelt with him at the altar and looked up at the statue of the Blessed Lady. She asked the Lady, with all the faith that she had, that this good man, if he should escape the war with his life, would find it in his heart to come back to her.

Dinner at "Hugo's" was always special. The food was wonderful, the service superior and the company, as usual, great. The place was always crowded. Josef sat next to Ludwik so he could pass the travel papers to him without drawing any attention. Ludwik saw Puskas with a gentleman off to his right. He was sitting with his back to the wall and had a clear view of the entire floor and making sure no threat had come into the restaurant after they had. He remembered Lupu saying that it always paid to be extra careful. As the evening progressed, Puskas's friend would leave the table and be gone for a time. Probably checking outside to see if anyone suspicious was hanging around. While Puskas and his friend gave him a sense of security, it also was a reminder that in a very short time, he and Josef would be back to the hide and seek game they had played in Romania and early on in Hungary. He forced himself to enjoy the meal of stuffed cabbages and noodles. And when the time came to leave, he reached under the table for Basha's hand, held it gently and told her quietly she was loved. He wanted to tell her before they left the restaurant just in case circumstances developed outside that wouldn't allow it. Puskas watched them leave. He casually scanned the dining area to see if anyone made a move to follow. No one did. He waited a minute before paying the bill. Another minute found him outside and walking slowly in the direction of the Erzsebet Bridge looming high over a slight bend in the river. The night air was cold but not uncomfortably so. It would be a lot colder on the river for the two escapees. A small price to pay! He saw his tablemate approaching. The man said there was a problem. An Army patrol boat had tied on to the barge and soldiers were swarming all over it.

412

The two couples were sitting on a bench not too far from the bridge and watching the action. Puskas told his man to wait here and keep an eye on the walkway past the restaurant. He moved quickly toward the two couples on the bench. He stopped in front of them and lit a cigarette. Looking down at the river and never turning to face them, he said, in Hungarian, they should wait until he found out what was going on. He added no one had followed them and that he had men on the walkway on both sides of the bridge keeping an eye open.

The barge's captain was yelling at an Army officer. He wanted to know if the officer was satisfied with his search. The officer apologized for the inconvenience. He then ordered his men to put the tarp back over the cargo of machine parts and prepare to leave.

Puskas walked over to the two men dressed as Ludwik and Josef who were waiting in the shadow of the bridge. He told them the plan would proceed as soon as the patrol boat left. Then he walked back to the two couples. He made sure the women couldn't see his face. He told them to wait until the patrol boat left and was out of sight before going under the bridge. He said it was a good thing the barge was being checked now. Ten minutes later it might have been a disaster. He said to go on with the plan as it had been laid out. He wished them all well and said he would stay here and help watch the walkway this side of the bridge.

The patrol boat's engines sputtered to a start, purred into a smooth gurgle and slowly moved away from the barge. It went upriver toward Parliament. A good thing. The barge would be going downriver. The goodbyes were quick and painful. A fierce hug, a kiss, a weak smile. Then the men were on board and in the secret hold under the captain's feet. The women watched them disappear then walked away with the two strangers dressed like their men toward the next bridge.

Thirty minutes into the slow-moving trip on the river, the captain opened the trap door to the hold where Ludwik and Josef sat with their luggage and backpacks in the dark. A crewmember helped them up into the wheelhouse. The captain spoke in Polish and told them the river patrol was not looking for them. They were looking for weapons that had been stolen from an Army base and thought to be on a boat somewhere along the Danube near Budapest. He said their time on the river trip would be a few hours. They would dock at a town called Dunafoldvar and spend the night there on the boat. Ludwik and Josef could either sleep outside on the deck in their sleeping bags or in the warmer confines of the hold. The thought of the stuffy, smelly and dark hold made their decision easy. Ludwik went down into the hold and handed the backpacks with the attached sleeping bags up to Josef. They brought the bags outside and laid them behind the wheelhouse wall to block the cold breeze as the barge chugged through the winter air. They used their overcoats as an extra layer of protection on top of the bags.

Settled comfortably in his bag, Ludwik went over the day's events in his mind. He wondered if there was anything that had been missed. The only thing that came to mind was that he wasn't exactly sure what was on the travel papers. The dates should have been added and stamped to coincide with their travel. He remembered his new name was Piotr Karski and Josef was now Jozef Hermanski. The pictures had looked good after they were taken. He was sure they had not been changed. Original birthplaces named him from Kurylowka, Josef from Krakow. Both were listed as entering Romania a few days apart in August and coming into Hungary last week. Josef was listed as a student in Bucharest, and he was listed as a locksmith in the city

He padded the papers in the inside breast pocket of his jacket. He hoped they would be good enough to get him out of Hungary. He was confident that once they made it into Yugoslavia, the papers would be fine and not questioned.

No one would be looking for him there. Puskas had said it would be unusual if papers were checked thoroughly at border crossings the rest of the way to France once out of Hungary. Ludwik hoped the man was right. He knew it would be trouble if the police in or near Budapest caught him, but there was a good chance that the police outside of Budapest would not be aware of who he was or that he was to be arrested and detained.

Long after Josef had disappeared into his sleeping bag, Ludwik wrestled with the best way to carry the papers. They had to be always on his person. The overcoat's two pockets were not deep enough, and pants pockets were easy targets in a crowd. The field jacket would be good. It had two large, zippered pockets on its inside. He would wear the jacket as much as he could the rest of the way; even sleep with it if he had to. Feeling the icy cold on his face, he tabled his worry about the papers and burrowed deep into the bag for the first time since the haystack in Romania. It felt warm; not Basha warm, but warm enough.

Dawn broke in a misty sunlight that covered the entire river. The barge bobbed gently against the dock it was tied to. The sound of men arguing loudly up in the wheelhouse was what woke Ludwik. He squirmed out of his bag to find out what was going on. The arguing stopped abruptly when he stepped inside the wheelhouse. The captain and two crewmen stared at him. The captain said the two men were nervous about them. They were afraid the river patrol would come again, and they didn't want to go to jail over foreigners. He told Ludwik to wake up Josef, get their possessions and put them on the dock. He said there was no food or coffee, but he did have some Hungarian advice for them. He said, "Ember embernek farkasa." One of the men howled like a wolf and pointed a dirty, oily finger at him.

Ten minutes later, a car came out of the mist and rolled to a stop at the end of the dock. Its headlights blinked twice. The signal for departure. The captain grunted, "Go!" Ludwik threw his suitcase and backpack onto the dock and climbed off the barge. Josef followed. Carrying their luggage, they walked quickly toward the black Peugeot sedan. A man opened the trunk and dove back behind the wheel. Josef had seen this drill before at the Citadella. He wondered if it was the same man. When the driver said, "It's nice to see you again, Josef," there was no doubt. It was the same man. Josef responded by saying, "Where's my hat?" The driver laughed and drove off. He told them they were going to a friend's house in Simontornya, a small village some twenty miles away. They would breakfast there and leave mid-afternoon for Kaposvar, some fifty miles further on toward the border. He would drop them at the train station there. They were to buy tickets to Zagreb, Yugoslavia on the early evening train. He said it was important for them to be across the border no later than tonight. The alarm would go out for Ludwik's arrest if he wasn't found at Basha's Sunday morning or on his way back to the Citadella Sunday night. By the time either one happened, they should be well across the border.

A few minutes into the drive, Ludwik's curiosity got the best of him. He wanted to know what advice the barge captain had given him just before they left the barge. He asked the driver if he knew what the Hungarian, "Ember embernek farkasa" meant. The driver said it was a warning; a little stronger than "be careful." It meant, "Man is a wolf to man."

Ludwik asked if the warning meant trouble for them in Yugoslavia. The driver said it was a sign of the times and that it would be wise to heed the advice, especially in the countryside. He said Zagreb would welcome them with open arms; the gypsies and outlaws in the countryside would be a different matter.

416

The drive on the bumpy, dirt road became a serious challenge when the fog began to thicken. The driver said if there was an accident, the two men were to be out in the fields and walking west by southwest to Simontornya on their own. They were not to hang around and have to answer questions from anyone, especially a local police officer. He said the "friend's house" would be easy to find. It was the third white house past the Simontornya Castle. The houses were the only buildings besides the castle on the street. Once at the house, they had to walk to the back and tap on the window next to the rear door. Not on the door. Either he or someone else would pick them up later. The precautionary directions of what to do in case of an accident or breakdown proved unnecessary. It wasn't without incident, however. On one occasion, a large herd of sheep scrambled out of the fog directly across the road and forced the driver to slam on the brakes. Brakes were applied again when the car came within inches of bashing into a tractor hidden in heavy fog ahead of them.

Ludwik was impressed with the skill of their driver. He did his job quietly and efficiently. He was all business. Ludwik thought he would have made a good pilot. He remembered the words from Jozef, Bodil's brother, just before his solo; "Understand the plane, be patient with yourself, stay calm and do what you have learned. Nothing else."

Eventually, the fog disappeared and took with it the anxiety created by being in it. Ludwik took the opportunity to review his papers. A half hour later, the village of Simontornya came into view.

The castle reminded Ludwik of the one in Mazanki where he would take his teenage sweetheart on Sunday afternoons after church for a kiss or two as they played hide and seek with their younger siblings. That was ten years ago. Memories of a better time.

417

The driver parked the Peugeot out of sight behind the house. He tapped the window a few times and the rear door opened. A heavy set, middle-aged woman with a plain brown "babushka" wrapped around her head grunted something at him, and he motioned for Ludwik and Josef to follow him inside. The woman led the three men into the kitchen and directed them to sit at the hardwood table by the wood burning stove. The fire that burned brightly in the stove heated the entire room. The warmth it spread was very welcomed. The driver and the woman exchanged a few words and then she went to work. As soon as they sat at the table, she set it. Beautiful, hand painted, blue and white plates accompanied by a fork and knife were placed in front of each man. Next came matching blue and white mugs. Hot coffee was poured. A loaf of black bread and a dozen small, thick squares of cheese were set down on the table. She avoided eye contact with Ludwik and Josef. It was as if she didn't want to know them. Understandable. When the men began eating, she put on a warm coat and left. She never returned.

When they finished eating, the driver collected the plates and utensils and placed them in a large pot. He said the woman had gone to work and the house was theirs until they left. He recommended they rest and read their papers. He said Josef needed to change into the clothes that fit his student profile. He disappointed Ludwik when he said he needed to keep his business attire on. Then he went out to the car and brought in the luggage and backpacks for inspection.

Ludwik and Josef moved closer to the stove, took out their papers for a review of everything on them, and then practiced pronouncing their new names and some of the places they supposedly studied or worked at during their time in Romania.

"What do we call you?" Ludwik asked the driver.

"Pan."

418

"That's more than I got from you the other night," Josef said.

"I was in a hurry then."

"Your Polish is good. Are you Polish or Hungarian?" Ludwik asked.

"Hungarian born and raised with lots of Polish friends."

"Polish family ties?" Josef asked.

"Just friends."

"Any new developments in the war you can tell us?" Ludwik asked.

"Some. You are aware of the Russians attacking Finland?"

"Yes. How is that going?"

"The Finns are giving them a hard time. The bear has had its nose bloodied."

"The Russians are after everything they can get," Josef said.

Pan shook his head in agreement. "The Finns won't hold on forever. But it's not the Russians you have to worry about right now. It's the Germans. They won't stop until they have stained most of Europe down to the Mediterranean and out to the Atlantic."

"Hungary?" Ludwik asked.

"My country will join Hitler sooner than later, I'm afraid. Others will also. It is good that you leave now. The evil has not spread entirely over the area you will probably have to travel across to get to France. Have you thought about how you will travel after Zagreb?"

Ludwik said he felt they had two options. They could travel overland from there into northern Italy and then into France. Or they could make their way to Split on the Adriatic and find a ship.

One that would take them around Italy and across the Mediterranean to France. He said they would decide once they got to Zagreb.

The tall, very thin Pan nodded and said, "In case you didn't know, both ways have been used by your countrymen. Most of the ones that escaped into Romania and Hungary boarded ships that took them into the Mediterranean and put them ashore in places like Palestine, Egypt, Syria, Libya and Morocco. Later, after being somewhat organized, they were loaded on ships again and taken to France. I'm happy to say that almost all that went by ship made it to France. However, traveling by ship is no longer a safe option. The Germans have put some of their U-boats into the Mediterranean. We have heard reports they recently torpedoed and sank a Greek steamer on its way to pick up refugees."

"And the overland routes?" Ludwik asked.

"Some of the men that escaped into Yugoslavia exercised that option. But that was in the fall. This winter has been extremely cold. And one cannot be sure how the Italians now feel about travel through their country. We do have information that groups opposed to Mussolini's fascism have been organized in northern Italy, the region in which one would go through to get into France. That would help anyone choosing that option. Hungary, Romania, Yugoslavia and Italy have all seen a dramatic increase in the number of German agents that have come into their cities to try and influence the authorities to hold all Polish military refugees. Hitler has also been ramping up his threats against those that are helping the Polish."

"So, what to do?" Josef asked to no one in particular.

"First things first. Let's get to Yugoslavia," Ludwik answered.

"Well said," Pan added.

"Do you have any new information about the Polish government?" Ludwik asked him.

"Well, Sikorski is running things out of Paris. General Sosnkowski has been organizing units underground in Poland."

"I didn't know about the underground organization. Anything else?"

"Do you know that England and France have refused to recognize the Soviet Union as an aggressor in its moves against Poland and now Finland?"

"What! What the hell is that all about!" squawked Josef.

Ludwik said nothing. He thought there had to be a reason for that. He knew England and France had to care what the Russians were doing, but they had to have a reason for not complaining about it. He wondered if someone from England or France was talking to Stalin about the danger of dealing with the likes of Hitler. He wondered if Sikorski had any idea of why there had been no complaints from the Allies. It was now almost seven months since they had declared war on Germany. Interesting! He changed the subject by telling Pan that Major Seles from the Citadella had recommended the Poles try for England rather than France.

Pan said he agreed with the major. He said the French seem to think the Germans will remember what happened in WWI and not attack them. He felt the French would only fight if they were invaded. He said they had the resources and numbers for war, but he didn't know if they had the will; that WWI had taken a lot out of them.

Pan spent a half hour grilling the two on their papers. Satisfied they knew what was on them, he suggested they inventory their possessions. All items in the packs were unloaded, inspected, and put back. Pan watched the entire process without saying a word.

When they had finished, he said he had a few questions and suggestions for them.

"You may have to prove to someone along the way that you are Polish pilots. Do you have any proof of that?"

Ludwik told him about the pilot wings they had hidden in their boots.

"Do you have money hidden in addition to the money you carry in your pockets?"

Josef said the larger denomination bills were tightly rolled into their boots. The rest was in their pockets. They hadn't done anything with the money he had given them two nights ago. Ludwik said he would alter the linings of some articles of clothing to hide most of that money. Pan was impressed. He said he was sure the woman who lived here had sewing material. He suggested they use it to get money into the linings, but have enough handy to buy things, bribe officials and anyone else that might need a little "incentive" to help them along their way. He told them to always try and stay within eyesight of each other. He said to remember what their travel papers said and NEVER misplace or lose them. Finally, he encouraged them to have a plan of rendezvous in case they became separated. He said there were many ways to achieve that; maybe to meet by the last pond or lake they had passed before separation. Maybe meeting under the last bridge or the last patch of woods they had passed along the road or trail they had been using. Maybe to meet in the closest inn next to a train station or inside the next train station down the line. It was like listening to Andrei and Lupu, the mountain men in Romania. Those two and this man, Pan, probably didn't know how to fly a plane, but they knew how to stay alive.

Josef took out the Yugoslavian dinara that Pan had given him and gave half of it to Ludwik. Pan found the woman's sewing material in

422

the small bureau next to her bed and gave it to the two Poles. Ludwik immediately cut open the lining of his overcoat and field jacket and began to slide bills into them. Josef followed suit. Hungarian and Yugoslavian currency quickly became a part of the garments. After neatly sewing the cuts in the linings back up, they gave the coats to Pan for inspection. He nodded his satisfaction. They had taken great care not to layer any of the bills. Each bill had its own space. There were no giveaway "lumps" to be found or felt. Then Ludwik went to work on his boot. Pan watched him pry open a slit in the heel of one of his boots and place a tight roll of several bills inside a shallow hollow next to two other rolls of money. When Ludwik closed the slit, it was almost impossible to see. Pan suggested more tar or mud be added to help seal the slit and for them to be very careful about not stepping in any dog shit.

Josef laughed and said he didn't think shit would be able to penetrate into the boot. Pan said he wasn't thinking about the money, or the pilot wings being tainted.

"What do you mean then?" Josef asked.

"The Yugoslavs like to use dogs to track people," Pan answered.

"And dogs like to smell shit," Ludwik interrupted.

"Exactly," said the Polish agent.

It began to snow just after two o'clock. It had gotten much colder. The three men watched the flakes fall and cover the car outside. Josef said it was tempting to stay inside by the stove, drink coffee and watch the world turn white. Pan laughed at his poetic plea and said, "Nice dream."

Ludwik and Josef each had two sets of gloves. One for hiking. Very warm. One for dress. Nice looking but not so warm.

Before loading the car and getting ready to depart, each chose the gloves that suited the profession his papers listed. Ludwik took the dressy ones, Josef the hiking ones.

It was seventy miles to Kaposvar. Pan drove slowly in the snow and stayed out of trouble. As he neared the large town, he reminded them to buy tickets for the last train to Zagreb. It was a semi-express and only stopped twice; at Gyekenyes, the last stop in Hungary and at Koprivnica, the first stop in Yugoslavia. He suggested it might be a good idea if each bought their own ticket and met on the train. He recommended they get on the last passenger car and sit in the last row; maybe across the aisle from each other. He said to keep all the luggage on one rack. If one had to leave quickly, he should grab his backpack and go. The other would stay and claim the remaining luggage belonged to him. After the train crossed the border and stopped at Koprivnica, the one with the luggage would get off and wait in the train station there. If the other didn't come later that night, he should find an inn near the station, stay, and check the station periodically during the next few days to see if the other had shown up. He also said there was a way to find out each other's location. They could relay their location to each other through the Polish Embassy in Budapest or through Basha and Bella, whichever they preferred. They would need telephones. Each person would call and give his location. They should repeat that once or twice a day until one location was chosen to meet at. They could work that out with the help of the embassy or one of the two women.

Ludwik stayed in the car while Josef went outside and retrieved his luggage and backpack from the trunk. Both Ludwik and Pan watched him crunch his way through the snow to the main entrance of the train station. As soon as he disappeared inside, Pan drove the car past the station, took the first street on the right and stopped a few buildings down. Before he let Ludwik out, Pan told him never to call Puskas. He said goodbye and wished him luck.

Ludwik watched the Peugeot make a left to circle back to the main road and head back to Budapest. He adjusted his backpack and walked slowly toward the station. The sky was dark with clouds. It was very cold. Halfway up the steps to the entrance, a strong wave of warmth suddenly surged through his entire body. He felt warm from head to toe. He felt strong and confident. It was exactly like the feeling he had experienced when he passed the crucifix on the way to the waterfall outside of Borsa with Andrei. He made the sign of the cross with his free hand and went inside. He had no problem buying his ticket. The ticket seller barely looked at him. He was on his way to Zabreb, Yugoslavia. Two hours or so more and they would be across the border. Safe from the Hungarian authorities. Seventy miles after that they would be in Zagreb.

Ludwik watched Josef board the train, waited a few minutes, then boarded the same passenger car. They sat on the aisle seats across from each other in the last row. The car behind them was closed to passengers. They kept their voices low and discussed setting up a rendezvous point if they became separated on this train before crossing the border. They decided to rendezvous at the station in Koprivnica, Yugoslavia starting at 0900 Sunday and every three hours after that until the station closed. They would leave open the option to call Bella at the embassy before noon on Monday and see if the other had called and given their location.

The train hadn't moved for a half hour. Everyone began complaining about the delay. The conductor came through the car and announced the train would be delayed. Ludwik heard the Hungarian word for "sick" and assumed the delay had to do with someone needing medical attention. Josef became suspicious. He wondered why they didn't take the person off the train. He worried this "sickness" might be an excuse to wait for the police. It brought back memories of the train ride months ago when the police had come in numbers to look for a fugitive on their train at Baia Mare in Romania.

425

He remembered the man running through their car with the police a few steps behind. He hoped that scene wouldn't be repeated here with Ludwik being the man chased. Getting arrested in Yugoslavia or Italy might mean a fine and a few days' delay. Here it would mean imprisonment for his friend. And maybe for him.

Soon, another announcement was made. Passengers stood up and began leaving the train. Ludwik and Josef watched them go into the station. Not sure of what was happening, they took their luggage and left the train also. Josef's fear of a repeat of the Baia Mare incident disappeared when they saw a man being helped out of the locomotive by two men. He looked extremely pale. He also looked like he might be the engineer. The delay really was a medical issue; not an excuse to wait for the police. They watched the two men carry the obviously sick man through the station and into an ambulance waiting outside. It became clear if it was the engineer, they would be waiting for another engineer to replace him. Ludwik knew by now the police were finalizing their operation to arrest him tomorrow morning or tomorrow evening. Probably hoping to find him in bed with Basha. He hoped that Basha would be treated with respect when the police found her alone. When they did, he knew an alarm might go out for him and train stations like this one would be alerted immediately.

It was a long and anxious wait. At ten o'clock, an announcement was made to reboard the train. A subdued cheer rang out from the passengers that were still in the bar. Ludwik and Josef finished their third beer, gathered their luggage, and followed the small crowd out to the train.

There was little activity on the streets as the train slowly made its way through Kaposvar and out into the cold, wintry, countryside. It was a relief to finally be on their way. Josef said he was concerned about the delay. He wondered if it would affect their train to Zagreb.

The conductor punched their tickets and inserted them in the top seam of the empty seats in front of them. Their tickets were the last ones he had to punch. Finished with his duty, he went into the empty passenger car behind them. Ludwik glanced back into the car as the man went through the doorway. He closed the door behind him but didn't bother to lock it. In minutes, the swaying of the train gliding over the tracks worked the door loose and it swung open. It thumped gently against Ludwik's seat. He leaned out into the aisle and looked back into the car. The conductor was slumped over, head resting on the seat next to the aisle in the first row. He was fast asleep. Ludwik scanned the car. There were boxes piled on the seats on both sides of the aisle near the rear door. Some were covered with tarps.

It was 11:30 when the train approached Gyekenyes. Josef saw them first. Two police cars in a parking lot away from the station. Ludwik knew they were there for him. The delay had cost him! The Budapest police must have changed their plans and come early for him. Just then, the conductor went by. He was in a hurry. Ludwik watched him enter the toilet at the front of the car. He didn't hesitate. He grabbed his backpack and punched ticket. He told Josef to wait for him at Koprivnica. He stepped into the vacant passenger car behind him, closed the door, and locked it.

Josef made sure Ludwik's suitcase was still on his side of the aisle. He was glad that Ludwik had taken his ticket and hoped the conductor wouldn't notice and start asking questions about the missing passenger. He felt relieved when the conductor came out of the toilet and immediately headed toward the front of the train. He never looked back into the car.

Ludwik went down the aisle of the empty car to the end and tried the exit door. It was chained and only opened a few inches. He could not slide the chain's end out of the catch. It was wedged tight into it.

427

He shouldered the door several times trying to break the chain. It held fast. There wasn't much time left. Maybe only seconds. Ludwik had to get through the door and off the train quickly. He told himself to stay calm and think. He remembered one of the backpacks carried tools. He hoped his was the one. He unzipped it. The first thing he saw was the hammer the manager of the Hotel Bristol had given him in Warsaw. Using the claw end of the hammer, he pried the latch off the door quickly and decided to do the same to the attachment holding the chain on the doorframe. He didn't want anyone to see the chain hanging and letting them know the door had been used. He pushed the door open and flung the hardware assembly out into the night. He grabbed his backpack and stepped outside on the platform. The lights from the station began to illuminate the slow-moving train. He shut the door, threw his backpack and attached sleeping bag off to the side away from the station and jumped. He hit the ground in good parachute landing form; legs and feet together, knees bent, and rolled away immediately on contact to absorb the impact. He rolled across the snow into an open area that sloped down to a stream. His backpack and sleeping bag lay five feet in front of him. He scrambled to his feet, picked up his backpack and trotted along the stream that ran parallel to the tracks. He needed to stay out of sight from the station. The train blocked anyone's view of the stream, and no one could see him outside in the dark from inside the lighted cars. His hope was to get back on the train by climbing on the same car he had jumped from. For him to do that, he needed to be out of sight from the station and at a spot where the train hadn't had enough time to pick up speed. He knew he would only have one chance to make it up on the platform. If he missed, he would have to cross the border on foot and walk to Koprivnika.

People leaving the train had their papers checked in the station before they were sent on their way. Two policemen boarded the train to check on the remaining passengers.

428

Josef was worried about his papers labeling him Polish but remained calm when the policeman asked for them. The officer didn't look to be that interested in him. He probably had a description of what Ludwik looked like. He quickly flipped through the document, handed it back to Josef and stepped to the door of the last passenger car. Finding it locked, he hesitated for a moment then stepped back. He motioned for Josef to get up and follow him to the front of the car. He pointed to a seat for Josef to sit on and then left the car. In a few minutes he was back with another officer and the conductor. Josef peered into the dark outside from his seat as they went by and prayed that Ludwik had made it off and was somewhere out there.

The conductor didn't think he had locked the door, but he wasn't sure. It didn't matter much to him anyway. He unlocked it and watched the two policemen enter with guns drawn. He knew there was nothing in the car, but empty wooden boxes covered by a few tarps. He watched them remove the tarps, open the exit door to check the platform then return complaining something about an exercise in futility. The train was then officially cleared to board any new passengers and be on its way into Yugoslavia.

Josef moved back to his original seat and thanked God that Ludwik had made it off the train. He was also thankful the police had not given him a problem about his papers. All he had to do now was get off at Kobrivnika and wait for his friend. He knew that Ludwik was probably somewhere on the tracks and headed toward the border.

Ludwik stayed close to the stream and away from the lights of the town. He needed to find a place near the tracks that wasn't far from the station. Too far away and the train would go by at full speed. Too dangerous to attempt a grab of the guard rail and climb onto the rear car platform. He was on the outskirts of town when he heard the whistle from the station. The train was coming! He scrambled up the bank to the tracks and ran along them to see what was on both sides.

He hoped the late hour and freezing cold meant no one from the town would be outside and spot him. He had only gone a few yards when he tripped and tumbled down the bank and landed in the stream and sank up to his thighs in the icy water. He scrambled out of the water and climbed back to the tracks and began running. He spotted the bridge the same time he heard the shriek from the train's whistle. He turned and saw the engine's light approaching. The ground on both sides of the track before the bridge was wide open. Nothing to hide behind. The train's whistle blew again. He turned and saw the light closing. In seconds he would be in it. His heart sank. The train was moving fast. Too fast! All he could do now was roll off to the side of the tracks, remain still on the ground and hope the engineer wouldn't notice or care if he did. He curled his body into a ball, pulled his cap down over his nose and waited. The ground shook as the train rumbled closer. The whistle shrieked again into the winter air as the locomotive approached the bridge. And then its light was on him.

The new engineer always slowed a train before crossing a wooden bridge. It was a habit he had picked up over his twenty years on the rails. Somewhere in his past, he had heard the structural integrity of wooden bridges, especially ones that crossed water, were to be questioned. He always throttled back when approaching that type of bridge so he could get a longer look at it. This time was no different. He eased back on the throttle, opened the window and leaned out into the frigid air to focus hard on the upcoming wooden structure. It looked fine. Just before the train made the bridge, he ducked backed inside to escape the cold and made ready to increase speed as soon as the entire train was across. He never saw the man lying on the ground some twenty yards from the track. He never saw him rise and sprint over to the train. And he never saw him grab the railing and swing himself up onto the platform.

Ludwik sat on the platform and untied the sleeping bag from the backpack. He didn't know why the train had slowed and didn't care. He was on! That's all that mattered.

He remembered the door opened outward. He reached up and gently pulled on the door handle. The door began to open. He closed it immediately. He thought about going inside and hiding under one of the tarps, but felt it was too risky. He decided to get in the sleeping bag and sit back against the door. It would be bitter cold, but he thought he would be safer outside. It was very unlikely the conductor or anyone else inside the warm car would open the door and let the freezing air in. And since there were no other stops before Kobrivnika, he didn't have to worry about getting off again. What he had to do now was take care of his lower body. It was like a block of ice. His wet pants, socks and shoes were frozen. He reached down into the bag and removed his shoes and socks. He rolled the wet portion of his pants up to his thighs and began massaging his legs and feet inside the sleeping bag. As soon as he felt the stinging surge of blood warming his legs and feet, he wormed his way down into the bag as far as he could. Only his face remained in the open air. He rolled over to one side and used the backpack as a headrest. It was uncomfortable lying on the steel platform, but the warmth generated by his body heat in the bag was well worth the position. He knew he would need the use of his hands to grab the railing if the bag slid so he kept them chest high inside the bag and rubbed them vigorously together to warm them. The fancy dress gloves were just too thin to keep his hands warm. His wet feet and legs were warming up a bit in the bag. He felt if he could maintain this position for most of the trip, he knew he would be fine when the train pulled into Kobrivnika.

The conductor tipped his cap to Josef as he went by. He was done with his work. It had been a very long day and he was tired. He would rest in the unused passenger car. Like he always did. They would arrive in Kobrivnika in an hour or so.

He knew the replacement engineer was a cautious one. Especially at night. He would not travel at top speed. Most of the passengers were either dozing or asleep. They wouldn't be needing him. It had been a long night for them also.

The first thing he noticed when he entered the car was the cold air. There was a draft somewhere. It hadn't been like that earlier, but that had been before the "search." He thought the police had probably done something to cause it. He walked back to the exit door and felt the seeping cold air on his feet. For some reason the door wasn't fully closed. He pushed hard on it and turned the knob to lock it into place. That seemed to do the trick. He grabbed one of the tarps that were piled on the storage boxes and laid it across the aisle in front of the door and kicked it a few times. That made it even better. Satisfied, he walked back to the front row where the seats were the softest and very comfortable to nap on.

Ludwik was startled by the pushing against the door. He wasn't sure what was happening. He was glad whoever was doing the pushing wasn't that strong. He remembered the conductor didn't look that hefty and his age had to be somewhere in the late fifties or early sixties. He also knew the man liked to take a nap in the car and figured to be the person pushing against the door. He heard something drop on the floor behind the door followed by a few hard nudges against the door. He wasn't sure what the person was up to but was relieved when the pushing and nudging stopped. Whoever was in there, probably the conductor, was trying to cover something on the floor just behind the door. He wasn't sure what to do. If he stayed and the man came back and tried to force the door open again it might be a problem. He decided to leave the platform and climb up on the roof of the car. He took a pen from his jacket and wedged it tightly under the door to keep it from opening too easily. He rolled his pant legs down and put on his shoes.

432

No socks. Too wet. He got out of the bag, wrapped it around his waist under the topcoat and pushed one end of it down into the front of his pants. Then he strapped the backpack on.

There were five rungs on the ladder bolted to the side of the car and one handle on the roof. He would have to be careful. His gloves were more for dress than comfort. He hoped they would be good enough for the climb. When he reached out for the middle rung, he was almost blown off the train. With one hand on the rung, he swung out to the side of the car. He hung there for a moment, the frozen rung stinging his hand. He reached up and grabbed the next rung and then climbed hand over hand up and onto the flat roof of the car. Sitting with his back to the wind, he took his backpack off, pulled out the sleeping bag and squirmed down into it. He slung one arm through the straps of the backpack and pulled it close to him. He reached out with his free hand and grabbed the roof rung so he wouldn't roll off.

Surviving the freezing cold and not rolling off the roof weren't the only problems he faced. The train burned coal and much of the black cloud of smoke and soot it spewed into the air landed on him. It was hard to breathe. Every breath he took was painful. All he could do to avoid the toxic, suffocating blanket of smoke was to close his eyes, pull his cap down over his face and press his mouth and nose into his overcoat. It didn't help much. He thought about going back down to the platform, but his hands were too numb from the cold. It was too dangerous. Coughing from the smoke filling his lungs and shaking from the freezing cold that seeped into the bag, he prayed for Mary to help him endure the trip. His misery lasted more than an hour, but his prayers were answered. When the train slowed for its stop at Koprivnika, Ludwik came out of the sleeping bag and stuffed his backpack down into it. He zipped the bag up and put it between his legs; the backpack bottom behind him, the other end secured under his belt in front.

When he saw lights in the distance, he climbed down the rungs with his frozen fingers barely keeping their grip and hung on the side of the car, his sockless shoes resting on the bottom rung three feet from the rails. There were buildings all along the track. None had lights on. He pushed off the car and jumped into an open area not far from the station. The landing was hard. He rolled across the snow and slammed into a stack of iron cables. He tried to get up but fell back and lost consciousness. He lay there for several minutes before coming to. He pulled out his backpack from the sleeping bag, swung both on his back and staggered down the tracks toward the station. The train whistle blew. It was leaving. He hoped Josef was still in the station. He knew his friend had to be thinking he was miles away. If he had left the station, he would be looking for a room in town and would come back in the morning. That was the rendezvous plan. Meet in the station tonight or tomorrow or the next day. Maybe Josef was still in the station getting information on a place to stay. He began to run. He watched the train disappear into the night. He got off the railbed and ran to a street headed toward the station. The buildings on both sides of the street were dark. He slowed to a walk. It hurt too much to run. The sound of the departing train had lessened to a whisper. And then it was no more. Only the sound of Ludwik's sockless shoes crunching through the thin layer of crusted snow interrupted the silence. This was a town long gone out of the freezing cold and under the covers. The only two lights he saw came from the station ahead. One illuminated the platform, and another dimly lit the entrance. He saw someone step outside onto the platform and light a cigarette. People were still there. That was good. Maybe one of them was Josef. As he neared the entrance, he saw fresh footprints in the snow leading away from the station. He hoped none of them belonged to his friend. The warmth that greeted him in the station lobby was wonderful. He sat on a bench a few feet to one side of the entrance, took off his shoes and slowly massaged his frozen feet. The station's one ticket window was closed.

Directly across the lobby was a door with light shining under it. He heard movement in there. To his left, on the far side of the lobby, a man sat on another bench next to the women's restroom. He was waiting for his lady. She appeared almost immediately, and they walked together toward the entrance and Ludwik massaging his bare feet. As soon as they spotted him, they stopped. The woman looked petrified. The man stared hard at Ludwik. He took the woman's arm and guided her quickly through the door and into the street.

Ludwik heard the footsteps approaching from the unlit side of the lobby. When they stopped, he heard a voice softly say, "You scared the crap out of them and me too. You look like something that came from hell."

Ludwik looked up and smiled. Josef was still here.

One look into the cracked, orange-stained mirror in the toilet/washroom told Ludwik why he had frightened the couple in the lobby. He was black from head to toe. Coal black! The only thing white about him were his eyeballs and a narrow strip of skin covering his Adam's apple. His frozen, coal-black hair stuck out sideways from under his cap. He looked like a troll that had come from the underworld; a "monster" turned loose on the good people of Yugoslavia. As he stripped down and shook off the coal dust from his clothes and sleeping bag, he told Josef about his ride through the frozen night. Josef listened intently and marveled at his friend's bravery and strength. He knew if he had tried to do the same, he would be lying dead somewhere on the tracks.

The creaking faucet reluctantly spluttered only cold water into the sink. Ludwik washed the layer of coal dust from his hair, face, neck and chest. The water thawed the ice in his hair enough for him to push it straight back over his head. He finished the cleaning by removing everything below his waist and washing his naked body.

435

He put on the clean underwear, socks, pants, and boots that Josef had taken out from his suitcase. He pulled a thick woolen sweater over his head and covered that with his hiking jacket. When he finished lacing his boots, he took out his travel papers from the overcoat and secured them inside a jacket pocket. He finished the clothing exchange by putting his filthy clothes into the suitcase.

"It's good to see that it really is you, my friend," Josef chuckled.

Ludwik rolled his overcoat and sleeping bag together and asked Josef if there was any coffee and food in the station. Josef said the restaurant was closing when he left. That there was a young man in there cleaning and was still there. He thought they might be able to coax him to open the restaurant with a little money.

Someone was still in the restaurant. They could hear furniture being pushed around. Josef knocked on the door. The knock was met with silence from inside. Suddenly the lights on the platform went out. Josef knocked a little harder. Again, no response. Then the light in the washroom went out. The station went dark except for a tiny sliver of light escaping from under the door of the restaurant. The message was clear. Time for you to go away! Josef dropped to one knee and took out a 2 denari note and slid it halfway under the door. He stood up and firmly tapped out the universal SOS signal on the door. They heard footsteps approaching. They watched the tail end of the two denari note disappear inside. Josef tapped out the SOS again and slid another two denari under the door. It disappeared immediately. The unspoken bargaining was working. They waited. Then the door opened.

He looked to be in his early teens. He quickly closed the door behind them and locked it. He smiled and tapped out the SOS signal on the door. He bowed respectively and asked them something in his native language. Josef spoke to him in Polish hoping he would understand.

He didn't. That began a conversation dominated by body movement, hand signals and a little Hungarian. In short order, their request for coffee and a little something to eat was granted by the young man. That was met with another two denari. The tall, slender lad smiled happily, thumped his chest and said, "Boris!" Ludwik and Josef introduced themselves in like manner. After the coffee was put on and some rolls brought out, Boris went out into the station and locked the front entrance while Ludwik and Josef finished their coffee and rolls. Four more denari later, both men unrolled their sleeping bags and cozied up in front of the stove on the floor. Ludwik used his to sleep on. It was too filthy to crawl into. Boris shut the restaurant lights off and went up a ladder into the loft above the small pantry behind the stove.

Ludwik was awakened by the sound of Boris clattering down the ladder in the pantry. It was 6:30. First daylight was seeping through the frosted restaurant window overlooking the station platform. The young man nodded a "good morning" to him then began turning on the restaurant lights. He pointed to Josef and politely jerked a thumb up asking Ludwik to get him up. He needed to build a new fire.

Ludwik and Josef rolled their sleeping bags onto their backpacks and made their way to the washroom. Boris prepared the morning coffee and brought out all the leftover pastries in the pantry. He and his two "guests" would breakfast before he opened the station.

Because of the lengthy delays at Kaposvar and Gyekennes last night and the fact that he believed the delayed train was probably still in Gyekennes, the custom official had left the station and gone home. When he arrived back to the station at 8:00 for the new day, he was surprised to find out the train had arrived. He wondered who the two men were with Boris. The young man said they were foreigners and had stayed in the restaurant last night. The official knew Boris had made a little money before by using the station as an "inn."

He didn't mind. He would get his cut later. He told Boris to bring some pastries and coffee for him and his aide who had just arrived. The official told the aide to check the papers of the two men before joining him.

The papers identified the two as Poles. They did not have their papers stamped for entry because his boss had left early last night. The aide suspected the two might be military. On their way to France to fight the Nazis; the bastards that had murdered his Jewish brother-in-law in Germany. There would be no questions from him. He quickly stamped their papers, wished them luck and joined his superior for breakfast.

Zagreb

Zagreb was a large city. It spread out to the foothills of the Mednevnica Mountains to the north and the Sava River winding its way in and out of the city to the south. A light snow was falling as the train pulled into the Glavani Kolodva, Zagreb's major railroad station. The two pilots found a large wall map of the city inside the station. It showed the location of several prominent places, the main plazas and more importantly, the location of several hotels. They chose the closest one to the station.

The hotel was perfect. Close to the train station, clean and inexpensive. It wasn't Warsaw's Hotel Bristol, but it was heaven compared to the floor next to Boris's stove. Or the top of a speeding train. The first thing Ludwik did was to draw a hot bath and scrub off the remaining coal residue on his body. Then he drained the tub of its filth and refilled it with more hot water. He lay in it, water up to his chin, and relaxed. It had been a miserable, freezing, roof top train ride, but he was glad he had done it. If he hadn't, he would still be out there, somewhere in the cold and miles from Yugoslavia and his friend, Josef.

Josef unpacked everything and separated the clean from the unclean. After he had his turn in the tub, they washed their clothes in it and let them dry hanging in the closet. The only things they couldn't clean were Ludwik's overcoat and sleeping bag. Too much coal dust from the train ride. They would have to be sent somewhere and that might take a few days. With that in mind, they decided to stay in Zagreb at least two days, maybe more. No need to rush. Time to rest awhile. Especially for Ludwik. His bruised body was still sore from his jumps off the train. They could also use the time to gather information for their next move. There were options now; train to Split on the Adriatic coast and find a ship sailing to France or go by train through Yugoslavia and northern Italy to get there.

As soon as Josef hung the few pieces of laundry he had washed, he went for the bed. He needed sleep. Last night's four-hour sleep on a hardwood floor had not been enough. He went out as soon as the blanket settled on his neck. Ludwik was close behind. The loud snoring of Josef didn't concern him. This was not hiding in the woods or haystacks of Romania. Or from the police in Hungary. He slept well.

It was mid-afternoon when they woke. Ludwik dressed and took his overcoat and sleeping bag down to the lobby to inquire about a place to have them cleaned. He also wanted to make a call to Basha. The clerk knew some Hungarian and was able to understand Ludwik. He recommended a cleaning shop just a few blocks away and wrote the directions to it. He also said a call could be made from the desk. Ludwik returned to the room. Josef was awake and smiling. Ludwik asked him to take the coat and sleeping bag to the cleaning shop while he called Basha before she left work.

Basha was ecstatic to hear his voice. "Az en-m draga!" she shouted.

"Yugoslavia," Ludwik happily replied.

439

"And Josef?"

"He is here. He is well. Is your father alright?"

"Yes. He will be happy to hear that you called."

"And the newspapers?" Ludwik asked.

"Not a word. Without you locked up, there will be no embarrassing news to report. Nothing but rumors and unproven speculation."

"Did the police bother you?"

"The fools busted into the apartment Saturday morning. I had stayed at Hugo's the night you left and wasn't home. They thought you were at the Citadella but came up empty. We heard an alert was sent out."

Ludwik asked her how the war was unfolding in Europe and in particular what she knew about the political situations in Yugoslavia and Italy. She said things were turning for the worse in Hungary and Romania. The Germans were influencing the politics in the two countries. She thought that Yugoslavia was holding on to its independence firmly, but Italy was lost except for the mountain regions north of Milan. She said that England continued to mobilize its forces with energy, but France had not shown the same intensity. She went on to say that the Germans had publicly recognized that some Polish airmen and soldiers had escaped to France in the past few months. They called them "Sikorski's tourists" and claimed they would pose no threat to their "Reich."

"What will you do if the Germans invade, or your government decides to join them?" Ludwik asked her.

"I am Hungarian. I will stay here with my family," Basha answered.

"But you worked for the Polish embassy and your father has been critical about the Nazi influence in the government," Ludwik prodded.

"If it becomes dangerous, I will call on the man that helped you."

Ludwik smiled at that and said, "How will you find him?"

"He has found us," Basha replied.

"He is a good man," Ludwik said as he watched the clerk approach with an anxious look on his face. "I need to go now. I will call you when this journey ends, my pet. I miss you."

Basha pressed her lips to the phone and whispered, "Be safe, my love."

Josef said the sleeping bag and overcoat would be ready in no more than two days. Maybe even tomorrow. He then left to call Bella to see if there was any news about his father. Ludwik wished him luck.

Ludwik sat on the bed and lit a cigarette. It had felt good to hear Basha's voice. Josef's news about the cleaner meant their hotel stay would have to be at least two nights. He felt it was time to watch their spending. Money in their pockets when they reached France would be wise. He had no idea what the pay was in the French Air Force or God forbid, what it was in their army. Like many others, Basha had said the French didn't seem too anxious to fight. And if that was the case, he didn't want to stay in France. The problem with that was if they joined the air force and then decided to leave, it would be desertion. And desertion would mean the firing squad. Then again, there was always the possibility the Poles would have their own units and not have to serve under the French. That would be the best scenario for him and all Polish airmen in France.

Josef said goodbye to Bella and slowly walked back up the stairs to the room. No news about his father. And sad news about Bella. He didn't know about Ludwik and Basha, but he knew he would never see Bella again. He heard it in her voice. She had moved on. It was the smart thing to do. They both knew it was. He would still call her when he could in the hope that she might have news about his father.

He agreed with Ludwik about watching their spending. They had been frugal up to this point, but the money was beginning to run out. They had to pay for the hotel, the phone calls, buy train or ship tickets, pay the cleaning bill and of course, they had to eat. Food from breakfast at the hotel could be brought up to the room and serve as lunch also. They could split a meal at dinner. They would have to find a place that wasn't too expensive. The desk clerk could help them with that.

The clerk made it easy. He walked them to the entrance and pointed across the cobble stone street at a three-story brick building. A sign over its main entrance read "Obiteljski Restaran I Delikatese." It was easy to translate; a restaurant/ delicatessen. Perfect. An easy walk in the cold and a choice of a "sit-down dinner" or a "take-out dinner."

The restaurant/delicatessen took up the entire first floor. The delicatessen was just inside the entrance. It was small. There were several customers lined up and waiting for service. A few were grumbling to themselves. To the right of the delicatessen in a separate room was a dining area. It held more than a dozen tables, each neatly covered by a white tablecloth with a single, yellow candle adorning its center. Only four tables were occupied. To the left on the back wall was a magnificent stone fireplace. A good-sized fire was warming the entire room. It was an easy choice for them. Lines never appealed to a military man. They went for the dining area's warmth and a clean table. If it was expensive, they would share a meal.

A well-dressed man in a dark blue suit with matching tie greeted them with a polished bow and led them toward a table close to the fireplace. Two men at a table on the way nodded at them as they passed. One was wearing a field jacket that resembled those of the Polish Army. Ludwik assumed the man was part of the local militia. He was proven wrong when he heard him say to his companion in Polish, "I wonder if these two clowns are here to hike the Mednevnina in this cold." Ludwik stopped, turned back to the two and said very politely, "We would prefer Mt. Rysy in the homeland, but I understand there is a heavy snow falling there." After a moment of stunned silence, the two strangers broke out into a howl. Handshakes and hugs were exchanged. Two chairs were pulled out. Beers were ordered. Mugs were brought.

One of the men, a Sergeant Tolski, said they had been part of an infantry battalion that had been pushed back toward the mountains along Poland's southern border by an overpowering German force. The situation had quickly developed into a race for survival when the Germans began to encircle them and cut them off from the safety of the mountains. Fortunately, they made it to the mountains before the Germans could do it. His battalion set up a defensive line and were waiting for the Germans to attack. That's when the order came down to "evacuate with all speed." He said some men refused the order. They went into hiding in the forests to continue the fight against the Germans. Others left the unit and set out to go home and be with their families. Ludwik said the same thing happened to them when that order came down to where they were on the Romanian border.

Josef asked the sergeant how they got to Zagreb. Tolski said that he and Corporal Ostrowski, the man sitting with him, had escaped across the Carpathians into Hungary, been arrested, and placed in an internment camp. They had quickly escaped the camp and made their way across Hungary into Yugoslavia.

443

They met up with a Polish captain here in Zagreb that had come with the permission of the Yugoslavian government to set up a way station in the city to help all Polish military with getting passage out of the country and into France. They had been helping the captain for the past few months and were now getting ready to leave with him and take a train to Split on the coast. From there they would board a ship sailing to France. They were just waiting for the right "arrangements" to be made.

"What arrangements do you need?" Ludwik asked.

"Finding the right ship for the right price with the right people," Tolski responded.

"Is that difficult to do?"

"Could be. One must be sure when giving money to someone you don't know. Especially in a foreign country. We heard a few stories of our men paying for passage on a ship and some bastards disappearing with their money."

"What happened to our men?" Josef asked.

"Some tried swimming out to the ship as it was leaving. They drowned. Others went back into the city to find the thieves. One was found and they killed him. The ones that killed him are still in jail as we speak. We need to be very careful. Our plan now is to wait for a ship to dock that will take us to France, take a train to Split and make arrangements with the captain for passage. Without giving any money up front."

"Sounds risky to me," Josef said.

Ludwik agreed, "Sounds like a train ride through Italy might be safer."

444

Tolski shook his head. "Safer? Maybe. Mussolini is not in love with us. He does love Hitler."

"How would one travel in Italy?" Ludwik asked.

"Stay out of the cities as much as you can. The fascist thugs are there in great numbers. You will have to be very careful if you get off in a city. The fascists are working with their pro-Nazi friends. German agents are everywhere. The fascists will turn you in to them for a price."

The conversation ended when two waiters arrived with steaming piles of food. Josef said they hadn't ordered yet. Tolski said that Ostrowski had signaled the "usual" for all four men some time ago.

"More beer?" a smiling Ostrowski asked.

During the meal, Ludwik thought about the possibility of joining the two soldiers and their captain when they left Zagreb for the coast. The problem he had with that was committing to a sea voyage. He wasn't sure about winding up in the hands of someone that might not have their best interest at heart. They would be at the mercy of the captain and his crew with no place to go once on the open sea. That had to be considered. He would discuss it with Josef after they returned to the hotel. They made plans for dinner with Tolski and Ostrowski for tomorrow. Same place, same time, and asked them to bring along the captain.

The night had turned brutally cold. A frosty reminder of the roof top ride on the train. Ludwik told Josef he would have a problem doing that again. Josef said he hoped that wouldn't be necessary, but if they had to, he would join him on the roof. Ludwik patted him on the back and said it was good to be with a friend these days. They discussed the choice of joining the three soldiers or taking trains through Yugoslavia and northern Italy on their own.

Distance, danger and time were the crucial elements in their decision making. Ludwik thought a map would help. He went down to the lobby to see if one was available. There was a new clerk at the desk. It was twenty minutes of broken Hungarian, some Polish, the local language and a myriad of universal hand signals before the clerk could help him. An old map of Europe was pulled out of a safe. Ludwik studied it while the clerk began drawing his own map of how to get to a church and a bank. As he waited for the man to finish, Ludwik noticed a woman entering the hotel. She smiled invitingly at him. He smiled back. The clerk caught the exchange and wrote a number on the map. Ludwik smiled and shook his head "no."

The map was good. Split was two hundred miles from Zagreb. Not that long on a train. However, the trip by sea from Split around the "boot" of Italy and across the Mediterranean to France was several hundred miles. Lots of water. Lots of time. Maybe lots of submarines. The trip from Zagreb through northern Italy into France was shorter. Not much water but lots of mountains, cold weather and a chance of meeting some unfriendly fascists and their Nazi friends. The discussion about preference of travel didn't last long. Despite the obvious dangers, both favored the overland route through Italy. If the train rides proved uneventful, they figured they could reach France in less than four days. A much shorter journey than a sea route. And Josef shared Ludwik's concerns about being stuck on a ship with nowhere to go if things turned sour. Going by sea was too long and the possibility of delay and trouble seemed just as great as the train rides. God forbid, they could even wind up back in Romania if the ship had problems. Josef put it bluntly, "I can walk across Italy, but I can't swim a hundred yards." It was settled. They would meet Tolski, Ostrowski and hopefully their captain tomorrow and let them know they wouldn't be joining them on the trip to Split. Josef suggested they talk to the three men over dinner and see what ideas they might have in planning a trip by train into France.

Ludwik wondered if there were any groups in Zagreb that might be of help to them. Even if it was only providing them with useful tips on what they might encounter here in Yugoslavia and the mountain regions of northern Italy. At the very least, he thought maybe Tolski or Ostrowski could help them plan the route to take. Josef said there was plenty to sleep on. Ludwik nodded in agreement and got ready for another much-needed night's rest.

The clerk's hand drawn map was easy to follow. St. Mark's church was beautiful. It sat at the rear of a snow-covered public square named in its honor. Its home-like design and beautiful bright white and sky-blue colors conveyed a welcoming, warm hello to anyone approaching its entrance. To Ludwik, it always felt good to be in the Lord's House. It didn't matter the location, size, style or color. Especially when he was praying to Mary, the queen of all saints; always reaching out to the world with her love. He thought of the woman in the mist, the shepherdess in the meadow and her "twin" outside Satu Mare. With the identical kind of dog, no less. His body tingling every time. Like no other time in his life. Feeling it was the Lady or someone sent by her.

They arrived late. Communion had just been administered to the faithful. There were only a few dozen people attending the weekday mass. One of them was Sergeant Tolski. Ludwik caught his eye across the aisle and nodded a greeting. After the priest ended the mass with a blessing, he and Josef walked outside with the sergeant. He said he was heading for coffee and would they like to join him.

Tolski was surprised to learn the two pilots had decided not to take the sea route to France. The short and stocky soldier felt that going by ship was the safer bet. Lots of fascist trouble in Italy. Ludwik asked him if he knew how the trains ran in Yugoslavia and could he recommend the best way to go. Tolski said he would be glad to help. Ludwik took out the hotel map and spread it open on the table.

Tolski finger-traced a route on it he thought was best considering the political situation in Italy. West to Ljubljana, southwest towards Trieste, get off at Divaca before Trieste and catch an express going northwest that would take them across the Italian border and into the city of Udine. Intrigued with Tolski's suggestion, Ludwik pressed him for help in finding a bank to exchange their Hungarian and Romanian currency in order to pay for the train tickets, hotel bill, a cleaning service, and most importantly, have enough of the local denari left to foot the bill for their dinner engagement with the Polish Army tonight. Tolski said he appreciated the dinner item. He said there was a bank two blocks from the coffee shop. He would not only take them to it, but he would also exchange their money for them. He said he had exchanged money many times while helping men out of the city and would be glad to do the same for them, while they were with him of course.

"You wouldn't steal money from an officer, would you?" asked Josef.

"Only if they were a pain in the ass, SIR!" a chuckling Tolski replied.

"Any chance you can help us buy our train tickets?" Ludwik asked.

"That's extra. It will cost you a beer or two more," Tolski replied.

"Done!" Ludwik laughed.

Josef took off his boot and laid it across his lap. He took out his knife and carefully pried open the heel and extracted the tightly rolled bills. He handed the bills to Tolski under the table.

"All this in one boot? How about the other one?" the sergeant asked.

That gave Josef an idea. It would be interesting to see if Tolski could tell the gapa was in the heel of the other boot. He slipped the boot under the table to him and told him to look for himself.

448

"Sole or heel?" the sergeant asked.

"You tell me," Josef answered.

Ludwik sipped his coffee and kept an eye on the few people in the café while Tolski examined the boot in his lap.

"I think there is something in the heel," the sergeant said.

Josef looked at Ludwik and said, "I'm sorry to hear you could tell."

Ludwik was surprised that Josef had given the sergeant his boot and then admit something was inside the heel. Probably better not to have done that. On the other hand, Tolski had detected the gapa rather quickly. He would have to fix that.

"Nothing in my boots," he lied to the sergeant as he slit out the money from the field jacket on his lap. The money in the boot would stay. He liked Tolski, but enough was enough. This was a public place. One never knew who was watching or listening. Best to end this little game.

The exchange of money went quickly. Tolski said there was enough money for the train tickets and a few more days in Zagreb. He wasn't sure if he got enough "lira" to take care of their needs in Italy. Ludwik acknowledged that and thanked him. He was pleased. Foreign currency was still in play in Europe. He would exchange the lei in his boot somewhere in France depending on their need.

It only took Tolski five minutes to get the train tickets. They were for tomorrow afternoon. This would be their last night in Zagreb. Tomorrow night, God willing, they would be sleeping in Udine, Italy. There was the matter of the two items in the cleaners. Ludwik needed the overcoat, but if he had to, he could use Josef's. Tolski suggested stopping at the cleaners now with a little extra money to see if that would speed up the process. And after taking much of his morning away from him, they could then buy him lunch.

Tolski rested his second mug of beer on the table and watched the pilots eat their lunch. He thought about their decision to go overland to France. It did have some merit and he began telling them just that. He said more than a few Poles going by sea had boarded ships that were only going to ports that had a French base on the southern coast of the Mediterranean. Once in those ports, they were placed into Army units whether they were Army or not. After some training, they were transported to Marseilles and dispersed throughout southern France for assimilation into the French Army. His captain had said most, but not all, Air Force personnel were sent to a couple of French air bases; one at Lyon in southern France, the other somewhere north of Paris. He didn't know the names of the bases.

Ludwik asked Tolski if he had any updates on the war. Tolski said the last briefing he attended with the captain and some army officers had been mixed. The French were sitting on their hands and hoping the Germans wouldn't invade. It was different with the British. They had a sizeable force stationed in northern France that was operational. In addition to that, they had sent a significant number of Indian troops from bases in England to join them. And unlike the French, the whole country of England was mobilizing for war.

"Any of our pilots in planes?" Ludwik asked.

"I don't know if anyone is fighting the Germans," Tolski said.

"I thought when you declared war, you fought!" Josef complained.

Ludwik calmly added, "We'll fight as soon as the French let us. I'm just hoping they don't make the same mistake we made by waiting too long to mobilize. They should have learned from our experience."

Tolski had declined to invite his captain to dinner. Instead, he had Corporal Ostrowski bring two of their favorite lady friends to enhance the night's festivities. One of them was the woman Ludwik had seen last night in the hotel. Eating at a regular pace became difficult with the ladies seated by their sides. Both airmen became the focal point of a little game the ladies played with strangers. While they ate with one hand and made small talk, the other hand was busy under the table caressing legs and other "parts" of the two pilots. The object was to see which of the men would "rise to the occasion" first. When that happened, the lady with the "winning hand" would lean over and kiss the man. Tolski and Ostrowski roared with laughter when both ladies leaned over and kissed the two airmen at the same time. They were aware of what the kiss signified. After Tolski explained the "entertainment," Ludwik asked him to thank the ladies for their attention and would they please put everything back in place.

While Ludwik was intrigued with the well-endowed, dark-haired gypsy that had fondled him, he was not interested in the offer to party with her after dinner. Josef was sorely tempted by his playmate, a long-legged red head, but understood Ludwik's caution. They were too close to their objective. France was only a few train rides away.

The soldiers insisted on paying for dinner. Thanks were exchanged. Ludwik and Josef stood, bowed, clicked their heels and kissed the hand of the lady that had caressed them; making sure that hand was the innocent one.

Crossing the street to the hotel, Ludwik began to chuckle and said, "My lady was a true gypsy. She had me unbuttoned and in her hand in five seconds. She must be a first-rate pickpocket."

Josef laughed and said, "My lady could have been a great pianist."

The train left Zagreb a little after two. Ludwik was dressed in his overcoat and "business" attire. Tolski's advice to stop at the cleaners after lunch yesterday with a little extra money had paid off. The coat and sleeping bag were delivered to the hotel early in the morning. The train would make four stops before reaching Ljubljana. They would change trains there and head for Divaca, a few miles east of Trieste, Italy. Trieste was to be avoided. Tolski had warned them it was too dangerous a place to stop. Instead, they would take an express from Divaca to Udine, Italy, crossing the border at Gorizia. Arrival time in Udine was 7:30 PM. They would have to stay overnight there and purchase tickets to Paris sometime the next day.

Ludwik and Josef spent most of the two-hour trip to Ljubljana discussing their options for the next few days. A lot depended on how much money they had after their night in Udine. If there was enough left for another night's stay, they would consider doing that somewhere in France close to the airbase in Lyon.

"I guess that means coffee and cigarettes for today," Josef complained.

Ludwik shook his head no. "Let's eat tonight, maybe buy a little food in Udine tomorrow for the rest of the trip."

Josef said, "I don't have much room left in my backpack and suitcase."

"We'll make room," Ludwik offered. "Take out your overcoat from your backpack and roll it into your sleeping bag. I'll roll my overcoat and put it into my bag. If for some reason we must hike and hide, we will have to eat. Water we can always find."

"I hope we don't have to hike in this freezing cold," Josef said.

"Let's hope that won't happened," Ludwik responded.

452

The train arrived on time in Ljubljana. Fifteen minutes later, Ludwik and Josef were seated comfortably in the 2nd class passenger car directly behind the dining car. When the conductor arrived to punch their tickets, Ludwik pointed ahead to the dining car and shook his head yes or no. The young man tilted the bill of his conductor's cap upward, thought for a few seconds, then pulled out a coin from his watch pocket and shook his head yes. The message was clear. All you needed was money to eat in the dining car.

"I wonder if it's expensive," Josef said.

"Let's find out," Ludwik answered.

The waiter working the dining car was happy to have customers. He usually didn't have many, sometimes none, on these mid-afternoon runs. It was different during the dinner-time hours. There were lots of customers then. Today, there were only four. Better than none. Two had first class tickets; a middle-aged woman impeccably dressed in winter finery, expensive jewelry, and a very fashionable fur coat. She sat across the aisle from an elderly priest dressed in his plain black, priestly garb. Both had just been joined by two men from the 2nd class car behind them.

The woman ordered tea and a small plate of cookies. The priest ordered a glass of wine. He was back with both orders in a few minutes. Finished with the two first class passengers, he turned his attention to the other two. One was dressed like a business man; the other like a student of some sort. Unfortunately, they ordered in a language he did not understand. When that didn't work, they pointed at the lady and nodded. He gave them a menu, but they just shrugged their shoulders. They couldn't read it. The waiter looked at the priest for help.

"I believe they want what the lady has," the priest said.

453

The bishop

The waiter bowed, said something to the priest and left. Ludwik and Josef didn't understand what was happening. The priest turned to them and said he had ordered what they wanted and hoped they didn't mind him doing so. His Polish was perfect. Ludwik said they didn't mind at all and thanked him for his help. He asked the priest if he was Polish. The priest said no, but he had had extensive training in languages other than Latin and his native Italian. Polish was one of them. He introduced himself as Father DeMonte. He was a bishop, but preferred to be addressed as "father." He worked in the Vatican in Rome as a translator and emissary for the Pope. He had just come from Vienna and was on his way to Paris to bring news of the political situation in Austria. His task had been to gauge the effect of the Nazi regime on the church there.

"Do the Nazis bother the church?" Ludwik asked.

"They have. Their main interest now lies with the Jews."

The conversation ended with the appearance of the waiter arriving with two orders of tea and cookies. The bishop blessed both and said, "Manga!"

"Will you bless mine, father?" the well-dressed woman said in Italian. The priest did so and accepted a small cookie offered in thanks. Before he could turn to resume his conversation with the two young men, she asked him if the church was going to fight the fascists. He said the church would do everything in its power to protect its people. The lady felt that bad times were coming. Bad enough for her to leave her beloved "Italia" and go to America. The bishop understood. He wished her luck and a good life in America. Then he turned his attention back to Ludwik and Josef. He translated what the lady had said and asked them what their plans were for the future.

454

Ludwik showed the bishop his travel papers. He couldn't lie to the man face to face. And didn't want him to know he wasn't the man listed on the papers. He hoped the papers listing his destination and employment would be enough to answer the question. The bishop stared at him for a moment then read the papers. When he handed them back, he said, "Now, my son, tell me who you really are." Ludwik could hear a voice somewhere in the back of his brain telling him not to trust anyone. He thought it might be the voice of Constantin Lupu, his Romanian friend. But this was a priest. A bishop no less. He could not lie to him.

"I am a Polish pilot. And so is my friend. We will be joining the French as soon as we find out where the Polish airmen are."

"And are you both going to Paris for that information?" the priest asked.

"If we have to, Josef chimed in."

"I will make inquiries in Udine. Both of you will stay with me tonight. I will get the information you need. Please, do not argue. There are those in my beloved Italia that would collect a sizeable sum for turning you over to the local fascist rabble. You will be safe with me. Your papers are well done, but it might not matter with the rabble. I think it is best not to take chances. What raised my doubt about the validity of the papers was when you didn't answer my question about your future. You just gave me your papers. Very odd, but understandable with you being Polish and probably Catholic, you did not want to lie to me face to face. I respect that. And while your papers look legitimate, the fact that they identify you as Polish, is enough for you to become a target for arrest and questioning. It is a reality of our time. I can assure you that after breakfast tomorrow, you will be safely on a train headed for France."

"Will you be with us?" Josef asked.

"No. I will be visiting with my family and friends for a while."

Given a handsome tip from the priest, the waiter allowed Ludwik and Josef to keep their luggage in the dining car and stay with him.

After making sure the lady didn't understand Polish, he asked the two men to tell him about their journey from Poland to Yugoslavia. He was especially interested in hearing first-hand accounts about the early days of the invasion from someone who had experienced them.

Their description of the indiscriminate bombing of civilian targets in Warsaw and the deliberate strafing of men, women and children fleeing for their lives on the open roads and in the fields, sickened the bishop. So much so, he waved for them to stop so he could pray for those who had died. When he finished, he asked them to continue.

They covered it all. From Warsaw across the Vistula into Praga, the bombing, the loss of their four new friends, the burning chicken coop, the lady sobbing in the mist, the massacre at the artillery base, the old man's cottage, the murder of the German pilot, crossing into Romania, Constantin Lupu, the hike over the mountains with Andrei, hiding in the haystack, the stowaway ride on the train, seeing the same young woman shepherding miles and miles apart, Budapest, their work there, the escape on a barge, the frozen train ride into Yugoslavia and their short stay in Zagreb.

The priest was fascinated with their story. He was especially taken by the number of people that had stepped forward to help the two men. The list was impressive. And encouraging. People from all walks of life and nationalities. Even a member of the German embassy in Budapest. The two men had been most fortunate. They had survived great evil with the help of great goodness. They had much to be thankful for. He asked if they had anything else to share.

Josef startled Ludwik when he blurted out that the Blessed Mother had helped them along their way. The bishop agreed that prayers to Mary were indeed powerful. Josef said it was more than prayer. That piqued the bishop's interest. He asked Josef how so. Josef said that Ludwik could better tell the story. The bishop turned to Ludwik and said, "You have a story to tell, my new friend from Poland." Ludwik gave Josef a concerned look then said it was complicated, but he would try.

"A day after the bombing in Praga, I heard a woman crying outside a farmhouse in Poland we had slept in. It was early morning. The darkness of night had just begun to wane. I went outside to investigate. A very cold, thick mist made it difficult to see anything past a few feet. I moved into the mist toward the sound of the crying. I had only walked a few feet when my skin began to prickle and my body filled with a warmth I had never felt before. It was then I thought I heard a voice say, "I am with you." And with that, the mist began to evaporate. There was no sign of anyone as it cleared. After breakfast, I asked the farm family if they had heard the crying. They said no, but there were stories about a young woman who wandered the forests and fields at night crying for someone. Some said it was for her husband. Others said it was for her son. No one had ever seen her. Then one day, a young woman began appearing in the hills tending a flock of sheep. Rumor spread she was the one that cried in the night. She was young and always dressed in a brown robe. And she was never without the largest dog people had ever seen. People were frightened of the animal. And they thought the young woman might be possessed. They stayed away from her. After we left the farm, we drove a distance before stopping to rest. We were hiding in bushes next to a stream. There was a long meadow on the other side of the stream than ran up to the crest of a small hill. Josef decided to stretch his legs and go for a walk up the hill on our side. I saw him stop, turn around and come running back to me.

He told me that a woman and her dog were approaching the crest with a small flock of sheep on the other side of the stream. He thought she fit the description of the woman the family had described earlier in the morning. I asked him what made him think that. He told me to see for myself. I watched the sheep come over the crest first. Not a large flock. The dog came next. It was the biggest shepherd that I had ever seen. Then the woman appeared. She was dressed in a long, brown robe with a hood folded on the back of her neck. She had dark hair and light brown skin. I couldn't make out the details of her face for some reason. The skin on my body began to prickle just like it had that morning in the mist. That's when we heard the plane. It was coming in just above the ground and directly at the woman and her animals. Then everything seemed to move in slow motion. The dog moved to the front of the flock, turned them and moved them quickly over the hill. They were followed by the woman. We saw the bullets tear into the top of the hill just as she disappeared on the other side. We watched the plane pull up and begin to circle back for another run. It went into a bank of clouds. We waited but he never came out of the clouds. We ran up the hill to see how the woman was. The meadow on the other side of the hill was empty. When we finally spotted her, she was making her way into a small line of trees. She had to be close to four hundred yards away. My skin was still prickling. I didn't know why then, and I don't know why now."

The bishop studied Ludwik carefully and said, "Is that when you thought the shepherdess might be our Lady?"

"No. It was when I saw what I thought was the same lady again in a place far away in another country. A woman tending a small flock of sheep with a huge dog beside her."

"Where was that?"

"Outside the train station in Satu Mare, Romania. Dressed the same. With that huge dog. My skin prickled just like it had the other two times."

The priest was silent. Then he said, "We must talk more about this. I have some thoughts. Perhaps after dinner at my church."

They carried the bishop's luggage along with their own to the train headed for Gorizia, the first stop in Italy. The bishop insisted they stay with him in first class for the trip into Udine. He wanted them to be with him when they left the train. There would be no official questioning then.

There were three custom officials and two border policemen checking papers in Gorizia. They did not bother with the bishop and his two "associates." They all knew his eminence; that he was from Udine and that he worked directly with the Pope in Rome. He was an important man. Anyone connected to the Holy See was to be revered and respected. There would be big trouble for them if any report reached their superiors that the bishop or his associates had not been treated with the utmost courtesy. So, when the bishop's party approached, they all bowed and moved out of their way as they walked to their next train. One custom official did come on the train to quickly stamp their papers as having entered Italy legally.

It was a short ride to Udine. There was a small group of black shirted men standing on the platform. They looked to be waiting for the passengers to detrain. Another group of black shirts, this one much larger, was out in front of the station marching back and forth shouting some pro-Mussolini/fascist propaganda. Both groups looked dangerous. The bishop and his small party of two were escorted off the train by two police officers to a waiting car in a private parking area.

St. Mary's had to be one of the oldest churches in the city. Ludwik was impressed with the wooden beamed interior that supported the building. The frescoes on the ceilings of the side chapels were spectacular. The statues and paintings of the Blessed Lady that adorned the side walls between the stained-glass windows were extraordinarily beautiful. This was more than a church. It was a monument to the Blessed Lady. Ludwik wondered how much of a coincidence it was to be here, surrounded by the Lady after discussing with the bishop how he believed she had been with him and Josef on their journey.

It was a quiet gathering by the priests of the parish in the dining room. They had waited all day for the return of his eminence. After the warm embraces and heartfelt words of welcome, the bishop introduced Ludwik and Josef as friends of the Church and himself. He made no mention of the fact they were Polish pilots on their way to France to fight Hitler and the hordes he had turned loose on Europe.

The "cjalcions," an assortment of stuffed pastas filled with meat and mints was the main dish. An ample amount of homemade bread and wine complimented the meal. Ludwik and Josef stayed busy eating at a quiet pace while the bishop entertained the priests with tales about Rome, the Holy Father and the state of the Church. Noticing the hour was growing late, Bishop DeMonte thanked everyone, especially the fine cook who had prepared such a wonderful meal and requested that dessert and coffee for three be brought into the library. He apologized to the priests for leaving them but said he had need to converse with his new friends in private.

Finished with the tiramisu flavored biscuits and coffee, the bishop made himself comfortable in his favorite chair in the library and began asking questions about the "Lady."

He spoke softly and listened intently to their answers.

What did she look like? Was she young? Old? Small? Large? Slim? Heavy? Delicate looking? Sturdy? Color of her skin? Hair? Did it sound more like a young girl, a young woman, or a mature woman crying in the mist? Did they believe it was the same woman tending her sheep with her dog that was attacked by the plane and the one they saw outside of Satu Mare?

Ludwik and Josef had basically the same answers: Not a girl. A young woman. Not very tall. Slim. Olive skin. Same brown, hooded robe. Dark hair. Same huge Shepard. Ludwik said he was taken by her beautiful smile and the grace with which she moved across the meadow in Poland. Josef added she seemed to glide over the ground in the meadow and never changed her gait. Even when the plane was streaking down at her. They both said she showed no sense of panic. Never screamed. Never ran. Just glided over the crest of the hill and disappeared. Ludwik felt certain the woman they saw in both places was one in the same. He said while the distance between the two encounters defied logic, his heart and body said it was so. The tingling of his skin and the surge of warmth in his body was exactly the same both times. As a matter of fact, it was the same feeling he had had once before when he was a boy. The bishop asked what the circumstances were then. Ludwik said it happened when he cleaned off a layer of dirt and grime that had accumulated on a statue of the Madonna outside their farmhouse in Poland. The bishop found that story intriguing. He then turned to Josef and asked him if he thought the two shepherdesses were one and the same. Josef said he did, that their clothes, the sheep and especially the huge brown shepherd, were just too much of a coincidence.

"Your faith has inspired me," said the bishop. "Logic does dictate coincidence in this instance, but at the same time, I believe faith

461

creates belief. I would like to share your story with my fellow priests here at St. Mary's. With your permission of course."

"Is it wrong to believe the Blessed Lady is with us?" Ludwik asked.

"She is always with us. So, I cannot question if she is with you. As far as appearing to you, the Church does believe the Lady has appeared many times before. You have heard of Lourdes, I presume. I was in Rome when Bernadette was canonized. So, it is possible the Lady has found favor with you. Perhaps it was your lifelong devotion to her. Perhaps it was the love you showed her when you cleaned that statue. It may have warmed her heart. Who am I to say or judge what is and what is not? I know your faith is strong. And as I have said, with faith comes belief. And with belief comes hope and that makes all things possible. And that is a good thing. Especially in the world today. Bernadette said the Lady promised her she would be happy in the next world, not this one. We can only hope your experiences will give you reason to believe the world will be a better place someday. However, it might also mean that you, like Bernadette, may have to suffer in this world before you find happiness in the next."

"How did the Lady appear to Bernadette?" asked Josef.

"She came with the sound of a strong wind that didn't move a leaf or a twig. She appeared dressed in a white robe with a blue sash around her waist. She had gold roses on her feet. And she was accompanied by a brilliant light that lit up the grotto behind her." The bishop paused and suddenly realized he was very tired. He stood up and said, "It has been a long day. I hope my words have given you some thought. I will awake you in time for breakfast. Inquiries will have been made concerning the train schedules and the location of your fellow Polish airmen in France. Now, let us pray to our Lady and ask her to help us find what is in our hearts."

The room was small. Just enough space for two narrow beds, a closet and a table. It had no lights; only a candle burning on the table facing the foot of the two beds. It shed a soft, flickering light up on the wall behind it that illuminated Jesus hanging on a wooden cross.

"What do you make of father's words?" Josef asked.

Ludwik gave the question some thought and said, "I think he was interested in our story, but had doubts about her appearing. His description of how the Lady appeared to Bernadette may have been his way of saying that the lady we described wasn't the Blessed Mother."

"How so?"

"Our lady was dressed in a brown robe. Bernadette's lady wore a white robe with a blue sash and had gold roses on her feet. The bishop said she came in a brilliant light accompanied by a strong wind that moved nothing. Not even a leaf. Our "lady" was in a meadow with sheep and a big dog."

"Are we fools to believe the Lady is with us?" Josef asked.

"We are not foolish in believing what we believe," Ludwik answered.

Ludwik went over to the candle and blew it out. Back in bed, he tried to picture the lady at Satu Mare. He could see her standing on the hill and smiling at him. His last thought before he slept was that he felt he would see her again. Maybe not in this life, but in the next. The bishop had hinted at that possibility earlier. It was a comforting thought; a good one to fall asleep with.

Dawn arrived with a gentle tap on the door. Ludwik answered it with a polite, "tak?" The bishop's aide said in halting Polish, "Sniadanie w ciago godziny." For an instant, Ludwik felt he was home in Poland and waking up to his mother's call to get up and do his chores.

He slipped out of bed, lit the candle, blessed himself in front of the crucifix and then shook Josef's blanket. His friend didn't move. That changed when he repeated the words he had heard; "Breakfast in an hour."

Ludwik enjoyed the warm water and the plush, white towels only a guest of a bishop might enjoy. Once again, he thanked God for his good fortune. It was good to be in a place that was clean, quiet, and above all, spiritual. It had been a while since they were forced to brave the elements and be completely on their own.

Bishop DeMonte said the bulk of Polish airmen were stationed at Sallon Field in Lyon-Bron and Le Bourget, just north of Paris. Lyon-Bron was not far from the Italian and Swiss borders. He said they would be glad to know that thousands of Polish servicemen were now in France.

"We live!" Josef exclaimed.

The bishop clasped his hands together in prayer-like fashion and said, "Yes, you do. Remember, my sons, with faith comes hope. And with hope all things are possible. A lesson from our Lady, perhaps. Be sure to keep your faith when life tests you."

"It already has, your eminence. And we are still here," Josef said.

"Yes, you are, my son, but the real test has yet to come, and it may last a long time. Maybe even a lifetime. At any rate, I believe if your faith remains strong and your prayers are sincere, our Lady, our Jesus and our God will continue to find favor with you."

Ludwik and Josef figured if they left Udine before noon, they might be able to get into France sometime tonight. Bishop DeMonte suggested it might be safer if they let him purchase their tickets. He said the fascists had a habit of hanging around train stations.

They were always looking for trouble and trying to impress travelers with their muscle and message. They liked to insult people, especially foreigners. He said he would send out one of the younger priests to purchase the tickets. The troublemakers never bothered a priest. Not yet anyway. Ludwik and Josef accepted the offer.

The bishop and priests watched with interest over their coffee as the two pilots cut open the linings of a topcoat and field jacket. All the lira extracted was laid out on the dining table. The bishop said it was enough for the tickets and food for a day. Ludwik was pleased. He didn't want to use the money in his boot. They would need it later.

It took an hour for the priest to buy the tickets and return. As the bishop had said, there was lira left over. They would indeed be able to eat tonight, maybe even tomorrow. The bishop offered them extra money. He said to consider it a donation in the fight for freedom. Ludwik said he would accept their prayers, but not their money. Josef said he would never forget what they had done for them. He shook everyone's hand in thanks; even tried to thank the portly cook who had just arrived with the eggs and bread for breakfast.

"Manga!" the surprised cook shouted as she backed away from this stranger. The bishop and his priests enjoyed the interaction. One of the priests gave thanks for the food. Bishop DeMonte blessed it all and asked the two guests to begin filling their plates. The cook, looking and acting like a taskmaster, stood behind them and made sure their helpings were large. She would not allow any of the priests to touch the food until they and the bishop had filled their plates.

The bishop and all the priests of St. Mary's were gathered at the rear of the rectory to say their goodbyes to the two Polish airmen. The bishop handed Ludwik a large brown envelope that contained, in his words, the tickets that would take them into the world of war and with that in mind, he had given each of them a gift.

A gift that would keep them close to their good "friend." Saying goodbye to the priests, Ludwik and Josef stepped out into the cold and got in the church's sedan. They hadn't driven more than a minute when Ludwik opened the envelope. He pulled out two sets of rosary beads. Perfect! Prayers to Mary, their "friend."

The tickets were to Paris. Ludwik noted they took them through Lyon-Bron. That was interesting. The Polish Air Force was in or near both cities. The bishop had done well. He had given them an option.

Four hours later, the train entered Milano. It was a large and impressive city. It looked to be one of those places loaded with a special charm. A place well worth seeing. As the train slowed nearing the station, the city's charm suddenly disappeared in a marching swirl of black and brown shirted men on the streets carrying signs and bristling with anger. The fascists in Udine were tame in comparison to this mob. They looked very dangerous. It was good they would be staying on the train for the trip to Turin. They would change trains there and head for the town of Bardoneechia. Another change there and then into France.

As the train sped its way to Turin, they discussed their options. Paris would bring them close to the High Command. The problem with Paris was money. They did not have any French francs. And there would be no place to exchange their lira so late at night. They did have a ninety-minute layover in Bardoneechia and could spend the lira there to eat. That might be risky if the fascists were around like they had seen in Milano. They would have to wait and see. Another consideration was to take the trains to Lyon-Bron, locate the Polish base, and report in. After some more discussion, that option seemed to be the most favorable.

The train station in Turin was quiet. The train to Bardoneechia was scheduled to leave in ninety minutes. It only had three passenger cars.

They all looked well used. There was already a sizable crowd waiting to board it. Ludwik told Josef he wasn't comfortable hanging around for ninety minutes with that crowd. It might bring unwanted attention. He suggested it might be better to make use of the time and their lira to get something to eat away from the station.

Carabinieri

The Corso Principe Oddone ran parallel to the tracks. The wide street was filled with cafes and restaurants. People were hustling about in the cold. Ludwik chose the café closest to the station. It was small and smoky. Only one room. Men drinking wine and playing cards were off to one side. Two of them were arguing with each other. Ludwik and Josef headed for a table on the other side of the room. No need to be close to trouble. That might bring the authorities and they might ask questions. Before they reached the table, the argument exploded into a fight between the two men who were arguing. They wrestled each other onto the floor and rolled right at them. The man on the bottom was biting the ear of the man on top of him. There was a lot of screaming. Josef saw the knife first. The brawler on top was taking it off his belt. Without thinking, he grabbed the man's wrist and twisted it sharply. The knife sailed out his hand. Ludwik jumped in, curled an arm around the face of the knife wielder, grabbed his belt with his other hand and threw him to the side. The man recovered and scrambled across the floor toward the knife. Josef beat him to it and kicked it away. It slid right into the waiting hand of a Carabinieri. He had come out of nowhere. He held the knife in one hand and his Beretta in the other. The combination soldier/policeman pointed his Beretta directly at the knife wielder. He yelled at the man to stay on the floor and for the other three to "SCENDI, ORA!" The Italian still standing dropped immediately. Ludwik and Josef hesitated, not sure what to do. The officer pointed at the floor with his weapon and yelled again. They got the message.

467

The officer shouted again. Three men and a woman shuffled out of the kitchen into the dining area. They were joined by two members of the local police entering the café. One of the men from the kitchen, a waiter, had witnessed the entire event. He explained to the officer what he had seen. His version of the event was roundly reinforced by all the patrons in the room. The officer motioned for Ludwik and Josef to get up and sit at the table he pointed to. As they sat, a police car, siren blaring, screeched to a stop outside. Three more local police entered. For a moment, Ludwik thought they were coming for all of them. When the police escorted the two brawlers out of the café, he began to breathe a little easier. The Carabinieri walked over to their table, pulled out a chair and began talking with them. When he recognized they weren't Italian, he pulled out his I.D and motioned for them to do the same. He studied their papers carefully then handed them back. He stood up, took a step back, clicked his heels together and saluted them. Bowing, he said, "Grazie I miei compagni Pollachi." Then he left.

"What did he say?" Josef asked.

Ludwik lit a cigarette and said, "I think he said, thank you, my Polish comrades."

The Cattle Car

They left immediately after that. Ludwik had the feeling the officer had an inkling they were military. His military salute was an unusual gesture to make to a civilian. They were surprised and disappointed to discover that the same old, three car, decrepit train would be the one taking them to the border. They had missed their meal, survived a dangerous fight, been fortunate not to have been arrested and now would have to ride a train that looked like it wouldn't make it out of the station. On top of that, the only car available was crowded and smelled like shit.

468

Josef almost gagged when he climbed into the crowded car. The odor was stifling. Ludwik knew exactly what the smell was. This was a converted "cattle car." He had to laugh at the pained expression on Josef's face. It was obvious he had not spent any time on a farm. Never had to muck a stall littered with three to four pounds of "fresh" cow and horse manure.

"Probably a good thing we didn't get to eat," he said to Josef.

"How so?" Josef asked through a hand covering his face.

"Think you could have kept your meal with this smell for your dessert?"

"No. This smell doesn't bother you?" Josef asked.

"I'm farm raised my friend from the city. Nothing like the sweet smell of hay, grain, dust and cow shit!"

Most of the converted cattle car was open space. Men were standing together or sitting on the stained, wooden floor. Ludwik and Josef stayed by the door. Josef insisted on cracking it open a bit to let some of the cold, winter air in. Anything to help with the smell. They stacked their luggage on the floor, sat on it and waited. It was a short wait. The train made its way slowly out of the station then accelerated impressively away from the city. The "cattle car" left a lot to be desired, but the engine pulling it seemed to be first rate. Hunger was a bit of a problem, but not serious enough to be a worry. The food that had been piled on their plates at St. Mary's would hold them for a while longer. There would not be any time for eating at Bardoneechia so their next meal would be somewhere in France either tonight or tomorrow. And only if the money they had could be exchanged. That meant once again, they would be scouting towns and cities looking for a bank.

The conductor didn't stay long in the car. He finished punching the fifty or so tickets in five minutes. When he left, Josef opened the exit door a little more to get some additional fresh air circulating in the car. There was a murmur of protest from the closest group of Italians, but one look at Josef's defiant face and Ludwik's broad shoulders kept their complaints to a minimum. They just turned their backs to the two men and huddled a little closer to each other.

Ludwik wondered, at first to himself, then to Josef, of what might be in store for them in France. He wondered if the Polish command had anything to say about the assignments of their men. He was also concerned that the two of them might be separated. Josef had another concern. He feared that because they were arriving months after most of the others, there might not be an opening in a squadron. And that might mean they would be put into the French Army. Ludwik said that was a possibility, but he preferred to think they might be assigned as reserve pilots in squadrons that reflected their past service; he in reconnaissance, Josef in bombers. At least that was what he was hoping for. Josef said it didn't matter where he was placed as long as it wasn't in the French army.

The train arrived ahead of schedule. Almost everyone on the train got off. Josef was the first one off the "cattle car." He walked quickly toward the entrance of the station thanking God, Jesus, Mary and Joseph that the "cattle car" agony was over. Ludwik had to yell at him to stop and join him outside the first car in the train.

"I thought you were going to run out of the station and not come back," Ludwik teased his friend.

"I could use a shower. Need to get this stink off me," Josef complained.

"Let me give you a farmer's tip on getting rid of a barn's smell. The smell isn't on your body. It's in your nose. Blow your nose every ten seconds for a minute. That'll send most of the smell out."

Ludwik went into the passenger car for a look while Josef did his best to blow out the stink. There were many empty seats. Good seats. He went back outside to get his luggage and see if Josef had finished with the nose. A large commotion from inside the station caught his attention. More than a dozen young men carrying skis and ski bags came running onto the platform headed for the "cattle car." The first ones in it were the first ones out. They were empty handed and jogging straight for them.

"Let's get a seat before they get here," Ludwik calmly said.

They were seated for only a few seconds before a wave of noisy, excited teenagers hit the door and scrambled for seats. Ludwik enjoyed their unbridled enthusiasm. He hoped they would find good snow in France. Josef commented on how nice it must be to be visit another country to ski instead of going there to fight a war. Ludwik said with Mussolini in power, many of them would be wearing a uniform soon. Then fun days skiing would be over. Downhill runs would be replaced by goose stepping in foreign lands like Africa.

Claude Moreau

It was warm in the passenger car. The wooden seats in the first row were hard but comfortable. There was enough leg room for them to stack their suitcases and backpacks on the floor against the wall and rest their feet on top of them. Compared to the "cattle car" it was a first-class accommodation.

Lights from Bardoneechia made it possible to see a few of the signs they were passing. The largest one read, "Trafuro a Frejus 1 KM." A few minutes later, the train entered a tunnel.

471

Ludwik felt his heart skip a beat. He didn't care for tunnels. He hoped the 1 KM on the sign meant the length of the tunnel. The idea of thousands of tons of earth above and around him sent chills through his body. It was too coffin-like. He needed some sort of distraction. He found it in the form of a diminutive, bubbling and very friendly, French custom official.

Claude Moreau had been in the border custom service for the past twenty years. He had been given the civil service position as a reward for his heroic action in the Battle of the Somme in 1916. He had suffered severe wounds in the battle and had spent more than a year recovering in a Paris hospital. He had hated Germany ever since and even more so now after their invasion of Poland. He knew that many Poles had escaped and were in France getting ready to fight back. He admired them. When he inspected the papers of the two men in the first row, he knew by looking at them, they were not what their papers said they were. He was sure they were military.

"Ah, Polonaise! Bienvenue a France!" Moreau's enthusiasm put Ludwik at ease almost immediately. That changed when the official said, "Monsieurs! Armee ou Armeede l'ar?" He mimicked a flying airplane. Both pilots understood his question. He was asking if they were Army or Air Force. As the train crawled deeper into the belly of the mountain, Moreau, still smiling broadly, repeated his question. Ludwik felt the truth was important now. In a short while, they would be in Modane, France. No need to hide who they were anymore. The French were their allies. He smiled at Moreau and said, "Oui. Armee de l'ar." Moreau almost jumped out of his black, ankle high, mountain boots. He snapped to attention, gave them his best salute and kissed Ludwik on both cheeks.

The posters inside the station at Modane told them exactly what the quaint, French village offered. Its draw was the natural beauty of the French Alps and its premier downhill skiing.

472

Other posters advertised this was the week of its annual "winter carnival" which featured ski racing. It didn't take them long to realize their arrival couldn't have come at a worse time. For one thing, they had misread their tickets. Their train was not leaving until the morning. They were now stuck with no way to exchange their money in order to rent a room. Their best hope was to find an inn that would take the Italian and Romanian currency. After a freezing hour of walking in the frigid night, they realized the "carnival" had attracted so many people there wasn't a room to be had. Their only hope now was the station or the train.

Finished with his supper, customs agent Moreau was walking the tracks back to the tiny equipment shack behind the station when he saw the men sitting on a bench under the platform light. When he heard them talking, he knew it was the two Poles. He wondered what they were doing out in this cold. Then it struck him. Carnival! Not a room to be had this time of year. They were waiting for someone to open the station. No chance for that. It would be eight hours before it opened. He decided to help the two who had come to France to fight the hated Germans; the ones that had killed so many at the Somme.

Ludwik and Josef weren't sure what the custom official was up to. They remembered him as a friendly sort and hoped his wave meant he could open one of the locked railroad cars for them to sleep in. They followed him into the dark across the railyard toward a row of freight cars.

The shack was tiny, filled with tools, railroad spikes, wire, cables and most impressively, a small, coal burning stove that spewed heat wall to wall. Moreau pointed to the open area next to the stove. They understood. They saluted the Frenchman and unrolled their sleeping bags. Moreau pulled a chained cot down off a wall and crawled under the covers. No words were spoken. They weren't necessary.

473

Breakfast was tea and a biscuit. They followed Moreau to the train and were introduced to the engineer and conductor as men who had come to France to fight the Germans and were to be treated with respect.

The first stop was at Chambery; Moreau's hometown. He was off duty now and going home. He waved to them from the platform, stiffened his back and saluted. They stood and returned his salute.

Grenoble sat on a high plain in the majestic, cloud-scraping French Alps. It was one of the premier ski resorts in all of Europe. They didn't have long to admire its beauty from their seats. The conductor came into their car and made an announcement. The few passengers that had boarded in Modane and Chambery got up and left the car. The conductor came to them and motioned for them to get their luggage and follow him off the train and into the station. He motioned to his watch and put up ten fingers. Ten minutes. A group of twenty odd passengers watched quietly as the "cattle car" train moved away from the station and a different train, one with several passenger cars, took its place. It was obvious the rail line officials were not going to allow the likes of the "cattle car" make an appearance in Lyon or Paris. The passenger car the conductor placed them in was first class. He was granting Moreau's wish for him to do that. Ludwik and Josef took the placement as another friendly gesture from another friendly human being. Ludwik thanked the conductor. The man pointed to himself and shook his head no, patted the seats and said, "Claude Moreau."

Money was still an issue with the two pilots. They would not be eating anything on the train. No francs. They would have to wait until Lyon. Then it would be finding a bank to exchange their money or getting to the air base at Lyon-Bron before they ate again.

As the train wound its way down from the mountains to the warmer plains of southern France, Ludwik sat in silence and thought of the journey they had been on from that first day in September. They had come far. Experienced much. Survived bombs, strafing, fire, cold, hunger, anxiety, fear and death. Lots of death. There was much to be grateful for. They were alive and uninjured. And soon, they would be with their comrades in arms. He thought all the people they had crossed paths with. So many of them. Strangers from so many different places that had helped them. Even to this day. People who they had met for only a few minutes. Like Claude Moreau, who had opened his tiny shack to them last night and kept them out of the awful cold. They had been fortunate to meet people like him throughout their trip across southern Europe. Common people mostly. Some of means and influence. Men, women, farmers, priests, soldiers, officials, policemen, even a German national, had all given them a helping hand. And of course, there was the Lady. She had been with them all the way. Had answered all his prayers.

Reunion

It was early afternoon when the train arrived in Lyon. They stood on the steps of the station in a bright sun. The air was warm. A welcome change from the frigid mountain air of Modane. It felt like freedom.

They weren't sure if Bron was a part of Lyon or a separate town by itself. Bishop DeMonte had said the Polish Air Force was located at a base called Lyon-Bron. They would make inquiries at the bank when they found one.

One of the first persons they saw outside the station was a Polish airman. He was standing across the avenue waiting to cross. The uniform was navy blue. The color was French Air Force. The cut wasn't. It was definitely Polish. As were the buttons and insignias.

The young sergeant saw the two men staring at him as he crossed the avenue. He could tell they were foreigners by their dress and the backpacks they carried. He didn't care for their stares and tried to avoid them. It didn't work. They moved directly into his path and seemed to be waiting for him. As he stepped on to the walk, one of them spoke.

"Sergeant, can you help us?"

The accent was Pomeranian. His part of Poland. He stopped and looked at them. They both had a "gapa" pinned to their jackets, the eagle and chain of a Polish pilot. He had only seen them on a Polish uniform. Not on civilian clothes.

"Yes sir. Sergeant Bohdan Kolinski at your service."

Ludwik smiled. The gapas Josef and he had dug out of their boots on the train ride had caught the young man's attention. The sergeant was polite and respectful. He clicked his heels together. Like a gentleman. He had class. It made Ludwik stand a little straighter just by looking at him. He tapped the gapa on his chest and said, "This is the only thing beside our word that we have left to prove who we are. We have come a long way to be with you and the rest of our countrymen here in France. We need your help."

Kolinski was impressed. The man doing the talking was older than the other one. The younger one looked to be about his age. There was no doubt who was in charge. He looked at Ludwik and said, "How may I help you, sir?"

"Can you tell us what it's like here?" Ludwik asked.

The sergeant began by describing his time in Lyon. He said the first four months had been a horrible experience for him. There had been nothing to do but hang around, drink, get drunk, fight and complain.

476

Their living quarters were awful. No beds, sleeping on straw mats, no heat, broken windows, bad food and very little pay. The French had no idea what to do with them. Didn't seem to care. They weren't even worried about the Germans. They did a lot of talking about how stupid it would be for the Germans to invade France. That they would never be able to penetrate the Maginot Line and the hundreds of thousands of French troops waiting for them. He said only a few of their top commanders seemed to understand the German threat. Then about two months ago things began changing for the better. General Sikorski and the Polish Command had convinced the French that their men would be an asset to France when the Germans invaded. He didn't say "if" they invaded. He said "when" they invaded. That got the ear of some influential government officials. They applied pressure on the French military command to begin listening more attentively to the needs of their "guests." When they asked Sikorski what he needed, he said the morale of his men needed to be improved. They needed a purpose. He suggested that better quarters, new uniforms and a little increase in pay would go a long way in improving morale. And more important than that, he said it was essential his men be put into training; get them ready to fight when the Germans came. That this was at the very essence of their being. Why they were here. They wanted to kill Germans. And they were willing to die with their allies in doing so. Die here in France if need be.

Kolinski said after Sikorski made his plea to the French, life changed for the better. Living quarters improved, the food got better, new uniforms were issued, and pay was increased. And most of all, men were placed into training squadrons. Poles were sent out to bases in France and French controlled areas in the Middle East and northern Africa. Plans were also in the making to send qualified Polish fighter pilots to England.

Ludwik thanked the sergeant for the information then asked him how to get to the base. Kolinski pointed to a group of Polish enlisted airmen who were gathering in front of the train station and told him a truck would be coming to take them back to the base. They could catch a ride with them.

The ride to the base was lively. The enlisted men were animated in their curiosity over the two men dressed in hiking clothes with a pilot gapa pinned to their field jackets. They were especially keen on finding out where the two strangers had been these past months. They kept repeating how fortunate they were reporting at this time. To a man, they echoed just about everything that Kolinski had told them; that the first few months in France had been hellish. They were not accepted by the French with open arms as an ally and some even blamed them for starting the war; obviously believing the Nazi propaganda that Germany invaded Poland in retaliation to a faked Polish incursion into Germany. They also concurred with Kolinski in saying things had dramatically improved. A few excitedly proclaimed they would be in operational squadrons soon. One of the older men, a high-grade sergeant, didn't share the younger men's enthusiasm. He said he had little faith the French would last in an all-out war with the Germans. He said all he heard from them was how much they had suffered in WWI and how tired they were of war.

It was a short trip to the airbase. The airfield itself was not big. Two things struck Ludwik immediately. Fighters were parked wingtip to wingtip in rows of six. Sitting ducks for a few strafing 109s or a well-placed bomb or two. The other worrisome feature were the fighters themselves. He knew them from the air shows he had attended with Bodil's family prior to the war. They were Caudrons, all C710s. He knew they were fast, but very brittle. They also had a bad reputation for stalling in a steep climb.

478

He didn't see any light bombers, his type of plane. There were a few medium bombers being worked on in a hanger. He wasn't familiar with them. He asked one of the men on the truck if the base was operational. The man laughed and said, "No, we are waiting for the Germans to invade first."

Major Sikora asked Ludwik and Josef to have a seat. He studied each of them for a moment. In his mind, he wondered where the hell these two had been all this time. He was anxious to hear their story. He kept in mind the possibility existed that they might be German agents. He knew the Germans were very interested in learning how big a force was in Lyon-Bron and how many Poles were here and what their role was with the French. But first, he would welcome them to the base without giving them any useful information. Then he would follow that up with questions concerning their background and the reasons for their late arrival. He would also have them interviewed by someone from Intelligence.

Lyon-Bron

"Gentlemen, welcome to Lyon-Bron. I want you to remember we are guests of the French government and at the present time we are under the command of its military. General Sikorski is working hard trying to have the French allow our forces be put under Polish command. We believe this will happen soon. You have arrived at a time close to when that may occur. You are fortunate. The first few months here were extremely frustrating for us. We lived in rags, received little pay, froze our asses off sleeping in dirt-bag quarters and had nothing to do with anything that resembled preparing to fight a war. All we did was fight among ourselves. The enlisted men pointed fingers at the officers, the officers pointed fingers at Command, and they pointed fingers at our government leaders, past and present.

Lots of criticism about our plan and readiness to defend the country when the Germans invaded. Fortunately, things have changed. Bickering has lessened. Morale has improved. Purpose has been established and training has begun. New uniforms and better pay have put pride into our men once again. They are now able to walk the streets of Lyon and other places with a sense of dignity instead of hiding in the shadows of shame with their ragged clothes and empty pockets. My point to this lecture is this; if we are to have a roll in fighting to regain Poland's freedom, we must act like men who deserve the chance."

"Couldn't agree with you more, sir," Ludwik said.

"The same for me, sir," Josef added.

Sikora rapped the knuckles of a very large hand on his desk and said, "Right! Now, tell me who you are, what your serial number is, your rank, what you do in the Air Force, where you come from and where the hell have you been since September 1st, 1939."

Ludwik answered first. He gave his name, rank, serial number and identified himself as a pilot in the navy. He gave the squadron he was in at Puck and how long he had been in the service.

"Alright, Navy pilot Skoczylas. You will need to fill out a form with that information. There will be other questions on the form. We will use it to try and verify your answers. Now, before you give me a little personal history, I will ring for my aide. He writes shorthand."

After the aide had been seated, the major began. "Tell me about yourself, Navy pilot Skoczylas."

"I was born in Kurylowka, Stanislawowskie, moved at an early age to Mazanki, Pomerania. I lived on a farm there, graduated from lyceum and went to the Naval Academy for one year.

480

I finished my university studies at Warsaw Technical University with a degree in Mechanical Engineering. I learned to fly with friends at their flying club near Sopot, joined the Navy, went to flight school and became a reconnaissance pilot in the Fleet Air Arm. After three years, the Navy sent me to Deblin to learn how to fly the Air Force's light reconnaissance bombers. That's when I met Josef, my friend here. He was learning to be a navigator. We went on pass to Warsaw from time to time. We were there when the invasion started."

"Why didn't you finish at the Naval Academy?" the major asked.

"Money, sir."

"Where did you stay in Warsaw?" Sikora inquired.

"The Hotel Bristol."

"Kind of expensive for your grade, wasn't it?"

"We always went as guests, sir."

"Guests of whom, may I ask?"

"My friends from the flying school in Sopot. Family named Pastula."

"Really! I am from Sopot. Can you tell me the first names of the family members?"

"Yes, sir. The father is Piotr. His son is Jozef and his daughter is Bodil."

The major was impressed. He had heard of Piotr Pastula. No German would have that information. Still, he would have that checked out. He asked what had happened to the Pastulas. Ludwik said he believed they had escaped to Sweden in their private plane.

481

Josef handled his own personal history quickly and then answered the major's question on where the two of them had been these past months. Sikora was particularly interested in the young man's description of their work in Budapest helping to facilitate the movement of army and air force refugees out of Hungary. After Josef had finished, he asked the major if it would be possible to call the embassy in Budapest to see if there was any news of his father making it across the mountains into Hungary. He had heard his father may have been guiding refugees over the mountains soon after the war began. The major promised him the call after they were interviewed by a Captain Sadowski at the transition center.

Sadowski was suspicious of the two late comers. The air force veteran had been hardened by war as an infantryman in the army during WWI and the subsequent Polish-Russian affair a few years later. He had lost his parents during the Russian war when Polish informants turned them in to the Russians for having a son in the Polish Army. He never saw his parents again. Ever since then, he had trusted no one. And these two "pilots" were no exception.

Sikora had vouched for Skoczylas, so he was alright for now. He hadn't totally endorsed the other man, a Josef Przyba. Sadowski decided to test him. He would ask a few questions concerning the form the man had filled out in the major's office. They would be pointed and asked in a semi-hostile manner to see how this Przyba handled them.

Ludwik handed Sadowski the forms they had filled out in the major's office. Sadowski scanned Przyba's form and said, "How is it your first name is spelled with an "s" and not a "z" like every other Polish man with that name?"

Josef was caught off guard by the question. He had asked his father that very same question as a teen-ager. And the answer to it had always made sense to him.

"My mother's name was Sophia. My father wanted some part of her name to be part of mine. He chose the "s.""

"So, Josef, with the "s," you pilot what type of aircraft?"

"Medium and heavy bombers, sir."

"We do not have many of those here. I see you were in Deblin training to be a navigator. So then, what are you, Josef with the "s? A pilot or a navigator?"

"I am a pilot, sir."

Sadowski glared at him and said, "You will have an opportunity to prove that in Africa soon."

Ludwik didn't care for Sadowski's tone. It was beginning to sound like an interrogation. He decided to divert the questioning to him. He asked the captain if there were any light bombers on the base. Sadowski paused and collected himself. He didn't appreciate the interruption, but it was an honest question. And it came from a navy pilot. No one knew much about them. A good cover for a spy. The short and stocky Sadowski eyed Ludwik carefully for a moment then said, "We do have a few light bombers here. I'm not sure you will be assigned to them but if you are, you will have to wait like the rest of us for our hosts to allow us to be operational. And before that happens, both of you will have to prove your worth as pilots. Now, I want both of you to report to the quartermaster next door, draw your bedding and report back here. You will stay in transition until we find a place for you. Przyba, you will probably be going to a bomber training base in Africa. I'm not sure about you, Skoczylas."

A minute after the two newcomers left, Sadowski called Major Sikora and asked him if he would expand a little on the reason why the two men had taken so long to get to France. Sikora briefly outlined their odyssey and long stay in Budapest working at the Polish Embassy helping to facilitate the movement out of Hungary of our personnel and getting them on their way to France. He said at this point, he had no reason not to believe them. He told Sadowski he had given Przyba permission to return to his office and call the embassy in Budapest to see if there was any word on his father who was thought to be guiding evacuees across the Carpathians into Hungary. He suggested to Sadowski that he listen in on the call to see if there were people there who knew him and were aware of his father. Sadowski agreed. He told Sikora it was bothersome to him that the two had stayed in Budapest for so long while everyone else was hurrying to France.

Once again, there was no word on Josef's father. Bella told him not to lose heart. The mountain passes were deep in snow and wouldn't be clear for some time. It was impossible for anyone to make it safely across. She said there were many friends in the refugee centers who were on the lookout for his father and for him to be patient. There was news about Basha. She had left her job at the embassy and gone to work for her brother. He had plans to open another restaurant and make her the manager. She said the police were asking questions about him and Ludwik, but she and Basha had feigned ignorance on the matter. She said there was also some talk that both of you had gone back into Poland to fight. Josef asked how the Jewish refugees were doing. He was thinking of the family with the two little girls he had sent to live with a willing Jewish family in Budapest. Bella said at the moment, everything was fine, but anti-Jewish rhetoric and articles in the newspapers were indicating a growing negativism toward the Jews. She said there had also been a surge politically to limit the amount of aid given to refugees. Especially Jewish refugees.

She felt that aid to Jewish refugees would end soon. Not so for the non-Jewish people. Josef said that was concerning. He told her about the exodus of Jews from Pulawy and how they had been massacred by German planes on the road outside of town. He described the horror he felt when he and Ludwik came across the site on their way to the Romanian bridgehead. There were bodies of men, women and children strewn all over the road. Everyone one of them a Jew. Bella asked if he thought that could happen in Hungary. Josef said if the Germans took over, it would. And that kind of cruelty wouldn't be limited to just the Jewish population. He said they wouldn't take kindly to people like her who had worked in the embassy helping Jews. He urged her to get out of the country before that day came. She promised him she would give that some thought. Before hanging up, Josef said he wasn't sure if he would be able to make another personal call like this one but would write her with his return address as soon as he could.

Captain Sadowski waited ten seconds before he hung up the phone in the office next door. He wanted to be sure Przyba had hung up. The Jewish captain from Lwow folded his hands together on the desk and stared blankly at the phone. He had been stunned to learn of the slaughter of Jews outside of Pulawy; gunned down like a pack of rabid dogs. He had heard of roundups and beatings, separations and harassment, but not the indiscriminate killing he had just heard described. He wondered for the thousandth time about his family who lived not far from Pulawy. He had tried many times to call them only to be told that all contact with that part of Poland had been lost. Przyba's phone call had made his anxiety over the family even worse.

As far as Przyba and Skoczylas was concerned, Sadowski had heard enough from Sikora and the phone call to believe the two had made good use of their time in Budapest.

They probably had contributed more to the war effort than he and everyone else in Lyon-Bron had while hanging around and doing nothing He decided it wouldn't be necessary to call the embassy in Budapest for information on the two men.

After two days of in the transition barracks, Ludwik and Josef received their orders. Josef was being shipped out to North Africa. His days as a promising navigator were over. He was back to being a bomber pilot. As for Ludwik, the only planes he was going to be in were the ones taxiing over to the maintenance hangar he had been assigned to. Sadowski said a personal recommendation had convinced headquarters that it would be good to have someone like him figuring out how to deal with the inferior planes the French had assigned them. Ludwik asked him if his orders had anything to do with him being a navy pilot. Sadowski said he should be grateful. Someone had spoken up for him. His initial orders had him being demoted to corporal and assigned to an army unit.

Josef was headed to a French airbase at Blida, Algeria and an unnamed bomber training unit under French command. He would undergo three months of training then either be kept there in reserve or brought back to France to join a different reserve squadron. Being a "reserve" meant he would only be flying bombing missions if there weren't enough pilots available to carry out the raids. The obvious question was, "What raids?" There had been no raids carried out against the Germans up to this point. The French had not made any offensive moves toward the German border since their declaration of war last September. They seemed content to sit behind the Maginot Line and play games with each other. French fighter squadrons did fly sorties along the German border but were seldom allowed to engage German aircraft. The prevailing thought in the French government and much of the military was that the Germans would not risk invading France and they didn't want any "incident" to provoke them into an invasion.

Ludwik reported to the motor pool as second in command to a Major Berk. They were responsible for maintaining and repairing a small fleet of land vehicles and the few planes assigned to the Poles at the base. He was told by Berk that his duty was temporary and as soon as more light bombers became available, he would be transferred out of the motor pool and into a training squadron. Eventually, once the squadron became operational, he would be back flying recon missions like he had for the Navy. When Ludwik asked what the chances were for that to happen, Berk shrugged and said while the French were not anxious to fight, things could change, and they needed to be ready. He said it was different with the English. They were dropping bombs on Germany and mobilizing, really mobilizing, all their forces for the war they had declared. It was his hope that Sikorski would somehow get them all transferred to England and into the fight. Ludwik asked Berk if he knew the man that had spoken for him at headquarters. Berk said he didn't, but heard it was an Army officer that met you at the Romanian border just before the order came to evacuate Poland. He happened to be in headquarters when your name came up for a demotion in rank and transfer to a French army unit. He pressed the assignment officer hard to keep you here in some capacity. He said you could repair everything from mess kits to motorcycles. Apparently, he was very convincing. He and your degree in engineering are the reasons you are here. Ludwik had no idea who the man might be but if what Berk had said was true, he was clearly indebted to him.

Josef had been gone two weeks. Ludwik missed his friend but had thrown himself wholeheartedly into his assignment at the motor pool. He supervised an exceptionally talented group of mechanics from the mother country and didn't mind getting his hands dirty alongside them. That quickly earned their respect. They were also impressed with his cleverness in finding solutions to mechanical problems that seemed insurmountable.

One day, he and one of his crack mechanics were having a difficult time analyzing a problem. They were working in a grease pit below a scout vehicle trying to find out why the vehicle's transmission could not be downshifted. They had been at it for over an hour without any success when they were interrupted by a loud and irritated voice that demanded to know, "How LONG is it going to take down there?" Ludwik told the mechanic to continue the inspection while he handled the "new" problem up on the floor of the hangar. His mechanic chuckled and told him to invite the "mouth" down here in the pit for suggestions.

Pelcz

As Ludwik emerged from his climb up the six, oil-stained steps of the ladder onto the floor of the hangar, he saw the source of the irritated voice. It was an Army captain. He stood with legs apart and arms folded across his chest. He was tall and well put together. His jaw was set, and he didn't look very pleased.

"Well, when will this vehicle be ready?" he asked. His tone was different. It was softer. Polite. It was also familiar. As he approached the captain, he recognized him. It was the scout commander he and Josef had met on their way to the makeshift camp on the Romanian border and later at the camp itself. He had repaired the captain's scout car at the camp and the man had returned the favor by bringing him some parts that he needed for the Volvo. It was Lieutenant, now Captain, Pelcz. Ludwik knew instantly he had to be the man who had spoken up for him.

"Pelcz!" Ludwik shouted.

"How are you, officer pilot, Skoczylas?" Pelcz answered.

488

"I am well. No sense complaining. No one is listening. I must ask you something. Was it you that made it possible for me not to be transferred to a French army company?"

"It was. I happened to be at headquarters waiting to speak to the base commander on a security matter when I heard the assignment officer's aide mention your name as he was adding it to a list of men that were being transferred to the French Army. Without thinking, I blurted out your name in recognition. The aide asked me if I knew you. I said I did and went on to tell him how you and your talented friends fixed everything from mess kits to motorcycles. The aide was impressed and scratched your name off the French list and added it to the maintenance list; with an asterisk saying you were Navy. I figured you being navy probably was the reason for the transfer to the French army."

Ludwik nodded and said, "I thought so. In any case, I want to thank you for speaking up for me. I didn't think a captain in the Army could have any influence on an Air Force decision."

"These are different times. We need to be one now. If we aren't, we should be. Most of our brothers at home have been lost. It's no longer you and me. It's we. Besides, how could I let a man of your talents be put in a forest or in a foxhole on the Belgium border with a bunch of malcontent French and Polish infantrymen?"

Ludwik suggested they go outside for a smoke and talk. They swapped stories of how they had made it into France. Pelcz said a week or so after he left Ludwik in Poland, his platoon engaged a Russian force in a firefight south of Lwow. Unfortunately, his scout cars were no match for their tanks. Most of his platoon was killed. He eventually made it across the Romanian border and was interned at Focsani, a hellhole of a place. He was only there a week before escaping with the remnants of his platoon.

They made their way to the Polish embassy in Bucharest. The embassy got them train tickets to the Black Sea. From there they boarded a transport to Syria. After a few weeks there, they bordered another transport that brought them to Marseilles. He had been in France for four months, been promoted to captain and given the responsibility of securing the perimeter of the airbase along with his French counterpart. He said he had also been assigned to scout the Italian and Swiss borders and look for routes to take in case things went badly for us in France.

Ludwik outlined the route that Josef and he had traveled to get to France. He talked in some length about their hike across the Romanian mountains with Andrei and their lengthy stay in Budapest working at the embassy. Pelcz was intrigued with the story. He had considered going to France via an overland route but had taken the embassy's quick help to sail the Mediterranean to here. He congratulated Ludwik on his trip and said, "So, my multi-talented friend, you not only fly airplanes and fix anything there is, you now qualify as a scout, a long- range reconnaissance man, a mountain man that has also dabbled in the diplomatic world at an embassy. I hope you can stay alive through this mess until we return home, and I can vote for you as our President."

Ludwik laughed at Pelcz's praise and said his words were not going to get the scout car fixed any faster. It usually took a day or so to remove a transmission, take it apart, inspect it, replace what they had to, clean it, reassemble it and put it back correctly. Pelcz said there was no rush. He said that most of what the French gave them was pitiful. He expected Ludwik and his men to be kept very busy keeping the second-rate vehicles running. Ludwik said it was no different with the airplanes. He stared out at the rows of Caudrons and antiquated Mureauxs neatly parked wingtip to wingtip on the grass just off the major runway.

These were the aircraft the Polish fighter pilots would have to fly and prove they were worthy of joining a French fighter squadron. Not too far off on the other side of the base he could see more orderly lines of parked planes. They had been parked that way for some time.

Pelcz knew exactly what Ludwik was thinking. It wouldn't take much to wipe out every plane on the base parked like that. He wondered if anyone had explained to the French how important it was for them to disperse their aircraft. Ludwik said they had tried. They had asked for permission to disperse the planes assigned to them and emphasized that having planes lined up like that was inviting catastrophic loss. The French didn't take the hint. They said there was no need for disbursement; that there would be enough time to get all planes airborne before the enemy got here. Pelcz shook his head and said, "Did anyone mention to them that it might be a good idea to have some of their planes put in secondary fields like we did before the invasion?"

Ludwik shrugged and said, "The French have a superiority complex. Many of them think we didn't make a serious effort against the Germans. They don't care we were outnumbered ten to one in the air and were flying against the most advanced air force in the world. They were not about to take suggestions from us. Sikorski believes that many in the French Command do not think the Germans are going to attack because France is too strong."

Pelcz laughed at that and said, "Some Frenchmen believe we started the war and are pissed that we are here."

"Not all Frenchmen believe that do they?" Ludwik asked.

"No. Most understand what happened in Poland. But I am not sure if the French military really appreciates the power of the German forces. I have to admit that attitude, unfortunately, was shared by many in Poland not that long ago. We know what happened after that. And how quickly it happened."

Pelcz and Ludwik became good friends over the next month. In that time, every scout vehicle was expertly repaired and elevated to a high state of readiness. That accomplishment gave Ludwik and his mechanics time to begin learning the ins and outs of the obsolete fighter planes the French had assigned to the Polish pilots.

Part Five

Preparing to Fight

Unfortunately, the success of the Polish motor pool, while grudgingly praised by the French, did not encourage them enough to give Polish ground crews a role in servicing any aircraft Polish pilots flew. That was left in the hands of French ground crews whose performance left a lot to be desired. Regular general maintenance checks were ignored. Cockpits were pig pens, gauges were too dirty to read, guns were not dependable, and some gas tanks were even left half empty.

Things changed dramatically after General Sikorski finally convinced the French to allow the Poles to organize a squadron of their own. Fighter Squadron 1/145 was assembled quickly and filled with veteran pilots and service crews that had fought the Germans in Poland. Sadly, the squadron's experience and talent were wasted by the French. It was assigned to protect the industrial plants in Lyon. Nothing more. All they were allowed to do was fly over the city. They never saw a German plane. In addition to their dull mission, they were given the obsolete Caudron Cyclone to fly. The plane had never been considered a capable fighter. Even the talented ground crews were having trouble keeping them in the air. Ludwik and his mechanics took some of the burden off their backs by doing what they could to help repair and maintain aircraft that probably belonged in a scrapyard. Nevertheless, the morale of the Polish airmen at Lyon-Bron rose considerably. Renewed pride of being a Polish airman had put a little zest into their life. They now had a purpose; not exactly killing Germans, but one step closer to it. Ludwik put it best when he told Pelcz, "We are flying again. We will be ready when the time comes."

It got even better for the Poles when they learned additional plans were in the making to form more all-Polish squadrons. The French had agreed to allow them to form three more fighter squadrons, three bomber squadrons and most importantly for Ludwik, three reconnaissance squadrons. Each squadron was to include all-Polish ground crews and the appropriate support systems. Everyone on the base believed the French had finally decided to get ready for a fight and they were going to be part of that fight.

In mid-April, Ludwik was transferred out of the motor pool to begin training on flying the French Potex 63.11 light bomber. It was primarily designed to fly recon and ground support missions. His training was to last three months. Ludwik hoped after that he would be able to fly recon missions into Germany or strafe and bomb German positions in support of Allied troops.

Most of the training in the first weeks was spent in classrooms on the base learning the ins and outs of the Potex; what it could do and what its limitations were. The diagrams of all its systems were straight forward. As a pilot, he was familiar with the function of each. The major problem was the language in the manuals. Everything was in French. It had to be translated by Polish officers fluent in French or French officers who could speak Polish. Those men were hard to find and that slowed the entire process.

One of the first assignments the pilots had was to memorize the entire instrument panel in the cockpit. French symbols and all. Failure to identify any one instrument might mean immediate demotion from pilot to crew member. And failure to pass any test on the day's lesson could also mean removal from the cockpit. Only the best and brightest survived the demanding requirements. Ludwik was one of them.

He spent most of his spare time studying the schematics in his manual. It was a habit he had formed in his training as a sport pilot with the Pastulas in Sopot, as a naval recon pilot at Puck, and later at Deblin learning to fly light bombers.

When not studying the manual, he wrote letters to his family in Poland and Basha in Budapest. The letters to Poland had to be written in a manner suggesting he was enjoying his life and work in Portugal. He was not allowed to mention anything about his service in the Polish Navy or his present duties with the Polish Air Force in France. He understood that all mail into occupied Poland was subject to search and if his service was discovered, his family would be persecuted or worse.

The French had all correspondence to Poland by Polish forces in France be sent via different postal locations in Portugal. It was believed that mail from a neutral country had a better chance of not being opened by Poland's occupiers. Ludwik knew it was impossible to get a response from Poland, but just wanted his family to know he was fine. He did expect to hear from Basha, still living in Hungary. Word did come from Budapest at the end of April. Not from Basha, but from Bella. She said Basha had gone on extended holiday with her family and she had not heard from her in weeks. There was concern they might have left the country. There had been mounting political pressure put on all outspoken critics of the government's growing pro-German posture. And Basha's father had become one of their favorite targets. His enemies were bound and determined to silence his voice. Threats had been made by phone and by mail to his home. Bella said she was hoping to hear from Basha soon and believed Ludwik would be hearing from her also if he hadn't already. She added she wouldn't be surprised if Basha showed up in Lyon to see him. Her letter went on to say that things had tightened up considerably in Budapest. The government had taken an even stronger pro-Nazi stance and life had become very difficult for all Jews, native or refugee and that she expected "hard times" were ahead for them. She said that Willie had disappeared and added the man who had been the first to meet him in Budapest had dinner with her recently. He had been pleased to hear you were doing well.

He also said there was a well-paying job waiting for someone after the war who knew how to fix things. Ludwik read the letter three times. He appreciated Bella's effort not to mention the jeweler's name. It felt good to hear from a friend. Budapest had been like a second home to him. He had made many friends there. He missed them. Especially Basha. She had stirred his heart strongly. It saddened him to think he might never see her and the others again. He thought of Josef, his good friend. What they had gone through together. Their time in Budapest. Brothers.

He folded the letter and slipped it back into the envelope careful not to wrinkle or crease it any way that might distort any of the words. It was now a small memoir, something he could always open and remember that special time in his life. He treated it like the prize it was; a gift of words that tied him to a place he would never forget.

He felt the need to give thanks for the letter, his friends and his good fortune. With the help of friends like the Blessed Lady, Josef, Basha, Bella, Puskas and so many others, he had made it to France and hopefully soon, would have the opportunity to fight for his country. He knew the chapel would be empty this time of day. It would just be him, his prayers and those that he prayed to; God, Jesus and most of all, the Blessed Mother.

Everyone in France and the western world was aware of Germany's advance into Denmark and Norway. The Danes had not made any attempt to fight the invaders. They did not have the military capability to do so. They were not "occupied" by the Germans but had become a "protectorate" of Germany. That agreement kept them away from bloodshed and destruction for the time being. Norway, on the other hand, had decided to fight. They had been surprised by a German airborne invasion, but by the end of April, with the help of British, French and Polish units, they were still holding out and giving a good account of themselves.

The men at Lyon-Bron were ecstatic to learn that Polish troops had landed by sea in Norway and were engaging the Germans. General Sikorski and the Polish Command were pleased to be a part of the fight but were deeply concerned that Norway and Denmark might only be the first stage of an attack on all of Western Europe.

Some French and Polish units in France were moved north toward the "low countries" of Belgium and the Netherlands to counter a possible German attack there. The French felt if the Germans did attack, they would strike there not through the rugged Ardennes Forest south of the two countries and certainly not at the "impenetrable" Maginot Line south of the forest.

Pelcz was concerned. He told Ludwik that some of his scouts had reported hearing a lot of motorized activity on the eastern side of the Ardennes. Especially at night. In addition to that, he had read reports from French recon pilots who had observed large numbers of tanks and tracked vehicles heading toward the Ardennes from Germany. It seemed obvious to him that something was going to happen there. The French, however, did not share his suspicions.

Ludwik's training had gone very well in the twenty days since he had left the motor pool. Both the French and Polish instructors he studied under were impressed with his ability. He was quicker than most when it came to understanding the function of all the different systems in the French planes he was learning to pilot. His time in the motor pool had been well spent. If it had been left up to the Polish instructors, his training would have been cut short by two months. They knew he was not only a smart, well-educated mechanic, but a damn good pilot. His experience in the Fleet Air Arm of the Navy was proof of that. The French might have cut his time in training also if he had been a fighter pilot. The demand for them was high. Not so much for a recon-ground support, light bomber pilot. Ludwik was going to have to do the entire three months of training.

The letters from Basha and Josef in came in early May. Basha had returned to Budapest but was leaving for good by mid-May. Her father had used his remaining connections in the government to obtain passage to Greece. Basha was going with him. Her brother was staying. She had closed by saying she would always love him.

Josef's letter was full of disappointment. He said all the Polish bomber pilots had requalified but had nowhere to go. As of now, there were no plans for them to return to France as reserve pilots because there were no plans to bomb anybody! He said most of their time in Africa was spent flying out over the desert and dropping bombs on makeshift targets in the sand. He said desert life was stifling. It was always hot, sweaty and dirty. He went on to say some of the men were renting women, sometimes girls, from native families, to serve as personal maids and bed mates. No one in Africa seemed to care that much about that sort of thing. Ludwik folded the letters carefully and added them to Bella's. The memoir of another time had just added two more chapters.

It was good to see Pelcz again. He had returned from scouting the Swiss border and the French side of the Ardennes. He had made his report and was settling back into the routine of maintaining security around the base.

"Anything interesting on the border?" Ludwik asked the captain.

"Nothing along the Swiss border. We were trying to map out routes we could take that were away from the main roads and still get across the border. The Ardennes was interesting. Especially close to the border of Luxembourg. We were assigned to get into the forest and have a look."

"See anything?" Ludwik asked.

"Saw nothing but heard lots of heavy engines. Sound travels well at night."

"Any ideas?" Ludwik prodded.

"Tanks. I'm certain of that."

"I heard there was a large buildup of German forces east of Belgium. North of Luxembourg," Ludwik said.

"Where did you hear that?" Pelcz asked.

"Our French trainers. They seem to think the Germans will come through Belgium. They feel heavy armor cannot get through the Ardennes."

"Maybe so. Maybe not. We'll have to wait and see," Pelcz quietly answered.

"Are the French in the forest?" Ludwik asked.

"Not enough of them," Pelcz answered.

On May 10th, Germany attacked Belgium, the Netherlands and Luxembourg. By the end of the day, Luxembourg was theirs. Pelcz was sent back to the border along the Ardennes. Ludwik continued to learn how to fly the Potex without actually flying the plane. It was frustrating for him; another fight he wasn't part of.

France sent thousands of troops along with some Polish units into Belgium. There were no reinforcements sent to the Ardennes. The word around the base was that the Germans were going to meet their match when the French and Polish engaged them in battle. Unfortunately, by the time they got to Belgium, the Belgians were retreating under the onslaught of a German blitzkrieg. To make matters worse, Pelcz's suspicion about the German buildup on the Luxembourg side of the Ardennes came to fruition.

The Germans had found a way to move an entire army through the dense forest surprising an undermanned French force on the French side. They quickly dispatched the French units and then swung north to cut off the rear of the French and Polish units that had joined a British force already engaged with the Germans. The Allied forces were now surrounded and heavily outnumbered on land and in the air. Everyone at the base understood the gravity of the situation; defeat there meant a German surge to Paris and south toward them some four hundred miles away.

At first, the news reports were positive. They had the French defeating the enemy and inflicting heavy losses on them. Ludwik was uncomfortable with the updates. It reminded him of the early days of the invasion of Poland and listening to the exaggerated and probably untrue reports of Polish victories over the Germans.

"Déjà vu!"

It didn't take long for the Germans to disprove all the "positive" French radio reports. They did it by launching an avalanche of air attacks on French airbases to protect their massive, armored incursion through the Ardennes and into France. While the Luftwaffe buzzed through the skies of northeastern France and the lowland countries, the blitzkrieg tactics of its armored forces began to overwhelm the Allied forces on the ground.

It was the German invasion plan for Poland all over again. Establish air superiority and overwhelm ground force opposition with quick, decisive and disruptive armored thrusts deep into enemy territory. To all the Polish forces in France it was a 1939 "déjà vu."

The Luftwaffe came early in the morning. Attacking with the sun at its back. Just as the Poles had experienced and warned the French about. The first wave of unopposed fighters methodically destroyed row after row of neatly parked planes. Thankfully, not all the planes were on the base. Someone had listened to the Polish warnings. Many fighters had been flown out of Lyon-Bron to a secondary field far from the base.

After most of the planes left on the base had been destroyed, the fighters went after the barracks and any personnel spotted on the ground. They were followed by screeching dive bombers that laid waste to the runways and other targets of opportunity. In minutes, the base was transformed into a cratered, smoking ruin. Ludwik had witnessed it all from the camouflaged bunker in the woods near the fenced perimeter behind the Polish sector. He had run from the mess hall to the fence behind the building and followed it to the bunker. From there he had watched men run for their lives across the airstrip; some making the fatal mistake of running by parked planes; the number one target of the Germans. Some had even tried to hide under the planes. They all died. The war had come to France. The hoped for "second front" had finally been opened. Unfortunately, it had come nine months too late. And it had been opened by the Germans, not the French or British.

Poland was gone. Carved up by the Germans and Russians. Denmark, Luxembourg and the Netherlands had capitulated and Belgium and Norway were on their last legs. The British had been pushed back to the English Channel and were facing annihilation. The French Army was still holding its own along the Maginot Line, but now faced German armies on two fronts with no support from the air. The Luftwaffe controlled the sky over all of France. It was only a matter of time before the fighting ended on the Maginot Line. Paris was also at the mercy of the Luftwaffe and Hitler's Panzer divisions were making steady progress toward the city. France's plan to fight a defensive war had proven catastrophic. The French arrogance in believing they had an impenetrable border anchored by the Maginot Line and the Ardennes had cost them dearly.

In addition to that miscalculation, they had been in no rush to organize and ready the reserve divisions they had at their disposal. By the time they realized that mistake, the Germans were at their throat. Surrender was inevitable.

General Sikorski moved the provisional Polish government from Paris to London when word reached him from Winston Churchill, the Prime Minister of England, that France had had enough and was about to surrender. Sikorski told Churchill if that happened, he would order his forces not to surrender, and with Churchill's help, he would continue the fight with the British. Churchill agreed to help, and with that, plans were put into place to put the Poles on the move again. This time, out of France.

For close to a month, Ludwik and the airmen left at Lyon-Bron spent their days helping to repair the airfield and dodging intermittent nuisance raids by the Luftwaffe. Ludwik noted the infrequent raids always seemed to avoid further damage to the runways and serviceable buildings still standing. It was a sure sign to him that the Germans felt they would be here soon and using whatever was left for their own purpose. At times, it made him feel he was working more for the Germans than the French, but at least it was something for the men to do. Some Poles left for the front up north to fight with the French army. With a few exceptions, pilots stayed at the base. A few did get permission to fly to Africa and join their comrades at the French bases there. Others decided to join the French underground that was organizing in the countryside. Most, including Ludwik, remained on the base and waited for an order from Sikorski. The order came on June 19th. Paris had fallen and the French were asking for an armistice. The order was eerily similar to the one the Poles had received last September in Poland. It didn't say, "Evacuate with all Speed!" It said, "Do not surrender! Move across the border into Switzerland and be interned or get to the Atlantic coast and wait to be picked up by ships and brought to England."

"Déjà vu," one of the mechanics said to Ludwik.

"Yes, it is," Ludwik answered. "For us and the Germans."

"What do you think, sir? Switzerland or England?"

"Internment is out of the question. I don't care for ship travel, but I need to fly and do some damage to those bastards."

"I'm with you, sir. I believe we all are," the mechanic responded.

Every available vehicle, top shape or not, was assembled and readied for departure that night. The plan was to convoy with parking lights only except for the lead vehicle. It would use its head lights. The hope was that any German night fighters flying over them would not see the entire convoy and assume the lead vehicle was a lone civilian going about his business. Every truck would carry extra gas cans strapped to its undercarriage. It was three-hundred miles to the Atlantic coast and the ports designated by Sikorski as the ones that Allied ships would be sent to. There had been no reports of Germans reaching the interior of France as of yet, but no one doubted they would be there soon. The Poles were counting on the French Army having enough fight left in them to delay the Germans from reaching the interior and cutting them off from the coast before the armistice took effect.

Food was a bit of an issue. They took only enough canned goods and perishables for three days and left the rest for the remainder of the men on the base to take when their transportation arrived for the last convoy off the base. The vehicles were covered with camouflaged nets and parked along a fence waiting for dark to fall. The men hung out in the woods behind the air raid bunker, smoked cigarettes and nervously waited for night.

504

Ludwik was commander of one of the last trucks in the convoy. It carried a full load of mechanics, most of whom he had worked with in the motor pool. His assignment was to repair any disabled truck from the convoy, get it back on the road and drive it to the designated rendezvous point. If they were unable to repair the vehicle, they were to wait for the last convoy to arrive and catch a ride with them.

Ludwik's map was one of the well-used ones the French had grudgingly given to Poles in their training classes. He scaled out the distance the convoy would cover getting to the ports on the Atlantic. It was 280 miles to Bordeaux and another 100 plus following the coast line south to the last port of St. Jean de Luz. Once they cleared Lyon, the convoy would use the main road headed west to the coast. It would take them through the city of Clermont-Ferrand and several small towns before reaching Bordeaux. All the travel had to be done during the short armistice agreed on by the French and Germans.

The last official briefing they received made no mention of German forces in the region of France they would be driving through. That was two days ago. The briefing did suggest that many roads might be crammed with refugees fleeing Paris and its suburbs. Ludwik knew refugees created problems. They would hinder movement on the roads. Definitely slow the convoy down. Make it an easy target. And if the refugees reached the ports ahead of the convoy, the congestion on the docks would cause delays in boarding and again create easy targets for the Luftwaffe. In addition to the congestion problems, it was going to be difficult not to help them; especially if children were involved. They were fleeing for their lives; just like he was.

Everyone was anxious for nightfall. Many were upset by the wait. Ludwik wasn't. He had seen firsthand what the Luftwaffe could do on a crowded, open road during the day. It was safer to travel at night. There were other matters that worried Ludwik.

He realized he would not have the freedom to move as he pleased like he had done with Josef in the Volvo. He also didn't care for his orders concerning truck breakdowns. It was one thing to be left behind to fix a problem; it was another thing to have enough time to do it. Better to just leave it.

Operation Ariel

During the last briefing before they left, it was revealed that thousands of English troops, surrounded by the Germans, had been successfully taken off the beaches at Dunkirk and transported across the English Channel to safety. It was also revealed that ships had set sail from England and would be waiting for them at ports on the French Atlantic coast. Scouts on motorcycles led the way as the convoy crept off into the night and onto a country road that would take them around a blacked-out Lyon. They would be the eyes and ears of the convoy and would report by messenger if the road ahead held any danger. Only a few, well-spaced lights could be seen off in the distance. Farmers, Ludwik surmised. Thinking they were safe from an air raid. Not realizing that being careless with lights could mean a quick death.

The Luftwaffe had returned with smaller numbers twice to destroy any planes on the base they had missed. Fortunately, none of the planes that had been sent to secondary fields had returned to the base. They were now being used to support French ground troops successfully repelling a failed invasion by Mussolini through the mountain passes bordering Italy and France. Ludwik had no respect for the Italians. They had waited until their prey was wounded before they got into the fight. He couldn't stomach that kind of cowardice. They wanted no part of a fair fight. They just wanted to walk in and pick up the pieces. Impress Hitler. The French pilots and soldiers were making sure they didn't get that opportunity. They had stymied the Italians at the border. Ludwik was thankful for that.

The trip to the Atlantic coast would be dangerous enough if the Luftwaffe decided to start hunting for them; they didn't need the Italians breaking through and cutting them off from the coast. Ludwik remembered what had happened in Poland after the Russians got involved. How perilous it was being caught in the middle between them in the east and the Germans advancing from the west. The Italians would have made it very difficult for them here in France if they were successful in their southern invasion.

Sitting quietly in the cab of the light truck, both feet on the suitcase that held his worldly possessions, Ludwik tried to relax. His backpack jostled from side to side on his lap as the truck slowly bumped its way along the uneven, dirt road. He focused his eyes on the dim, bouncing taillights of the crammed truck some twenty yards ahead of them. He thought about his friend, Pelcz, sent off into battle up north and the friendly French customs agent, Claude Moreau, who had saved him and Josef from freezing to death that frigid, winter night in Modane. He wondered how they were faring; if Pelcz was facing tanks once again and if Moreau was at home and out of danger from the fighting on the Italian French border.

Before long, the convoy moved off the dirt road and onto a wide, paved highway that led to Clermont-Ferrand some eighty miles away. Convoy speed was increased to forty miles an hour. That would get them clear of Clermont-Ferrand a little after midnight. They were to rendezvous with the second convoy in a forest some ten miles west of the city. All men would offload and sleep for a few hours there. Before dawn, they would be on their way again. The password for the night and the rest of the trip was "ARIEL." It wasn't a Polish word. Some officer from Command had linked it to the code name of the evacuation which was "Operation Ariel." One of Ludwik's fellow pilots said the word was from a play written by Shakespeare. Ludwik had never heard the word before but would make sure all his mechanics on the truck knew it before they reached the forest.

More than a few people had lost their lives at night because they had forgotten a password.

Ten miles outside of Clermont-Ferrand, the convoy stopped. All drivers let their engines idle. Ludwik tried to continue his nap. The driver's attempt at conversation made that impossible. Ludwik just sat there in the dark and listened to the young man lament the fact that he had been forced to leave, in his opinion, the most beautiful girl in Lyon. And he was worried that somebody else, at this very moment, was enjoying the girl's considerable ability. Ludwik told the young man to pray hard to God that it wasn't happening. And do it in reverential silence. The driver got the message. He sat back, lit a cigarette and fantasized making love with his French beauty. Ludwik enjoyed the respite and tried, unsuccessfully, to nap.

The smell of the driver's French cigarette was sweet. Enjoyable. A little intoxicating. He got out of the cab and lit one for himself. The murmur of men talking quietly in the back of the truck drifted out into the night. An occasional snore from someone lucky enough to sleep under the circumstances, brought on a quiet chorus of chuckles from the men. Ludwik smoked his cigarette slowly. He made sure to cup his hands around the burning tip to cover the bright glow it made when he inhaled. Without thinking, the survival training portion of learning how to survive undetected as a downed pilot in enemy territory had kicked in. "Good training," he thought just before crushing out the remaining inch of the cigarette. Then he heard the motorcycle and saw the bouncing beam of its headlight approaching the truck.

"Here comes trouble," Ludwik's driver said.

The motorcyclist stopped next to the truck and yelled at the driver, "I need Skoczylas. They want him up front."

"I'm here," Ludwik said as he walked around the front of the truck.

Ludwik got the story from the motorcyclist as they wound their way back to the front of the convoy. Something had happened to one of the lead trucks. Ludwik was needed to assess the situation and determine if it was worthwhile to spend the time fixing what needed to be fixed.

The captain heading the convoy was standing in the field just off the side of the road next to the disabled truck. As soon as Ludwik got out of the sidecar, the captain yelled to someone to get the order out to "mount up" and "move out." He welcomed Ludwik by reminding him that every truck was needed in the evacuation and to see what he could do. He said to get the men and equipment he needed from the truck he had come from. If they fixed the truck, they should use it for themselves. If they couldn't, they should wait for the next convoy and hitch a ride. Ludwik didn't care for the idea. He was being asked to identify and repair an automotive problem in the middle of the night. And there was no guarantee the next convoy from Lyon would not get lost and go a different way. Still, he did what he was ordered to do. He had the driver of the disabled truck bring him the truck's tool kit. He hoped by the time his truck got to them, he might be able to identify the problem.

While he inventoried the tool kit, one truck after another stopped to pick up men from the disabled truck. They had to stand on the running boards on each side of the cab and hang on to the doors. It was going to be a long and rough ride for them.

The disabled truck had slid sideways down into a depression in the field. It sat leaning dangerously toward its downside. It was going to be difficult opening the hood without tipping the truck over. He realized the lower side would have to be jacked up so he could stand safely on the front bumper, open the hood and get a look at the engine. He tried to look under the cab with the flashlight from the tool kit, but its beam wasn't strong enough to penetrate the thick grass that had been rolled up like a rug underneath when the truck slid down into the field. He was going to need at least two jacks and something solid to place them on to lift the truck up level enough to get a view of both the engine and what might be under it.

The driver, a sergeant, explained to him what had happened. He described losing power on the road and hearing a loud scraping noise followed by a sudden lurching, almost hopping, of the truck off the road and sliding down into the field. After the truck came to a stop and tilted to the field side, he put the transmission into low gear and tried to drive back onto the road. But no matter how easy or hard he pressed the accelerator, the truck wouldn't budge. Its engine just roared like it was stuck in neutral. His description reminded Ludwik of an experience he and a friend had one evening outside of Deblin. They had driven into a muddy field by mistake trying to find a secluded spot to snuggle with their lady friends. They got stuck and no matter what they did, they couldn't get the car going. All they got was a roaring engine and no movement; very similar to what the driver had just described. They found out later the driveshaft on the car had broken off.

A truck stopped to pick up the remaining three airmen from the disabled truck and quickly moved ahead to catch the convoy. Ludwik watched them disappear into the night. His truck was nowhere in sight. He lay down on the sweet- smelling grass in the field and waited for the truck to arrive. He looked up at the beautiful show of stars overhead. The sight took him back home to the many times he had spent outside on a night just like this. Lying in a field and admiring the very same alignment of stars he saw here.

"I see them," the sergeant said. Ludwik got up and spotted the truck. It was moving a little faster than convoy speed. Its headlights were on. He wondered why it was so far behind the other trucks that had already passed. He picked up the faint parking lights of two other

510

trucks behind the lead truck. All three seemed to have the proper convoy spacing. It was a mini convoy. He told the driver to take the flashlight and get up on the road to let them know where we were. Just as the sergeant started up toward the road, the single headlight of a vehicle appeared far off in the distance coming fast in the opposite direction. As it quickly closed the gap between them, the distinctive tell-tale hum of a motorcycle gearing down, let them know some news was about to arrive. A lieutenant in the motorcycle side car jumped out and told his driver to turn off the headlight and wait for him there. He told Ludwik the truck with the mechanics had been moved to last in the convoy and fitted with a trailer loaded with an assortment of tools, transmission fluids and motor oil just in case they were needed. That had caused the short delay of the three remaining trucks. He said any men and the equipment needed had to be unloaded as quickly as possible. He gave Ludwik a map that outlined the route the two convoys were to take to the Atlantic coast and circled the rendezvous point in the large forest ten miles west of Clermont-Ferrand. He said if for some reason, the second convoy didn't make it to here, or the rendezvous point before the first convoy left, scouts would be sent to look for them. He said to make sure they went to Perigueux, then on to Bordeaux and follow the coast road south checking all ports for ships; the last port being at St. Jean de Luz.

"And if the truck cannot be repaired?" Ludwik asked.

"Wait for the next convoy. They will probably come this way."

"Probably?" asked Ludwik.

"And where are the Germans?" the sergeant asked the lieutenant.

Ignoring the question, the officer asked the sergeant to remove anything in the cab that might identify the unit they were part of and where they had come from.

"I can't get in the cab," the sergeant said.

"Then see if anything of value is around the vehicle," the lieutenant ordered.

The sergeant shook his head and walked slowly down the grassy slope to the truck. Ludwik waited until he was far enough away from them.

"So, where are the Germans?" Ludwik asked.

"They are close and headed this way," the lieutenant answered.

"Why didn't you tell the sergeant that?"

"That information could cause a panic."

"We are getting to be experts in the art of retreating and not panicking," Ludwik said.

"We are also experts in fighting the bastards in the air. We will prove that once we get to England," the lieutenant responded.

"If the English give us the chance," Ludwik muttered. "They may be our last hope."

The lieutenant thought for a moment and said, "Yes. England. The island of last hope. Let's pray they like to fight."

A minute after the lieutenant left, the lead truck pulled up. The headlights were turned off. Before Ludwik asked for volunteers, he made sure everyone in the truck knew there was a risk that anyone left behind might not make it to the coast. Despite the warning, everyone stood up when he asked for volunteers. He took the first two men seated on each side. When the jacks, shovels, saws, hammers and crowbar had been brought out from the equipment trailer, Ludwik told two of the men he knew to be excellent

512

mechanics to stay. He thanked the other two men and put them back on the truck. As the truck pulled away, someone in the back yelled, "See you in England!"

"See you in England," one of the two mechanics echoed as he watched the three trucks roll away.

The ground under the downside of the truck was soft with one small exception. Halfway down the carriage was a firm patch of soil. Ludwik thought it might keep a jack in place. One of the mechanics agreed and suggested jacking the truck up there just enough to keep the vehicle from rolling over onto its side. Ludwik agreed. As soon as the jack was in place, Ludwik and one of the mechanics went to the other side of the truck and leaned against it with their hands to see how stable the truck was. It wasn't that stable. Ludwik decided one man should get in the back and carefully rip out the first section of seats with the crowbar. The lightest man volunteered. He climbed into the back, lay a lit flashlight on the floor, and took apart the back section of the bench on the high side of the truck. It took ten minutes. Once it was outside, one of the other men sawed the section in half. One half was put under the carriage in front of the rear wheel on the downside, and the other half was placed under the cab behind the back wheel of the truck on the same side. In minutes, the jacked truck was level and stable. Ludwik stood on the front bumper and opened the hood. He scanned the engine carefully with the flashlight for any sign that would indicate a reason for failure. There were none. All wires and hoses were in place. There wasn't any fresh stains of oil or other fluids on the engine. He had each of the mechanics take a look to confirm what he had seen. They both agreed the problem wasn't with the engine. Then Ludwik decided to look at the driveshaft. It took a few minutes to cut back the high grass that obscured what was under the engine. It only took a few seconds to see that Ludwik's suspicion about the driveshaft was correct. It lay disconnected at the front end with the coupling missing.

The sergeant shook his head and said, "That's the reason the truck is in the field. The drive shaft must have caught on something when it dropped off and caused the truck to hop off the road and slide down into the field."

"Hard to believe," one of the mechanics said.

"Whatever. We're not fixing this vehicle," Ludwik said.

"What's the plan?" the mechanic asked.

"We wait for the next convoy," Ludwik answered.

"How much farther to the rendezvous?" the sergeant asked Ludwik.

"Ten miles to Clermont–Ferrand and another ten to the forest west of the city."

All four agreed to rest in the field away from the truck; maybe even catch a little sleep. Ludwik said he would take the first half-hour watch while the other three rested. The sergeant was the third man on watch and nearing the end of it when he saw the approaching lights. They were far away. He yelled for everyone to get up. Ludwik thought it was about time they got here. He put his backpack on, picked up his suitcase and walked toward the pile of tools they had left near the truck. That's when he felt the trembling. His heart sank. He knew trucks would not create that kind of vibration. There was only one kind of vehicle that could. And it wouldn't be driven by a Polish airman.

"How come they all have their lights on?" one of the mechanics asked.

"Because they are German tanks," Ludwik answered. "Leave the equipment. Keep your packs and whatever you have and follow me."

He turned and began to run through the field away from the road and disabled truck. The ground was really shaking now. The tank column was closing. Ludwik knew there would probably be a command car and some scouts in front of the tanks. He hoped they would not pay attention to the truck. One man passed him and headed for some waist high grass. Ludwik yelled for him not to go in there. He knew if the Germans got interested in the area around the truck and saw the tools and jacks, they might deduce that someone had been working on the vehicle and were still in the area. He did not want to leave a trail of bent grass for them to follow and find them. He saw the stone wall at the end of the field and thanked God for his gift of seeing in the dark. He made for it as fast as he could. The others were right behind him. They heard the tanks stop and saw the search light off to the right beginning to sweep the field in their direction. It would be on them in seconds. Ludwik dove over the low stone wall and lay still behind it. The others piled over and did the same. They waited, heads down, and prayed. The searchlight swept overhead and kept going. It stopped on a small patch of trees a hundred yards away. Like an owl screeching in the night to startle prey into movement, the beam of light flicked off and on among the trees. The Germans were hunting. After a time, the searchlight slowly began making its way back across the field. It stopped along the stone wall in places, searching for any movement, anything out of the ordinary. Then it went out. Ludwik peeked over the wall and watched helmeted men leave the abandoned Renault and return to a truck. They were carrying the tools and jacks that had been left there. He watched them load everything onto the truck and climb aboard. He ducked down as the night suddenly came alive with lights and roaring engines. Searchlights sent beams of light into the fields and up into the sky. It was if they were sending a message to anyone who might be out there hiding; "We are here and have nothing to fear. Listen to our engines and tremble as does the earth around you and see how we light up the sky."

Small stones tumbled from the top of the wall onto their heads and bodies as the ground shook from the departing tanks. Ludwik thought if the Germans intended to make an impression with the noise and light displays, they had succeeded famously. He wondered if this confident show of arrogance and lack of fear meant that a surrender had already occurred. He figured there were now around two hundred men between them and Clermont-Ferrand. All armed and lethal. They had four pistols and maybe a knife or two between them. They would have no chance against the Germans. All contact had to be avoided.

He waited until the last German vehicle was gone and silence had returned to the night before asking, "Who's the one that said, I'll see you in England?" One of the men said it was he. Ludwik got to his feet and said to him, "Then let's get on with it, shall we?"

There was no question as to who was going to lead. Ludwik was an officer and the only one that had extensive experience traveling overland on foot. Everyone at the airbase had heard of the long trek across southern Europe by him and Josef. Their story was legendary.

Before making any decisions, Ludwik said he was open to suggestions from any of the three; anytime, anywhere. The sergeant said they were ready to follow him. He asked what the plan was. Ludwik said the first thing was to get away from the main road here. It stood to reason that if more Germans were coming, they would probably be using the same road. He stressed it was critical not to be seen or heard.

The fields on the other side of the road stretched out for some distance. The four men jogged across them at a steady pace until they reached a shallow stream. It was a challenging run for Ludwik. He was hampered by the heavy suitcase he was carrying. It was stuffed full of clothes, blankets and shoes.

They filled their canteens in the stream then crossed the knee-deep water and headed for the woods on the other side. Once there, Ludwik pulled out his rain poncho, map and flashlight from his backpack. He spread out the poncho and crawled under it to hide the light of the flashlight while he checked the map for clues as to how they might travel. He wanted to avoid the city of Clermont-Ferrand. He felt there was a good chance that was where the Germans were going. He decided to take the men south of the city, stay in the countryside and work their way to the rendezvous point in the forest. They had about four hours of darkness to use as cover. He figured they could make ten miles before dawn and that would put them somewhere close to the rendezvous point. It was not likely their convoy would still be there, but there was a chance the second convoy might. Corporal Mazlanka, one of the mechanics, said he doubted they could cover ten miles in the dark walking through unfamiliar country and not be noticed. Ludwik said they would do what they could. He said they had about a mile more of crossing these fields before they reached the town of Lezoux. From there, they could use a country road that went southwest to St. Bonnet-les Allier, a village not too far from the rendezvous forest. Once they got into the forest, they would have plenty of cover. If the convoy was gone, they could either rest there or make the two-mile trek through the forest to the village of Orset. Two more miles after that would get them to the main highway that led to Perigueux and eventually Bordeaux, their destination. Somewhere along that highway, they would have to find transportation to take them the final one hundred and thirty miles.

"It's not going to be easy," Ludwik warned.

Mazlanka and Private Zablanski, the other mechanic, nodded their heads in agreement.

"I should have put a little more effort into the physical training they gave us on the base," Zablanski said.

"They should have just left the truck there," Mazlanka grumbled.

"We need to keep our talking to a minimum the rest of the night," Ludwik ordered. He explained the three hand signals he would use on their trip; fist raised, stop, get down. Hand waved forward, get up and continue. Arm pointed left or right, go that way and find cover fast. Ludwik took the point. He had the eyes. Zablanski and Mazlanka, the two mechanics, followed. Sergeant Hoydra was the trailer.

Lezoux was a small town. There was no blackout. A few buildings along the streets still had lights on inside. Careless civilians begging for trouble. The four of them kept to the rear of the buildings as much as they could. They moved quickly from one shadow to the next. They saw no one. Only an occasional dog's bark gave evidence of their passing. In twenty minutes, they were through the town undetected and onto a narrow, country road that headed southwest toward the rendezvous forest. Ludwik immediately quickened the pace on the dirt road. He was hoping one or both of the convoys was still in the forest, maybe hiding from the German tank force. Whatever the case, he knew it was best they be in the forest as soon as they could. In less than an hour, they were in Vertaizon. They went through the tiny village without a sound. The next three miles took them by several farms. Each one welcomed them and said goodbye with the gift of silence.

The route Ludwik had chosen was going to put them on a major roadway soon. They would be on it for two miles before turning east on a road that led to the rendezvous forest. From there, they would be able to access the roadway their convoy was supposed to use. The plan was to use that same road into the forest and see what was there.

He had a few questions to consider. Had the Germans been pursuing his convoy? And if they had, had they caught them? If not, were they still in pursuit? And maybe the Germans were not aware of the convoy and were just headed for Clermont-Ferrand. If that was the case, the convoy would be safe in the forest now and leaving for the coast in a few hours with the second convoy. He wondered about the second convoy and if they had avoided trouble with that column of German tanks. He would know when they reached the forest.

Dawn found the four approaching the small village of Le Crest. The village was spread out at the base of a hill just off the road they were on. High above the village was an old, partially walled-off chateau that looked down into the village. Vineyards, separated by a road that curved its way up to the chateau, covered the hill on both sides of it. The rendezvous forest was no more than two hours away.

Someone in the bell tower of the lone church began ringing its bell. Their presence had been detected. There was no place to run so they didn't. They kept walking toward the village. A group of men and boys began gathering in front of the church. They stood there and watched them approach. A small boy left the group and ran into the church. He returned with a priest.

Le Crest was like countless other villages throughout this region of France. It depended on wine making for its income. The men assembled in front of the church were the farmers and workers that lived in the village and walked out into the vineyards to do their work every morning. This morning had started out differently. Four strangers, dressed in unfamiliar uniforms, were approaching their village. They didn't look armed, but why were they here?

Ludwik saw the priest emerge from the church and begin walking up the road toward them. They stopped and waited for him.

"Bonjour," the priest said enthusiastically.

"Bonjour," answered Ludwik politely. "Nous sommes Polonaise."

The priest smiled broadly. He turned to the crowd anxiously waiting for answers. "Polonaise! Nos amis," he shouted. That was greeted with a cheer from the group. They ran up to the priest and their new "friends." Each of them welcomed Ludwik and the other three with a "Bienvenue, mon ami," and a handshake. Ludwik thanked them with a, "Merci, mon ami." The exchange was simple. Basic but meaningful. It was appreciated by the airmen.

Sergeant Hoydra mentioned it might be good to eat in the village. They hadn't eaten since their supper at Lyon-Bron yesterday and they did not carry any food with them. One of the things they had left in the field next to the disabled truck was the case of rations that had been left for them by the convoy. Ludwik agreed. He knew his convoy must have moved on; with or without the second convoy.

The priest brought them to an inn and had them wait on the porch while he woke up the owner who was also the cook. The man wasn't happy but changed his mind when he saw the four strangers counting their francs; just like the priest had suggested they do to motivate him.

Boiled eggs, sausage, bread and steaming, black coffee energized the four. Ludwik and the sergeant lit up a cigarette and waited on the porch for the two mechanics to finish an extended breakfast. It was a warm, early summer morning. The village had come to life. Women came to draw water from the well in the dirt plaza before them. They glanced nervously at the strangers on the porch and whispered to each other about them. A young boy chased a puppy around the plaza and two little girls giggled as they played with each other's pigtails.

"Been a while since I've been in a place like this," the sergeant observed.

Ludwik didn't answer. He was home in Poland, brothers and sisters at play in the village square. Sunday after church. Men sharing a drink and arguing. Women watching their children and sharing some gossip.

The ringing of the bell was loud. It sounded urgent. Someone else was headed their way! Someone that the person up in the bell tower didn't recognize and was alerting the village.

"There," said Sergeant Hoydra, pointing down the road on the other side of the village. Motorcycles! Two of them.

"Let's get inside," Ludwik calmly said.

Inside the inn, Ludwik opened his backpack and took out the binoculars. He went to a window and focused on the approaching motorcyclists. He watched them stop. Both men dismounted. One of them was looking at the village with his binoculars. Ludwik laughed with relief. He stepped out of the inn and walked to the middle of the plaza. He waved to the two Poles sitting out there on the road. The one with the binoculars waved back. Ludwik motioned for them to come in. Then he shouted for the others. They were the only people in the plaza when the two scouts arrived. The women had run off with the children at the first sound of the bell. The owner of the inn had locked the door behind his guests as soon as the last one left. The priest was the only villager still outside.

The motorcyclists were scouts; part of an Army/Air Force convoy that had come from one of the secondary airfields south of Lyon. They had taken almost the same route Ludwik had walked last night. One of the scouts said that France was about to surrender. All resistance by the French was ending. He said the French and Germans had agreed to an armistice. It was going to go into effect tomorrow. He wasn't sure how long it was going to last, what the terms were or how it was going to affect foreign troops like them.

521

The two scouts left to make their report on Le Crest. It was simple and to the point.

1. No Germans in the village. Clear sailing.
2. Four Polish airmen having breakfast at the local inn. Request transportation be sent for them to join the convoy.

Four motorcycles with side cars roared into the village a half hour later. Ludwik, Sergeant Hoydra, and the two mechanics each squeezed into a sidecar, their back packs secure on the floor between their legs. Ludwik was the only one that had a suitcase. His driver hinted it might be a good idea to leave it so they could have a safer trip. Ludwik would have none of that. He had enough clothes in it to cover a week's worth of wear. He was determined to keep them.

There wasn't much room in any of the trucks parked under the shade of the trees next to the road. The convoy's commander, a Captain Slisz, offered Ludwik a seat next to him in the cab of his truck. The other three men were offered a choice between a sidecar and a standing room only spot on one of the trucks. They all chose a sidecar.

Ludwik was concerned about the convoy making its way across open country in daylight. Easy targets for the Luftwaffe. Captain Slisz said it was imperative they get to the coast as soon as possible. He didn't want be left stranded in France and at the mercy of the Germans. He said Command in London had made the determination that the Germans, on the last day of fighting, which was today, would be keeping most of their planes in the areas being contested. At least that was what they were hoping. Slisz also said there were Germans in Clermont-Ferrand, only ten miles away. He wanted to put as much distance between them and the convoy as he could. None of the Poles knew what the armistice meant for them. All they knew was not to surrender and get to the coast for evacuation.

Slisz said he had been warned that French authorities, local gendarmes and the sort, might be ordered to stop any Poles, Czechs, English or even their own French forces and civilians from trying to escape. He said the fear was the Germans would soon send forces to all ports along the coast of France to stop evacuation attempts. He was concerned that the tank force in Clermont-Ferrand might be one of many sent to block the run to the ocean. They had to make it to the coast and get out of the country before the Germans got there. He said the armistice might last for only a few days and that would mean trouble for anyone that had not officially surrendered.

Command had been right. Not one German plane appeared on their trip to Bordeaux. The only problem they encountered were the hordes of refugees on the road. They numbered in the thousands. The ones walking, riding bikes or on carts drawn by horses, were easy to move off the road and out of the way. It was the cars, buses and trucks that slowed them down. When they stopped, the convoy stopped. And that was problematic. For everyone. Civilian and military. Ludwik remembered how the Germans had slaughtered helpless men, women and children on the country roads and in the fields of Poland, how that 109 pilot had tried to kill the woman and her sheep in the meadow and how their pilots had even machine-gunned Polish airmen parachuting to earth. He knew there were no limits to their mayhem. He had heard stories of that sort of thing in France. He knew French civilians had died on roads like this. And armistice or not, civilian refugees, as well as troop carrying trucks, might be fair game for the Luftwaffe once they spotted the convoy.

It took the convoy most of the day to travel the one hundred and thirty miles to Bordeaux. When they reached the docks, they were met by hundreds of other Polish airmen. They were the leftovers from a large force that had boarded two ships earlier in the day and had been told to wait for other ships that were on their way. They were expected to arrive tomorrow or the next day.

Ludwik wasn't invited to the meeting held by the officers in the convoy. The decision was made by them to stay the night in Bordeaux and wait with the others for the arrival of a ship; hopefully sometime tomorrow. That all changed when a lone German reconnaissance plane appeared and made several passes over the docks before departing. Their presence in Bordeaux was now known to the Germans. And that meant an attack might be forthcoming. Maybe even today.

Everyone from the group that had been left on the docks earlier was immediately ordered back into their trucks and driven away from the docks. They were to reassemble in a large park outside the city that afforded them some cover. It was close enough to the docks to return everyone quickly and board any ship that came for them. Scouts were sent out along the roads leading into Bordeaux. Their job was to set up observation and listening posts to warn the Poles in the city of any advance by the Germans. The officers in Ludwik's convoy changed their minds about staying overnight in Bordeaux. Captain Slisz advised Ludwik and his three men they were free to stay or join them. Ludwik didn't want to be caught on the docks in an air raid. He and his men chose to stay with Slisz and go down the coast to other ports in the hope of finding a ship in one of them ready to board troops.

No one knew for sure how many ships were involved in Operation Ariel. It was said to be many. And not just from England. Ludwik wondered if some of the ships might begin their pickups from the southern-most ports first. A check of his map showed the southern-most port to be St. Jean de Luz, only a few miles from the Spanish border. The convoy made good time. The number of refugees moving toward the coast diminished considerably the farther south they went. There was no German activity in the sky. It began to feel like a trip to the beaches along the Baltic Sea back home in Poland; a sunny holiday with friends and family.

They passed one sparkling, sandy beach after another. Sometimes the road wound its way along high cliffs that provided spectacular views of the blue Atlantic, the white beaches and the multi-colored rooftops of quaint French villages nestled just off the beaches.

Word came via radio from the Poles that had retreated to the park in Bordeaux that German dive bombers had arrived and were attacking the docks. While that was disturbing news, it underscored the decision to leave and go south had been a wise one.

The port of St. Nazaire was empty. Not even a fishing boat anchored in the bay. Bayonne had several fishing boats tied to the docks. Nothing out in the bay. Two Polish officers that spoke French went into each port to find out if any ships had been there or were expected in the next few days. The story was the same in both places. Ships had been there. They had taken large numbers of French and Polish troops out to sea. They were supposed to return to both ports as soon as they could. One fisherman said he had seen two great passenger ships filled with men sailing north past Bayonne a day ago. If that was true, then those two ships wouldn't make it back for at least a week. Probably too late to help. Their last hope lay at the port of St. Jean de Luz.

Bednarz

Bednarz and Ludwik shook hands for the last time in Campo Casale. The doctor had spent the better part of two days listening to Ludwik's story of his long odyssey from Poland to France and eventually, England. He had written hundreds of notes and added them to Ludwik's file with the promise of giving him the note-filled file that included his comments. He would send Ludwik the file before he left with the suggestion that he use it for referential consideration by a professional psychiatrist if the need for one arose in the future. It wasn't much, but it was the best he could do.

525

Ludwik was leaving Campo Casale in two days. Special Duties Flight 1586 had been disbanded and was now part of Squadron 301 Transportation. He was going to fly an American-made Dakota C-3 to a base in Morocco and pickup Polish airmen who were going "home" to England. Bednarz hoped Ludwik would be able to shake off the disappointment of being let down by the Allies. Most Poles, himself included, would not be going home to a Poland that had been given to the Russians by them. They would have to find a new home.

Standing at the window in the library, Bednarz watched Ludwik slowly make his way across the field to the airstrip. An interesting individual, he thought. Intelligent. Boundless ability and promise. Unusual spirituality. He would have liked to discuss more of this business with the man's stated belief that the Blessed Lady had actually helped him in his journey through the war. But time and his personal loss of faith had made it impossible for him to attempt it. He had felt it best to let it go. He stayed in the library, took out his pipe, and filled it with sweet Jamaican tobacco. In minutes, the air was filled with its pleasant aroma. He relaxed. He would finish his work on Ludwik's file here.

France, the Final Days

He opened his notebook to go over the final list of notes that covered Ludwik's last few days in France. The wait at St. Jean de Luz must have been very nerve-wracking. So close to freedom yet so close to captivity or worse. A race against time. An excruciating wait. Waiting for a ship to arrive. Then waiting for the ship to board everyone and hoist anchor. Three days of waiting that were filled with anxiety, fear and frustration. Learning the Germans were coming for them. Waiting for their bombers to arrive. It had to be frightful. He knew Ludwik would never have surrendered. He would have died first.

Ludwik had said their options were poor if they were forced to flee the port. Going across the border into Spain, a few miles away, was out of the question. Internment there meant being imprisoned in a jail system known for its cruel treatment of prisoners. Switzerland was a possibility, but it was too far away. Joining the French resistance was a consideration. Some Poles had already done that, but he felt he needed to be in a plane to do what he was trained to do.

Ludwik's convoy had arrived in St. Jean de Luz on the first day of the armistice. Reports had the Germans standing down during the length of the armistice said to be three days. Ludwik said that news had been well received. And then even better news had followed. The Arandora Star, a large ocean liner, was expected to make port in St. Jean de Luz sometime the next day.

Later that afternoon, scouts returned to the convoy with reports that the German army was far away and the tank force that had passed Ludwik and the disabled truck that first night close to Clermont-Ferrand, had left that city and was headed back east towards Paris. Away from the coast. It was estimated it would take two or three days for any German ground force to reach St. Jean de Luz once the armistice ended. That news produced an immediate sense of relief to the thousand or so men waiting for the arrival of their "freedom" ship. Ludwik said that relief began to wane during the second day. The only thing that showed up at St. Jean de Luz besides thousands of more Polish airmen was a German recon plane. Just like the one that had flown over Bordeaux. And Bordeaux had been attacked by dive bombers later in the day. Everyone was put on high alert. All personnel were withdrawn from the dock area. They were met by more arriving Poles. The number of men looking to escape had grown close to five thousand. They were dispersed into the village and up into the hills that overlooked the port. Scouts were sent out again to watch the roads for Germans.

As the day progressed, the weather took an unfavorable turn. A strong wind blew in over the water. The ocean began to roll. White caps covered its surface far out into the bay. The sky went dark. Torrential rain began pummeling the village. The storm had come out of nowhere. It was huge. That's when the Arandora Star appeared. The two stack, luxury liner stopped and dropped anchor on the ocean side of the long stretch of sandbar shallows that guarded the entrance to the port. Her captain evidently realized that any attempt to enter the bay in a turbulent sea might result in the ship running aground on the sandbar and rendering itself useless and at the same time making it an easy target for dive bombers once the storm blew over.

Ludwik said it had been frustrating. The ship had arrived but couldn't enter the bay. Thousands of men sat and looked out through the rain at their "escape" anchored far from shore. No one seemed to know what to do. Eventually, someone, either a Pole or one of the natives, came up with the idea of hiring all the small fishing boats in the bay to ferry men out to the ship. With their shallow draft, the small boats would be able to cross the sandbar line and reach the huge luxury liner. Within an hour, the docks were filled with Polish airmen anxiously waiting in a steady rain to board one of the fishing boats lining up in the bay for them. As the first boat approached the docks, three police cars streamed out of the village, sirens wailing. They pulled up to the dock entrance. Six gendarmes stepped out of the cars and demanded to know what was going on. When they learned an evacuation of the Poles was about to begin, they became upset and ordered it to stop. They said under the agreement of the armistice, they had the legal right and duty to arrest all foreigners attempting to leave France. That shocked the Poles and most of the locals that had come to their aid. One of them, a village leader, came out of a crowd of airmen waiting on the dock and spoke to the gendarmes.

He said a business arrangement had been made to get these men out to the ship and the village stood to make a great deal of money. He said he would be able to arrange a little money for them if they looked the other way. And if they didn't, they would be facing some thousands of very angry, armed Poles.

After a short conference between themselves, the gendarmes agreed to accept the money offer and leave. They did have one condition; if the Germans approached the village before the ship left, they would have to return and impose their authority on the Poles still on the docks. If they didn't, they would be in serious trouble themselves.

Ludwik found the whole situation incredibly disgusting. Not only had the French government quit on their country in a relativity short period of time, but they had also agreed to help the Germans against their former allies. It was unbelievable! He remembered thinking how ironic it would be that he had spent nearly a year of his life getting to France to fight the Germans only to be turned over to the Germans by the French government.

Bednarz puffed a small wisp of smoke out into the library air. He tried to imagine waiting days to escape with your means of escape sitting in your view and not being able to get to it. And not knowing how much time for sure they had before the enemy arrived. Wondering if your turn would come to board before they arrived. Ludwik had said only a third of the men made it out to the ship before nightfall that first day. He hadn't been one of them. Not even close. He spent that night sleeping in the cab of a truck parked feet away from the dock. He said the storm worsened during the night and made the ferrying of men out to the ship very difficult the next day. By the end of that day, only half of the men were on board. Again, he wasn't among them. After eating that night, he walked the streets alone until he found the local church.

He spent hours praying the rosary and asking Mary to end the storm. Then he stretched out on a pew and slept there the rest of the night.

Dawn arrived on the third day carrying an overcast sky and a calm sea. The Arandora Star moved slowly and safely over the shallows assisted alongside by two tugboats. Ludwik said he anxiously watched the luxury liner make its way toward him. There were more than a thousand men waiting, most of them behind him. Space aboard ship had become a problem. More than four thousand men were already on board. An order came to leave all luggage. No space for it aboard ship. Backpacks were allowed. He said the scouts were the last ones to board. They clambered up the gang plank with news that the Germans were closing and only hours away. That spurred the ship's crew into getting underway. Within minutes, it was steaming out to the open sea and heading for the cover of a large fog bank that had suddenly materialized. The ship slipped quickly into the fog and disappeared. Perfect cover! Less than an hour later, the unmistakable drone of bombers above the fog filtered down to the crammed men on deck. Ludwik said he heard many of the men say how lucky they were that the storm had ended, and the fog had appeared. Ludwik said he didn't believe it was all luck that saved the ship. He was convinced the fog that had suddenly appeared was an answer to the rosary he had said along with the thousands of prayers that he knew were being said by the other men waiting to be evacuated. He believed the Blessed Lady had heard them. That belief was bolstered by an English-speaking Polish officer who had overheard a conversation by some crewmen saying they had never seen a fog appear so suddenly.

Bednarz felt that Ludwik almost had him on the cusp of actually considering that the mother of Christ may have indeed intervened on his behalf more than a few times on his odyssey from Poland to England. Especially with that story of the fog coming out of nowhere and saving the five thousand men on the Arandora Star.

530

He had to admit the fog appearing so suddenly like that would undoubtedly reinforce a man's faith in the power of prayer. He shook his head and sat back in the chair. He stared at the handcrafted bookcase in front of him. He remembered Ludwik's account of standing before it admiring its woodwork and how he had turned to see a young woman passing by the doorway in the corridor. Now, here he was in the same place. He was almost afraid to turn and look at the doorway; half believing she might be there. When he did look, he saw no one. He waited. Nothing happened. He smiled to himself. Of course, nothing happened. Not to a man of science. Maybe to a man that possessed a vivid imagination. Or maybe to a man that possessed a phenomenal amount of faith. Maybe to a man like Ludwik Skoczylas. He sighed, tamped down his pipe, gathered his notes and walked back to his office. He would finish Ludwik's file tonight. He began packing some of the files of the airmen he had seen over his time here in Italy. Most of them were gone. Ludwik would be gone in a few days. The base was to be turned over to an occupation force by the end of the month. Special Duties Flight 1586, now Transportation Squadron 301, had left Italy. Forever. And very soon, so would he.

Peace

It had been almost four months since the Liberator had crashed into the Adriatic. Hospital care, rest, physical therapy, medication, conferences with Bednarz, letters from home and prayers had worked well for Ludwik. The physical ailments had almost all disappeared, and his nightmares had become less and less intensive. He slept enough now. The war had ended, and he was going home. Much of his rest had come on the sandy beaches along the edge of the airstrip. He had spent countless hours relaxing in the sun and reading the almost daily letters he received from Nellie. He loved her letters. Especially the way she used words to paint pictures of their son, Kazimierz and the family in Carlisle. The letters were very encouraging. It helped to know they were well and waiting for him.

A great deal had happened during these last few months. Special Duties Flight 1586 had been disbanded. It had flown its last covert mission. A few of the 1586 crews had been sent to Africa. Others sent home to England. He had said goodbye to his crew a few days ago. Like him, they were now all members of Squadron 301 Transportation. They would all fly again but hopefully never in a combat situation. He had given each one his address in Carlisle and said they would always be welcome. There were only a few pilots left in Campo Casale. He was one of them. After tomorrow, he would be gone. His orders were to fly one of the American Douglas Dakotas across the Mediterranean to Blida, an air station in Algeria, stay overnight and fly some airmen and himself back to England the next morning. Blida was the very same station Josef had been transferred to from Lyon-Bron some five years ago. He had not heard much from his friend since then. He hoped that he was still alive and with the grace of God, he would see him again.

So many questions now. Questions that he had put aside for the most part while trying to stay alive. Now that the war was over, he had the time to ask. How serious had the tuberculosis been for Nellie? Was she fully recovered? How had his family in Poland managed during the war? Had Josef ever found his father? What about Basha, the love of his life for months in Hungary and her friend, Bella? How about Puskas, the jeweler, the undercover Polish agent in Budapest, Bishop DeMonte from Udine, Bodil Pastula and her flying family, Constantin Lupu and his man, Andrei, the Jewish families in Old Town Warsaw, the doctor and his family in Pulawy. What about this relationship with the Blessed Lady? She had saved him from the dark waters of the Adriatic as his plane sank toward the bottom. Of that, he was sure. What about the young woman he had seen twice on his escape from Poland and once here in Campo Casale?

532

Who was she? Was she really the Blessed Mother or a vision she had sent? Or were they three different women who looked alike? Of this, he wasn't that sure. He wanted them to be the Lady, but his need, bolstered by his faith, may have demanded he believe they were when they were not.

Questions about his family in England would be answered. Questions about his family in Poland would not. And then there were the questions about himself. Bednarz had warned him that life after war might have serious repercussions. That it might take time to acclimate to a world at peace. Bednarz had advised him not to dwell on the past but not be afraid of it. His past was to be owned. All of it. The good and the bad. He had to respect what it was. And learn from it. To try and make the world a better place for his family by being open to his experiences. Not to repress the madness he had witnessed and be man enough to recognize the need for help if it began to overpower him. He had promised Bednarz and himself, to do just that.

The twin engine Dakota roared down the corrugated runway toward the Adriatic. It was the second takeoff Ludwik had done with a Dakota since he had been cleared to fly. It was an easy lift off. The plane rose quickly over the sparkling, clear water. Ludwik leveled off at five thousand feet and began a slow turn to the south that would eventually put him on the westerly course he would follow across the boot of Italy. He took a last look out to his left as the plane flew over Campo Casale. He stared hard down at the water where his Liberator still sat submerged beyond the runway.

"Can you see it?" Sergeant Pilot Tysko asked.

"Only in my mind," Ludwik answered the young co-pilot.

"Think they'll ever pull it out?" Tysko gently prodded.

533

"I'm thinking it might belong there," Ludwik responded.

"How many of the crew were lost?"

"Three. Three good men."

Tysko recognized the emotion in Ludwik's quiet response. It was time to get busy with the charts and double check all the gages that sat in front of him.

Ludwik kept a comfortable hold on the controls. It was a beautiful day. In more ways than one. He was flying and on his way home. He appreciated that. Home. The place the three who had died in the crash would never see again. Edward Gagala, tail gunner, Stanislaw Slowik, radio operator, Witold Zurawska, navigator. Three young men. All in their middle twenties. "I am with you," Ludwik said quietly.

Tysko never took his eyes off the gauges. No need for questions. He understood who the words were meant for.

The flight from Campo Casale would take them over Naples, the southern tip of Sardinia and across the Mediterranean to Blida, Algeria. It was a four-hour flight. His orders were to refuel at the base, stay the night and fly out early in the morning with a full load of Polish airmen that had arrived a few days earlier from their base in Bari, Italy. After a final refueling, he would take himself, the crew and the thirty airmen from Bari, back to England.

It was almost five years since Ludwik had sailed on the Arandora Star out of France and gone to England for the first time. He hadn't any idea then what life was going to be like on the island most men aboard ship had called, "the island of last hope." The transition to the English ways and customs had been difficult in the early going.

As time went by however, England became a warm and welcome "Home away from home."

He thought about his first day there. It was on June 27, 1940. The day he and thousands of other Polish airmen and assorted refugees had walked down a gangplank onto an old, greasy, oil-stained dock in Liverpool. Besides the clothes he wore, he had nothing, but a backpack filled with socks, undergarments, a few cigarettes and items he always carried for survival. A band was playing the Polish national anthem. People were waving Polish flags and cheering as they marched proudly through the streets to trains waiting to transport them to their camp.

He remembered working a while helping to build barracks for German POWs captured in France. Then being sent to Blackpool to learn English culture and how to fly the English way in English planes. And after that, spending a fortuitous six weeks at Kingstown Aerodrome just north of Carlisle, a city close to the Scottish border. A city that happened to be the home of a young woman named Nellie Smith. Carlisle had been fortuitous indeed. For two reasons. First and foremost, he had found Nellie, the "love of his life" there. Second, he had been given six weeks to show he knew how to fly. And that had been easy because the plane they gave him to train on was a "Tiger Moth" biplane. Just like the one he flew in Poland.

He met Nellie and her friend, Jean, while on a walk in Carlisle with another pilot. She didn't like him at first. She told him that later. The walk along the river Eden that afternoon in 1940 helped to change the young lady's opinion of him. When he was sent to South Cerney to begin bomber pilot training, he found himself spending every weekend he could traveling the hundred miles to Carlisle to be with Nellie, the girl he had fallen in love with.

After completing his training on the small, three-man, Air Speed Oxford at South Cerney, he had been sent to Bramcote to learn how to pilot a Fairey-Battle bomber. He was riding a bike back to his barracks after completing a night training mission when he was hit and run over by a drunken driver. He suffered multiple injuries; the worst being to his face. He had to undergo an extensive series of reconstructive plastic surgery operations. That's when he learned Nellie loved him. She was at his side frequently at the hospital. When he was released, he was put on administrative duty until he was medically cleared to resume training. He had to travel to London every month and have adjustments made to his wired jaw. Nellie accompanied him on each visit. It was during that time he asked her to marry him. She had hesitated because she wasn't sure of herself. She said she loved him and wanted to marry him, but she didn't know how to be a good wife. Her parents felt the same about their young daughter but changed their minds when he convinced them how much he loved her. On September 5, 1942, with permission from Mr. and Mrs. Smith and the Polish command, they were married.

"Correct course 15 degrees west, cruising speed eight thousand feet," co-pilot Tysko recommended.

"Roger that," Ludwik responded. He changed course, climbed to eight thousand feet, leveled off and nudged the Dakota into its cruising speed of two hundred fifty miles per hour. That would get them to Blida in approximately three hours. After an hour at the controls, Ludwik had Tysko take over. All gauges read normal and both engines were humming smoothly. He relaxed and thought back to 1942, the marriage and the honeymoon in the Lake District. Best days of his life! Soon after the honeymoon ended, he was cleared to finish his training at Bramcote and then move on to Finningly for advanced training on the Halifax bomber. Nellie came with him then. It was an interesting time for her.

536

Living in a boarding house in Doncaster with thirty Polish airmen. And loving every minute of it! It was there she had learned her Polish. Some of the units at Finningly had become operational and were conducting night bombing raids into France. He remembered waking with Nellie every time the bombers returned to the base; usually around five A.M. He taught her how to count the number of planes by listening to their engines. He remembered how difficult it was for them when their count didn't add up to the right number of planes. He would wonder if he knew any of the men that hadn't made it. It always made Nelly cry. They would pray that the missing had not died or been captured; that they would make it back one day to this base and if not here, to their families back home in Poland. After Finningly, he became operational and was assigned to 301 Bomber Squadron at Blackpool. When he got there, he discovered the squadron had been given Wellingtons to fly. No one in the squadron had flown one before. That meant a new training cycle for him and everyone else. The squadron was taken off operational status pending completion of their training with the Wellington. That was fine with Nellie. She said the Wellington was a gift from God. It kept him close to her and away from the dangerous bombing missions over the mainland. Then Nellie became pregnant. Weekends strolling the boardwalk on the beach and frequenting Blackpool's amusement park, dance halls and restaurants came to an end. Nellie went home to be with her mother during her pregnancy. He tried to see her on weekends, but the training had become extremely demanding. There was an urgency in Command to get the squadron operational. It had to be a matter of life or death before a pass was given to any airman. With little or no hope of getting a pass, he decided to concentrate on learning everything he could about the new bomber. One of his instructors, a Polish officer, had noted his exceptional night vision. And while excellent vision was a prerequisite for any pilot, the instructor thought that his superb night vision qualified him for Special Operations. They always flew their missions at night.

He was urged to volunteer for 301 Squadron's Special Duties unit. It was operating out of Africa. He said while the unit didn't do any bombing, its work was extremely important in the war effort. When he added the fact that they flew missions into occupied Europe, including Poland, he volunteered. He was accepted and was transferred to Tempsford, the RAF's Special Operations base, the day after he finished training at Blackpool.

"I like the way the Dakota handles," Tysko said. "One of the better planes I've flown."

"I'd like to see how she handles with a little turbulence. That's the real test for me," Ludwik answered.

"How many planes have you flown?" Tysko asked.

"Many. From the old Tiger Moth up to this one. The Halifax, Fairey-Battles, Wellingtons, Liberators, gliders and a few sport planes."

"Going to fly for a living after this?"

Bednarz had asked him that question a little while ago. His answer was the same. "I don't think I'll be flying anymore. There are other things I would like to try."

Tysko replied, "I'm considering going back to Poland to be with my family, but I'm not sure if that's the right thing to do now. What do you think?"

Ludwik chose his words carefully. He did not want to influence the young pilot one way or the other. "A beautiful thought, Tysko. To be home again. May be a bit risky though. Your family will welcome you warmly. The Russians will not. As you know, our history with them hasn't been very pleasant."

Tysko sighed and said, "We gave so much blood in this war. And what do we have to show for it?"

Ludwik nodded. He remembered the Italian bishop's advice to him concerning the same subject. He repeated it to Tysko, "You know with faith, comes hope. And with hope, anything is possible."

Tysko replied, "I believe that, but I worry that the Russians don't."

Ludwik could not argue with that. He knew it might be a long while before Poland regained its independence. The Russians were not going anywhere soon. He still had faith that Poland would find its freedom in time. But he believed it would be in God's time, not his.

"Africa," Tysko announced as he jabbed a finger ahead at a thin outline of land appearing on the horizon. The word jolted Ludwik. It was the same reaction he had had the first time he saw Africa. That was in March, 1944; a few days after he had seen his son, Kazimierz, for the first time. He had been granted two days to be with Nellie and their newborn boy before leaving for Derna, Libya and "special duties."

He spent less than a week in Libya before shipping out to the squadron's new base at Campo Casale in southern Italy. When he got there, he learned his squadron had been renamed Special Duties, Flight 1586. From there he had flown many missions into occupied Europe including Poland. He remembered with special pride how he had dropped agents, food, medicine, ammunition and a multitude of other supplies to the partisans in Poland; his brothers and sisters who had been fighting against the occupiers since the early days of the war.

"ETA is 1430 hours," Tysko stated as he turned to follow the African coastline eastwards toward Algeria and their destination, Blida Airfield.

It was hot at Blida. Very hot. There wasn't much relief from the heat in the barracks. Ludwik knew that would change as soon as the sun went down. Night in the desert was cold. There wasn't much to do in the desert besides drink, play cards, and frolic with some of the local women who rented themselves out for the night. Ludwik hadn't been interested in the local women the first time he was in Africa, and his lack of interest hadn't changed.

All the work to accommodate the thirty airmen with a place to sit was completed before midnight. Breakfast was at 0630 hrs. The Dakota was in the air at 0800 hrs. To a man, the thirty passengers were buzzing with excitement. They were going home.

Ludwik felt the excitement also, but he had the job of getting these veterans home safe and sound. He would allow himself to feel the joy of home as soon as he stepped onto the tarmac at Blackbushe. He would receive his orders there and hopefully be granted some time off to go home. He wasn't sure how much longer he would be required to remain in the service. He had heard there would be options; stay on as a pilot in Squadron 301, leave the PAF and join the RAF as a pilot, or leave the service and make his way as a civilian. There was another possibility. One that all Polish servicemen were a little nervous about. There had been a rumor that the English government might try to convince the Poles to get in the fight against the Japanese. That rumor was started the day the Germans surrendered. Ludwik was confident the Polish government in London would have none of that. He did wonder what was going to happen to his government now that the war had ended. He knew they would not be going back to Poland. The Russians would probably have them shot.

The flight to Rabat, Morocco was short. Everyone was allowed off the plane for a two-hour break while the Dakota was refueled for the long trip to England. It would take eight hours to cover the fifteen

540

hundred miles. The entire trip would be flown over the Atlantic. It would still be daylight when they touched down on English soil. He would be debriefed, eat, assigned a cot somewhere and then call Nelly to tell her he was back in England and would be coming home soon.

During the war, he had been on many long flights into occupied Europe. Each one had taken a piece of him. A little from his heart. A little from his soul. One flight had almost killed him. The Lady had saved him then. He remembered what it felt like when he was approaching enemy territory with only the cover of night his defense. The silence in the plane. The loneliness. The cold. The fear. The unknown. That was all gone now. There was only happy, joyous anticipation. The cockpit door wasn't thick enough to block out the animated conversations and occasional songs that broke out among the veterans.

The excitement lasted for a few hours then gradually dissipated into quiet conversations about their families, women and plans for their future. Eventually, the entire plane grew quiet. Ludwik knew why. If the men weren't sleeping, they were thinking. Like he was. The war was over. Thank you, God. What about my family back in Poland? Will I ever see them again? Should I go back to them? What would I do there? What about the Russians? How would they treat me and my family if they knew what I did in the war? Troubling thoughts!

The two pilots alternated the flying. Each took a two-hour shift. Tysko had the last two hours. When they spotted the English coast, Ludwik announced over the intercom, "England in SIGHT!" A tremendous roar erupted in the passenger area. It echoed continuously back and forth inside the plane. Men were crawling over each other to get a look at the island. Someone shouted, "The Island of Last Hope!" The expression was a familiar one. He hadn't heard it in years; the last time being on the Arandora Star, the ship that had rescued them from a defeated France in 1940. Dark days, indeed. Bishop DeMonte had been right. Faith had brought hope. And hope had brought days like today.

England

The welcome home ceremony at Blackbushe was relatively quiet. All four crewmembers of the Dakota lined up with the thirty men from Blida and were addressed by the base commander. He didn't take long. After a personal welcome, he thanked the men for their service and then read a prepared statement from the Polish government in exile that did the same. Finished with that, he outlined what would be happening in the next few days. He said officers, including sergeant pilots, were to report to one area for billeting, and enlisted men to another. He said all personnel would eat together in the officer's mess tonight; there was a real Polish meal being prepared for them. That brought a cheer from everyone. When the cheering subsided, he told them they would be provided with a partial pay tomorrow to hold them over for a few days; a sort of "bonus payment" for their service. That brought another cheer. Then he advised them to take the time to listen carefully and understand what options they had for the future. He said those options would be discussed in the morning, but for now, and the near future, the crew were members of Squadron 301, Transportation and the men from Blida would be assigned to a unit shortly. He closed by saying that the English attitude toward the Polish presence in England had changed somewhat over the past two years. The English press had been complaining about what the Polish presence on the island might mean for a peacetime England. He said Churchill had maintained a strong and steady support of the Poles for what they had done for England and that he was backed by most of the country's military. Especially the RAF. The problem was the trade unions.

They were nervous about Poles staying on in England and taking jobs away from English veterans returning from the war. And that had begun to resonate with the English population. With that he dismissed them.

Ludwik and Tysko were led by an officer on the commander's staff to the debriefing area. The debriefing was short. No problems with the flight. Everything at Blida and Rabat had gone smoothly. The officer had orders for both of them. Tysko was given a four-day leave. He was ordered to report back to Blackbushe and resume his duties as pilot. He would be flying men, equipment, supplies and surplus material from one part of England to another. He would also be flying both Polish and English servicemen back to England.

Ludwik's orders were different. Because he was married with a family in England, he was given a two-week leave. And in respect for his almost decade long service to his country, he was offered the option of resigning, with honor, from the PAF or staying on as a pilot with the same duties as Flight Sergeant Tysko. If he chose to resign, he would be required to report back to Blackbushe after his leave and wait for his official discharge.

Martin Smith, Nellie's father, answered the phone. He recognized the broken English and Polish accent of Ludwik immediately. Each man was glad to hear the voice of the other. Nelly was upstairs with her mother and son. Martin called for her, saying there was a Polish "lad" waiting to speak with her. She asked her mother to take care of the boy and hurried downstairs to the phone. She was anxious to hear if this "lad" was the same one she had talked to earlier in the week; the one who had been with Ludwik for months traveling across Europe after escaping Poland. He had somehow found out that she and Ludwik had married, and she was living in Carlisle. When he said his name was Josef Przyba, she knew instantly who he was.

543

Ludwik had talked about him many times. She was hoping it was him on the phone and that he had some news concerning Ludwik. She began crying as soon as she heard his voice. It had been a long time. Hundreds of letters had passed between them over the past year. Phone calls had been a different matter. This was the first time they had talked to each other since he had left England for Special Duty operations in Italy. He had survived and made it back. Now, he was just hours away. They would be in each other's arms tomorrow.

Plans were made. He would train to London in the morning, board another train to Carlisle and hopefully arrive there sometime in mid-afternoon. He said he would call her from London and give her the time of his arrival. She said they would be at the station waiting for him.

Nellie kissed the phone before she hung it back on its cradle. She turned to the group that had gathered at 21 Dalston Street for supper and smiled. Her mam, dad, sister Molly and Ludwik's two nephews, Franek and Karol Krach, just home from the war themselves, all returned her smile with a loud, "Hoorah!"

Ludwik hung up the phone and stared at it. He picked it back up and listened. He wanted to hear Nellie's voice again. Maybe some sort of echo still lodged in there. He took out her picture from his billfold, looked at it and quietly repeated what he had said before hanging up, "Cheerio, my pet. See you soon."

Ludwik joined Tysko for supper at the officer's mess. The young man said he was off to London in the morning. Ludwik said he would join him. They agreed to meet at the paymaster's office thirty minutes before it opened. Just in case a long line was in the offing. They didn't want to waste a minute of their leave.

"Much to be thankful for, my friend," Ludwik said to Tysko. Tysko agreed and said it was time to celebrate.

He walked toward the building with the sign that read, "Pilot's Pub." Ludwik headed for the chapel.

Nellie went to her closet and looked for something to wear that Ludwik liked. She hadn't spent a lot of the money he sent her every month, but when she did, she made sure it was on necessary things like food and clothes. Clothes for her and their son. She picked out the black, yellow flowered dress that had been his favorite when they were together on the boardwalk in Blackpoole a few years ago.

Ludwik sat mesmerized in the front pew before the altar. Just beyond the altar was a marble statue of Mary, the Blessed Mother. She stood majestically in an alcove some five feet off the floor. Her arms were reaching out to him. Welcoming him. He stared at her. He had never seen her like this in a church. She was not clothed in the usual white robe with the blue sash. She was in a long brown robe. Her upper body was covered by a light brown mantle that ended in a hood folded back on her neck. It was the dress of a peasant girl! Her face intrigued him. He thought she resembled the woman by the library in Campo Casale and the woman with the large dog and small flock of sheep in Poland and Romania. He stood up, looked directly into Mary's eyes and thanked her.

Nellie decided to really make Ludwik's return a grand occasion. A day no one would forget. She would invite Ludwik's nephews Franek and Karol to the train station. And with the number he had left her, she would call Ludwik's friend Josef Przyba, and have him join them. It would be wonderful! She would give her father money to buy what was necessary for the reunion. Mam and she would cook. Molly would entertain Kazimierz. The dinner would be wonderful. The men would talk and have a beer or two. Ludwik would play with his son. It would be perfect. And when all the celebrating was finished, she would say goodnight and take her husband to bed.

Every station the train stopped at on the way to London was flush with the Union Jack. Dozens of them hanging proudly everywhere. Victory! He could envision people hugging, crying and dancing in the streets when the news came that the war had ended. Five years of hoping and praying for that one moment and exploding with joy when it arrived.

He didn't see one red and white Polish flag the entire trip. None in the villages, none in the towns. He knew it would be the same in Poland. Very little dancing in the streets there. The Russian occupiers would be hard on those trying to remind the world that Poland still lived.

The English countryside showed little evidence of war. It remained, for the most part, a gentle, pastoral reflection of what life had always been in rural England before the war.

Tysko mentioned how everything seemed untouched as the train sped on its way toward London. Ludwik knew that was misleading. While the fields and gardens flowered with potential, many of the people that had tended them in prior years were gone. Taken by the war. It was going to be hard for their survivors to go on without them. But while the chill that death had brought them would be difficult, it would diminish in time under the comforting blanket of peace and freedom that had finally made its way back into their lives.

Not so for his Poland. While England, France, America and others had shed their blood and suffered like the Poles, they were now free to rebuild and improve what they had been. Poland and other eastern European countries were not free to rebuild. They had been abandoned by those very same allies to appease the power-hungry despot, Joseph Stalin and his communist henchmen.

The serenity of the English countryside changed dramatically as the train entered the outskirts of London. Remnants of the "blitz" that

546

had terrorized London began to appear; a bomb cratered, unused road spattered with unkempt wild grass, a tenement reduced to a few rows of bricks and looking more like a fence than a building, burnt out vehicles mashed into piles of scrap and a windowless, abandoned warehouse. The physical scars of war. A haunting reminder.

The early days of the war had been a terrible time for the people of London and other major cities in England. But they had survived. The RAF had done its job. They had defeated the Germans in the sky over their country. And they had done it with the help of Polish pilots. He and Nellie had the opportunity some years ago to witness one of the Polish fighters in action. They had come to London for a routine checkup on the plastic surgery that had been performed on his face after the near fatal accident at Bramcote. They were taking a walk along the Thames when the sound of an air battle caught their attention. Spellbound, they watched as two planes went after each other. Ludwik's keen eyesight let him know who was who up there. When one of the combatants began trailing smoke and losing altitude, he smiled. A few seconds later, the Messerschmitt burst into flames and the pilot bailed out. His burning plane spiraled down out of control and crashed on the opposite bank of the river. Nellie wasn't sure what had happened. She wanted to know who had "won." Ludwik said Poland had. She asked how he knew that. He pointed to a plane coming low over the river to inspect the burning hunk of twisted metal that was the Messerschmitt. It whizzed by a few feet above the water. It was a Hurricane with the red and white Polish insignia on its wings, tail and fuselage. It had been a proud moment for him.

Josef was delighted and excited to hear that his dear friend, Ludwik, had returned. He told Nellie he would wait a day or so before coming to visit. He did not want to interfere with the homecoming being arranged by the family. Nellie would have none of it. She insisted on him being at the station.

She asked to meet him thirty minutes before Ludwik's train arrived so they could become acquainted and have some time to talk.

Euston Train Station in London had been hit several times during the blitz and still showed the effects of it. The roofing that covered the tracks still in use was in desperate need of repair and the entire interior of the station begged for a thorough makeover and cleansing. Nonetheless, it was the northbound stepping off point from London and Ludwik never took notice of the station's condition. He was too excited. A transfer in Castleford for a train to Carlisle would be the only change he would have to make. He would be in Carlisle at 4 PM.

Before Euston, the train had stopped briefly at Charing Cross station in central London to empty its passengers and pick up new ones headed north. The station was near Buckingham Palace and Trafalgar Square. All three iconic British landmarks stood as they always had in marked contrast to much of the Euston neighborhood. The English had proved their worth in a few short years when it came to rebuilding that historic part of London. Ludwik wondered about the other major cities in England and on the continent. Especially the ones in Germany. Berlin was probably still smoldering. Hundreds of thousands of civilians killed. Innocent civilians. He was glad he had gone into Special Operations. He hadn't dropped a single bomb on anyone; just agents and supplies to partisans who brought the fight to the enemy and not the civilian population. He could live with that.

He had said goodbye to Tysko at Charing Cross. Outside of the sergeant-pilots remarks about the English countryside, each man had been content to sit quietly with his own thoughts. Tysko's thoughts were those of a young man; London, what to do, what to see, where to go, who to find. Ludwik's thoughts were those of a family man; his wife, his son, his English in-laws. The last time he had seen his son, the boy was only two days old. He had received pictures of him while in Italy, but pictures didn't walk, talk, laugh and cry.

He couldn't wait to look his boy in the eye. To hold him. And to hold Nellie. His cyganka! His slim, black haired, little gypsy. His beautiful, young bride. So many thoughts and dreams of her. All becoming real today. He thought about Carlisle. The city had been spared a bombing during the blitz. Only one bomb had fallen there, apparently jettisoned from a German bomber returning from a raid on the Newcastle shipyards northeast of the city. It hadn't exploded. It was discovered, nose buried, sticking upright in a garden just behind a farmer's house. Not that far away from Dalston Street where Nellie lived with her parents. Good fortune for the farmer's family; a bomb landing only feet away and not exploding. And good fortune for his own family on Dalston Street. Not one bombing raid during the war. Much to be thankful for. God had been spared them. The family was safe and waiting for him. And thanks to the Lady and so many others, he was alive, in good health, and would be with them today.

Nellie's plan for a grand reunion was falling into place. Josef Przyba had agreed to meet her at the English Street station at three thirty. She had given him a description of the dress she would be wearing and that she would be with her son, Kazimierz and Ludwik's two nephews, Karol and Franek. She was happy for the opportunity to meet Josef and spend a little time with him. To talk with him. To thank him for being her husband's friend and companion in the early days of the war and on the long odyssey they had taken together to reach France. Ludwik had not talked much about that time, but did mention that Josef had been with him all the way. She had also heard her husband call out Josef's name in his sleep. She had never asked Ludwik about his journey from Poland to France or his time in Hungary and she never would. If the day came when he wanted to talk about the war, she would listen. Until then, she would concentrate on helping to build their future together.

Ludwik walked up the passenger car aisle past some British soldiers and toward a woman and a young girl sitting together near the back. He headed for them eyeing the last row behind them. He would be comfortable there. He liked to have everything and everybody in front of him, an old habit from riding trains in uncomfortable places with fake travel papers.

The woman sat quietly with her daughter and watched Ludwik approach. She was impressed by the cut of the blue uniform and the well-postured man who wore it. Her husband had worn one similar to it with honor and distinction. He had been killed in a bombing raid over occupied France in 1942.

"Mother, he looks like father!" the young girl whispered.

"It's the uniform, my dear," her mother answered.

As Ludwik passed, she saw the chained eagle on his chest and the flash on his shoulder that read, "POLAND." He was a Polish pilot. One that cut a dash. Just like her husband had.

An hour into the ride, a loud shouting match erupted between two of the British soldiers up front. It didn't last long. It ended with one of the men saying, "It's none of your business, Eddie." The silence that followed lasted a minute or so. It was broken with a loud, "Dammit! I'll make it my business!" With that, a man wobbled up from his seat and staggered up the aisle toward the rear. He was obviously very drunk. He was a big man. Tall and barrel chested. Somewhere in his early forties. He wore the stripes of a sergeant. He took a seat across the aisle from Ludwik.

"Speak English, Polack?"

Ludwik didn't answer. He stared out the window at the countryside.

"Are you deaf, you bloody, cabbage eater?" the drunk slurred.

Ludwik made eye contact with the man, "I am not deaf. And I speak English. What is on your mind?"

"I want to know when you and your filthy Poles are going to leave our country. You have done nothing but cost us money."

Ludwik eyed the man carefully. He was not dangerous. Too drunk to do anything that would cause a problem for him. Still, he knew he would have to answer the man. Before he could, the woman sitting in front of him with her daughter beat him to it.

"The only filthy person on this train is you, sergeant. And I believe it's because of the drink and not the man. Go back to your seat. This man has as much to do with our victory as you and the rest of our boys have."

A voice up front yelled, "You heard what the lady said, Eddie. Come back and take a seat." And just like that, it was over. The sergeant stumbled back to his mates without a word. Ludwik got up and went to the woman. He clicked his heels, bowed and introduced himself. Then he thanked her for defusing a situation that probably was going to end in a physical confrontation.

"I am not used to having a woman step into a situation like that. You were very brave. I am grateful. I did not want to hurt the sergeant. We have done enough fighting."

The woman smiled and said, "I am sure you would have handled yourself well. I didn't mean to step on your toes or insult your manhood. The sergeant was insulting your people and the uniform you wear. I know what happened to your country...... My husband wore a uniform like yours. He was a captain, a bomber pilot in the RAF. He was shot down in 1942. Declared "Killed in Action." If he was here, he would have done the same thing."

Ludwik watched the soldiers make a concerted and genuine effort to help the lady and her daughter with their luggage as they detrained in Castleton. Even the drunken sergeant carried one of their pieces. He was doing a good job of restoring his honor to the widow. God only knew what the man had gone through in the war. Ludwik hoped he would do well. The incident made Ludwik think of Bednarz, his friend and doctor confidant. Demand for his kind of services was going to be great in the peaceful aftermath of war. Men and women who had experienced the horrors of conflict would now have ample time on their hands to reflect and digest that experience. Many would have problems with that. He had already experienced it. Bednarz had helped him cope, but he wondered about the future. Would the dreams come back? Would he be able to handle them if they did?

Carlisle

She was standing just outside the entrance to the station. The dress was just as she had described it. Black with bright yellow flowers. It clung to her body in an attractive manner. She had an abundance of curly black hair. Her face was kind, her eyes bright. It was Nellie.

"So very pleased to meet you, Mrs. Skoczylas," Josef said. He bowed, clicked his heels and kissed her hand. Like a true Polish officer. Very gallant. Very Ludwik.

"Josef. The man I know helped make it possible for Ludwik to escape Poland and live. I want to thank you for being there for him."

"He was there for me. I would not have made it but for Ludwik."

Nellie introduced her son Kazimierz to the slender man. She picked him up out of the carriage and introduced Josef as "Uncle" Josef. The young lad smiled at the man in the blue uniform and then squirmed his way back into the comfort of his carriage.

"Milo cie poznac, Kazimierz," Josef said to the boy.

"He has never heard a word spoken in Polish, so I'll answer for him. "Nice to meet you, also."

Josef laughed and said that was going to change when Ludwik was home. He said he never saw a man with so much pride in his homeland.

"You speak our language now?" he asked.

"Yes. But until today, I had no one to speak it with. I will speak it with Ludwik when he wishes to, but if we are to make our home in England, it is important that he, like you, speak English. Tak?"

"Tak!" Yes! Of course," Josef chuckled.

He liked this young lady. She was having fun and so was he.

Ludwik was tired and a little stiff from the long ride. The train was a corridor train. All cars were connected. That allowed any passenger to walk the entire length of the train and back if he or she chose to. The train was crowded. Many of the passengers were British military. Some were with their families. Their laughter was loud and hearty. Infectious celebrations! Happy reunions! He wanted to join them; be a part of it. But he would have to wait. He would celebrate at the station in Carlisle. And that would be with his wife and son. The most important celebration! He would hold Nellie in his arms, look into her dark and beautiful eyes and say, "Hello, my pet." He would kiss each eye softly and then move to her lips. He would then hold his son, kiss both of his cheeks and say, "My son." Another celebration would come later on Dalston Street. That's when the laughter and good cheer in that house would resemble what he was witnessing here; a picture of love and joy painted within a frame called home and family.

There were a few Polish soldiers in one of the cars. He stopped to chat with them. They had been to London for a few days of rest and relaxation. Their unit had taken heavy casualties in Germany and had been relieved and sent back to England just before the war ended. When Ludwik asked about their time in London, he was disappointed to hear about the change in attitude of the English toward them. They hadn't felt welcome. There were fights in the pubs. Insults on the street. Women were available, but for a price. And they had to find them. When their money was gone, so were the women. It hadn't been like the early days when a man in a Polish uniform was treated with respect by most and sought after by many on the distaff side of the population.

It was the dress that caught his eye. His favorite! She was standing in a crowd next to a carriage that held a young child. His son! By the time he crossed the aisle to the station side window to wave, the train had slid past her. It stopped down the track a few seconds later.

Departing the passenger car was a slow process. When he made the platform, he found himself behind a large group of servicemen moving toward the station entrance. Many of them carried a service bag on a shoulder. For the moment, he couldn't see Nellie because of them, but he knew where she was. He would surprise her.

All the uniformed men looked the same coming up the platform toward her. She watched each man enter the station. More than thirty of them. No Ludwik! Disappointed, she turned her attention back to the track and the simmering, hissing steam train. And there he was. Standing straight. Smiling. His service bag at his feet. Staring at her. Tears streamed from her eyes. He left his bag and came to her. He kissed each of her eyes softly and said, "Hello, my pet."

Josef and the Krach brothers had left Nellie alone on the platform. They had decided not to interfere with that part of the homecoming.

554

It was a time for husband and wife. Special for them! None of the three had married. There was no one waiting for them in England. Their families and friends were still in Poland. Josef had received word possibly concerning his father while training in Africa. Bella had learned from a refugee that a man matching the description of Josef's father was involved in guiding Polish refugees across the Carpathians into Hungary. And while that had been more than four years ago, it had been enough for Josef to maintain the hope he had in his heart that his father was still alive. Unfortunately, he had lost contact with Bella. She had stopped answering his letters years ago. Basha, Ludwik's lady, was thought to have fled to one of the Greek islands with her family a few months after he and Ludwik had escaped Budapest. His only hope now was to continue writing to his father's address in Krakow and hope that one day he or one of his sisters would return and find one of the letters with his return address on it. The three uniformed men sat on a bench away from the entrance to the train station. Franek wore the wings of a paratrooper, Josef the wings of a pilot and Karol the patch of an artilleryman. They sat quietly and waited. The brothers for their uncle. Josef for his friend.

Kazimierz was having difficulty in Ludwik's arms. He was trying to escape from this stranger he did not know. Ludwik understood. He put the boy gently back into the carriage and kissed his head.

Nellie was very familiar with the scene she was witnessing between Ludwik and their son. Six months after Ludwik had left for Italy, she had become ill. She developed a lingering, sometimes violent cough and began experiencing frightful episodes of losing her breath. Her doctor diagnosed the illness as tuberculosis and ordered a stay in a country sanitarium in the Lake District west of Carlisle. With the illness known to be highly contagious, she left immediately to begin a treatment of isolation, lots of fresh air, rest, wholesome food and exercise. Her son was left in the care of her mother and younger sister, Molly. The treatment lasted almost a year.

Nelly saw her family and son only twice during that time. Physical contact was not allowed. When the coughing and shortness of breath disappeared, she was cleared by her doctor to return home. She thought about that first day back in Carlisle. Walking into the house and seeing her sister, Mollie, holding Kazimierz in her arms. She remembered her son staring at her then looking away and pressing himself closer to Mollie. Mollie put him down on the floor and said, "Your mam is home." She remembered her shock when the young boy shook his head and ran crying into the arms of his grandmother exclaiming, "My mam!"

It took two months of bonding with her son to earn back her place as his mother. She knew Ludwik, just a stranger to Kazimierz now, would be going through the same process she had for a while.

"Does he walk?" Ludwik asked.

"Yes, he does," Nellie answered. "I brought the carriage because it was too far for him to walk from the bus to the station."

Mother, father and son made their way through the station and out into the city. Nellie knew there were three sets of eyes watching them. Somewhere nearby. She wondered when the three men would appear.

The family had to pass by them on their way to the bus stop. Franek had convinced his brother and Josef to stand far away from the bench with their backs to the walkway. He wanted to surprise his uncle when they exited the bus on Dalston Street. Ludwik never gave them a glance. He was too busy pushing his son in the carriage. Nellie didn't notice them either.

Ludwik folded the carriage and brought it on the bus. He paid the fare and took the first bench that faced the aisle. He didn't pay any attention to the people shuffling by on their way to the rear.

All three men turned sideways, faces away from Ludwik, as they passed him. He was too preoccupied working the bulky, folded carriage under the bench to notice. Nellie held Kazimierz on her lap and watched the three tiptoe by and take their seats way in the rear.

The extended Smith family of Nellie Smith Skoczylas. Ludwik, back row in uniform, with hands on Nellie's shoulders. Kazimierz in the arms of Mollie, second row, third from the right.
Carlisle, England
1945

The bus ride took ten minutes to reach Dalston Street. The Smith house at number 21 was a short walk from the stop. The three men exited the back door of the bus and stood waiting for the family to exit the front. It took a little time for Ludwik to get the carriage off the bus and set it up for Kazimierz.

He saw three men approaching out of the corner of one eye and politely moved the carriage so they could pass. Nellie put a sleeping Kazimierz in the carriage and asked Ludwik if he was ready.

"Of course, I'm ready. Can't wait to see everyone," he said.

"I don't mean that, my darling," she answered.

That's when Ludwik realized they were not alone. The three men he had moved the carriage for had not passed. They were standing behind him. He turned to look. It took a few seconds to process who they were. He just stared in disbelief at them. They were all grinning at him.

"Hello, uncle," said the paratrooper.

"Hello, uncle," the artilleryman repeated.

And then from the one he had shared so much with, "Hello, my friend."

Ludwik began to tear up. His hands trembled slightly. He felt shaky. It was like being in a dream. Franek, Karol and Josef! Here. In England. With Nellie and Kazimierz. How was this possible? He composed himself, stepped forward and hugged each one. Kissed them on their cheeks. Stepping back, he said, "It's a miracle!"

"The Lady is still with us," Josef said.

"Tak! Yes, of course!" Ludwik answered.

"And what lady would that be?" asked a joyously happy Nellie.

There wasn't time to answer that question and all the other ones they had for each other. Those would have to wait. For now, it was enough to know they had survived the war and were here. Together.

The house at 21 had two signs handcrafted on the gate that opened to the walk leading to the front door; one in English that read, "Welcome Home," and the other repeating the greeting in Polish, "Witaj w domu!"

A man and his wife working in their front yard across from 21 paused to watch the small, military ensemble make its way into the Smith house. They nodded approvingly at each other as the celebratory cries of reunion made their way out onto the street.

A toast to the return of their Polish son-in-law and his comrades was made by Nellie's father. The spindly WWI veteran begged everyone's forgiveness for borrowing Churchill's inspiring, "Never was so much owed by so many to so few," tribute in honoring the four Polish veterans for their roles in the defeat of the Germans. He said how proud he was of all the men and women who wore the uniforms of both the British and Polish forces; especially the ones who had come together early in the fight when the outcome was in serious doubt. He raised his glass to each man at the table and said, "Thank you. Welcome back."

The dinner lasted two hours. No one left the table for any length of time. Much of the talk revolved around the family, life in Carlisle and what the future might hold for the country and themselves. There was little discussion of the war and what part of it each had played; only the places they had served and the units they had belonged to. At one point during the dinner, Mr. Smith offered his home to the three men to meet with Ludwik and catch up with each other any time they wanted. He said it was the least he could do.

Ludwik stood with his arm around Nellie's waist and looked down at his son sleeping peacefully in his crib. It was a moment to be revered. He had thought about this scenario many times in the past year. And now it had arrived.

"So peaceful," he said.

Nellie agreed and added, "He's a good boy. He'll be needing his own bed soon."

"I will make one for him," Ludwik replied.

He lit a cigarette and watched her undress. It was their time now. Husband and wife. She was naked for a few seconds before slipping into the pink nightgown she had bought for this moment. She climbed into bed and lay there waiting for him.

Ludwik slowly, methodically, undressed. He talked to her as he did.

"Do you remember our first night as a married couple?" he asked.

"I do. I knew nothing. You were so kind to me. So gentle."

"And before the bed?" he asked.

"We prayed."

"Will you join me again to thank our God and our Lady?"

"Of course. Is she the lady that Josef was talking about?"

"She is. But for her, we are not. I will explain someday."

They knelt together by the bed. Each took a turn thanking God and the Lady in their own words. Then they prayed for their families and friends here and in Poland and for those who had lost their lives and suffered in the war against Germany and Japan.... Ludwik finished by asking God, Jesus and the Lady to help his Poland regain its independence someday.

A New Life

War with Japan ended in August. It took two American atomic bombs to convince the fanatical Imperial Command and their emperor/God Hirohito to call it a day. At home, Winston Churchill, the beacon of English defiance and pride throughout the war, fell victim to the swirling winds of politics and was forced out as Prime Minister by the anti-immigrant Labour Party.

The question of what to do about the substantial Polish presence on the island became quite controversial. The government of England, now labeled a debtor nation and influenced by nationalistic trade unions, tried to encourage their former allies to return home to Poland or find other countries to go to. Supporters of the Poles objected strongly to that idea and reminded everyone of the sacrifices the Poles had made and the role they had played in the defense of England. That response and support moved the government to do something for the Poles besides asking them to return to Stalin's Poland. That "something" was called a Resettlement Plan. It was a two- year plan designed to teach each man a skill and make him a productive member of England. The plan would keep the Polish vets in the British reserve with pay commensurate with their reserve rank, gave free medical care to them and their family members and provide all with government housing. The plan would go into effect the day after all Polish forces were disbanded by the English government. The government also offered the Poles the opportunity to join the regular British Army or Air Force. They could also choose to leave the country or stay on their own without joining the Resettlement Program. If they chose to be on their own, they would be required to establish a residence and obtain a job. If they failed to do so they could face deportation. The Polish forces were disbanded in March of 1946. Hundreds of former Army and Air Force bases, both English and American, were converted into family housing for Polish servicemen who had opted to join the Resettlement Plan. Ludwik remained a pilot in the RAF, Squadron 301, until it was disbanded in 1946. He was discharged as a Warrant Officer Pilot. With a residence firmly established in Carlisle, he began a career utilizing the "good turn of hand" he had developed as a farmer in Poland and later as a pilot and mechanic during the war.

Thanks to low interest loans from the USA and Canada, the government was able to help finance many industries in the country. Construction was one of them. Demand for skilled workers was high. That opened the door for Ludwik. He was able to find work immediately. He began as a carpenter and brick layer for a construction company. In addition to that, he created a watch and jewelry repair business that he operated out of his home. He bought a sewing machine and made clothes, drapes, tablecloths and other household linens and sold them. He became an expert in making and selling leather goods like pocketbooks, gloves, sandals, shoes and wallets. Eventually, he made enough money to co-invest in an automotive repair shop with a local Englishman. They rented a garage in Carlisle and began a very successful partnership. The Englishman took care of the books and investments while Ludwik brought in the business with his uncanny ability to service and repair any form of motor vehicle. Word spread quickly. Business boomed. He hired his two nephews, Franek and Karol as mechanics. He prospered. By 1948, the family was renting their own home, drove their own car, dressed well and could afford to add another family member. They named her Wanda May.

While Ludwik forged successfully ahead in his many business ventures, Nellie took care of keeping order in their growing family and tending to her flower and vegetable gardens.

Part of the new construction taking place in post-war Carlisle and throughout much of England, was the building of pre-fab housing. The new housing, designated as council housing, was owned and rented out by the respective town or city government it was located in. Nellie's doctor was an influential member of the council that oversaw the rentals in Carlisle. He had been the one that diagnosed her acute cough and loss of breath as tuberculosis and sent her away to a sanitarium for treatment. He had been indelibly impressed by the manner in which the young woman had carried herself while enduring months of isolation in the sanitarium and having to do it without her son, a little more than an infant at the time. That had taken courage, resolve and discipline. He respected that. So, when Nellie came to him and asked if she and Ludwik might be considered as tenants in the new prefab duplexes being built on Dalegarth Avenue, an attractive new community, he was more than happy to put a word in for them. Ludwik's talent in automotive matters coupled with his growing reputation as a fair and honest man made it easy for the council to consider him. And when his books proved the thirty-six shillings a week rental would not be a problem, they quickly approved the ex-pilot.

The approval brought some criticism from the community. There was resentment that a "Polish family" had been accepted while other more "worthy" English applicants had not. Many felt the Poles should just leave and go back to Poland or find another country. Fortunately, the doctor and the council hadn't agreed with them.

The family was to live in their new home for six years. It became a friendly rendezvous point for visitors, Polish and English alike. It was not unusual for a young Polish vet to knock on their door looking to talk with Ludwik about a job, getting advice, maybe borrowing a little money until he found work. None were ever turned away. They were always welcomed. Some stayed the night. Some stayed a week. Franek and Karol stayed for two years. Josef remained in the RAF as a pilot, married a young schoolteacher and had begun raising a family in Carlisle. Not far from Ludwik and Nellie.

Word spread in the area that the Skoczylas home welcomed ex-Polish servicemen that needed a place to stay occasionally. With an OK from Ludwik and Nellie, some even used the Dalegarth Avenue address as proof of residence. As stated in the Resettlement Plan, it was one of two things a man needed to possess after the Plan ended or when he was discharged from the military. The other was to have a job. At one point, there were five ex-Polish vets using the Dalegarth address as their home residence and working at jobs that Ludwik had found for them. With the money they earned, they were eventually able to establish their own residence. Initially, Nellie was not happy with all this. In time, however, she began to understand that these men were like brothers to Ludwik. Castaways of a sort. With no one to turn to. Except Ludwik. She loved him for that and decided to help. It was she who came up with the idea of leaving a key outside the house for any of their Polish friends to use if they arrived after everyone had gone to bed. And for almost a year, she gave up her bed in the morning to Franek and Karol when they returned from their midnight to morning night shift in a factory. That lasted until Wanda was born. Then they slept on cots in the garage during the summer and on the same cots by the furnace in the coal room during the winter.

Whenever the family took a vacation, usually to the Lake District during the summer, the house was kept open for any "homeless" or needy Polish veterans. By early 1950, most of the Polish vets had either made their way in England or had left the island. That's when the house ceased to be a haven for needy vets and instead became an occasional gathering place for veterans like Josef and others who had served with both him and Ludwik. From time to time, the family entertained a wide circle of family and friends that included Franek and Karol, who had moved into their own place, Ludwik's business partner and wife, two English teachers that were tutoring Ludwik and Kazimierz, a Polish lad that Ludwik had helped begin a successful jewelry business and a priest that Ludwik worked with to find a place to say mass for the local Polish population.

There were many happy reunions and fun-filled Saturday night parties. Card playing, football pool arguments, Nellie's dad on the piano, everyone singing songs like "TOO RA LOO RA LOO RAH," (Ludwik's favorite) all became the standard party entertainment. And, of course, a pint of this and a pint of that was always available for those who liked to hoist a glass or two. Sometimes the late Saturday nights made the Sunday morning trip to mass a challenge, but challenge or not, the family never missed a mass. It was far too important to Ludwik.

By the end of the '40s, the economic problems for the Poles remaining in England began to dissipate. While acceptance into the English culture was problematic for many, most Poles had found employment. Mining, farm labor, construction and rejuvenated factory work took in the most. Hundreds, like Josef, remained in the British military. Many others left England to start a new life in places such as Canada, the USA, Australia, Malta and New Zealand. Some, choking on the bitter taste of homesickness, even decided to risk it all and go back to Poland.

Genek Louden, a friend and fellow pilot from 301 squadron was one of them. He left money with Ludwik in case something happened to him. He was never heard from again. When the Skoczylas family left for the United States, Ludwik left the money with the parish priest with instructions to use it for the church if Genek didn't return. He never did.

Marion Krol, one of Ludwik's oldest friends, a decorated war hero who had saved his entire crew from a fiery death by making a miraculous landing, left with his Maltese bride to live in Argentina.

Olec Obelewicz, a Polish refugee and brother of Albert, one of Ludwik's closest friends, left for the United States and became a very successful shoemaker. He made custom shoes for some of the most popular radio and television personalities in the United States. Arthur Godfrey was one of them.

Piotr Gai, Ludwik's best man and commander of his training squadron at Bramcote, left for Australia to become a private pilot.

Albert Obelewicz joined Josef as a pilot in the RAF.

Franek and Karol Krach, Ludwik's nephews, left Carlisle and went to the United States for better job opportunities.

By 1951, Ludwik and Nellie had lost most of their Polish friends to a foreign land or the British military. Nellie's mother, father and sister moved to Dalegarth Avenue to be closer to Nellie and the two children. Then life took an unexpected turn.

In 1951, Nellie's father died.

In 1952, Nellie's mother died.

Their deaths had a profound effect on Nellie and Ludwik. Their most loyal supporters were gone. For Nellie, it was almost too much to bear. In addition to their passing, there had arisen a resurgence of anti-immigrant sentiment in England. And while Kazimierz had done well in school up to then, Ludwik became concerned that he and Wanda might become targets of school bullies because of their mixed blood.

Ludwik and Nellie had been through anti-Polish sentiment before; much of it just after the war had ended. They had weathered that period well. Even the embarrassing and humiliating refusal by the English government to allow Polish veterans to march in the massive victory parade in London had not deterred them.

It had hurt Ludwik's pride to be excluded, but he had thrown himself into his work and improving the lives of Polish veterans in the city.

Both he and Nellie became involved in organizing Polish social activities like teas and dances at the Polish social club they had started in Carlisle. Ludwik also established a sport flying club with Josef and some of the other former pilots that had made their home in the city. They used the training base at Kingstown where Ludwik had flown in 1940 to prove his skill to the RAF. There had been no thought of leaving England then. Now, with the loss of Nellie's parents and a growing resentment against non-natives, Ludwik considered leaving, but wasn't sure where they might go. Then the letter arrived.

It was from Franek. He was in the United States in a place called Connecticut, not too far from New York City. He was living with his future wife, Olesia, and her parents in a town called East Hartford. He felt that Ludwik, with his skills, would do very well there. He said the schools were filled with students from countries all over the world and thought that Kazimierz and Wanda would excel because they spoke English already. He, Olesia and her parents even offered to share their home with Ludwik and his family for as long as they needed if they chose to come.

America

The letter lit a fire in Ludwik. The United States of America! A big country. A free country. Welcoming so many strangers. A country that was sharing its abundance with a crippled Europe via its generous Marshall Plan, breathing new life into much of the war-torn continent. Even helping the encircled citizens of Berlin. This was the country that had tipped the balance of power in favor of the Allies; the only one that had the means and will to look Stalin in the eye and defy him. And lest he, Ludwik Skoczylas, forget, this was the country whose soldiers had lifted him out of the sea and helped to save his life.

567

Plans were made to leave for America soon after Franek's letter. At first, Nellie was opposed. She was a proud Englishwoman that loved her country. But she loved her husband even more. Much more. When Ludwik faced a lengthy delay in booking passage because he was not an English citizen, Nellie used her citizenship to get it done.

In 1953, the four members of the Skoczylas family boarded the "SS Ile de France" in Liverpool and set sail across the Atlantic for America and the United States. Their cabin was in first class and they were treated like royalty. They arrived in New York on a cold and misty March morning. The family joined hundreds of others on deck to get a glimpse of the New York skyline and the Statue of Liberty. Young Wanda warmed the hearts of many by pointing at the lady holding the torch and asking, "Why is she wearing her nightgown?"

Ludwik felt full of life. He saw the excitement in the eyes of everyone around him. A new world! Opportunity! He thought of his family back in Poland. A wave of guilt swept over him. They were behind the "Iron Curtain." And here he was staring across the water at the skyline of New York City and the famous Statue of Liberty. It was an awesome moment in his life, one to be shared with loved ones. He so wished his family in Poland were here standing alongside him, Nellie, Kazimierz, and Wanda and sharing the excitement that flowed from bow to stern on this great ship.

One of the benefits of traveling first class was the "preferred treatment" those passengers received as they went through the immigration process on shore. Most of the necessary paperwork had already been completed at the U.S. embassy in London. What was left to process was done in a speedy and very respectful manner at a government office in a place called Manhattan. The United States welcomed everyone regardless of economic status, but to the ones whose appearance and tickets symbolized wealth, a little extra attention fell in their path. It had been no different in London. Basic manners, courtesy, proper dress and a little money went a long way.

The medical "exams" took less than thirty seconds each. All papers were checked for authenticity with just a few questions. In short order, an "Alien Registration Receipt Card" or "green card" was issued to each member of the family with instructions to carry it on their person at all times. The card guaranteed each holder the right to permanently reside in the United States and citizenship would be an option they could entertain in time.

Within an hour, the family was reunited with Franek and his brother, Karol. They met Olesia who greeted them warmly. All luggage was loaded into Karol's 1947 Buick sedan. Ludwik rode with him. Nellie and the two children rode with Franek and Olesia in their 1949 Mercury. The trip from New York to Connecticut was like a sight-seeing tour for the family. As the steel, concrete and glass towers of New York City slipped from sight, they were replaced by the gentle, snow-covered hills and wide fields that separated the many small towns of western Connecticut. The picturesque countryside the Merritt Parkway took them through was very similar to their beloved Lake District back home in England. It made the three-hour drive to Hartford a thoroughly enjoyable one.

Ludwik and Karol talked about Nellie for some time on the ride. Karol was impressed with her change of heart in agreeing to come to America. He knew she didn't want to leave her home, her sister, and her extended family in England, but here she was. In the United States. Ludwik smiled and said it was one of the many reasons why he loved her so much. Leaving Hartford, Karol crossed the Connecticut River into East Hartford where Franek lived. He followed Franek to the center of town, took a left onto its Main Street and drove a few minutes more to his brother's street. His house was the last one of a dozen on the left.

It was appropriately shingled in the Polish colors of red and white; red covering the second floor and white, the first. A small, snow-covered stadium sat in a park within walking distance behind the house. Karol said it was a baseball stadium for youngsters that belonged to something called the "Little League." Ludwik had heard of baseball. He knew it had something to do with a "Babe Ruth" and the sport of cricket.

They were met with warm embraces from Olesia's parents who lived in the house with Olesia and Franek. After dinner and a few shot glasses of vodka, the tired Skoczylas parents took their children upstairs for their first night of sleep in America.

Lying in bed, Ludwik and Nellie exchanged bits of information they had learned from the Krach brothers on the ride to Connecticut. Franek was working in a factory in Hartford. Karol had a factory job for a time in upstate New York, but the weather had been a problem. Lots of snow and freezing cold. He left after the first winter and came by train to Connecticut where he had heard there were large Polish settlements in towns called Manchester and New Britain. He found a job and a small apartment in Manchester. It was only five miles from Franek.

Ludwik liked the location of Franek's house. It was on a bus line, within walking distance of a playground, a church, two schools, a movie theatre, a supermarket, a drug store and several retail stores. It was perfect. He immediately thought of finding a home in the same area. He had saved several thousand pounds over the last five years and had sold his half of the automotive repair business in Carlisle to his partner. He had come ready to buy a home in America. There was little need to buy clothes. Nellie had brought the entire family wardrobe including some very warm, winter clothing. They had recently weathered one of England's worst winters a few years ago and were well suited for the cold, winter climate of Connecticut.

They stayed six weeks with Franek and Olesia. In that time, Ludwik found a job and the house he wanted to buy. The job was in a machine shop as a welder in East Hartford. The house was on a dead-end street a half mile from Franek and less than that to the center of town. The street ran parallel to an elevated bank of railroad tracks that came from somewhere across the Connecticut River to East Hartford and other towns beyond. It wasn't the prettiest of locations, but the price was right. He knew there would have to be something "special" about the house before Nellie would consider living so close to a railroad track. He felt it had that "special" appeal.

As they passed the house on Ranney Street, Nellie said "NO!" Living on a "dead end" street only fifty feet away from the rumble of a train wasn't going to work. He turned the car around at the dead end and headed back toward the house. It was time to point out that "special" appeal. Just before he reached the house, he slowed the car to a stop in front of a large open lot. There was a stand of trees that spread out all along the rear of the lot. Nellie liked the trees. She also liked the size of the lot. Plenty of room to have a nice, English garden. She asked if the lot was for sale. Ludwik said the lot came with the house. That did the trick. The property was theirs by the end of the week.

Ludwik took over a part of the basement to pursue his hobbies and sharpen his "turn of hand." The workbench he built along one wall became his refuge from the rigors of the world. He created works in bronze that emphasized the family's Polish heritage and his service as a Polish naval pilot. He hung them upstairs in the parlor and small dining area. He created leather pouches, wove baskets, made sandals, and fashioned clothes, drapes and linens on his sewing machine. He made beds and toys for the children. Outside in the back yard, he became the farmer he used to be. He converted an old barrel into a small, smoke house to smoke his sausages from the pigs he had butchered. He built two chicken coops and filled them with the hens and roosters that provided a continuous supply of eggs and chicks.

571

He built a trellis and planted the grapevines that eventually crawled up and over it carrying the sweet, smelling grapes that he converted into his home-made wine.

As for Nellie, she quickly adapted to the tremors of the occasional train that rumbled slowly by across the street with all its creaks and groans. Besides keeping the house clean and cooking for the family, she kept herself busy knitting, sewing and reading everything she could get her hands on. Outside in "her" part of the yard, she created an "English" flower garden. It was the envy of the neighborhood and even won a prize for its originality, arrangement and beauty. She was showing her husband and the world that she too, had a "good turn of hand."

Life was good for the family in their early years in Connecticut. Ludwik had changed jobs and became a mechanic for an imported motor car dealership in Hartford.

Kazimierz and Wanda had settled into the routine of attending public school in America and making friends. Karol had married and was living in Manchester just a few miles away. Nelly's sister, Mollie, had come to live in America with her husband, David Maxwell. They lived with Ludwik and Nelly for a time. Franek and Olesia were still just a short walk away down Main Street. The extended family of Polish ex-patriots and English citizens that had lived together in England, had been reunited in the United States of America.

Having Ludwik's family in Poland come to America was an entirely different matter. Both the American and Polish governments had major concerns about that. Ludwik held out hope that one day things would change, and he would be able to see his parents and siblings again. He knew from their letters the family had made its way back to their farm in Mazanki. He also learned that he had actually helped them survive a terrible period of hunger and sickness.

572

They had found the supplies he had dropped on his uncle's farm in Kurylowka where they had been living since the Germans forced them off the farm in Mazanki. Both his parents, brother, stepbrother and all his sisters had survived the war. For that, he was immensely grateful. He knew his father, once back at his farm, would never leave, but he hoped some of the others would be able to visit someday. He also knew it was out of the question for him to go to Poland. Too many had tried only never to be heard from again. He could not afford to take that risk. He had a family to take care of. For the time being, he would continue what he had started with that unauthorized drop from his plane. He would send to Poland what he could to help the family. Money and scarcities like clothing, shoes, boots, aspirin and other medicinal items were what the family needed most. In addition, letters and pictures of family life in America and back on the farm in Mazanki were exchanged on a regular basis.

Nellie wrote short letters in Polish about the children and the extended family that had come together in America. Ludwik wrote about his work and what life was like in in their new home. The war was not discussed. Everyone knew it meant trouble if the Russians learned Ludwik had been a Polish pilot.

The new American family became members of St. Mary's, the neighborhood Catholic Church. Ludwik joined the Men's Guild and became active in church affairs. The predominately Irish and Italian parish welcomed both Nellie, the English mother, who spoke fluent Polish and Ludwik, the Polish father, who spoke a heavily accented English.

There were many veterans in the parish. On certain occasions, they wore their uniforms. When Ludwik wore his, the impressive row of medals on his chest opened many an eye.

Ludwik, Franek, Karol and other former Polish soldiers and airmen in the Hartford area decided to keep their Polish culture alive by supporting three prominent Polish organizations in Hartford. One was the Polish Army Veterans Club, Post 119. The other two were the Polish National Alliance and the Polish National Home; all open to anyone of Polish heritage. All three organizations gave the Polish community a place to gather and celebrate their culture.

For Ludwik, the opportunity to bond with his fellow Poles and share their Polish heritage and pride was welcomed with open arms; especially with those who had served in the war. Men he could share his experiences with. Men who understood what it had been like.

There was one drawback to those kinds of exchanges. They sometimes shook loose memories that had been safely stored away on some deep and dark shelf in his mind. He began having some of the old dreams and nightmares that he had experienced years ago in Italy. They came off and on, maybe once or twice a week. Flashes of incidents he had experienced in the war that made for a restless night of sleep. Sometimes they made the next day at work a little harder to finish. Nothing more than that. That all changed when the flashes became full-fledged nightmares. That's when the war came back with a vengeance. It lasted for more than a week. The last nightmare had him biting Nellie's arm in bed. He had grabbed hold of one of her arms with his two hands; one at the wrist and one at the elbow while he bit her forearm to free himself from the "man" that had grabbed him in a railyard. The man was dragging him across some railroad tracks toward a platform filled with thuggish looking brutes holding ax handles. They began jumping off the platform and running toward them. A few seconds later, Nellie's cry of pain woke him. After treating Nellie's arm, Ludwik kissed her wound and apologized again and again for his actions. Then he got up and left. He went to Kazimierz's room. Moonlight spilled through the window onto his son; a handsome young man now. He was sound asleep.

Ludwik left him and went to check on Wanda, his little angel. She was sleeping peacefully also. He stepped back into the hallway, crossed himself and thanked God, Jesus, Mary and Joseph for his family. There were no men carrying ax handles here. His family was safe. Returning to Nellie, he whispered he would be just a few minutes more. He kissed her gently. She threw her arms around his neck and whispered that everything was going to be alright.

He sat quietly in the dim light from the bulb that hung suspended over the workbench in the basement. Nellie's whispered words still echoed in his head; "Everything is going to be alright." He wondered about that, hoping it was true. Everything had been just fine for the longest time. These past few weeks had been very different. He pulled a cigarette out of the half empty pack of Lucky Strikes that lay on the bench. He lit it; took a heavy drag and exhaled. The smoke rose and mixed with the dust from the dirt floor that always hung in the basement air. Ignoring the pungent smell it created, he looked at the crumpled pack of cigarettes on the bench. Instantly, his mind took him back to Brindisi, Italy. A weekend on pass. Watching a young Polish airman, a pack of Lucky Strikes in his hand with an older Italian woman. Ludwik knew she wasn't as old as she looked. The war had done that. The sergeant handed the woman the pack of cigarettes. She took him by the hand and led him into the dark shadows on the beach and gave him the pleasure he had paid for. When she finished, she rose, brushed the sand from her knees and left with the cigarettes; the cigarettes that would buy her children food the next day. Ludwik remembered how sad he had felt for the woman, any woman, who had to do things like that so she could feed her family. The Brindisi recollection wasn't a nightmare like the one he had just experienced upstairs, but it was the second unwelcome and unpleasant memory of the war in less than an hour. Until recently, he had successfully shut the door on the war for almost a decade. Now, that door had been reopened.

He thought about Bednarz, the good doctor who had helped him when nightmares began to shake his confidence as a pilot. Sleeping pills, good counsel and friendship had gone a long way in helping him sleep. He wondered if Bednarz had moved on. He knew the man had his own demons. He had lost the faith that he once had in God and in the goodness of man. The war and his work with the victims of war had put him in that place. He had sensed that right away when he had decided to confide in Bednarz about his "relationship" with the Blessed Mother. While the doctor had consistently lauded him for his faith, he remembered the doubt that always appeared in his eyes every time the subject of the Blessed Lady came up. It had been no surprise to him that Bednarz had never really pursued any of the "encounters" he had experienced with the Lady or who he thought might be her. Even so, the good doctor had served him well in the few days they had spent together at Campo Casale.

A strong breeze suddenly rattled a small pane in the basement window. A whisper of confidence from the good doctor? He peered into the darkness that lay outside the window for a moment then switched off the light and went back upstairs to Nellie.

She was waiting for him. She had laid there thinking about her husband and what he must have gone through in the war. She understood what had just happened and wasn't afraid. She prayed for Mary, Ludwik's spiritual anchor, to rest her holy hands on his spirit and drive the dreams away. She asked God, Jesus and the Lady to give her the strength to help her husband through this bad time.

As for Ludwik, he accepted the dreams as a part of who he was. To take ownership of them. Bednarz had taught him that. He had also taught him he would be able to handle things like tonight and far worse because of his spiritual strength and unwavering faith. Faith that had been fostered by his love and adoration of the Blessed Lady.

576

The latter part of the 1950s proved eventful for the family. For one thing, the nightmares had disappeared, and Ludwik had convinced his district representative in Congress to help him bring his mother to America. She arrived in October of 1958 on a one-year visa. As luck would have it, Nellie gave birth to a second son named Christopher on the day she arrived. Their home now had two new members and housed three generations of the Skoczylas family.

Ludwik was pleased beyond words. He had a new son. His nightmares had disappeared. His mother was with him for the first time in twenty years. His son, Kazimierz, was becoming something of a local celebrity with his skill as a duckpin bowler. His daughter, Wanda had become his "right hand" in marching alongside him in parades honoring Polish heroes and holidays. Nellie was, and always would be, the "rock" he could lean on. He had become the lead, white jacketed, "master mechanic" at the Russ Sceli foreign imported auto company in Hartford. His reputation for servicing and maintaining foreign cars with excellence had expanded to all corners of New England, down the Atlantic coast and inland up to and including Rochester and Buffalo, New York. He had become a well-respected officer in the Polish Alliance and was a regular with his family at many of the social affairs put on by the Alliance and the Polish National Home. Life was good.

Ludwik's mother returned to Poland in October of 1959. Kazimierz had set a national record for scoring in a single duckpin game for his age group. Wanda was becoming an expert in rehabilitating injured wildlife. Nellie had become a leader in organizing Polish social events and Christopher had learned enough words to talk with Ludwik at home and on the phone during his father's lunch break. The family had successfully joined the millions of other immigrant families that had come to America in the hope of finding a new life; one that offered freedom and opportunity.

From time to time, Ludwik subbed as a replacement bartender at both the Polish National Alliance and the Polish Veterans, Post 119 in Hartford. He was bartending at the Alliance during a 1949 pre-Christmas party when disaster struck the Skoczylas family.

For six months prior to that night at the Alliance, Ludwik had been working with a chronic backache. It didn't affect his job at Russ Sceli because he was hands-off when it came to the actual work on a motor car. His job was supervisory; determine the cause of the car's problem, evaluate the extent of it and then supervise the work to fix it. If a problem required a part that was not readily available or no longer existed, he would make the part himself, give it to his mechanics and then supervise their work. He had little to do with any heavy, manual labor. At first, the back issues were little more than a nuisance. As time went by however, he began to experience an increase in pain. When he began having problems walking the short distance to church without becoming tired, it was decided a visit to the family doctor was in order. He was diagnosed as being in the early stages of chronic back pain and advised to take some time off from work, rest at home and limit what he did with his many hobbies. And most importantly, he was to stay away from any form of heavy lifting.

It was difficult for Ludwik to rest and do little. Not his nature. He was a little concerned about getting tired so easily, but felt any man, especially himself, could live with a little back problem. He told Nellie not to worry. Everything would be fine. Nellie wasn't so sure. She knew he wasn't sleeping well and having a hard time finding a comfortable position in bed. She also noted how much of an effort it was for him to climb the dozen stairs every night to their bedroom.

Ludwik managed to keep his work schedule in Hartford and rest a little more than usual at home. He spent a lot of time with his son, Christopher, who had just recently learned to walk.

Nellie kept an eye on both until Wanda returned home from school. Then she took care of Christopher while Nellie tended to her housework and her husband. Kazimierz, a young teenager now, was usually out with a friend after school doing whatever teenagers did after school.

The season of Advent found Ludwik feeling better. There was a grand social planned at the Polish National Home on Saturday, December 12th. There would be dining and dancing. Despite the objections of Nellie, he decided they should go and enjoy the festivities. Maybe even do a little dancing. He told Nellie not to worry. They would have a nice day of rest after mass on Sunday. And Monday, he was going to have his regular checkup with the doctor.

The social at the Polish Home went well. Ludwik even danced a few obereks and didn't have any ill effects from the spins the dance called for. He did have the usual uncomfortable night in bed, but still had a decent sleep.

The walk to church Sunday morning was difficult. Ludwik had some difficulty breathing and had to stop a few times. Kazimierz and Wanda scooted ahead of their parents to find an open pew and save some seats. Father Dial said the mass and delivered a message of hope. It tied in neatly with the coming of Christmas, less than two weeks away. The walk home was fine. The phone was ringing as they walked through the door. Ludwik picked up the receiver and engaged the caller in a short conversation. Nelly heard him say, "Of course, I will be there," just before he hung up. She wasn't pleased to hear those words.

The regular bartender at the Alliance was out sick. Ludwik had agreed to sub for him. He had never said "no" to Stanley Mucha, the president of the Alliance, whenever he was asked to help. He told Nellie he had to go. He said he felt fine after the walk home.

Nellie said she was worried about his shortness of breath on the walk to church earlier and the fact that he would only have a few hours rest before he left to bartend. Ludwik told her not to worry.

The Alliance was filled with people celebrating like they always did on a weekend. The atmosphere was festive with Christmas less than two weeks away. Smoke hung thick in the bar room. People were shouting more than talking. They were lined up two, sometimes, three-deep at the bar clamoring excitedly for their drinks. Beer, wine and hard whiskey went from Ludwik's hands onto the bar and into the outstretched hands of the eager drinkers. It was non-stop. It had been like that for most of the afternoon. Ludwik began to feel tired and a little dizzy. He asked Stanley to spell him while he went down into the cellar where it was cool, quiet and smokeless. He would rest there for a while then bring up a needed case of cold beer from the cooler. On his way down the stairs to the cellar, Ludwik suddenly felt weak. His legs were wobbly. He steadied himself on the railing. He felt woozy and out of breath. As he reached for the railing with his other hand, a sudden shock of pain rippled across his chest and wrapped itself around his back. Stunned by the pain, he managed to stumble his way to the cellar floor and the chair next to the cooler. He sat there until the pain left him. Feeling better, he went into the cooler for a case of beer. He lifted it to his waist and started back up the stairs. He was halfway before the pain ripped through his upper body again. He dropped the beer and collapsed on the stairs covering his chest with both arms.

Stanley heard the case of beer crashing down the stairs above the din at the bar. Everyone in the bar heard it. One of the patrons ran to the entrance of the stairs and yelled, "Ludwik is hurt!" Stanley and the patron ran down the stairs to their stricken friend. Ludwik was sprawled out on the last few stairs. He was on his back and unconscious. The patron climbed over him and took hold of his legs. Stanley bent down and got a firm grip under Ludwik's armpits.

Together they lifted and carried their unconscious friend up the stairs and into Stanley's office. They laid him gently on the couch. His face had no color and he wasn't moving. Stanley walked to his desk to call for an ambulance. Before he could dial, he heard someone say, "What happened?" It was Ludwik. He was sitting up and looking at the two men in the office.

"You blacked out on the stairs. I'm calling for an ambulance," Stanley told him.

"Don't do that," Ludwik responded. "I'm going home."

He stood up. His legs were shaky; his face ashen. His heart was beating rapidly. He said he had no pain.

"You don't look good," Stanley said.

"I'll be better when I get home," Ludwik mumbled.

Stanley looked at his friend and said, "You're taking a cab, Ludwik."

After the cab call, he called Nellie and told her what had happened, and that Ludwik was coming home in a cab. He said someone would drive their car to East Hartford. Nellie asked to talk to her husband.

Ludwik listened for a few seconds then said, "I will be fine, my pet. I will be home shortly."

Ludwik said nothing during the short ride home. He never changed his position. He sat in the back, bent over at the waist, both arms across his chest. It looked to Stanley like he was trying to hold something in place.

It was early evening. Dark. Very cold. Nellie, Kazimierz and Wanda stood outside on the porch. Waiting. Christopher was napping in his crib upstairs. As soon as the cab came around the slight curve on the street, Wanda ran to the gate and opened it for her father.

Nellie watched in horror as her husband staggered from the cab, both arms fixed across his chest. She ran to him and helped Stanley get him up the stairs to the porch and into the parlor just inside the door. They laid him on the couch. Nellie told Wanda to check on Christopher upstairs. Then she took the knitted blanket off the rocking chair and covered Ludwik up to his neck. He opened his eyes then and smiled at her. She leaned over and kissed him.

Two cars stopped in front of the house. One was Ludwik's. A man got out of each one and approached the porch. One of them had Ludwik's jacket and car keys. Just as the two men entered the house, another car pulled up outside. Nellie's sister, Mollie and her husband, David, had arrived.

Stanley and the man that had driven Ludwik's car said their goodbyes and wished the family well. Nellie walked them out to the porch and thanked them for their efforts. Then she rejoined everyone that had gathered around Ludwik on the couch. Mollie took Nellie aside and said that Ludwik needed to be in the hospital. Nellie agreed. She called their family doctor who lived a few minutes away to come and have a look at Ludwik. Dr. Murphy walked into the house fifteen minutes later. He took one look at Ludwik's ashen face and blue lips and calmly said, "He needs to be in a hospital, NOW!"

It was quiet in the intensive care wing of the Veteran's Hospital in Rocky Hill. Nellie was alone in the room with Ludwik. She sat in the chair next to the zipper side of the clear plastic oxygen tent that covered Ludwik from his waist up. She stared at her husband and prayed that he would wake up and see her. It was Monday morning, December 14th.

Dr. Kelly, one of the physicians at the hospital and a personal friend of Ludwik's, had ordered the move to intensive care immediately after diagnosing that Ludwik had suffered a massive heart attack and was in dire need of the oxygen he needed to survive. He had not mixed his message to Nellie. He said Ludwik's enlarged heart was beating out of control and had not responded, as of yet, to the medication used to slow it. He said the pure oxygen being pumped into the tent would help to keep Ludwik alive, but his heart could give out at any time. He did not feel Ludwik's chances for survival were good.

David Maxwell, Nellie's brother-in-law, brought Kazimierz and Wanda to the hospital later in the day. Young Christopher stayed at home with Mollie. Ludwik had been in and out of consciousness for most of the day but was able to see his two eldest children and Nellie for a few minutes before falling back into a deep sleep. Later, he woke again to see a smiling Nellie sitting just outside his oxygen tent. He was able to smile back at her before falling back into another deep sleep, exhausted from the wracking his body had taken from his enlarged heart. Nellie was grateful they had been able to exchange smiles. She had wanted so very much to let Ludwik know how much he was loved. The smiles had accomplished that. She slept that night on a cot brought in for her and placed beside Ludwik's bed. It was her first real rest in more than thirty-six hours.

Tuesday, December 15th was a difficult day. Ludwik thrashed about in unconscious agony under the cover of his tent. Nellie was forced to watch her beloved husband suffer his pain. It was an unbearable watch. She had to close her eyes from time to time. Dr. Kelley recommended she leave the room and get something to eat. To take a break. To do something else and then come back. Nellie refused.

Ludwik screamed in silence at his heart to stop jumping all over his chest. He begged the Blessed Lady to help him. It seemed to work. While his heart still throbbed strongly in his chest, he felt no pain. He slipped into a blissful, supremely beautiful quiet.

Peaceful images began to float by; a teenage Nellie on the river walk in Carlisle, Kazimierz rolling a little ball at some little pins at the local bowling alley in East Hartford, Wanda, bedecked in a native Polish dress, marching alongside him on Pulaski Day, little Christopher running around the yard on Ranney Street and strangely enough, the face of a smiling Dr. Bednarz, hand on his corn-cob pipe, standing on the beach at Campo Casale. With it all came the distant sound of singing. It was moving toward him. The words were familiar, "Silent Night, Holy Night. All is calm, all is bright. Round yon Virgin, mother and child, Holy infant, so tender and mild. Sleep in heavenly peace, sleep in heavenly peace." Beautiful words. Beautiful verse!

The young carolers, angels from above in his mind, moved slowly past the room and down the corridor towards the stairway. The words "sleep in heavenly peace," resonated softly off the tiled walls in the corridor until the "angels" turned and made their way down the stairs. Then all was still, the only sound a diminishing beat from his heart. He wondered where everyone was and what they were doing. He wanted to see them again; be with them. He didn't like this quiet. It was strange. Very different.

Then he heard footsteps.... He saw himself in the bell tower of St. Stephens in Budapest. Basha was there. They were playing the game of who could accurately describe the person whose footsteps they could hear echoing in the spiral staircase as he/she drew closer to the landing. He listened carefully and knew it was a woman. Soft steps. Nellie. He felt his skin begin to prickle. His body began to flush with a familiar warmth. Sensations he hadn't felt in sometime. He opened his eyes, turned his head and saw her standing in the room.

It wasn't Nellie.

She was dressed in a long, brown robe and wearing sandals. A soft glow of light behind her began to rise and grow in brilliance.

584

He knew her. The shepherdess in the meadow! The smiling, young woman on the hillside at Satu Mare. The girl walking by the library at the base in Campo Casale. The majestic Lady in the Light under the waters of the Adriatic! She smiled and approached his bed. Halfway there, she stopped and reached out for him with both arms.

Nellie was pleased that the young boys and girls had been allowed to walk the halls of the intensive care wing and bring a little joy with their sweet, angelic voices to the patients here. Especially to her husband. She knew how much Ludwik loved Christmas. She knew how much he loved the Holy Family, especially Mary, the Blessed Mother. She looked at her husband. He seemed so at peace now. She thought she saw a faint smile on his face. She got up and went to him. As she came close to the plastic tent that covered him, he sat up, reached for her and cried with joy, "Moja Pani, Moj Boze!" then fell back on the bed, closed his eyes and went from his world to theirs.

To Mary and God

Epilogue

Ireland

It was nearing midnight. The sound of a storm came rumbling across the sea. It swept over the cliff and past the mossy, stone cottage that overlooked the Atlantic. A cold December rain began to quietly pepper the old cottage.

Bednarz wondered how far away the storm was. Sometimes a storm stayed at sea and sometimes it found its way onto land. One never knew for sure. But storm or not, the rain guaranteed a wet walk in the morning along the cliff with his lab, Teagan. And that was fine with him. Both he and the dog loved the cold, wet, Irish mornings. It made one feel alive. But now it was time to reorganize the mess of paper, books and notes on his desk. They had to be in their proper place and ready for the next day's effort. Finished with that, he went to the fireplace and stoked the smoking wood gently, sparking it into a large, warm blaze. Another whiskey in front of the fire was in order. It was comfortable here; a place where a man could think. A place where a man could write. Whiskey in hand, he sat back in his rocker and stared into the flames. It had been fourteen years since the war had ended. He had stayed in England and worked in one of the "resettlement" projects the English government had established for Poles that had chosen to remain in the country after the war. He had worked out of Blackpool, the old Polish transition center. His job was to provide counseling for former Polish airmen struggling to escape the after-effects of war. He did it for twelve years. And after those twelve years of listening to men suffering from not only the pains of war, but the loss of their country, their family and their own identity, he began to struggle himself. He found it increasingly difficult to remain objective and professional toward the veterans. Their pain slowly became his pain and that took away his impartiality.

When he realized how ineffective he was becoming, he took a leave from his position and went home to regroup and spend more time with his family. It didn't help. He became increasingly distant, moody and withdrawn. He found himself at odds with his English wife of nine years, his in-laws, his friends and even his two sons. He began to feel like a stranger in his own home. Their marriage disintegrating, both he and his wife decided it might be best for them to separate for a while. Give him some time to find himself. He left the busy city of Coventry and went to the island of Achill, just off the west coast of Ireland, in search of a quiet place to stay. It was there he found the cottage on the cliff overlooking the Atlantic.

Bednarz hoped the cottage and the solitude it offered, would reenergize him. He felt if he was to find himself, it would be here; far away from people and their troubles, his only neighbors being the sea and the creatures that belonged to it. His dog, Teagan, was bought from a farm just outside the tiny village of Dooega, some three miles away. He was to be his companion. And a good companion he was.

Writing became his therapy. He had been at it for some months now. He focused on the Polish airmen he had treated during and after the war. They were the people he knew best. He could fill a dozen books with their stories. His plan, if successful, was to donate a portion of any money he made to the few Polish outreach organizations that had been set up to aid Polish veterans in England. He wanted to do something for them and at the same time, channel his energy in a way to help find himself. He quickly discovered that writing was a way to accomplish both. He never revealed the identity of his patients; just told their stories. Some were about men that had survived the war but had developed emotional problems coping with the experience. Others, maimed, burned, disfigured and crippled, had been left with a life filled with alcohol, drugs, pain and misery.

All together, they made up what he called, "The Legion of Lost Souls." It would be the title of his first book.

A third group of Polish veterans were the ones that had escaped injury and seemingly had not suffered any emotional consequences from their war experience. They had managed to find a new life in England. Many had married and were raising a family. Like he was. They had somehow learned to carry the burden of war. Bednarz worried about them. He believed the day would come, like it had for him, when that burden would prove to be too much to carry.

His former patients were like an extended family to him. He loved them. A few had dominated his thoughts recently and he had poured his energy into writing about them. In the last two days, his thoughts and words had centered on Ludwik Skoczylas, the Polish Naval Academy student turned Air Force pilot. He had dreamt about him recently. And last night, after some serious drinking, he thought he had seen the man's face in the flames of the kitchen fireplace. He hadn't known the man very long, but in that short period of time felt a spiritual kinship had developed between them. His last name alone had brought back boyhood memories of hearing stories of a spirit world that God had created to reward people of exceptional faith. One of the spirits was a woodsman named Skoczylas. His name would come to mean, "The woodsman who leapt from the forest to save the maiden from an evil dragon." Bednarz felt that description fit Ludwik Skoczylas perfectly. Ludwik hadn't chased any scaly dragons away from maidens, but he had helped to rid the swastika-clad dragons of Hitler from the world. And he had done that with a strength and will that had come from a deep, spiritual faith. A faith centered on his devotion to Mary, the mother of Christ.

Ludwik had not been rewarded a special place in the spiritual world, if there was such a thing, but had been rewarded nonetheless, with his life. The doctor felt sure the man's incredible faith in God, Jesus and Mary was the reason he had survived the war. It would be interesting to knew if his friend still possessed that wonderful faith.

He thought about Ludwik's face in the flames. He wondered if it had been the result of too much whiskey, a very late night and nodding off thinking about his old friend. Whatever it was, he hoped it wasn't a harbinger of bad news. There had been no joy in his eyes.

A rising wind began to rattle some loose shingles on the roof. The storm was approaching. Time for bed. The last thought he had before sleep overtook him were the pale, blue eyes of Ludwik Skoczylas staring at him sadly from within the fire.

The blast of thunder shook the entire cottage. Pouring rain hammered the roof. Lightning was everywhere. Jarred wide awake, Bednarz threw off the duvet and slid quickly out of bed. Teagan was by his side immediately. He shuffled slowly toward the kitchen, half expecting to see the roof missing there after that bomb-like clap of thunder. Every step he took seemed to be synchronized with the lightning strikes that illuminated the cottage interior. He stepped into the kitchen. The ceiling was still there. Moving past the fireplace and its dying fire, he crossed the room to the small, latched window that faced the Atlantic. He opened it and stood there for a while watching the lightning dance its way far out to sea and disappear. The storm had gone. Stars began blinking their way back into the now clear night sky. He started to relatch the window when a soft "whoosh" from the fireplace startled him. A flame had suddenly burst up from the dying embers igniting a pile of dry wood chips that had dropped to the bottom of the fireplace. The kitchen was filled with a blanket of warm air and the sweet smell of burning cedar chips. He locked the window and went to his rocker to enjoy the unexpected new blaze. Teagan followed and took his customary place lying on the floor next to him. The soothing whisper of crackling wood chips made its way around the kitchen.

Bednarz quickly added some wood and returned to his rocker. His body slumped comfortably in the warm air. Sleep came quickly. It lasted two hours.

The sound of the approaching plane woke him. It was low and coming fast. Multiple engines for sure. He opened his eyes just as the plane roared over the cottage and headed out to sea. So much for a quiet, remote spot on the island, he thought. He reached over the side of the rocker for Teagan. He was gone. It took a few coaxing whistles to bring him out from the bedroom where he had fled. He lay next to the rocker again; this time a little closer to it. Bednarz smiled at the look on his dog's face. It mirrored his thoughts. It seemed to say, "What is going on here?" Suddenly, the wind began to swirl outside. It quickly grew in intensity. Teagan was up and whining. "Here we go again," Bednarz thought. The wind was howling now. It began to batter the front of the shaking cottage. In seconds, the front door blew open under the assault and a rush of cold air raced inside. It flew by the rocker and dove into the fire snuffing it out in an instant. The startled doctor stared into the darkened fireplace. Nothing left but a smoky smell of a dead fire. The fierce wind had stopped as soon as the fire went out. The cottage was cold. Very cold. Bednarz felt the skin on his body begin to prickle into little bumps. The hair on his arms began to stand at attention. For a moment he was afraid. He felt something beside the weather was happening here. Cautiously, he got up and turned to face the door. It was wide open. Empty. Nothing there. Relieved, he went to close it. Before he could, something far out on the sea caught his eye. A light. Moving across the water very slowly and away from the island. Getting dimmer and dimmer. Then disappearing. Probably a ship, he thought. One that had crossed over the horizon or had just slipped into a dense fog. He closed the door, locked it and grabbed the woolen throw hanging off the back of it.

He returned to the rocker, covered his body up to his neck with the thick Scottish throw and sat quietly in the dark. Thinking.

He thought about the light on the sea. Something about it intrigued him. Something familiar. He wondered if it was a ship. He wondered if the plane that had flown over the cottage had something to do with it. Everything had happened so fast tonight. One thing after another. His instinct told him something was going on here, but logic dictated he accept the reality of what had actually occurred, a storm, the lightning, the wind, the plane and the light on the ocean. Most likely a ship. What was there anything to wonder about? Maybe he was making something out of really nothing. Maybe his imagination had been turned loose by overwork, too much drinking, a lack of sleep and the forces of nature. While that was certainly a possibility, his body was telling him something different. It was still tingling. And it wasn't from fear. It was from something else. He decided to forgo sleep for a while. Maybe even for the rest of the night. He needed to come up with something that made sense out of these last two nights. Especially tonight. First, he would need a fire. He didn't think well in the cold. He used some dry, sweet smelling thicket branches for kindling and added a few small, splintered logs once the flames grew high. He poured himself a strong one from the almost empty bottle of Bushmills. Time to make some sense of it all.

Rocking gently in the glow of the fire, he sipped the smooth whiskey and began to relax. He needed to formulate a process that he could use to objectively evaluate what had occurred during the past two nights. He decided on a "standard question approach." He would ask himself three questions. One, was there a relationship between the events that had occurred the last two nights? Some kind of connection? Two, was there a common element that existed in all the events and three, was there anything he had experienced himself or learned from someone else that was evident in the events?

He began with the sad face in the fire last night. The face of Ludwik Skoczylas. He would see where that led. He thought back to Campo Casale and their talks about life and Ludwik's concern about being a good pilot. He put his whiskey down on the floor, stared into the fire and listened to his friend. He heard him speak about his youth on the farm. Cleaning the statue of the Madonna. The day he saw his first airplane. The Academy. His friends. The invasion. The retreat and escape. Josef. Romania. Basha and Budapest. France. England. The automobile accident. Nellie. Italy. Special Duties, Flight 1586. The crash. The light in the water. The light in...the water! Saved by Mary, the mother of Jesus! The prickling of his skin. Like his had! He picked up his whiskey and finished it. He thought for a moment. If there was a common element to all of this, it might well be his friend, Ludwik Skoczylas. He fit into everything. His face in the fire, the storm, the crash of thunder, the sea and of course, the LIGHT in the sea. Was the storm tonight like the one Ludwik had flown in desperately trying to find the airfield at Campo Casale and eventually crashing into the Adriatic? What about the plane that zoomed so low over the cottage heading out to sea? Did it crash? And hadn't he been thinking about Ludwik recently? The man had been on his mind for the last two days now. Maybe the two days and too much whiskey had fueled the flame of his imagination. He decided to try and extend this train of thought. He had a few questions.

Why was Ludwik's face so sad? He took a deep breath, exhaled, and thought about his friend. If he was as spiritual as Ludwik, he might be guessing that his face in the fire was his way of saying something bad had happened. Next question. Was his friend dead or alive? He remembered the interesting stories of the man's "experiences" with the Blessed Lady and the unbelievable faith that he had in her. That she had appeared to him in a bright light and saved him from drowning in his sinking plane.

He remembered Ludwik telling him that he hoped to see the "Lady" again in this world, but if he didn't, he was sure he would see her in the next. He never thought that Ludwik lacked a sound mind. He did believe that his strong faith was one of the reasons he had survived so much. He thought how interesting it might be to write about a man's relationship with the Blessed Lady, real or not, and how instrumental it was to his surviving almost six years of war.

Dawn was breaking. Bednarz decided to table his thoughts about the previous two nights and his imagined connection between them and his friend, Ludwik Skoczylas. It certainly had been "food for thought." Worth considering for use in writing an interesting and unique story. He took Teagan outside and walked to the cliff's edge. The sea was calm and the air suddenly warm in the rising sun. He thanked God for the day and for all his days. Then for some reason, he thanked Ludwik Skoczylas for his service and what he had done to help win the war. He would tell the world the man's story. It was a story worth telling. He made a mental note to pull out Ludwik's file later and add the following:

"December 15th, 1959. Ludwik Skoczylas visited me to say goodbye. He was a gifted man. A true Polish Patriot."

REMEMBRANCES

"He taught me how to be a woman, a wife and a mother. I told him I didn't want to be married. I wanted to be home with my mother. I said I knew nothing. He said he would teach me. He said I would learn. Then he taught me. How to cook, how to sew, how to bake, how to garden and how to be a woman. And I learned. I used to walk down into the cellar and stand by his bench and watch him work. He could do anything, and he did it for anyone that asked. A few days before he died, he held my face in his hands and told me he loved me and not to be afraid of dying. When he did die, I thought my whole world had died. But it didn't. I survived and lived on. He had taught me that, too."

Nellie, his wife

"After all these years that have passed, I still feel the loss of my father. I was "Daddy's little girl." He took me everywhere. He was a good, caring father. I remember having a high fever that wouldn't break. He kept piling blankets on me and changing my sweat-soaked clothes until the fever broke. Once I had a huge wart on my knee. He went to a farm and brought back some horsehair. He wrapped it around the ugly wart and tightened it every day. It fell off in a week. My dad was kind to everyone and everything. Once I brought home a wounded pigeon. Dad put it in a large box and dressed the wound every day until it was healed. Then he let me release it outside. He never raised his voice or swore. He never missed Mass and truly believed in loving one another. He was very proud to be a Polish veteran and Polish patriot. He always wore his Polish Air Force uniform marching in Hartford's Pulaski Parade. I was proud to march with him in my Polish dress and vest. I only wish he could have lived to be a hundred."

Wanda Skoczylas D'Agostino, daughter

"We were friends for so many years, during the war and after. We met at the beginning of the war in Warsaw and were together, up and down, until we came to France. Ludwik was the finest man that I ever knew. Quite a lot of people in Carlisle asked me if I knew him. All of them feel very sorry he died so young."

*Josef Przyba, friend and fellow Polish pilot.

*Josef accompanied Ludwik from Poland to France after the Germans had overrun Poland. He eventually joined the Royal Air Force in England as a bomber pilot. After the war ended, he continued flying for the RAF. He and his English wife, Frances, became best friends with Ludwik and Nellie in Carlisle, England.

The simple marker in St. Mary's cemetery in East Hartford, Connecticut reads:

WWII
Ludwik Skoczylas
WO RAF/PAF
Died 12/15/59
Age 45

"Ludwik served in WWII as a Warrant officer in the Royal Air Force and the Polish Air Force. He was an educated man, a man who could fix anything from a simple watch to a complicated combustion engine. Someone who had literally built the family's first car, a man who cured his own pork, hanging kielbasa and sausages in the basement after smoking them in an open 55 gallon-drum. He was a man who emigrated from England to the United States with his family of four to start a new life after the communist takeover of his Polish homeland. He was a dedicated man who when fixing things, always fixed them right. The clientele where he worked as a Master Mechanic on foreign cars trusted him above all. Powerful men, well-heeled and very wealthy, entrusted their prized automobiles for Ludwik to care for, much as they trusted their doctor or lawyer. Liked by all, Ludwik worked long and hard to support his family but never forgot his heritage. He also was an officer in the Polish National Alliance, a group dedicated to supporting Poland and hoping for their return as a sovereign nation. Everything positive one can say about Ludwik can be summed up in two words; he was a **Polish Patriot** until the day he died!"

Kazimierz L. Skoczylas, son

About the Author

e is a retired teacher of History and long-time
ack coach at Hartford Public High School in Hartford,
icut. He is a former U.S. Army recon specialist. His first
, "Stories from the Fifties, East Hartford Style," was self-
lished in 2015. He lives with his wife, Pat, in Manchester,
Connecticut.

Jack L
football,
Connec
book
pul